George Frederick Masterman

Seven eventful Years in Paraguay

A narrative of personal Experience amongst the Paraguayans

George Frederick Masterman

Seven eventful Years in Paraguay
A narrative of personal Experience amongst the Paraguayans

ISBN/EAN: 9783743340312

Manufactured in Europe, USA, Canada, Australia, Japa

Cover: Foto ©ninafisch / pixelio.de

Manufactured and distributed by brebook publishing software (www.brebook.com)

George Frederick Masterman

Seven eventful Years in Paraguay

Seven Eventful Years in Paraguay

A NARRATIVE OF

PERSONAL EXPERIENCE AMONGST THE PARAGUAYANS.

BY

GEORGE FREDERICK MASTERMAN,

LATE ASSISTANT-SURGEON,
LECTURER ON MATERIA MEDICA, CHIEF MILITARY APOTHECARY, GENERAL HOSPITAL,
ASUNCION DEL PARAGUAY.
FORMERLY OF MEDICAL STAFF OF HER MAJESTY'S 82ND REGIMENT.

SECOND EDITION.

WITH A MAP AND ILLUSTRATIONS.

LONDON:

SAMPSON LOW, SON, AND MARSTON,

CROWN BUILDINGS, 188, FLEET STREET.

MDCCCLXX.

[The right of Translation Reserved.]

PREFACE TO THE SECOND EDITION.

I am glad to avail myself of the opportunity presented
by the issue of the Second Edition of this work for the
correction of many faults in style, and a few inaccuracies
which existed in the first; which, being written somewhat hastily, and almost entirely from memory, contained
many errors, which are, I hope, now thoroughly eliminated.
Several friends, and not a few severe critics, have assisted
me in this revision; to both I beg to express my sincere
acknowledgments. And especially I have to thank the
many reviewers to whose favourable notices of my work,
rather than to any merit it possesses, I am indebted for
the rapid sale it has met with.

When my story first appeared it was, as I had anticipated, but half believed, but I was scarcely prepared for
the violent attacks made both upon my book and upon
myself by one or two newspapers. I had imagined that
a tale so simply told would have carried ample internal
evidence of its truth and trustworthiness; and much as

b

they might quarrel with my style, or dissent from my opinions, that my critics would be satisfied with attacking them, without proceeding to question my veracity also. However, I can well afford to wait for the confirmation of my statements, which time and fuller information will certainly bring me; indeed I may say which they have already brought, for, with the exception of the editor of one journal, who still writes, and professes to believe, that Lopez is a hero and a very ill-used man, the press of the whole country has expressed a detestation of his enormities and personal character in even stronger terms than any I have ventured to use.

There is another point I think I ought, in justice to myself, to allude to: one literary journal accuses me of great presumption in venturing to criticise the conduct of the foreign representatives in Paraguay. Now, two of these gentlemen have been recalled by their respective Governments, and—we may suppose—for very sufficient reasons. Moreover, as I happened to know one of them very intimately, and another tolerably so, ought it not to be conceded that I may be quite as good a judge of their conduct as my critics can be of my judgment? and, as I suffered very severely, both in purse and in person, by what I cannot but think their mismanagement—to use the mildest term—surely I have good reason to complain of it! In regard to the first American minister, and his successor also, it must be remembered that the class of men following politics as a profession in the United States is not, as a rule, recruited either from the better educated or the more respectable; and especially, that those who are placed in subordinate posts, although representatives in one sense of the word, are by no means so in the other; a truth of which the higher classes in America are painfully aware, and not a little anxious that foreigners should fully understand.

I have also been roughly handled for my opinion of the Brazilians; I regret I cannot alter it, although I have—in deference to the wish of some well-wishers of theirs whom I esteem—softened the somewhat rude asperity of the terms in which I spoke of them; still I can but think that negro slaves do not make good soldiers, and that the Emperor—who is unquestionably the best ruler South America has seen for many a long year—was singularly unfortunate in his choice of officers, and they, also, in their mode of conducting the war.

I regret also that the greater part of my book is devoted to descriptions of scenes of cruelty and disaster, but with the marks of the sufferings I had endured still fresh upon me, and from the anxiety I felt for the fate of my friends who were then prisoners in Paraguay, such scenes would necessarily constantly recur to my memory and give a sombre tinge to all I wrote of the country; although I gladly dwelt upon every incident illustrative of the people which, trifling in itself, would serve to introduce lighter and brighter touches into the picture. The history of South America, like that of Mexico, has hitherto been written in blood and tears, and I fear will continue to be so written until Anglo-Saxons or Teutons shall there out-number the Indio-Spanish race. And with a soil so fertile, a climate so beautiful, and a shore of such ready access, I trust some of our swarming millions may now be tempted to emigrate to a country where success and prosperity cannot fail to reward the most moderate industry and perseverance.

But before emigration on a large scale to the Plate can be looked for, Englishmen must be assured that they will be effectually protected there in their lives, liberties, and property; fortunately this can be done at little expense. Let the authorities of those so-called republics be but convinced that England will protect those who are best entitled to claim her protection, and there will never be any difficulty in the matter; the mere threat of active operations will be sufficient to render them unnecessary. Even Lopez himself, lawless and reckless as he seemed, at once agreed to the demands of the United States when Admiral Davis plainly told him that, if he did not, the guns of his ships would immediately open upon the batteries before him. And if the despatches of Mr. Gould to Lord Stanley had evoked an order similar in tenor to that sent from Washington, some forty British subjects would have been set at liberty, the lives of several of them would have been saved, and I should have been spared the cruelties and indignities I suffered so long and so unjustly; and, moreover, without the expenditure of an additional shilling, for the squadron lying idly at anchor in the estuary of the Plate would, by its mere appearance in the Paraguay, under the command of an officer who had had imperative instructions to demand our unconditional surrender, have been sufficient, and more than sufficient, to effect our instant liberation.

Sussex Villa, Croydon,
March, 1870.

CORRIGENDA.

Page 29, line 22, *for* seite *read* siete.
  ,,   ,,   ,,   30, Ipegtata *omit the* g.
  ,,   66, line 16, *for* Parana   *read* Panagua.
  ,,   75, ,, 2, ,, Itugua   ,, Itagua.
  ,,   76, ,, 21, ,, rubiaceta ,, rubiacita.
  ,,   77, ,, 13, ,, hül   ,, hill.
  ,,   115, ,, 17, *dele* "and was then executed."
  ,,   194, ,, 8, *for* muerto *read* muerte.
  ,,   225, ,, 6 from bottom, *for* Lavalle *read* Delvalle.

DEFEAT AND DEATH OF LOPEZ.

THE present edition of this work had already left the printer's hands, when the news of the death of Lopez reached England, therefore I am compelled to leave much in the present tense which should have been written in the past, and to insert at the beginning of my story that which should have formed its conclusion.

After the retreat from Cāācupè, on the 18th of August, 1869, Lopez fell back to the woody fastnesses of the central cordillera, and, for a time, escaped the search made for him by the Brazilian cavalry; so much so that the most conflicting accounts of his force and whereabouts appeared in the newspapers—he was in "the wilderness," wherever that may be; he was making his way to the eastern Paranà; he had escaped into Bolivia, and so on; and his army was at one time a mere handful of starving fugitives, and at another, numbered several thousand well-armed men, reinforced by the nomadic Indians of the Gran Chaco. But the truth is, he retreated only far enough to secure himself from the danger of immediate pursuit, and was hidden so close to Villeta that he could send parties of men to collect arms from the battle-field, where, strange to say, they were found in abundance, and then made his way slowly to the north; keeping always close to the flanks of the hills so as to avoid the river Paraguay, from which his movements could have been watched and checked by the gunboats, and to be able to cross its affluents with his artillery before they became deep or wide enough to make the passage difficult. His intention, most probably, was to reach Bolivia, which he could have easily done with a small party; but I fancy he lingered on the way in the hope that the Brazilians, believing him dead, would withdraw their army from the country, or that some political convulsion would compel them to reduce their force so considerably that he could re commence the war with a fair chance of success. Be that as it may, by the end of February of the present year he had reached the banks of the river Aquidavana (or Aquidaban, Page), a stream which falls into the Paraguay in lat. 23° 10′ south, about two hundred miles above Asuncion and a few leagues to the north of the town of Concepcion, and was there encamped when the Brazilian general Camara came up with him on the 1st of March. It is said that the Paraguayans were taken by surprise, and were dispersed and cut to pieces before they could be formed in order of battle; but I have little doubt that they were so completely exhausted by hardships and starvation that they were then too weary and too weak to fight, and that they only waited apathetically for their fate. For it is impossible otherwise that a thousand Paraguayans with seventeen guns could have been " defeated by a handful of our heroes, with the loss to us of only five men wounded," as the aide-de-camp of the Comte D' Eu writes to his chief.

The battle, or massacre, was a decisive one; Lopez and his officers vainly urged the men to fight to the last, and then, as before, he tried to secure his own safety by flight, but was pursued and called upon to surrender; he refused to do so, and was thereupon run through by the lance of one José Diabo, a corporal of lancers. Madame Lynch was at some distance, protected by a division under General Caballero, a cousin of the colonel of the same name who defended Piribubuy, but she was captured with four of her children, after enduring the agony of seeing her eldest son Panchito cut down and killed at her side. The mother and sisters of Lopez were also taken, and were led to where his corpse was lying; the señora threw herself on her knees beside it, weeping bitterly, but one of her daughters, remembering only that terrible day at San Fernando when she saw her husband shot pitilessly before her eyes, and the smart of the ignominious punishment inflicted upon herself, raised her impatiently, saying, " Madre, do not weep, this monster was neither a son nor a brother."   A shocking story, which I would gladly believe to be untrue.

It will be seen that four Englishmen were detained by Lopez after the majority of their companions had escaped; of Mr. Skinner (surgeon) nothing has been heard, and it is said that the others* were put to death, as the Brazilians were advancing, by order of the Dictator.   Caminos the Foreign Secretary, my old friend Col. Aguiar, Solis, and many other officers, are mentioned amongst the slain; in the *mélée* the poor old Vice-President Sanchez was also killed.†   Resquin was taken alive, so was Father Maiz; of his brutal colleague nothing is said. Delvalle (*not* Lavalle, as I have called him in mistake) escaped; I am glad of it for the sake of the loaf of bread he gave me; Caballero and the negro Aveiro were still at large, but I have no doubt that long ere this they have been captured; I trust that the former will meet with generous treatment, for the latter I have no pity, whatever his fate may be.   Don Venancio's name does not occur in any of the late despatches, so I have no hesitation in saying that he was put to death, probably shortly after the execution of his brother Benigno Lopez.

I would have gladly given fuller and more exact particulars, but I have only the meagre newspaper accounts to copy from, supplemented by a private letter from Buenos Ayres.

April 20*th*, 1870.

---

* They are Mr. Hunter, draughtsman; John Nesbit, mechanic; and Taylor, a son of the Mr. Alonzo Taylor, whose story will be found further on.

† Rumour had already killed him twenty times, and even at the last he was sabred in mistake; Francia ordered him out for execution as a conspirator, one morning some fifty years before, but, at the last moment, discovering that he was innocent, reprieved him and afterwards set him at liberty.

INTRODUCTION TO THE FIRST EDITION.

In October, 1861, I entered the service of the Republic of
Paraguay as Chief Military Apothecary, and reached Asuncion
on the Christmas-Eve of that year.

Don Carlos Antonio Lopez was then President, and under
his administration there seemed little fear that the peace which
Paraguay had enjoyed for many years would be interrupted.
I was assured by his English agent, moreover, that the country
was a civilized and advancing one. Outwardly, perhaps, such
was the case; the Paraguayans were polite in their manners,
ready in conversation, and the better classes usually well
dressed; but it needs more than these to constitute a civilized
people. They—as a people—were advanced, also, when compared with the Indians of the Chaco, their neighbours, the
Payaguàs and the Guaicùrùs; and it would be unfair to judge
them or their acts by European standards, by rules only
applicable to communities long in the enjoyment of absolute
civilization.

I say thus much to show that I did not wilfully run into
danger, and, on the other hand, to deprecate too stern a judgment of a people I esteem and pity.

It must be remembered that two classes, related, but distinct, formed the population of Paraguay: the descendants of the Spanish settlers, more or less tainted by admixture with the Guaranis and other Indian tribes, the aboriginal .inhabitants of Paraguay, and the descendants of these Indians themselves. Of the latter, necessarily more numerous, the bulk of the people consisted, and they were raised but a step above the savage of the pampas.

The former and superior class was almost exterminated during the first year of the war, and hence one reason of the blind obedience of the rest to the orders of Lopez, an obedience almost as unreasoning as that of an ox to his master, but which has been mistaken in Europe for devotion and patriotism. For, owing to the system adopted by the Jesuits, who first gathered them into communities, and gave them just sufficient knowledge to enable them to feel the immeasurable superiority of their instructors, a system which threw the whole management of their affairs, even to the minutest details of their lives, into the hands of their priestly masters, they have never tried to think or act for themselves, and to obey unquestioningly had become almost an instinct with them. Deprived of the aid of the only men who could have successfully resisted the tyranny of Lopez; by education, by habit, by many years of most repressive despotism, trained into the belief and taught assiduously from the pulpit and the confessional that any opposition to the will of their ruler would be the worst of crimes; and never doubting the story that the Brazilians wished to enslave them, they fought against all hope and chance of success, for four long years. And even now, reduced to the one-hundredth part of their original number, they still fight in defence of a man who has repaid their devotion by ingratitude, their obedience by merciless cruelty.

It reduces our admiration of their courage and endurance very materially to learn the truth of this matter. The spectacle of a people fighting valiantly, hopelessly, in defence of their liberty, and dying to the last man rather then yield it up, is one to excite our noblest sympathies. But that of slaves madly resisting the very men who offer them freedom and independence, and, blind to their own degradation, clinging to the chains which bind them, is one we can only view with mingled pity and indignation.

Lopez has been regarded as a great general, an unselfish patriot. He is neither the one nor the other. The incapacity of the commanders opposed to him, the constant quarrels, the rivalries and jealousies of the Allies, and the difficulty of carrying on a war in a country the geography. of which was almost unknown to the invaders, and the conformation of which gave every advantage to their adversaries, not any military talent of his own, has deferred his destruction so long; and with the Indio-Spanish obstinacy and tenacity, which he possesses in so remarkable a degree, it is very certain that he will never yield, although he knows that his cause is irretrievably lost, so long as he has a man to fight for him. As for his patriotism, the war itself sufficiently disproves its existence.

The same men who would fight for him so devotedly would, of course, make the kind of police a tyrant would choose. The pitiless cruelty with which they executed his orders may also be traced partly to natural ferocity, and partly to the gratification which men treated with repressive severity feel in trampling upon those superior, either in birth or in fortune, to themselves.

I have retained the Spanish spelling of the names of places and of Guarani words, but I have marked the accented syllable with a grave accent, as Paranà, in all cases ; in Spanish words I have, as a rule, only used the accent, and then the acute, when they vary from the usual accentuation of that language ; in which, by the way, j (and sometimes g and x) is a guttural aspirate. It must rather astonish a Spaniard to hear how Juan, Juanita, and our old friend Don Quixote, are generally miscalled by us.

I may remark that the diphthongs ai and ay should be pronounced exactly like the *i* in thigh, so Paraguay should rhyme with why, or more exactly with why-i, and

> " The town of Buenos Aires
> Built all in the mire is,"

(which it is not) writes a local poet of Hibernian extraction.

It is remarkable that the Indians of South America almost invariably accent the last syllable, as in Tuyutì (white mud-water), a marsh ; Tuyucuè (mud-that-was), a dried up marsh ; Tatàmi (a little fire), give me a light ; Yaguàretè (a big dog), a tiger ; whilst those of the North generally place the stress of the voice on the penultimate, *e.g.*, Mohican, Potòmac, Shamòke, and so on.

The word Paraguay means a fishing-net, or a hide-bag for carrying water, and should have been written paragua-eù. The last syllable, *eù* (*water*), however, cannot be represented by any combination of letters known to the Spaniards ; indeed it is almost unpronounceable by Europeans, so they wrote it as we see. But it was a blunder altogether. The discoverers of the river under Gabot found some natives fishing, and pointed to the river to ask its name ; the Indians thought they indicated the net, and replied, paragua-eù, and the mistake was not found out till it was too late to alter it.*

G. F. M.

CROYDON, *August*, 1869.

* I should state that Mansfield and Page are my authorities for this derivation, and in confirmation of it, I noticed that the soldiers always called the vessel —of whatever material—in which the water for the prisoners was brought, *paraguà-eù*; but Thompson, who speaks Guarani fluently, says that it is from *para*, the sea; *gua*, pertaining to; *eù*, a river = the river of the sea. Lopez, on the other hand, said, one day, that Paraguà was the name of a great chief, once the ruler of the Guarani Indians, and that the river was named after him. *Quien tiene razon ?*

CONTENTS.

CHAPTER I.

CHAPTER II.

CHAPTER III.

CHAPTER IV.

CHAPTER V.

CHAPTER VI.

CHAPTER VII.

CHAPTER VIII.

CHAPTER IX.

CHAPTER X.

CHAPTER XI.

CHAPTER XII.

CHAPTER XIII.

CHAPTER XIV.

CHAPTER XV.

CONTENTS.

CHAPTER XVI.

PAGE

BOLIVIANS—REGIMENTS OF WOMEN—BOMBARDMENT OF ASUNCION—EVACUATION OF HUMAITA AND RETREAT TO SAN FERNANDO 188

CHAPTER XVII.

THE PLOT—MR. WASHBURN CHARGED AS A CONSPIRATOR—HIS CORRESPONDENCE—I AM DENOUNCED AND AGAIN ARRESTED 197

CHAPTER XVIII.

JOURNEY TO VILLETA—I AM PUT TO THE TORTURE—EXECUTION OF CARRERAS AND BENITEZ 211

CHAPTER XVIII.—*Continued.*

THE NARRATIVE CONTINUED—ATROCITIES OF LOPEZ—MY RELEASE 242

CHAPTER XIX.

MR. TAYLOR AND CAPTAIN SAGUIER'S NARRATIVES . . 259

CHAPTER XX.

BATTLES OF YPANE AND ITA-YVATE—DEFEAT AND FLIGHT OF LOPEZ—ESCAPE OF THE ENGLISH—CONCLUSION . . 283

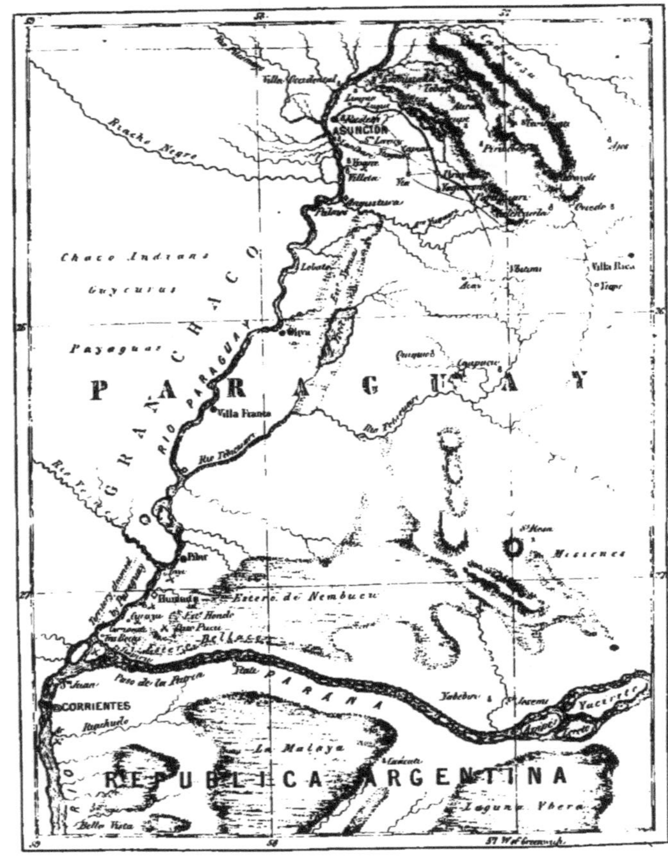

THE SEAT OF WAR IN PARAGUAY.

SEVEN EVENTFUL YEARS IN PARAGUAY.

CHAPTER I.

Since the commencement of the disastrous war between Brazil, the allied Republics, and President Lopez, public attention has been drawn so much to the district of La Plata, that it is no longer necessary to define exactly the geographical position of Paraguay.

But five years ago few Europeans had any clearer idea of its locality, than that it was situated somewhere amid the bewildering network of rivers radiating from the Plata, and close to Brazil.

Now, however, the position of this jealously guarded republic is well known, and the name of Humaità, the Sebastopol of South America, is familiar to all newspaper readers.

I may shortly state, therefore, that Paraguay is a tract of country about four hundred and fifty miles long, by two hundred in average breadth, bluntly wedge-shaped in form, and almost in the centre of the great southern peninsula. It is bounded on the east and on the south by that river of islands, the Paranà, and on the west by the river Paraguay. Its northern margin is not well defined ; for neither a large river nor a continuous mountain chain divides it from the Brazilian province of Mato Grosso.

Lopez claimed as far as the Rio Blanco, in lat. 21° north, and there can be no doubt that this was the original boundary between the Spanish and the Portuguese possessions, and so far he had right on his side. The Brazilians, on the other hand, would shift it to the Rio Apa, a degree further south.

Paraguay claimed, also, some territory to the south-east of the Paranà, but that clearly belongs to Corrientes; and a considerable part of the Gran Chaco, an almost unexplored district on the west of the Rio Paraguay, apparently a dreary waste of lagoons and marshes traversed by rapid, muddy, and tortuous rivers. The only value of this latter claim lay in the fact, that Paraguay thus commanded the mouth of the river Vermejo, a narrow, impetuous stream, which, flowing from Bolivia, may one day become the highway of a large trade, and one of the most important outlets for the produce of that country. At present, not even a canoe floats on its turbid waters.

The south-west of Paraguay, the side from which it is generally approached, is low, flat, and for many a long league marshy and impassable; it is the district of the *esteros*, as these flooded lands are called. Even beyond them the soil, a stiff clay containing much selenite, retains the rain on its surface, and in the wet season immense shallow lakes form, simulating the *esteros* themselves, but drying up in hot weather, and leaving a grey dusty soil, full of cracks, and covered with wiry grass and low shrubs.

When the river is high the water extends far and wide beyond its crumbling banks, and were it not for the melancholy palms standing as landmarks above the flood, it would be difficult to trace its former boundaries, or navigate the muddy lakes, almost illimitable in extent. The immense lake Ypoa, which is rather a series of marshes and shallow lagoons than a continuous sheet of water, occupies nearly the whole of this district, as the still larger lake Yberà does the northern division of Entre Rios on the opposite shore of the Paranà. A dreary malarious waste, only separated by a narrow strip of higher land from the river when the latter is low, and continuous with it at other times.

Above the Tebiquari the country is higher and more diversified; a long range of distant hills can be seen from the river, which culminate, a hundred miles above, in the cordillera of Cerro Leon. The landscape also becomes bolder and almost picturesque. Vast woods, broader and denser as we journey to the north, vary, and at length occupy, the entire breadth of the picture, and a dark red sandstone, easily disintegrating into sparkling grains, replaces the grey clay of the *esteros*.

The south-eastern division of the republic, known as the Misiónes, the old Jesuit settlements, or *reducciones de los Indios*, as they were called, is perhaps the most fertile and valuable in the whole country. Before the war the richest and oldest families in Paraguay were to be found there ; and the climate being cool, the land high, the soil deep and crumbling, the province was celebrated for its salubrity and productiveness. Large churches, comfortable homesteads, and innumerable herds of cattle were then to be seen, where now is but a desolate wilderness, abandoned to the fox and the heron.

Of the eastern division, bounded by the Paranà, very little is known; pathless and almost impenetrable forests defy exploration on the land side, whilst the falls and rapids of Curitibà cut off the upper waters of the river from navigation.

The north of Paraguay is hilly, but it has been scarcely explored; and as I have not visited it I am unable to describe it, except near the large town of Concepcion. There, however, gneiss and mountain limestone replace the basalt, sandstone, and clays of the south ; and there, if anywhere in Paraguay, the mineral wealth South Americans are always dreaming about should be looked for. The Government, and the people generally, showed a singular distrust and reticence whenever this subject was mentioned ; I received several specimens of copper ore to analyse and report upon, but could never learn where they came from, except that it was " up the river." And when I told them that neither yellow mica nor rhombic iron pyrites contained gold, I was supposed to be intentionally misleading them with some ulterior purpose. As an example of their suspicious behaviour, whenever the precious metal was in question, I may relate the following affair, which annoyed me greatly at the time.

In 1866 we were without sulphur in the Hospital, and I wrote to Mr. Charles Twite, the Government mining engineer, who was then searching hopelessly for coal, to send me in a few *arrobas* of the above pyrites, which yield sulphur abundantly when heated. He succeeded in getting me about a hundred-weight of the mineral, and sent it to the commandant of the *partido*, with orders to forward it without delay. That functionary, however, finding the box to be very heavy, opened it, and the bright yellow stones at once excited his suspicions. He reported what he had seen to the Minister of War, and when the box arrived in the capital an investigation took place, and a sample of the mineral was sent to an Italian apothecary in the Plaza for examination. He reported that it was only a compound of iron and sulphur, and almost without value. This was not satisfactory; another specimen was sent to him with the information that it certainly contained gold, of which " el señor Boticario Ingles " and Mr. Twite intended to rob the republic. He replied, as before, that it did not contain a particle of gold; and through a mutual acquaintance informed me of the whole affair. I had commenced the distillation of sulphur from the pyrites, which had, meanwhile, been sent on to me, but I at once ceased working when I heard of the suspicion entertained concerning us, and called upon the Minister of War to request an explanation. He, Paraguayan-like, had the hardihood to say that he knew nothing about the investigation he had himself ordered, although a specimen of the mineral lay upon his table as I entered!

One feature of the rivers of Paraguay, and a very depressing one to the traveller, is the absence of life from their banks. One steams up for league after league against the turbid stream, and no sign of man or his industry, or scarcely, indeed, of any

living creature, is visible. Here and there an alligator is bask-
ing on a sand bank, and disappears, as the boat approaches,
with a lazy plunge into the water; a few melancholy storks
watching with dreamy eyes for the chance of seizing an unwary
fish, or a vulture waiting with folded wings for the mangled
remains of a carpincho, are, perhaps, all one sees in a long day's
journey.

There are the high clay banks, if the rivers are falling, or the
lagunas, if at flood, with the meadow-like pampas beyond,
covered with a short dry turf, scarcely green in the foreground,
except shortly after rain, grey and then blue, as the plains
recede to the horizon, and, save for the shadow of a passing
cloud, without one interruption to the gradual change of tint,
and as silent and unpeopled as when they first rose from the
bottom of the sea.

If, when the Paraguay is ascended, it should be at flood, the
view is but of endless swamps covered with *camalote* and other
aquatic plants, or half-drowned trees showing but their tops
above water, and only upheld by the twisted cables of lianas
which bind them firmly to each other, or floating in natural
rafts, corded and moored by their tangled strands. The tepid
water between them is almost hidden by white and blue lilies,
perhaps by the broad leaves and snowy flowers of their
queen, the Victoria Regia. Flocks of small aquatic birds are
seen, it is true, fishing amidst the network of creepers and
branches, but they give little animation to the scene, and utter
no sound, save a low, warning cry of alarm, if we approach
them too nearly. It is only at sunset, when the parrots are
flying back after a raid on the orange trees, that the death-like
silence is broken. Then their harsh screams, softened by
distance, as they wing their way far overhead, sound almost
musical, and light and life seem to fade out together, as the red
disc disappears and the last straggler passes.

On the Gran Chaco shore (the right bank of the Paraguay)
and on both sides above Humaità for a hundred miles, there are
palm groves, and little else, as far as the eye can reach, not,

however, with the tall column-like stems, rising slender and arrowy to the feathery crest of foliage, as one usually pictures that most graceful of trees, but with thick bulging trunks, rough with spines, with a thin ragged crown, and great bunches of last year's dead leaves rustling dry and withered beneath the new growth, till the high winds shall sweep them away.

When the river is very high, it is difficult for a person on it to believe that it is not flowing in a canal raised above the general level of the country; for, no banks being visible, and the water extending without definite margin between the trees, the land appears to slope down on both sides of it.

I should, however, be giving an impression foreign to my intention if the banks of the river should be imagined to be dull or uninteresting; the rich luxurious vegetation, the vivid contrasts of form and colour, ever changing and developing into a thousand combinations of both, give them a beauty of their own; but they have withal an air of sadness and desolation, and it was that which most strongly impressed me at the time.

The absence of life and activity is not peculiar to the scenery of the Paraguay; it is the same the whole way from Buenos Ayres. The few sleepy towns on the Paranà scarcely vary its monotony, but seem rather to intensify it. Little evidence of activity is to be seen in them, and the broad sandy streets, save for wandering fowls or goats, are almost always still and lifeless; and if by chance a few passers-by should be met with, they are only idly strolling without an apparent purpose, or even a pretext of business. The towns themselves have a singular concentration about them, speaking of the time when they were surrounded with stockades, and their inhabitants crowded together for mutual defence against the Indians of the pampas. Not only so, but they seem to be thoroughly isolated, and were it not for the domes of the churches seen afar on these vast plains, one would come upon them absolutely without warning. There are towns there, of five or ten thousand souls, in the midst of an unpeopled waste, scarcely a road, not a trace of a suburb around them. To me they always looked like some ancient centres of civilization long abandoned to the owls and the fox, rather than the homes of a large, often increasing, but siesta-loving population.

After leaving Corrientes, a hot, dreary, sandy city, there is not a single town for nearly three hundred miles. Between Humaità and Asuncion are—or were, for the war has left but the names of several of them—only a few villages, a little cluster of huts around a *comandancia*, or perhaps a barn-like church; for all trade being confined to the capital in order to facilitate the collection of the custom dues, they had no chance of increasing in size beyond the needs of their few inhabitants.

Paraguay was first colonized by the Spaniards in 1536, shortly after the destruction of the first settlement in La Plata, now the site of the town of Buenos Ayres. For a long time there was but a stockaded fort, dependent upon external supplies for food and other necessaries; for the Indians around them were so warlike and intractable that all agricultural operations—for which however the Spanish settlers never seem to have had much taste—were out of the question, and the garrison was several times reduced to great straits for want of provisions.

A native friend of mine lent me for a short time a book entitled, "La Historia de la Conquista, por Ruidiaz de Guzman. Conquistador." It had been printed by order of Don Carlos Lopez, the late President of Paraguay, from the original manuscript in his possession. I should have liked to have translated the whole of it, for it gives a most vivid picture of the toils and difficulties of the first settlers; and coming from an eye-witness, these stories are of greater value. In one place he tells a tale which is so curious that I give it here from the original :—

"In the year 1535 they suffered cruel hunger in Buenos Ayres, and since proper food was utterly wanting, they ate toads, snakes, and putrid animals, which they found on the plains; and coming at last to the same extreme famine which the inhabitants of Jerusalem suffered in the time of Titus and Vespasian (when they devoured human flesh), so it came to pass that the miserable people sustained the life of the living by eating the bodies of the dead, and even of executed criminals, leaving nothing but the bones, and there was one man seen eating the corpse of his own brother.

"At last almost all the people died, and it happened that a Spanish woman, who could no longer bear such terrible suffering, was constrained to leave the town to seek amongst the Indians some means of sustaining life; so she journeyed along the bank and up the river till she reached Punta-gorda in a great wood. It was then night, and she looked out for a place to lie down in, and spying a cave in the river banks, she entered it, and found herself face to face with a lioness; the terrified woman, nearly dead with fear, fainted away, and when she came to she laid herself down humbly at the animal's feet. The lioness, although dolorously ill, when she first saw her, sprang forward to tear her in pieces; but her royal nature prevailing, she felt compassion for her, and laying aside in a moment the ferocity and fury with which she was about to rend her, gave food to the poor woman (who had now lost all care for her life) in a caressing manner. The woman then assisted the suffering animal, which shortly afterwards gave birth to two cubs. In their company she remained for several days, being fed by the lioness on the flesh of animals she killed, and gratefully feeling this hospitality, nursed the little animals. At last, one morning as she was going down to drink of the river, some Indians, who were passing, surprised her and carried her off to their village, where one of them took her for his wife.

"Some time afterwards, a captain and his company making an excursion into the neighbouring territory, brought in this same Spanish woman, who through hunger had fled to the Indians. When Francisco Ruiz Galan (the captain) saw her, he ordered her to be cast out into the wilderness, that she might be torn and eaten; his order being carried out, they led off the poor woman and tied her firmly to a tree, and left her there alone about a league from the town. At night a great number of wild beasts collected to devour her, and amongst them came the lioness which she had assisted in her trouble, and, recognizing her, she defended her from the other beasts which sought to tear her in pieces; and remained guarding her that night, the next day, and the following night, until at last, on the third day, some soldiers had gone out by order of the captain to see what had become of the woman, found her alive, and the lioness, with her two cubs, at her feet. Without being attacked, the animals withdrew a certain distance to allow the men to approach; and they, admiring the instinct and humanity of the wild beast, went up, untied the woman, and took her away with them, leaving the lioness roaring furiously to show how she felt the loss of her friend, her royal generosity and gratitude being very different to the want even of humanity shown by the men.

"The woman, who thus escaped from the fate intended for her when she was left in the wilderness, I know; she is named Maldonada, but she ought rather to have been called Biondonada.

"However, from the result, we see that she did not deserve such a punishment, since necessity had been her only reason for leaving her own people and going amongst the barbarians. Some attribute this hard sentence to Captain Alvarado; but whoever it might have been from, it was, as I say, of almost unheard-of cruelty."

We gather from this narrative that the Spanish women were not allowed to mix with the natives, although the men very generally did so, and with very lamentable results. For the Spaniards committed two grand mistakes in South America: enslaving the aborigines, and intermarrying with them. The first, a cruel wrong to the Indians; the second, an irreparable injury to themselves, for in place of raising the race they mingled with, they sank themselves to the lower level. And the folly has brought retributive punishment for the crime.

The endless intestine wars of the turbulent, indolent, and lawless *mestizos*, their wholesale butcheries of each other, which have depopulated whole provinces, are but the result of that primary error. Nor will they cease, I fear, until the whole mixed race has disappeared, until the descendants of the oppressor and the oppressed shall have been alike annihilated by the terrible vengeance demanded for the atrocities of the conquerors.

Had they only acted as wisely, in that respect, as our colonists did in North America, and had "no dealings with the heathen," how different the result would have been!

There is another story from the same source which I am tempted to quote, although the tragedy it recounts took place lower down the Paraná on the Argentine side of the river, for its own sake, and for that of the quaint language it is told in, and which I have endeavoured to preserve in my translation.

"Sebastian Cabot having left for Spain, to the great sorrow of those who remained, for he was an affable man, of great prudence and valour, and very expert as a practical cosmographer, Captain Don Nuño de Lara endeavoured to preserve the peace with the surrounding Indians, particularly with the Timbùes, men of mark and good-will, and especially with their two chiefs, who, helping to support this good understanding, supplied us with food and never-failing labourers. These chiefs were brothers, one called Mangorè, the other Siripò, both lusty young fellows of about thirty years of age, expert and valiant in war, and greatly feared and respected by all. Mangorè, the most powerful of the two, was greatly attached to a Spanish woman in the fort of Santo Espiritu, named Lucia de Miranda, the wife of Sebastian Hurtado, a native of Ecija. The chief made many presents to her, bringing her fruit and flowers, and such-like things, which she received kindly [and graciously: this, with her beauty, inspired the barbarian with such fondness and disorderly love for her, that he determined to carry her off at the first opportunity. So he invited her and her husband to his village, promising them a hearty and friendly welcome; but Hurtado, from right motives, declined it. Mangorè, seeing that his plan failed, from the prudence of the husband, and the honest faithfulness of his wife, lost all patience, and in his savage indignation and guilty passion arranged a treacherous plot (under the disguise of friendship) by means of which he hoped to get the poor woman into his power. So he tried to persuade his brother that it did not do to submit so suddenly and completely to the Spanish rule, for they were already so lording it over the land that in a short time they would overtop every one, as their acts plainly showed, and that if they did not put a stop to this in good time, afterwards, however much they wished, it would be impossible, and they would remain slaves for ever; therefore, it seemed to him, that they ought at once to kill and destroy all the Spaniards whilst they had the opportunity. To which his brother gravely replied, ' How can you possibly treat the Spaniards in this way, when you have always shown so much friendship for them, and loving Lucia so much?' and that for his part he had no intention of doing anything of the kind, for he had received no provocation from them, and had been always treated well and kindly by them, and therefore could find no reason for taking up arms against them. To which Mangorè indignantly replied that he ought to do it for the common good of their people, and because his own wish ought to be respected by a good brother. And he knew so well how to mould his brother, who was a great warrior of generous and open countenance and heart, that he persuaded him to enter into the plot, and he only waited for an opportunity to carry it out, which Fortune soon afterwards gave him, to the height of his wishes, in this way. There being a scarcity of food in the fort, Captain Don Nuño sent forty soldiers in the brigantine with Captain Rui Garcia to seek for it in the river islands, with orders to return as soon as possible. So the brigantine having left, Mangorè had a good chance, and the more so because Sebastian Hurtado, the husband of Lucia, had gone with the rest; so he soon collected under their chiefs more than 4,000 Indians, who were placed in ambuscade in a grove of willows, on a bend of the river, about half-a-league from the fort; then, to carry out his design more easily, and facilitate their entrance, Mangorè went to the fort with thirty strong young men carrying fish, meat, honey, maize, and butter for the garrison, and with great show of friendship divided these things amongst them, giving the greater part to the captain and officers, and the rest to the soldiers; the present was gratefully received, and, as it was near sunset, the bearers stayed that night in the fort. When the traitor knew that all, save the guard and sentinels, were sleeping, he gave a signal to the men in ambuscade, who had silently surrounded the walls, so they within and those without attacked at the same moment the sentinels, set fire to the magazine, in an instant seized the gates and killed the guards, and those of the Spaniards whom they met hurrying in terror and the greatest disorder from their quarters to the place-of-arms; for the force of the enemy was so great that some ran here, others ran there, and many were killed in their beds without being able to offer the least resistance. But a small band fought valiantly, particularly did Don Nuño de Lara, who ran to the courtyard with his sword and shield in the midst of the enemy, wounding and killing many, and causing such terror that none dared come near him. Seeing that he slew all who approached, the chiefs and warriors therefore drew off, and attacked him from a distance with darts and lances till he was covered with wounds and bathed in blood. At the same time the sergeant-major, in a suit of armour and armed with a halbert, fought his way through the ranks of the Indians to the gate, intending to make himself master of it; he cut down and wounded his foes on all sides, receiving himself many blows, and had reached the threshold, but there was surrounded, shot through with arrows, and fell down dead.

"Also Ensign Ovieda, and a few of his men well armed, sallied out and attacked a large force of the enemy, and tried to drive them out of the magazine, and pressed forward with great courage, but were all mortally wounded or cut to pieces; valiant, however, until death, they sold their lives in this cruel battle at the cost of numberless of the barbarians. Their captain, Don Nuño, wounded, bleeding, standing alone without succour, threw himself into the densest throng of the enemy where he saw Mangorè; he cut him down with his sword, and making sure with two other blows left him dead at his feet. He killed many other chiefs and Indians; but at length, exhausted and bloodless from his many wounds, he fell to the earth, and died cheerfully under the blows of the savages, since like a brave man he had manfully done his duty. After the death of this captain the fort was soon taken, the Indians leaving none alive save five women, amongst them the too dear* Lucia de Miranda, and some three or four children who were taken as prisoners.

"A pile was then made of all the spoil for division amongst the warriors, but rather that the chiefs might more easily take what best pleased them. Which being done, Siripò gazed on the dead body of his brother and the lady who had cost him so dear, and burst into tears as he thought of Mangorè's ardent love and how he had longed for her; and when the spoil was divided he would take nothing, save Lucia. She was thus his slave, yet she was the ruler of his free-will, as I shall show presently. When she was given up to him she wept bitterly, and although she was well treated by Siripò and his servants, nothing could console her for being in the power of a savage. One day, seeing she was so unhappy, Siripò tried to console her, and said to her with great tenderness, 'From to-day forward, dear Lucia, I will not have thee for my slave, but for my dearest wife, and as such thou wilt be mistress of all I possess, and do with it as best pleases thee, and I now give thee the most valuable trea· sure I have—my heart.'

"This speech completed the misery of the hapless captive, and a few days afterwards her sorrow was augmented by the arrival of Sebastian Hurtado, who was brought as a prisoner to Siripò. He had returned with the rest in the brigantine to the fort, and saw it sacked and ruined and the bodies of the dead lying un- buried there; but not finding that of his wife, he considered within himself, and resolved to go over to the savages, and remain a prisoner with her, preferring this, or even death, to living apart from her. So, without telling any one of his intention, he set off on this errand, and the next day was taken prisoner, and

* *Caro* has, in Spanish, the same double meaning as its English.

presented with his hands bound to Siripò, who, looking angrily on him, ordered him to be taken from his presence and put to death. This was heard by his unhappy wife, who threw herself, dissolved in tears, at the feet of her new husband, and prayed him to spare his life, and let them both be his slaves for ever. Siripò at length granted this prayer, moved by the earnest supplications of her he was so desirous to please, but on a very hard condition : that, under pain of his indignation, which would cost the lives of both, they should hold no communication with each other. Moreover, he promised to give Hurtado another woman for a wife, with whom he would live very happily, he said, and that he would not treat him as a slave, but as his friend. They both agreed to these terms, and for some time nothing particular occurred ; but as there are no bonds which can prevent lovers following the road to which their passion would lead them, they never lost an opportunity of conversing together; and as Hurtado ever had his eyes fixed on Lucia, and she on her true husband, they soon attracted attention, especially as they were jealously watched by an Indian girl who had been the favourite of Siripò, but repudiated for the sake of her Spanish rival. So, one day, this girl said maliciously to Siripò, ' You are very contented with your new wife, but she is not contented with you ; she values more a look from her former husband than all the affection you can give her. But this you deserve for casting off her who by blood and love belonged to you, for the sake of this vile stranger whom you have taken in her place.' Siripò changed countenance when he heard this, and none doubted but that he would immediately punish the lawful lovers atrociously ; but, wishing to have full confirmation of what he had heard, he concealed his resentment, and from that day watched them carefully.

"At length he caught them together, and he, with infernal cruelty, at once ordered a great fire to be made, and the good Lucy to be burnt alive. The sentence was carried out, she suffered it with great courage, bearing the burning which put an end to her life like a good Christian, praying that God our Lord would have mercy upon her and pardon her great sins, and so her gentle spirit flew away. Then the cruel savage ordered them to kill Sebastian Hurtado ; so he was delivered to a number of young men, who tied him hand and foot and then bound him to a tree, where he was shot with arrows by these barbarians until life was departing ; when, his body all rent and torn, he raised his eyes to heaven, imploring our Lord to forgive his sins, and so died, and from His mercy we must believe that husband and wife are now united in His holy and everlasting glory.

"All this happened in the year 1532, and was told me by an Indian who witnessed it, and was afterwards my servant."

CHAPTER II.

The climate of Paraguay is an important question for foreigners who may think of visiting it, and one which, but for an accident, I should have been able to enter into at some length ; for I took careful and systematic observations of the barometer, thermometer, pluviometer, and other instruments used by meteorologists, but my register was unfortunately lost with my instruments in 1866.

However, I can give as much information as the general reader will care for from memory and the observations of Captain Page, U.S.N. This officer gives as the maximum height of thermometer 95°, Jan. 3rd; minimum 46°, May 16th. Mean annual range 76° ; ditto of barometer 29.07. But I have registered temperatures both very much higher and lower than these. In December I have frequently seen the thermometer at noon above 100° (up to 110°) in the shade, and in the winter, that is to say in the months of June to August, during the night as low as the freezing point, but the latter circumstance is rare. The climate is that of the southern Mediterranean coast, but very much damper. The wet-ball thermometer often· indicated an extraordinary amount of moisture in the air ; this would be expected from the immense extent of river and marsh surface in the country; and was most disagreeably shown by the dampness of rooms which had been shut up for a day or two, and the thick coating of fungoid growths found upon our clothes, and especially boots, if left in them under the same circumstances. The rain-fall averaged 150 inches per annum; the greatest quantity I measured in one day was 7·85 inches. Storms were very frequent, and deaths from lightning by no means uncommon; on one occasion three men and five horses were killed by a single flash. I satisfied myself by frequent observation that the electrical discharge most to be dreaded was the one from the earth, and I had a good opportunity of verifying this opinion by the flash proceeding several times from a very circumscribed piece of damp ground near my quarters, situated on an excessively arid upland. Usually the lightning played almost constantly during the storm from cloud to cloud, accompanied by a continual roll of loud thunder; but at intervals of about fifteen minutes there would be a flash of blinding intensity, and a perfectly simultaneous crash, more deafening than the near report of a battery of heavy artillery. This would restore the electrical equilibrium for a time, and there would be a temporary lull in the storm, which only gradually reached its former violence. Now on two occasions men were killed within a few yards of me, and by a flash of this kind, and there was no appreciable interval between the discharge and the detonation which accompanied it. The odour of ozone was remarkably strong each time. The rain meanwhile would be pouring down in torrents, and sweeping in a raging flood down the steep hill-side. But in an hour or two the sun or the stars would shine out brightly, and, except for the deep gullies torn in the sandy streets, not a trace of the tempest would be left.

The prevailing winds are from the east and north-east; it must be remembered that the ocean and equatorial conditions are the reverse of ours, that from the south is often bitterly cold, and so dry that it affects the skin most disagreeably. It is usually presaged by a sudden fall of half-an-inch or more in the barometer, and often blows with extreme violence—*a pampero*, as the natives term it.

I should be departing from my plan if I entered into any detailed account of the fauna and flora of Paraguay, and will only say that the extraordinary variety and strangeness of both make the country alike interesting to the naturalist and the botanist. I should but disappoint the scientific reader by entering slightly upon these subjects, and at the same time I should fail to give any adequate idea of the beauty of the trees and flowers growing under that fervid tropical sun, and bathed in a warm moist air which seems to give them a higher vitality and development than they can reach in our colder clime. So I shall devote this chapter to a few random notes on these subjects, referring those who would have fuller information to the "Republique de la Paraguay" of Du Graty.

One of the favourite topics of conversation amongst my native friends was that of the Indians who roamed, or were supposed to roam, in the prairies and woods to the north and east of Paraguay; and I wish I could now recall some of the legends, half whimsical, half pathetic, they told me about them; their strange forms, and sometimes terrible, sometimes ludicrous, ferocity.

These were, of course, but idle tales, and the Guaicurù and Payaguà Indians I saw in Asuncion were but savages of a very uninteresting kind indeed; there is, however, one tribe living in the vast woods to the north of Concepcion I should have liked to have studied; whilst I was in "seclusion" a few of them were brought down to Asuncion, and, as they were attacked by small-pox, my friend, Dr. Rhind, enjoyed the opportunity I lost. They would seem to be of a very low type. Stunted in growth, and with almost black skins, and lean slender limbs, they reminded him painfully of monkeys; and their intelligence seemed to be hardly greater than that of those animals. They neither build huts, nor use clothes, nor do they know the use of fire; they live in the woods on fruits and roots, occasionally stealing the fowls of the settlers near their domains, and eating them uncooked; and the soldiers told him that if they were put in a cattle pen they had no better idea of escaping than oxen would have under the same circumstances. They appear to have no articulate language, and Señora Leite-Pereira* assured me that

* The wife of the Portuguese consul.

she had had two of them (about six years of age when caught) some years in her house, but that they could never be taught to speak. Several of the men under Dr. Rhind's care died, and the women showed their grief by putting their heads between their knees, and rolling over and over, around the bodies, uttering, at the same time, groans and short jerking shrieks.

I saw a man, when I was a prisoner, standing opposite the door of my cell for some time, exactly resembling an ape in features; there was the same muzzle-like projection of jaw, the depressed curve between the tip of the nose and the brows, the eyes close together, with long tubular upper-lids, which he was incessantly winking; and he grinned and showed his strong close teeth when spoken to, just as a tame monkey would. I am inclined to think, however, that the Guaiquìs are cretins, resulting from the constant, perhaps incestuous, interbreeding of a few Indians of a higher type, lost in the woods. But the wonderful intelligence, the sad expression, and almost human actions of the monkeys on the one hand, and the ape-like features, and mere animal lives of many of the natives on the other, affected me most disagreeably. I could never shoot a monkey, though the Paraguayans did the Guaiquìs without compunction, saying they were not "*cristianos*," and were incorrigible thieves.

Whilst I was in the U. S. Legation I had an excellent opportunity of studying the habits of the gregarious spider, which is an apparent exception to the rule that the Araneæ are the most unsocial and blood-thirsty of animals. These spiders when full grown have bodies about half an inch in length, black, with the exception of a row of bright red spots on the side of the abdomen, four eyes, remarkably strong mandibles, and stout, almost hairless legs, nearly an inch in length. They construct, in concert, immense webs, often thirty feet long and eight deep, generally between two trees, and ten or twelve feet from the ground.

Across a roadway is a favourite station with them, and when so placed the webs are invariably at a sufficient height to allow equestrians and bullock carts to pass beneath; but I could generally touch them with my whip, for if too high they would have missed the flies and moths, their principal food, which do not rise far from the ground.

In the *patio*, the grassy courtyard of the Legation, was a small garden, the beds bordered with bricks (exactly like one of Lord Paulet's in Charles the Second's time, I was reading of the other day) and fenced in. It was rarely entered, except by a stooping old crone, one of the servants, and the spiders had stretched six of these huge nets between a large Cape jasmine and a clump of orange and peach trees about forty feet apart. They had extended two strong cables, as thick as pack-thread, to form the margin of each of the webs, the lower being only four feet from the ground, and between them was a light, loose network, imperfectly divided into webs, each presenting about a square foot of surface. Each of these sub-webs was occupied by a spider from sunset till a little after sunrise, the six containing, I should say, two thousand of them altogether. But they often changed their location, and a double stream was always passing along the cables, apparently strengthening them as they came and went, and sometimes three or four would be lying in wait within a few inches of each other; but I noticed that they always gave the lines a quick, impatient shake whenever a companion left the main rigging, which formed the public gangways, and ventured on to the lighter threads. In passing, they crawled over or under each other without hesitation, unlike beetles and ants, which always pause when they meet.

Soon after sunrise they left their webs, and retreating to the shade formed two or three large masses, under the thick foliage of the jasmine ; there they remained motionless till sunset, when the black lump crumbled to pieces—it was a curious sight to see the process—and then, in a leisurely way, the spiders scattered themselves to their aërial fishing. The air swarmed with mosquitoes, which were caught in great numbers, but were too small game, and were hastily swept away by the spiders, for they made the webs conspicuous. The larger flies, and especially the moths, were at once pounced upon and devoured by the nearest spider, or several of them; and I have often seen half a dozen feeding amicably together on the body of the same insect.

I also satisfied myself that they are not content with merely sucking the juices of their prey, but devour the soft parts altogether: of moths they would leave but the wings; of beetles, all but the abdomen. Their fangs and jaws are greatly developed (I have several times allowed them to strike the former into my finger, but I felt no pain beyond the slight prick as they entered), and are well suited for tearing and comminuting.

Another peculiarity is, that they swallow any part of their web which may be broken or torn by the wind. If such an accident occurred, the nearest spider gathered up the loose threads, rolled them into a ball, and immediately ate it. I have arrested them in the act, and found that the silk had been abundantly moistened with clear saliva preparatory to doing so. I was long puzzled by the difficulty, how was the first thread, often sixty or seventy feet long, thrown from tree to tree? For intervening bushes made it impossible to adopt the native theory, that they made fast to one trunk, descended it, travelled over the ground to the other, ascended, holding on to the line, and then tightened it. I was fortunate enough, one day, to see how it was accomplished. There was an arch of iron work over the mouth of the *algibe*, to hold the bucket-chain, and I saw a spider perched upon it, busily forming a loose, light ball of silk, nearly as large as its own body, which was soon borne away by the wind, and caught in the leaves of a neighbouring tree; when the spider after a time tightened it, and then hastily crossed back and forth on the line, adding to its thickness on each journey, until it was strong enough to support a web. If the weather were wet or windy, they remained huddled together until it cleared up, and the next day the webs which had been blown away were replaced.* Several others had been thrown

* The main lines were rarely blown away, so this was easily done.

from the trunk of one tree to another, in the grounds ; all high enough for the horses to pass underneath ; but although I several times demolished those in the garden, they were invariably woven as low as before. They were tenanted about two months, and then every spider suddenly disappeared ; but I found soon afterwards, under the leaves of the trees, several large bags of eggs, evidently left by them.

I have said that these traits—working in concert, and meeting without fighting—are but apparent exceptions to the general rule ; for I am of opinion that whilst they thus labour amicably together they are immature, and that so soon as the reproductive function is developed, the usual ferocity of the order appears. There is then a sanguinary battle ; the few survivors, all females probably, devour some of the slain, provide for a future brood, and then die also. I think so, because they are all of one size in the same web, crowd together to sleep exactly as young spiders generally do,* and they disappear suddenly, leaving no stragglers behind them. I could find no remains of the slain, I must admit ; but the activity of the swarming ants, those scavengers of hot climates, would account for that.

There are two wasps which provide in a most singular way for the wants of their future brood. One, a large and extremely handsome insect, forms rude pitchers of earth roughly massed together, in which it deposits its eggs, and fills the space above with living spiders, stung, however, so that they are completely paralyzed. I found from ten to fifteen in each receptacle, and all of one kind, with large bodies and short legs, which would, therefore, give the greatest amount of nutriment in the smallest space. The grub of the wasp feeds upon them until it passes into the chrysalis state. The other, a smaller insect, beautifully banded with black and yellow, builds up most elegant little vases of sand and mucus, supported on slender stems, but filled in the same horrible manner.

* All must have noticed that spiders for some days or weeks after being hatched remain on friendly terms together, and spin an irregular web common to all.

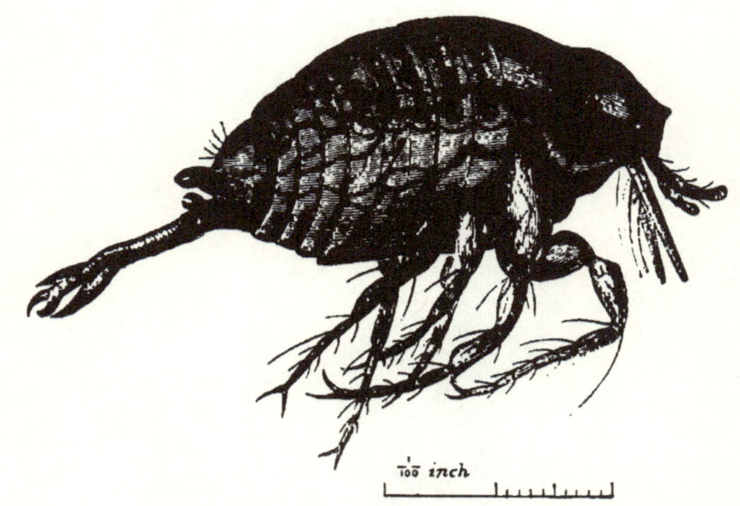

Sand Flea (*Pulex Penetrans*).

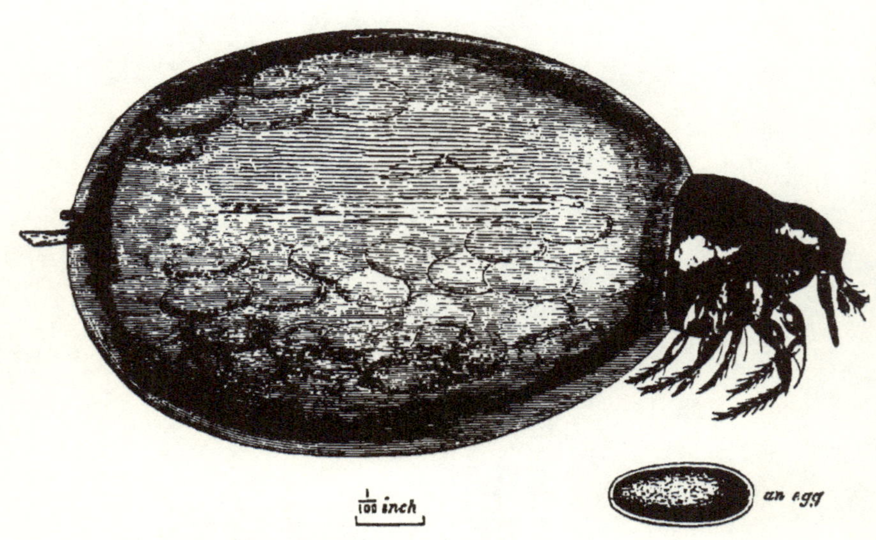

Sand Flea distended with eggs.

It is singular, also, that a true wasp there stores up honey in cells formed of resin.

There was a question I tried to clear up: why does the piqué, chigoe or sand-flea *(Pulex penetrans)*, bury its eggs beneath the skin of living animals?   " Ce vilain insecte," as Du Graty calls it, is very minute, not exceeding one-twentyfifth of an inch in length; it burrows beneath the skin, or rather between the cuticle and true skin, and there, as is commonly supposed, lays its eggs, producing a swelling containing a bluish-white sac, about the tenth or the eighth of an inch in diameter, filled with them.   But I find that the case is not so simple, the sac is not merely a bag of eggs, but is the developed abdomen of the flea, which preserves its vitality after the death of the rest of the parent; and when that event takes place, the eggs are mere germs which ordinarily would perish at the same time.

Under the microscope the sand-flea presents a marked difference to the common flea *(P. domesticus)*: its head and thorax are welded together, the first pair of legs by no means so developed, and there is an appendage to the anal extremity, armed with double hooked forceps.   Its cutting apparatus consists of two scimitar-shaped lancets placed in a common sheath, with which it slices out a space beneath the skin, large enough to bury itself entirely, anchors firmly by its hook, and in a day or two dies.   But the abdominal section still lives ; it absorbs nutritive material through its walls, and grows rapidly at the expense of the serum poured out by the irritated skin into which it is inserted ; it increases in thickness as well as in diameter ; strong ligamentous bands are developed in it, and, more curious still, the eggs which now fill it grow also, enlarging their tough membraneous envelopes at the same rate, and the mature eggs are each of them fully half as large as the perfect flea.

The reason why it does not form and deposit its eggs like the rest of the family I believe to be this ; that in its ordinary habitat, the sand, it finds no food ; that it takes away with it on leaving the eggs all it needs for its own development, but not sufficient to provide for a new brood, and that only those females which can succeed in lodging themselves beneath the skin can produce fertile eggs. The males I have never met with ; I expect they die as soon as they have performed their part in creation.

I examined great numbers of the fleas, to establish these points, when I was waiting for the police to arrest me, and I was fortunate in finding a subject which interested me so much. Apart from the scientific interest attached to them, they are simply a great nuisance, and neglected children suffer a good deal from them.; so do the dogs, who almost tear their feet to pieces in biting them out, and often they get into their lips and outer nostrils, from which of course they cannot dislodge them.

El Tigre, the tiger of Paraguay, the jaguar of naturalists, is a most formidable animal, both for its size and untamable ferocity. I never measured their dimensions exactly, but I had a rectangular mat fully six feet in length cut from the skin of one without the head. One was kept alive in the capital for some time, and fed upon stray dogs caught in the streets by the police. In Humaità, Lopez had two, both immense brutes, in a cage near the cable-capstans. It is said that three Brazilians, supposed to be spies, were thrown alive to them. The story is very likely to be true ; and even such a death would be a most merciful one compared with those endured by others caught and charged with the same offence.

I saw there, also, a fine specimen of the lion, or puma, as it should be called (*Felis Caguar*); an animal very easily tamed, and then almost as docile as a dog. The one in question used to walk about the camp as he pleased. He took part in a ludicrous scene one night.

One of my friends had an almost morbid fear of tigers. Once, when engaged surveying in the *esteros* near Villa Oliva, he had to camp out far from any house ; he sent his native servants in search of food, and lying down near his picketed horses, went to sleep ; he was awakened by the latter straining at the *sogas* to break away ; he tried in vain to soothe them, and at length, snapping the strong hide ropes, they galloped off at their utmost speed. He suspected a tiger must have frightened them, and might return; so he built a large fire, and keeping within its glare fired shots from his revolver at intervals as a signal of distress. His position was certainly a trying one; his servants had apparently forgotten his whereabouts; there was not a tree nor a house for miles, to travel the *estero* on foot was a task the hardiest of pedestrians would have shirked, and the danger from snakes was serious and far greater than that from tigers, which never, to my knowledge, attacked a man; but the tardy morning came at last, and his servants also. After this adventure the very name of a tiger was sufficient to disturb his equanimity, and every large animal imperfectly seen assumed the shape of one.

Close to the quarters of Lopez was a narrow passage between two walls, and late one night my friend was passing through it, carrying a lantern. Half-way its light fell upon two glaring eye-balls, and an unmistakable growl saluted his ears. Forgetting all about the puma—indeed, all else than that wretched night in the *estero*—he dropped the lantern, gave an involuntary yell, fled for very life across the *patio*, and rushed breathlessly into the quarters of Dr. ——. The puma very composedly trotted after him, contemplating with amazement the singular spectacle of a stout middle-aged gentleman fleeing with more than the traditional speed of a lamplighter, but without his lantern, across the moonlit courtyard.

Several tiger cats and an ocelot are found in Paraguay, all with very beautifully marked skins. The natives have made a singular blunder in naming the larger animal: they call it Ya-guàretè, that is, the big dog, Yaguar being the Guaraní for the latter; but they name the others correctly, Mbaràcayà, that being the name given to cats generally.

A fine wolf, with a handsome black mane (*Canis ruber?*), I have once seen, and foxes are plentiful.

Du Graty mentions three species of monkeys, one three feet high; but I have only seen very much smaller ones.

The most remarkable animals, however, are the anteater and the carpincha. The former reaches a large size: the girls use its stiff mane-bristles for piercing their ears, believing that a puncture so made is not liable to inflammation. The latter is the *Capybyra palustris, or Sus hydrochserus.* Linn. It is the largest of existing rodents, and is a most singular animal. Its quick and yet clumsy gait, and its droll truncated face, one can scarcely look at without laughing. I had one for some time ; it was so fond of warmth that it used to singe off its fur by creeping too close to the kitchen fire, made, as usual, on the ground ; and at length burnt itself to death. It is obliged to triturate its food—grass and herbaceous plants—for a long time, for the œsophagus is so contracted that it will hardly admit a goose quill, although the animal sometimes weighs more than two hundred pounds. Its destiny seems to be to feed tigers, for they live principally upon them.

There is another rodent, the *Tapiti buruchá*, or chinchilla, very common in the fields and *esteros*. I tamed one, and had it running about my room ; but like most pets it came to an untimely end. I tried all kinds, from alligators to tapitìs, from the most blindly ferocious to the gentlest and most timid of animals, and with very variable success.

The *Cuatì* (*Viverra Nasua*) I found the most amusing of them all : restless as a monkey, but without that pathetic seeming of a lower humanity shown by the latter, it was ever leaping and climbing, now and then pretending to go to sleep for a moment, but with its sharp little eyes sparkling under its brown fur, and springing up like a squirrel, which it strongly resembles, if the slightest sound caught its ear. It used to leap on my shoulder, and, twining its long prehensile tail round my neck as a support, drive its sharp flexible snout into my pockets in rapid succession, in search of something to eat.

I had, for a few weeks, a fine specimen of the great heron, *Tuyùyù* in Guaranì, that is, one which walks in the mud. He was nearly five feet in height, and with a bill more than a foot in length. I kept him tied with a hide rope, with a heavy paving brick fastened to the end of it. One day, frightened by a peon suddenly galloping into the courtyard, he flew off with the *soga* and brick ; and the latter, striking the wall, broke off and nearly killed a soldier who was lying asleep under it. He flew across the river, into the Gran Chaco, the rope streaming in the wind behind.

To a sportsman Paraguay offers a thousand temptations: herds of deer roam in the open glades between the rivulets and the forests; droves of wild pigs are found in their leafy depths; partridges like our own, and another, *Yñambù guazù*, as large as a pheasant, and *Mutùs*, quails, larger still, are seen in flocks in the *esteros*, with snipe and wild pigeons, the latter surpassing in flavour anything of the kind I have ever tasted.

Should he be a man of an adventurous spirit, there are the great falls of the Paranà, El salto de Guyrà, in lat. 24° 6′ S., which no European has seen for more than a century, and which for magnificence must rival Niagara itself. He would find difficulties sufficient to give the zest of danger to such a journey, and mountain, forest, and river scenery grand and wild enough to satisfy the most *blasé* seeker of the picturesque. He could journey easily from Asuncion to Villa Rica, and crossing the cordilleras of Caàguazù, cut his way through the virgin forests on their flanks to the waters of the Rio Mondaì, and then float down its rapid stream for a hundred miles to the foot of the great falls, the half-mythical *Salto de las seite caidas*. On his way he *might* meet some Guyracuì Indians, who have short tails, they say, of inconvenient stiffness, necessitating the wearers to carry a pointed stick, with which they make a hole in the ground in order to sit down conveniently. But at any rate he should carry a good rifle, and have a few companions armed in the same way; for other tribes he would certainly meet with are expert, and by no means particular, in the use of poisoned arrows. At night, that wonderful bird, the Ipègtàtà, *might* be seen flying like a meteor over the tallest trees, and illuminating them with a brighter light than that of the full moon; for does it not feed on fire-flies, and exhibit in an intensified form their marvellous brilliancy?

The countless islands of the Paranà he would find swarming with tigers of the royalest dimensions; and if he came upon tapirs as large as I have seen them, he might make a "bag" such as a Gordon Cumming would envy.

The natives say that armadillos of extraordinary size are found in the *yerbales*, but I have not seen a specimen. There is one with every scale of its armour fringed with stiff hairs.

Snakes are numerous, but the danger from them is exaggerated by the natives; several of those brought to me as most venomous I found had no poison fangs at all. I have been assured that it is hazardous, however, to attempt to gather the wild vanilla which grows on the Upper Paraguay, because its scent attracts the rattlesnakes.

Lizards are common, and some are of large size. I found their lungs worthy of study, exhibiting, as is well known, a most simple form of breathing apparatus, scarcely more developed, indeed, than that of insects. The iguana, for instance, has two perfectly undivided membraneous sacs, on the internal surface of which the pulmonary blood vessels ramify, and absorb through their thin walls the oxygen of the air, which enters by the wide trachea. It is, in fact, a single cell of a human lung greatly magnified. The natives make a singular use of them; they put the liver of the reptile, which is loaded with fat, into them, and hang them in the sun until the oil flows out. This they believe to be a sovereign remedy for sprains and bruises, exactly as goose-grease is still regarded by rustics in England.* The tail of the iguana is esteemed as a great luxury, cooked, like *carne con cuaro*, in its own skin. But I am not fond of gastronomic experiments, and never tried it.

The natives showed extraordinary courage in attacking tigers of the largest size, armed only with a knife, and guarded but by a poncho. Two men usually went together, with a few yelping curs to bring the tiger to bay. Then one of the men, rolling his

---

* This is not to be wondered at, when we find Captain Page, U. S. N., in his "La Plata," gravely recording the ridiculous story that "The vast growth of sarsaparilla on the borders of this river (the Rio Negro, Uruguay) discolours its waters, and at the same time imparts to them such medicinal properties that invalids resort to Mercedes for the benefit of their curative power."

woollen poncho over his left arm, and with his long, keen-pointed knife in his right hand, met the infuriated animal as he made his spring, and drove his weapon between the vertebræ of its neck, generally with unerring aim. Should he miss, his companion comes to his assistance, and in a moment the huge brute would lie disabled at their feet. But the more usual mode of destroying them was, catching them in large wooden cages with sliding doors, like an old-fashioned rat-trap, and then killing them by a thrust with a lance.

CHAPTER III.

Asuncion, the capital of Paraguay, is situated in latitude 25° 16′ 29″ south, and longitude 57° 20′ 53″ west. It is built on a gentle slope, which rises from the river for about a mile, and then falls gradually away to the south, but reaches a higher elevation beyond the town in the opposite direction. Before the war the population was about twenty thousand.

From the river it makes but a poor appearance, owing to the absence of lofty buildings, and as the houses are rarely more than one story—a ground-floor—in height, there is little to be seen from a distance but red-tiled roofs, with here and there a white-washed *mirador* rising above them. There was but one really handsome building, the Palacio, built by Don Francisco Solano Lopez for his own residence, but destined to be never occupied by him.

The quay, the first point seen by a traveller, showed but little appearance of business, and except for a few lounging soldiers or smoking market women, was often nearly deserted, and the ships seemed to be rotting at their moorings, rather than taking in or discharging cargo. Yet there was a considerable trade carried on in an idle, irregular way.

The wharves, being built on the outside of a bend which the river makes there, are being gradually abandoned by its waters, the opposite bank is compensatingly eaten away by the current, and the channel will soon be far from the city. A hundred years ago the landing-place was more than a mile above its present

site.   Now it is far from the business part of the town (for the
merchants have not retreated with the river), with a sandy waste,
a shallow muddy brook, and a dilapidated bridge intervening.

To the right, as one lands, is the Arsenal, a large unfinished
building, with a number of rough sheds clustered around it.
The engines, machines, and materials all came from England,
and the work was directed and principally performed by Englishmen.   The chief engineer, Mr. W. Whytehead, was a man
of remarkable skill and administrative ability; his death, in the
first year of the war, was an irreparable loss to Lopez.

Above it, on a gentle eminence, stands the Hospital, a long
low building, with a colonnade of heavy pillars in front, and a
red-tiled roof.   In a line with it, but overlooking the river, is a
brick battery, which used to mount eight guns, and is the one
attacked by the iron-clads in 1868; lower down is a formidable
earth-work.   The unfortunate hospital is so placed regarding
these defences that a shot missing either of them was pretty
sure to pass through some part of it.   At the other extremity
of the river-wall is another battery, a brick casemate, well and
solidly built.   Close to the latter is the Aduana or Custom-house,
which, like all else in the country, is unfinished, and is, moreover, so hideous, that one can only regret that it was ever
commenced.   The ground on which it is built slopes at an angle
of about ten degrees, and, as a Paraguayan sees no beauty in,
nor necessity for, level lines, the whole front of the very long
building follows the slope of the ground!   To make matters
worse, there is not a single break or projection to hide the
defect, and the piazza, with its twenty-two arches and heavy
cornice, looks as if it were sliding into the river.

To an Englishman, who cannot bear to see even a picture
hung awry, the indifference which the Paraguayans show in
their houses and streets to levels and symmetry is very curious.
In a row of windows, one or two would be higher or wider than
the rest to a certainty, and in the cornices of rooms, the patterns of wall paper, and panelled woodwork, the same glaring
defect is met with.

On the other hand, the streets themselves are laid out with the utmost regularity as regards plan, always crossing each other rectangularly and at equal distances. The squares, or *cuadras*, thus formed, are built upon externally, the centre being occupied by domestic offices and sometimes by gardens.

The better streets near the river are well built; the roadway is but sand, it is true, but there is a pretty good foot pavement for the greater part of their length, the houses have a respectable appearance, and some attempts have been made at architectural display. But the higher part of the town is intersected by several ravines, which have only been filled up here and there; and in wet weather each becomes a lake, or the bed of a torrent, and then it is often difficult, for several hours, to visit one's opposite neighbour.

With a few exceptions, the houses consist but of a ground-floor, and are generally built of *adobès*, sun-dried bricks, of about the form and size of Roman tiles. I was greatly struck, when I first entered Asuncion, with the remarkably Pompeii-like appearance of many of the old Spanish houses. The panelled external walls decorated with pilasters in low relief, and coloured a delicate buff or violet, the wide and lofty doorway, not opening into the house, but into a broad vestibule, and showing the pillared courtyard beyond; the roof, covered with semi-cylindrical tiles in two layers, the handsome reception rooms, and the miserable, often windowless bedrooms, the dark and sooty kitchen with its earthen fireplace, the arrangements for an almost out-of-door life, and the absence of those domestic conveniences which make the old Roman dwellings seem to us so comfortless—all gave me the idea that one sees there the homes of eighteen hundred years ago reproduced with almost perfect exactness. The Moorish *algibe*, it is true, has taken the place of the Roman *compluvium*: the graceful decorations, the wall paintings, are wanting; it is a Pompeian house as the builder left it, and which the artist has never entered. But, like the sonorous tones of the Spanish language, it carries one's thoughts back to those old-world days, and but little aid from the imagination is needed to bring them with almost startling reality again before us.

I have often thought, too, that the debased Romanism practised in Paraguay (and in S. America generally) must be very like the old heathen worship, as it would have been seen in some remote district or mountain hamlet of the empire, where rude images would be worshipped with ruder rites, by rustics who had half forgotten, or never understood their original meaning.

Religion in Paraguay is Christian only in name ; practically it is but a bare idolatry, a fetish worship. The priests are ignorant and immoral, great cockfighters and gamblers, possessing vast influence over the women, a power which they turn to the basest of purposes, but they are little respected by the men.*

The favourite idol is the Virgin, an incongruous compound of Venus and Diana, but with scarce a trace of the poetical beauty of her antitypes. A virgin mother with the air of a courtezan, a poor, wooden-looking queen seated on a half moon, crowned with stars, and dressed in tawdry, paltry finery, is there worshipped, and fêted, and grovelled in the dust before, whilst, except in salutations or expletives, the name of our Lord is never heard. I verily believe that, if the words of the catechism did not unconsciously recur to them, they would reply, if asked of the creation, that "La Virgin Maria" made the world and all around it. And she often takes most literally the place of the Paphian Queen. A Paraguayan Phryne, instead of begging a necklace for her Venus, caressingly asks a golden rosary for the image of La Santisima.

But to resume our tour of the town. The public buildings are few in number, and, with the exception of an unfinished church designed by an Italian, very paltry in appearance. The

* One day a friend of mine was talking with Mrs. Lynch and Bishop Palacios, whilst her children were playing with the figures out of a Noah's ark; presently one little fellow commenced crying because he could find two only of the patriarch's sons. Mrs. Lynch scolded him, and told him to take more care of them, but the Bishop turned to her, and said in his blandest tones. and with an air of paternal correction, "Pardon me, senora, there could not have been three, for Noah had only two sons, Cain and Abel."

façade of the cathedral, and of the church of San Roquè, is carried up to a great height above the roof, in order to give them an adventitious loftiness, which disappears most ludicrously when viewed from behind. The Cabildo, or town-hall, is a tasteless two-storied building, used for the *Beso-manos* or levées of the President. A new theatre, designed by the same Italian architect, was half built when I reached the country, and so it still remains ; in fact, it would be too large for the population for a century to come, and the architect frankly confessed to Mr. Whytehead that he was unable to roof it. Lopez had a most childlike habit of going into any new scheme with wonderful ardour, but soon getting tired of it, and trying something else. Thus, he had a palace, a new church, a railway, a new arsenal, a new custom-house, a post-office, and a plan for a fine block of government offices and an esplanade, all commenced, and none finished, when, in fact, any one or two of them was quite as much as he could properly manage at once ; and the result is, that the hastily constructed front of the railway-station is already crumbling to pieces, the massive-looking cornices of the Aduana were half demolished by a heavy hail-storm, and remain so, and the theatre is a mere wilderness of lofty walls and arches. There was a so-called Public Library, but the books were nearly all theological, and I never heard of any one reading there. Lopez found, however, a most characteristic use for them : he had the ponderous tomes cut up for rocket and squib cases ! I saw them one day serving thus a folio Hebrew Bible, with an interleaved Latin translation—a most South American mode of diffusing useful knowledge.

The windows of the houses, throughout the country, as in South America generally, are guarded by strong iron gratings, giving them a most prison-like appearance ; and the shutters and doors, with their fastenings, are of singularly ponderous make.

But I like these old Spanish houses, with their massive walls more than a yard in thickness, lofty rooms, and doorways so wide and high that one could ride in without stooping, and dismount in the *sala* itself, if so minded. Their heavy roofs, supported by beams of enormous size, the small, deeply-recessed windows, the broad piazza, were all thoroughly suited to the climate, excluding the heat, and subduing the light, in a manner that was inexpressibly grateful after riding at mid-day through the streets of glaring white houses, or over roads of sparkling sand. But, unfortunately, one of the results of the ostentation and extravagance introduced by Francisco Lopez was a fondness for a meretricious style of house-building of the most flimsy and pretentious character. The fronts of the houses were carried up to a great height above the eaves; very large windows, with the inevitable *reja* or grating, became the fashion, in order that the furniture and carpet of the *sala* might be readily seen by passers-by, and all interior comfort, even stability itself, was sacrificed to obtain a showy front to the street.

Nearly in the centre of the town is the Plaza, or market-place, a large square surrounded by low one-storied houses used as shops. They had, however, no windows for the display of the goods within, the wide doorway serving both for entrance and the admission of light. Being at the lower part of the town, and quite undrained, half the space was a fœtid marsh; there the carts of the country people were ranged in rows, whilst the produce was displayed for sale on the higher ground beyond. Most of the sellers were women, and on a busy day the sight was a very pretty one; for the strange intermingling of colour, which in obedience to a tropical instinct was shown in their clothing, and made the more vivid, but never glaring, by its contrast with their snowy *tupois* and raven hair, produced an effect quite kaleidoscopic in brilliancy and changefulness.

CHAPTER IV.

THE Paraguayans are Indio-Spanish in blood, and descended from the several tribes which inhabited the country before the conquest and which intermingled with their Spanish invaders, and of a few Spaniards who had preserved their blood untainted, and married only amongst themselves. Therefore in speaking of the Paraguayans as a people, it must always be remembered that the upper and lower classes were almost distinct races; the former differed in little, save the antique Castilian they spoke, from their countrymen in Europe; they were *creoles*, that is, the descendants of Spaniards born in the colony; not *mestizos*, as the children of Europeans and Indians should properly be called, and which formed the bulk of the population, and were, I take it, the Paraguayans proper.

The latter are below the average height of Englishmen, but well developed, with broad chests and muscular extremities; head, rather small; face, round; nose, short, somewhat flat; cheek-bones, very prominent; hair, strong, black, thick, and straight; iris, dark, and conjuntiva, yellowish; with little hair on the face or body; and skin, olive to dark brown.

They showed a remarkable endurance of cold, far greater than we. One very cold day I was riding, wrapped in a thick overcoat to shelter me from the bitter south wind, when I met a native sauntering unconcernedly along with his poncho barely covering his shoulders, and I asked him if he were not cold. "Is your face cold, señor?" replied he. "No." "Then why should my body be?"

The women, when young, are often very pretty; their slender graceful figures, large lustrous eyes, to which long lashes give an air of languid gentleness, and thick tresses of jetty blackness, produce a style of beauty which harmonizes well with the brilliant flowers and sunny skies of their native land. But like them they soon fade, and having little or no education, no accomplishments to fall back upon, their charms are soon gone for ever; and the early age at which they become mothers often hastens this premature decay.

Their complexions are usually dark olive, but I have often seen Paraguayans of pure native descent—that is to say, without any recent mixture of European blood—of remarkable fairness; *rubias* they are termed. I have met with some as fair as ourselves, with blue eyes and yellow hair; descended from Biscayans, I expect.

The dress of the men is similar to that of the *gauchos* of Buenos Ayres. Fringed drawers, a kind of kilt of white cotton, a broad belt, or rather double apron of dressed leather; a white shirt, often handsomely embroidered, and a poncho, which is simply a piece of woollen cloth about two yards square with a hole in the centre to put the head through. A straw hat, and enormous silver spurs, weighing perhaps two pounds apiece, and worn on the bare feet, complete the costume.

In the capital, all who could afford it wore European dress, and they showed a great weakness for patent-leather boots; that article of dress being a distinctive one, the phrase *gente calzada*,* or the reverse, being often used to indicate the upper or lower classes.

The dress of the women is very simple, but remarkably becoming. A long cotton chemise, called a *tupoi*, cut very low in the neck, with a deep border of embroidery, in black or scarlet wool, to its upper edge, and loose lace sleeves, and a skirt of muslin or silk, puffed out by stiffly starched petticoats, and fastened round the waist by a broad sash. Except in the capital, very few wore shoes.

* People with shoes.

They dress their hair in two long plaits, sometimes worn wreath-like around the head, or else simply rolled at the back, and fastened by a large tortoise-shell comb, heavy with gold and jewels. A rose, or a plume of soft silky leaves worn droopingly, would be sufficient to complete their very pretty head-dress. Large ear-rings of native workmanship, and so long as to rest on the shoulders, one or more massive gold chains around the neck, and rings enough to cover every finger, were added on gala days.

This costume has, however, almost gone out of fashion amongst the wealthier families, and a *peyneta-de-oro*, or golden comb, now means a woman of the lower class. The change is to be regretted, for the old dress is extremely picturesque and well suited to the climate.

It is singular that the language of the conquered, and not of the conquerors, was alone spoken by the people amongst themselves. With us, and in the presence of foreigners generally, the better classes spoke Spanish; but the bulk of the people used Guarani, and understood no other. The phrase "mother-tongue," had there its full significance; for it was only during adolescence that children of even the best families learnt Castilian.

I have mentioned how much some of the houses reminded me of those of Pompeii. The resemblance became almost an illusion if sitting, when night was falling, in a saloon dusky with shadow, I saw a servant, clad in a *tupoi* falling from her shoulders in snowy folds, the whiter from the black arabesques on its edge, bearing a vase-shaped water-jar on her head, and with rounded pendant arms, elastic and silent step, passing through the pillared corridor. I could almost believe that a caryatide had left her heavier burden, and had come, in living flesh, before me.

Children of both sexes are very wisely allowed to go quite naked, except in cold weather, until eight or ten years of age. The girls of the lower class are taught to carry water-jars on their heads as soon as they can walk steadily; when grown up they scarcely ever carry a burden in any other mode. I have often seen women swiftly threading their way through the crowded market-place with a bottle of wine thus poised on the head, and as safely carried as if it were in a basket.

I one day saw a charming study: a child of about eight years of age coming up from the springs, without her *cantaro*, but evidently thinking that she still carried it, bearing a long plume of white *nardo* blossoms in her hand and sloping over her shoulders, like a pictured St. Catherine; the setting sun, the broad waste of glowing sand, lay behind her, a golden background to the graceful figure of the little maiden as she passed me, with her large melancholy eyes fixed abstractedly on a cottage before her.

I cannot recall ever having seen Paraguayan children at play, I mean engaged in a regular game; and toys seem to be almost unknown amongst them. I got from England some dolls and other playthings for distribution amongst some of my little friends; but the latter were first called "*ipoindite*" (very pretty), and then broken to pieces from sheer inability to get any amusement out of them, whilst the dolls were at once appropriated by the elders, and soon appeared as most gorgeous and fashionable saints. One Christmas-eve there was in the cathedral a side-altar decked out as a *pesebre*, that is, a manger, with the contents of a " Noah's Ark" arranged to represent the procession of the Magi; Shem, Ham, and Japheth, in their cylindrical wooden coats, doing duty for the three kings.

The children of both sexes learn to smoke cigars almost as soon as they could walk alone, and the boys to gamble as soon as they can talk together. These vices of their elders take the place of the more natural amusements of the young.

Once I found a group of children busily engaged in burying a live baby; they had scooped a hole in the middle of the road, and had covered the little creature as far as its neck. It looked somewhat scared, as might have been expected, but lay quietly enough in the warm sand. Two or three of their companions, about five years old—too old, I suppose, to take part in such childish amusements—were sitting on the edge of the path, smoking their cigars and watching the proceedings with the utmost gravity.

Next to smoking and sipping *yerba* (the native tea), the great amusement, one may almost say business, of Paraguayans is dancing, and I never met with people who devoted themselves so thoroughly to its enjoyment. One reason why the *señoritas* like it so much is, perhaps, that it is the only opportunity they have of listening freely to their admirers; for at all other times they are subjected to the strictest *surveillance* by their mothers and aunts—I am sorry to add, not without good reason ; so much so, that before marriage one can scarcely speak to them for a minute alone, and they never walk in the streets with their male friends, not even with their brothers.* But at the public balls, the *dueñas* sit in the ante-room by themselves. I often pitied the poor old ladies : they could not even smoke, and seemed to watch their charges at a distance so anxiously. However, they had their turn at supper, when they not only ate all they possibly could, but carried off all they were able. I actually saw one stout matron maraud an entire pagoda of barley-sugar some two feet high ; and roast fowls were pocketed with the utmost coolness.

I have mentioned that the women, except a few of the higher classes, are quite uneducated, so much so that it is rare to find one who can read and write. The men, however, nearly all do so. In each town and village there was a primary school supported by the Government, where the boys were taught these simple accomplishments and the easier rules of arithmetic ; but I never met with a native who could do properly a sum in compound division, and the facility with which we, the foreigners in the

---

* One native lady paid us Englishmen a great compliment. I frequently accompanied her and her daughters—very pretty girls, by the way—in their evening rides from her house in the capital to the *quinta*, a mile or two out of it ; one day she said to me, " You know, Don Federico, that it is not the custom in this country for young ladies to ride alone with gentlemen: but my nephew, Captain Fernandez, who has been in England, has given me so high an opinion of your countrymen, that I shall be glad if you will accompany mine whenever you please." I was intensely amused, and I think they were also, with the horror and astonishment shown in the face of an ancient spinster aunt, when she met her nieces and me riding together a few days afterwards.

service, handled figures was a source of never-ending wonder to
them.

Shortly after my arrival in Asuncion I went to the Treasury
to draw my pay, and as it was the first time I had seen *el Señor
Colector*, I took a translation of my contract with me, and a
statement of the sum I required. I found him in the pay-office,
a room about ten feet square, but very lofty, with whitewashed
walls and a ceiling of rough palm trunks, festooned with cobwebs, and with a huge white-ant's nest in one corner. In the
centre was a baize-covered table, very dirty and inky, and behind it sat the paymaster, a mild-looking old gentleman, very
brown, and wearing an air of perpetual perplexity. At his side
were two clerks, in the light civilian costume of the country.
On the table was a pile of treasury notes, an inkstand full of
flies, some very scratchy steel pens, and the inevitable sand
box; in the rear was an open cedra* trunk containing a few
books, a heap of silver dollars, and a tray of dull, heavy gold
doubloons. At the door, guarding the whole, stood a sentry,
clad in red baize, with a hat made of leather and brass, shaped
like and strongly resembling a child's drum, who first glared at
me with ferocious *hauteur*, and then, as I did not take off my
hat to him as a native would have done, saluted me with great
humility. I shook hands with the paymaster, gave him the
papers, accepted a cigar and a chair, and waited for them to
verify my statement, and pay me the money. It is scarcely
credible, but they were actually more than an hour trying to do
the simple sum of dividing so many dollars and rials by twelve.
I could scarcely help laughing outright to see them figuring in
hopeless perplexity on the official whity-brown paper, whilst to
add to the absurdity of the scene some idlers volunteered to assist
them, and showed wonderful and intricate modes of calculation,
unknown to Cocker; and even the sentry, fired with generous
ardour, put down his clumsy flint-lock, and scrawled fearful nu-

* The Cedra tree, a variety of mahogany, has been very naturally, from the
similarity in their names, confounded with the cedar, which it resembles only
in the colour of its wood.

merals with the stump of a pen, to explain how he calculated *his* pay, about a dollar a month, when he got it, poor fellow, which was not very often.

I sat with my chair tipped up Paraguayan fashion, listening to the band playing in the Plaza; and when they tendered me wild shots at the amount, which they did occasionally, I told them quietly I wanted so many dollars, and should wait till I got them. At length, when my patience was pretty well exhausted, I saw the surgeon-major crossing the square, and he was kind enough to come to my help, and assure them that they might trust in my arithmetic, and I received the sum I had claimed.

In the Plaza I have often seen the country people reckoning up the price of a sack of maize with the aid of red and white grains of it; the former representing dollars, the latter rials, or sixpences. Arithmetic is essentially a science indicative of culture and civilization, and we always find, I believe, amongst races still in a semi-savage state, although outwardly polished, either an inability to express a high number, or an extreme vagueness in the use of the terms employed. In Guarani there are only cardinals as far as four, above that number the Paraguayans used Spanish integers; but I often noticed how little they were able to realize the amount they represented; a thousand or a million would seem to them only as a great many, and a great many more.

CHAPTER V.

WHILST under the rule of the Spanish monarchs, the province of Paraguay included the whole of the territory to the east of the Andes and the south of Brazil. But when the colonists threw off the yoke of Spain in 1811, all to the west of the Paranà and the (river) Paraguay was separated under the name of the Estados Unidos del Rio de la Plata, or the Argentine Territory; that between the former river and the (river) Uruguay as the Province of Entre Rios; and the remainder, to the east, as the Republic of Uruguay, or the Banda Oriental; leaving to Paraguay, as then constituted, only the small territory I have defined in the opening chapter.

The Spaniards and *mestizos* of Paraguay proper were the last to revolt from the mother country, and when the new Republic of La Plata sent a small force under General Belgrano, to "invite them" to co-operate with them for that purpose, or, if they declined, to make them accept freedom by force, the Paraguayans attacked and actually defeated the very men who offered them liberty and independence.

A skirmish took place near the river Tacuari, in the first case, but it only temporarily delayed Belgrano, who marched on to Paraguari, a village ninety leagues to the north of his first position, and was there finally defeated. But as the Paraguayans were only armed with sticks and stones—notwithstanding the presence of the Virgin, who, mounted on a white horse, led them on to victory—I can scarcely imagine that the battle was such as to deserve the prominent place it has since held in the annals of the country.

Paraguay, however, a few months afterwards, followed the example of the Argentines, and, having declined to enter into the Confederation, was declared a free and independent republic in 1811.

Velasco, the Spanish governor, was not deprived of his rank, but two counsellors were elected to assist and control him in the administration of the law. One was named Zevallos, and the other was a certain Dr. José Gaspar Francia, a tall, thin, saturnine gentleman, who has won for himself a place in history. The latter acted as secretary, and in that capacity managed to embroil his indolent colleague and Velasco in so many difficulties that they were glad to leave to him the task of extricating them therefrom, with the inevitable result of investing him with the supreme power he coveted. After a few months, a bloodless revolution occurred, Velasco and Zevallos were deposed, the former died in prison, and a wealthy Spaniard, named Yegros, was elected in their place. In the following year (1813) Francia suggested to his co-ruler the advisability of retiring into private life, and Yegros, who seems to have been a popular, but not an ambitious man, and certainly a very weak one, resigned accordingly.

Francia was thereupon named Consul; in 1814, Dictator for five years; and in 1816, Supreme and Perpetual Dictator of Paraguay: a title not a little singular, to say the least of it; but, nevertheless, not a whit more remarkable than the man who bore it.

Of his personal history we know very little: his father was a foreigner, probably a Frenchman, who had settled in the fertile Spanish province and taken an Indian girl as his wife. She bore him three sons and two daughters; but he could not have been happy in his children, for one son and both the girls were insane. José Gaspar seemed, at least in his earlier years, to have escaped this terrible affliction, and was sent to the Jesuit college of Cordova to be educated, from whence he returned after a few years with the title of Doctor of Laws, and commenced practice as a lawyer, in Asuncion. He soon gained the name of an honest, courageous, and skilful advocate; and it is not extraordinary, therefore, that although a young man he was chosen for the important post which he made the stepping-stone to irresponsible power.

At first he ruled with justice and moderation; he did much to improve the condition of the people, introduced a better system of husbandry, established schools, and reduced, by the very summary process of pulling down all houses which projected beyond a certain line, the streets of the capital to regularity.

In the meantime the neighbouring republics had commenced quarrelling amongst and within themselves; on the seaboard there was nothing but confusion and bloodshed, plots and revolutions; and, in order to prevent such a disastrous state of things occurring in the hitherto peaceful regions he governed, Francia determined to completely isolate Paraguay from the rest of the world, and succeeded in doing so.

He collected, and drilled personally, an effective army; established forts and *guardias* at short intervals along the frontier rivers, and defeated the Indians of the Chaco, who were getting troublesome. He shut up the country so completely that not a single native could quit it, and the few foreigners who succeeded in getting in, had marvellous difficulty in getting out again. He allowed only a few trading vessels to ascend as high as Nembucù, a town a short distance above the embouchure of the Paraguay; he examined the manifest of their cargoes, selected what he needed, arms and ammunition especially, paid for it in *yèrba* tea, and sent them away immediately.

I think this was, under the circumstances, a wise measure; and I believe that had the people been of a more advanced type, he would have ruled the country well.* But he, a talented and self-reliant man, had no patience with their love of talking rather

---

* One of his maxims was, "That liberty must be won to be valued; and that it should be proportioned to the education and advancement of the people."

than doing, and their utter inability to think and act for themselves. He found that they could not respect, but only fear, and he adopted, therefore, a most repressive tyranny as his system of government. I am his apologist thus far, for I know how sorely my own patience was tried in Paraguay, in endeavouring to teach men who would make no effort to learn, who could talk well, even eloquently, and yet seemed to have no power of ratiocination or of acquiring useful knowledge; and, moreover, how difficult it was to restrain myself from using the power of punishment I held. Francia did not exercise this forbearance, and he made his name infamous as that of a most cruel and remorseless tyrant.

He raised money by forced contributions from the wealthy, and shot those who appealed against his estimate of their means; but he did not appropriate one farthing of it to his own use, and remained poor, although the whole revenue of the republic passed through his hands. Too intelligent to fear the sensual and illiterate priests, who administered the offices of the Church, he curbed their power, laughed at their dogmas, and despoiled them of their wealth. He abolished the *diezmo*, an unequal and oppressive tax, and compelled the indolent farmers to adopt a better system of agriculture. He did much good, but was terribly severe and irritable; and, haunted by a constant fear of assassination and revolt, in his later years he became a moody, bitter, and cruel tyrant, absolutely without a friend or a single joyous hour.

It is difficult for an Englishman to realize the power that a man of strong will and unscrupulous character can exert amongst a race so pliable as the Paraguayans; during his lifetime, and long after, the slightest expression of his will seemed a law that none could question. This was shown, perhaps, most strangely and revoltingly in the zeal with which every man played the part of a spy on his fellows; the most sacred relations of life were disregarded; sons would denounce their fathers, even mothers their children.

He scarcely allowed any, save his body-guards, to approach

him, and when he passed through the streets he ordered the people to retire within their houses, and close the doors and windows, on pain of death; and any found loitering in the road leading from his house to the barrack of San Francisco, almost the only one he traversed, were severely beaten by the soldiers.

An old lady told me, that one day, when a child, having been sent to the market-place to buy some oranges, she was running back with her apron full of them, and, hastily turning a corner, came unexpectedly upon the terrible Dictator. She fell on her knees, the oranges rolling in the sand around her, and begged him not to kill her. Francia smiled, and said gently, " Go my daughter, you have done no wrong," and rode on his way.

On another occasion, a funeral procession crossed the road as he approached; the bearers immediately dropped the bier, and with the priest and mourners hid themselves behind a hedge at the roadside until he had passed.

So he ruled alone, and with irresponsible power, for twenty-six years, and died on Christmas-day, 1840, at the age of eighty. He was buried in the Iglesia de la Incarnacion, the oldest church in Asuncion, in a tomb built on the floor of the choir. The next morning the bricks were found scattered about in all directions, and his body had disappeared. What became of it remains a secret; but the priests told to trembling listeners that the evil one had carried him away bodily during the night. I suspect, however, could the alligators speak, they would clear up the mystery, for, without doubt, his body was thrown into the river, which flows to the base of the walls of the church.

The terrible dread his very name inspired did not die with him. A native will never willingly speak of " *el defuncto*," as they call him; and to this day will look round fearfully if Francia be mentioned, and only to intimate friends tell " with bated breath," tales of his cruel deeds and supernatural wisdom.

After a short interregnum, two consuls were again chosen, Don Carlos Lopez and Don Mariano Alonzo, and they entered on their office in May, 1841. Three years afterwards, it is said,

Don Carlos offered his colleague the option of death or retirement; he wisely choose the latter, and by an extraordinary congress Don Carlos Lopez was named the first President of the Republic, on the 13th of March, 1845.

He was a *mestizo*, the son of a poor shoemaker, who lived in a thatched cottage opposite the church of the Recoleta, about a league from Asuncion, who had married a Guycùrù Indian girl.

A Spanish carpenter, his neighbour, took a fancy to him when a child, and sent him to study at the Colegio, the old Jesuit college of the capital. He was a clever, engaging boy, and his progress did credit to his benefactor. When his education was finished he commenced practice as a lawyer—rather an anomaly, by the way, in a country the only law of which was the will of the ruler; but his occupation was principally that of drawing up petitions, and, at rare intervals, title-deeds and agreements. He used when engaged on the former to whisper cautiously to his clients how happy the country would be if it had but a liberal government, and especially that pan'acea of South Americans—a Constitution; hinting, at the same time, how willing and able he was to provide both if an opportunity occurred. When Francia died, Don Carlos put himself forward, and was, as I say, elected with Don Mariano.

To prevent any misconception, it may be as well to explain that the President nominated the officers, who chose the deputies, who nominated him; so he not only re-elected himself at the end of each nominal ten years of office, but secured their perfect acquiescence in any laws he might lay before them. However, his administration was stained with few deeds of cruelty; he removed most of the restrictions on the free navigation of the river, introduced European workmen, established the arsenal, and a line of fortnightly steamers between Asuncion and Buenos Ayres, and, on the whole, he may be regarded as one of the best of the bad rulers South America has had.

He had little difficulty in his internal government; for the people had been so thoroughly drilled by Francia into unquestioning obedience, and his office was looked upon with such reverential awe, that his decrees, however harsh, were obeyed with timorous submission.

He always spoke of the Government as a vague and terrible abstraction, saying that he was not it, but only represented it, and for that reason received visitors, even of the highest rank, seated and with his hat on.* And he never acknowledged a salute, because that sign of respect was not paid to him as an individual, he said, but to *el gobierno supremo*, of which he was but the visible type.

He made but little difference in the severe laws of Francia, but he administered them more mildly; he did not restore, except to a very trifling extent, the property of individuals which had been forfeited to the state during the former admini-stration; he re-established the " diezmo," and acquired enor-mous wealth by the sale of the *yerba maté*, which was still a monopoly of the government.

The police regulations were excessively severe ; and especial pains were taken to prevent many people meeting together un-watched. For instance, if one wished to give a ball or an evening party it was necessary to get a license from the chief of police to do so ; and when the time arrived a row of lanterns was hung up in the front of the house to notify the fact ; and the doors and window shutters were left open in order that the guests might remain under observation. We English were tacitly exempted from this annoyance, but we were closely watched, and our card parties were not interfered with only because none beside ourselves were invited to them ; our ser-vants, however, were generally policemen in plain clothes, and any natives we visited were closely questioned as to our topics of conversation. The better families had the most perfect faith in our discretion and trustworthiness, and would tell of things they would not have dared to speak of to one another. I was often surprised at the acute sense they had of the cruelty and

* He so received Sir Charles Hotham, but Mr. Christie, who was afterwards Her Majesty's Minister in the Plate, compelled him to receive him standing and uncovered.

injustice of the Lopez family, and yet that they never made a national effort to rid themselves of it.

In the year 1859 a conspiracy against him was discovered, or, at least, was said to have been. Many Paraguayans and one British subject, named Canstatt, were arrested. He was, however, soon set at liberty, owing to the energetic action of Mr. Henderson, then Her Majesty's Consul in Asuncion ; but the natives were imprisoned for years, and two of them were shot. The story of one of the victims is so tragical that I shall relate it.

I should premise, that it is common to see by the roadside rude wooden crosses, painted black, with a lace scarf wound round them, a low fence to keep off the cattle, and an earthen jar sunk at the foot, in which a candle may be placed, and burn sheltered from the wind, at night. Foreigners generally imagined that they marked the spot where a murder had been committed, but this is not the case ; deeds of violence were rare among the people, and murder was, like the *yerba matè*, almost a monopoly of the Government. They were simply memorials of friends who were sleeping in their peaceful graves in the distant cemetery.

There was one on the road from Asuncion to the Recoleta which often attracted my attention. The lace around it was so delicate, such beautiful flowers were strewn at its foot, and, pass when I would after dark, the light of a candle was invariably to be seen shining from the buried *cantaro*. But I never found any one tending it ; there was a little cottage with a few fenced fields close behind, but I saw no other evidence of life within or without its walls than an old man labouring occasionally in the fields.

I often wondered who could bring and arrange the flowers so carefully—too beautifully, I was certain, to be the old man's handiwork ; but more than a year elapsed before the mystery was explained.

I had then some native friends residing near the Recoleta, and sometimes I stayed late. One night a *fiesta* had induced me to remain much longer than usual, and as I approached the cross—it must have been near midnight—I was surprised to see a girl dressed in black kneeling before it. The road was deep and sandy, my horse was unshod, and I was riding slowly, so that I had reached almost near enough to hear the words of the prayer she was murmuring, before I was noticed. She was half kneeling, half crouching, with averted face and pendant arms, in an attitude of hopeless sorrow, and was sobbing bitterly.

Shocked at the idea of intruding upon, indeed of witnessing, grief so sacred, I was turning slowly away to take another road, when my horse suddenly swerved, my sword rang sharply against my spur, and with a scream the mourner sprang to her feet in terror.

I shall never forget the beautiful face, beautiful still, in spite of the sorrow which was wearing life away, which in the bright moonlight was turned to me. Had she not spoken I should have believed that I had seen a vision of even a sadder world than this. In a few words I expressed my shame and regret for disturbing her. "It is nothing; may God be with you, señor," she said in reply, and passed hastily through a gap in the hedge towards the cottage.

The next day I rode over to my friends to ask who the midnight mourner might be. The mocking, half-incredulous look with which my tale was at first listened to soon changed to one of sorrowful pity, and the señorita I was questioning said, "Ay de mi! that is a bad omen: you have seen Carmelita; she is mad, poor girl." I begged she would tell me her story, for my curiosity was heightened by the unusual gravity of the light-hearted Paraguaya. "A few years ago," she began, after seating herself beside me, "Carmelita was the prettiest girl in Asuncion, the best dancer and the merriest talker. She had lost her father when a child, but her mother was rich, and she had many suitors, but she favoured only Don Carlos Decoud. He was to have married her in a few weeks, when, in an evil hour, she was seen by Don Francisco Lopez, then a colonel in the army;

he fell in love with her, made proposals of the basest character, and was scornfully rejected.   He left her, threatening revenge.

"A few days afterwards Carmelita heard, with indescribable terror, that her lover and his brother had been arrested by the police, and thrown into prison; on what charge no one knew; and soon many others shared the same fate. Weeks passed away: one of the prisoners, a countryman of yours, señor, was set at liberty, and it was then known that a conspiracy had been discovered."   The narrator paused, looked round cautiously to see that none were watching, and then continued in a lower voice: "The rest remained a long time in prison, and at last two of them were shot. They were executed in the Plaza de San Francisco at daybreak; Carlos was one of them; and, horrible to tell, his body was stripped naked, and thrown into the street before his mother's door!*   Carmelita was in the house at the time; she ran out on hearing a noise, and fell senseless on the corpse of her murdered lover. For many weeks, in fever and delirium, she hovered between life and death; but at length she left her bed. Better that she had died! for she was hopelessly insane. She shortly afterwards lost her mother; and, left an orphan, is supported only by the labour of the slave, who cultivates the fields you pass so often. She is never seen by day, and lives only to adorn the cross she erected to the memory of poor Carlos, to pray for the repose of his soul, and for that happy day when death and Our Lady of Sorrows shall dry her tears for ever."

*   *   *   *   *   *

The only other event worth notice during the administration of the late President, is the visit of the United States' exploring expedition in 1854. It was commanded by Captain Page, U.S.N., and under his able management the river Paraguay was thoroughly explored, and the Paraná would have been also but for an unfortunate misunderstanding about the right to pass through a certain channel under the guns of the fort of Itapirù, which

---

* I can vouch for the truth of this part of the story.

the Paraguayans would allow none but their own vessels to enter. The "Water Witch" was fired upon, and one man killed. At the same time, a trading and cigar-making company established in Asuncion by the U.S. Consul, Mr. Hopkins, got into difficulties with the Government. The company was broken up, the *exequatur* of the consul was withdrawn, and for some time hostilities seemed imminent. The affair was, however, amicably settled, but in a way not very honourable to either of the disputants.

In person, his Excellency Don Carlos Lopez was short and extremely stout, with rather good features, but showing strongly the taint of Guycùrù blood he derived from his mother. I never spoke to him, and I fancy that he disliked dealing directly with foreigners. All arrangements with us, as *employés* of the Government, were made by his son Don Francisco. His manners were imperious, and, to his own people, rude and overbearing. The way in which he treated his own officers of state may be judged of by the following incident.

When Mr. Doria, Her Majesty's Chargé d'Affaires, went to Paraguay, I think to settle the Canstatt claims, he addressed an official letter to the Minister for Foreign Affairs.* "A. S. Excelencia, Señor Don Francisco Sanchez," etc., as is usual. The next day the minister called upon him privately, and told him in some trepidation that he must not give him the title of Excelencia, lest it should offend the President. Mr. Doria said that it was the usual way of addressing men in his position, and he could not see how "El Excelentisimo" could be offended by it. Señor Sanchez replied that he feared he could not accept it, and asked him to mention the subject to the President the next time he saw him. He did so, and Lopez gruffly answered, " Call him what you please, he will remain but a blockhead still."

Don Carlos Lopez died on the 10th of September, 1862, aged seventy-two years, and was buried with great pomp in the church of La Sma Trinidad, about four miles out of Asuncion.

* Who was afterwards Vice-President of the Republic.

CHAPTER VI.

By the will of the late President it was provided that at his
death a triumvirate, consisting of his eldest son Don Francisco-
Solano Lopez, Judge Lescano, and Colonel Toledo, should hold
office until a new ruler had been selected by the people; and
within a month of his death, an extraordinary congress of the
Diputados del Estado was ordered to assemble, in order to elect
a new president; all knowing perfectly well beforehand who
would be selected, or rather accepted, as their future lord and
master.

The election was but a farce: the deputies from the ninety-two
partidos of the republic met in the capital, and sat in the Cabildo,
which was surrounded by a strong body of troops, commanded
by the very man who asked their votes, and of course all free
action or even discussion was out of the question. One member, it is true, had the temerity to say that the office of
president was declared by the "organic law" of the country
not to be hereditary, and that, therefore, Don Francisco was
ineligible: he was listened to in ominous silence. Another suggested that the present time was a good opportunity for
modifying the laws of the country; he was going on to explain
how, when he was angrily told to hold his tongue by Lopez
himself, who reminded the deputies that they had not met to
consider the laws of the country, but to elect a new president.

That same night both disappeared, and have not been heard
of since.   It is almost superfluous to add, that the next day
"the citizen Francisco-Solano Lopez was unanimously chosen
Gefe Supremo y Generàl de los Exercitos de la Republica del
Paraguay."

He was invested on the 16th of October, 1862, and one of
his first acts was to require that his salary should be raised to
$50,000.   His father had been contented with one-fifth of that
amount.   One must admit, however, that even this demand was
a moderate one; for he had the absolute disposal of the whole
revenue of the country in his hands: no budget was ever discussed, no return of the annual receipts and expenditure given,
and the only thing of the kind which appeared was a monthly
return of imports and exports, and the revenue of the custom-
house.   But Lopez always tried to make it appear that he ruled
constitutionally, and any one unacquainted with the country,
reading the reports of his speeches in the " Semanario," would
have regarded him as one of the justest and most liberal of men,
and a jealous guardian of his country's liberties.

A series of sumptuous feasts, balls, and spectacles followed
his election, and for more than a month endless processions and
felicitations, until the merchants and shopkeepers were half
ruined, and everybody was heartily tired of them.

The new president was born on the 24th of July, 1826, and
was, therefore, thirty-six years of age when elected.   Personally,
he is not a man of very commanding presence, being but five
feet four in height, and extremely stout—latterly most un-
wieldily so.   His face is very flat, with but little nobility cf
feature, head rather good, but narrow in front, and greatly
developed posteriorly.   There is a very ominous breadth and
solidity in the lower part of his face, a peculiarity derived from
his Guycùrù ancestry, and which gives the index to his
character—a cruel, sensual face, which the eyes, placed rather
too close together, do not improve.   His manners when he was
pleased were remarkably gracious; but when enraged, and I
have twice seen him so, his expression was perfectly ferocious;

the savage Indian broke through the thin varnish of civilization, as the Cossack shows in an angry Russian. His address was good, both in public and private, although his articulation was imperfect from the loss of the lower teeth, and he spoke in so low a tone, except on one memorable occasion, which I shall refer to presently, that only those standing near him could catch the purport of what he said. Until he went to Humaitá he always received me most graciously, rising, if he were not standing, when I entered, and shaking hands with me—an honour rarely accorded to a native—with great friendliness.

In 1854 he went to France and England as Minister Plenipotentiary, to negotiate a·treaty of peace and commerce between them and Paraguay. In Paris he remained for some time, and from thence he imported two novelties—the French uniform for officers, and a mistress for himself; the latter the most fatal step in his life. As that lady occupied a very prominent place eventually in Paraguayan affairs, and, I believe, by her evil counsels and boundless ambition was the remote cause of the terrible war which has utterly depopulated the country, it is necessary to devote a few lines to her.

She is of Irish parentage, but was born in France, and married a surgeon in the French army: he still lives, I understand, so I will not give her real name, but that by which she was known in Paraguay—Madame Eliza Eloisa Lynch. She was, when I first knew her, a tall and remarkably handsome woman, and although time and climate had then somewhat impaired her beauty, I could well believe the story that when she landed in Asuncion the simple natives thought her charms were of more than earthly brilliancy, and her dress so sumptuous that they had no words to express the admiration they both excited. She had received a showy education, spoke English, French, and Spanish with equal facility, gave capital dinner parties, and could drink more champagne without being affected by it than any one I have ever met with.

A clever, selfish, and most unscrupulous woman, it will be readily understood that the influence she exercised over a man so imperious, yet so weak, so vain, and sensual as Lopez, was immense. With admirable tact, she treated him apparently with the utmost deference and respect, whilst she could really do with him as she pleased, and virtually was the ruler of Paraguay. She had two ambitious projects : the first, to marry him ; the second, to make him "the Napoleon of the New World." The first was a difficult one, for her husband as a Frenchman could not sue for a divorce ; but should the second succeed, it would not be very hard, perhaps, to obtain a dispensation, and her equivocal position would be exchanged for a secure one. Therefore she gradually and insidiously imbued Lopez with the idea that he was the greatest soldier of the age, and flattered the vain, credulous, and greedy savage into the belief that he was destined to raise Paraguay from obscurity, and make it the dominant power of South America. It was necessary for the realization of this ambitious project that a war on a grand scale should be undertaken ; and with neighbours so encroaching as Brazil, so turbulent and lawless as the Argentine Confederation, it was not difficult to find a pretext for hostilities ; nor had he long to wait for an opportunity.

Long before his election his intentions were sufficiently manifest, and even during the lifetime of his father, who said that he would rather lose a fourth of his territory than enter into a war to defend it, he had gradually collected a vast amount of materials and ammunition, and during the first year of his magistracy he formed near Cerro-Leon (in a beautiful valley near the cordillera of that name, to the south-east of Asuncion, and about fifty miles from it) a vast camp of instruction, and by June, 1863, the army numbered 80,000 men. These preparations produced a feeling of great uneasiness amongst the foreigners and the more intelligent natives ; and some of the latter must have expressed their ideas somewhat too freely, for an extraordinary number of arrests were made at this time by the police. On two occasions, returning to my quarters late at night, I saw a group of them with fixed bayonets hurrying respectably dressed men to prison—probably never to be seen by their relatives again, and only to be spoken of in terrified whispers.* Two priests of the capital were amongst the first to suffer, Padre Corbelàn and Padre Maiz; the former belonged to one of the first families in Paraguay, and the other was a man of unusual talent and attainments. I must except both from the sweeping condemnation I have passed upon the priests; for they were highly respected, and deservedly so. They had, however, spoken disparagingly of the President (all the old Spanish families regarded him with contempt from his low origin and half-Indian blood), had been overheard, and within a few hours found themselves inmates of a dungeon. Father Corbelàn remained for years a prisoner, and was treated with horrible barbarity, perishing at length in the general massacre towards the end of the year 1868. His companion had, it is said, been denounced by a priest named Palacios, who for that, and his dutiful zeal generally, was made Bishop of Paraguay. Maiz remained three years in prison, and was then set at liberty and taken into high favour. He was made chaplain to the army, and afterwards a member of the terrible tribunal appointed for the trial of those accused of conspiring against Lopez in the above year. In that capacity he condemned the bishop himself, the very man who five years before had thrust him—imprudent but innocent—into a felon's prison. I cannot vouch for the truth of the former part of this story; but if it be well founded, a fearful retribution fell upon Palacios : he was tried, tortured, and found guilty ; guilty of a crime which he could not have committed. His sacred office, his devoted service, could not save him, and he fell, with a bullet through his heart, on the blood-stained turf of Villeta.

Many other arrests were made, and it was with indescribable anxiety men watched and waited to see what turn affairs would

* The exact charge against political prisoners, and their sentence, were rarely known ; the evidence, the names of the denouncer or witnesses—never ; and their family and friends were shunned as if plague-stricken, for to be suspected was to be condemned ; and seldom did one fall into disgrace without dragging half his relatives with him.

take. To a passing visitor to Asuncion all would appear, however, prosperous and happy. The "Semanario"—the only newspaper of the country, and written under the immediate inspection of Lopez—was filled with glowing accounts of the advancing greatness of Paraguay, and the virtues and wisdom of the "heaven-sent ruler," who was making her the greatest and most enviable of republics. Every *fiesta*, every day remarkable in the history of the country, was seized upon as an opportunity for banquets, balls, and patriotic speeches; and those who could see nothing of the strings, and the hand which moved the puppets, would have said that the Paraguayans were indeed the happiest of people, and Lopez the greatest and most beneficent of rulers.

On the occasion of the first anniversary of his election, a large amount of money was expended in architectural decorations, fireworks, and feasting. A handsome triumphal arch was erected in the principal street, and an immense saloon of wood and canvas in the Plaza del Gobierno. The expense was principally borne by the State, but many wealthy natives contributed heavily to it.

I have mentioned that the river is gradually receding from Asuncion ; it has left to the north of it a series of shallow lagoons, a favourite habitat of the Victoria Regia ; and when the water is low, a broad sandy shore, called the *ribiera*, stretches for miles between the edge of the lakes and the high banks above. There an immense circus was built for the bull fights ; so large that standing room and seats were found for several thousand people. The arena, some fifty yards in diameter, was open to the sky, but a broad zone of canvas, edged with wreaths of flowers, flags, and palm branches, encircled it, and shaded the spectators from the sun. Opposite the *corral*—the place where the bulls are kept—was a row of boxes draped with scarlet cloth and muslin curtains, the centre one for the President and officers of state, the others for the *élite* of Asuncion, whilst the rest of the space was thrown open freely to the people, who swarmed and clustered from the barriers to the topmost beam ; and, as a living girdle to the disc of glittering sand, glowed with crimson and green, with gold and azure ; the colours thrown out brightly by the snowy *tupois* and *cherifes* in the hot sunlight, which flashed restlessly from fluttering fans and jewelled hair.

The site had been most happily chosen, close to the lagoons, teeming with lilies and bright green *camalotè*, where the smooth sand, or smoother turf, extends from the steep banks till it dips almost imperceptibly beneath the water; whilst the river bank on the other side rose like a wall forty or fifty feet high, crowned by the Cathedral; the tottering old Cabildo, and a few houses as ancient, and part of the city could be seen above them. Beyond the lakes one saw the broad rapid river winding to the far-distant horizon, fringed with dense woods now high above the water, with a thatched rancho or a handsome quinta at intervals half buried in their shade, and veiled in a trembling purple haze, which seemed to enlarge the landscape, and melted it into the softest and sunniest of pictures.

Here, then, Asuncion had turned out in high holiday ; for, in addition to the bull fights, there were races, music, and the *sortija*, that spirited Moorish game all South Americans enjoy so heartily. A gold ring *(sortija)* is suspended by a slender ribbon from an archway, and he who riding full gallop can carry it off on the point of his sword, or a painted wand if a civilian, claims it as a prize, and a triumphant flourish from the band salutes his victory. Two butts of wine were also broached, and with plenty of *caña*, the native rum, distributed to all who would take them.

The spectacle within the amphitheatre, apart from the spectators, was a very poor one. The *picadores* and *matadores* were but herdsmen in their usual dress ; picturesque it is true, but not showy enough for an arena. The bulls were very tame, and showed only blind terror. The greatest amusement was contributed by the *cambá rangàs* (literally, black images), grotesque maskers, who danced and played absurd antics in the ring. But they were all policemen, and I fancy the money the people threw was more to propitiate than to reward.

The races were, according to our English ideas, conducted in a very odd style. A line of posts and rails stretching about two hundred yards marked the course. Only two horses started at a time, one on each side of it, and but for the difficulty of getting a good and fair start, each race would have been over in a minute. All the jockeys tried for was some advantage in starting, which, from the shortness of the course, decided the race. They did not wear spurs, and set off by mutual consent, kicking the ribs of their horses with their bare heels; but it was not adjudged a fair start unless both used their whips. So, of course, if one horse went off well, the rider of the other would not raise his heavy double-thonged *latego;* and his opponent, in a very bad temper, and spluttering Guaraní expletives, had to come back to the starting-point. This occurred so often that an hour or more was lost in wrangling and mutual abuse, before one race could be decided. There was little betting or excitement amongst the crowd.

In the Plaza two large marquees were erected, and gaily decorated with evergreens and banners. There, for two days and nights, the heavy throb of the *gomba*—an immense Indian drum which I could never hear without a shudder—beaten in turn by hundreds of willing hands, sounded incessantly; and as ceaselessly danced the common people, as only savages can dance; whirling, shrieking, and wildly gesticulating, as the huge drum pulsated louder and quicker, till at last they staggered out, trembling in every limb from exhaustion and fierce excitement, only to make room, however, for others eager to take their places. But in that crowd of perhaps ten thousand people, in spite of gleaming eyes and frantic yells, in spite of strong drink for all who would take it, there occurred neither accident nor quarrel till the last day; when a herdsman, who had been jilted by some coquettish *morenita*, stabbed her and his rival to the heart, and then, throwing away his blood-stained knife, gave himself up unresistingly to the police.

CHAPTER VII.

CHARACTER OF THE PEOPLE—MANUFACTURES—YERBA MATE.

In spite of their long isolation from the rest of the world, their want of education, generally speaking, and always thinking in a language which has no words to express "thank you" or "if you please," they are remarkably polite in their manners and address.

Francia made a law, that all males should wear a hat of some sort, if it were but a brim (as I have often seen) it would do,* "in order," he said, "that they might be able to show proper respect to their superiors by taking it off." And a civilian, whatever his social position may be, never passes an officer, even of the lowest rank, without so saluting him. This is the key-note in Paraguay. The military are supreme, and are treated with far more respect than the priests or any civil *employé* of the Government.

In the country, if one asks for a light for a cigar (*tátamè*, a little fire) or a cup of water (*eumí*), at the door of a house, an invitation to dismount and take a seat invariably follows. A cigar is then offered you, and if the place should belong to a family of the middle class, but still one which we in England should consider very poor, a *refresco*, a glass of lemonade, or sweet liqueur. In approaching a house, especially if the door should be shut, there is a little ceremony to be observed. You

---

* In very many cases the rest of his costume, if a child, would be but a tooth-pick suspended from his neck by a string : realizing the old story of an African chief's full-dress suit.

should stop, and shout out "*Ave Maria*," then wait for the reply, "*Sin pecado*" (Without sin), to which you answer, "*Por siempre*" (For ever), and then you receive the invitation, "*Adelante, señor*" (Come in, sir). No well-bred native would think of knocking at a door without shouting out "Ave Maria" previously. It is considered rude to decline a cigar, but you are not obliged to smoke it. The habit is, however, almost universal—men, women, and children of both sexes all indulge in it; the women of the higher classes were, however, getting ashamed of it, and only smoked in secret.

The Paraguayans are excessively fond of dress, and an ostentatious display of it, but they show a singular disregard for domestic comfort. As a *medico*, I saw a good deal of their private life, and the privilege was a saddening one. It reminded me of going behind the scenes during a morning rehearsal. To meet, say, the wife of a colonel at the club ball, dressed in last year's Paris fashion, with glossy hair, and murmuring the most courtly of Spanish, and then to see her the next day in the midst of her family, clad in a very scanty cotton gown, and without shoes or stockings, sitting in the midst of her slaves, with dishevelled hair, and scolding in uncouth Guaraní, whilst her children, with dirty skins, were tumbling about, with cigars in their mouths, amongst the goats and the poultry, was not one of the least curious sights in Paraguay.

Next to smoking, sipping the infusion of the *yerba maté* was the great excuse for idling time away. Early in the morning and after the *siesta* were the legitimate hours for indulging in it; but those who had plenty of yerba, and, as usual, little to do, passed half their waking hours *maté* in hand. Yerba is the dried and powdered leaf of the Ilex Paraguayensis, a tree in size and foliage resembling the orange (that is, as the latter grows there, often thirty feet high), and with small white clustered flowers. It belongs to the holly family, but contains a bitter principle similar to, if not identical with, *theine*, the alkaloid found in tea and coffee. It is taken in a somewhat singular way, the *maté*, a gourd stained black, which would hold three or four ounces of water, is nearly filled with the coarsely powdered *yerba*. The *bombilla*, a silver tube with a bulbous end pierced full of fine holes, is then inserted, the gourd is filled with boiling water, and the infusion sucked through the tube immediately, exactly as one would take a sherry-cobler, except, of course, that it is scalding hot. Some take sugar with it, but a true matè drinker prefers it unsweetened. As soon as the gourd is emptied, a servant who has been standing, with the arms formally crossed, before you, refills it with water from a little kettle and again hands it to you. If several are taking it, the *matè* is passed from one to another, all sucking from the same *bombilla*, a fashion I had some difficulty in accustoming myself to.

When we were invested in the Legation, we used it in the place of tea, and prepared in the same manner, and liked it pretty well. On my way to the United States afterwards, I fell in with an American who had been cultivating it in Paranà, in the south of Brazil, and was then on his way to New York to introduce it there. He was quite enthusiastic on the subject, and was certain that it had but to be tried to displace at once both tea and coffee ; I had used it for years, and become fond of it, but I cannot agree with him. I have seen it stated in an English scientific work,* that the reason why it is taken in such an unusual way is, that the infusion has a disagreeable colour, and blackens on exposure to the air. This is not the case ; the infusion is a greenish brown, and certainly does not blacken until it becomes mouldy. The fact that the leaf is in powder, and that the *bombilla* strains the infusion whilst it conveys it conveniently to the mouth, is sufficient to explain why that mode of taking it is preferred. I have sometimes seen the leg bone of a fowl, with a tuft of cotton wrapped at the end, doing duty as a bombilla. Like tea it is slightly stimulating and astringent, and, if Liebig's theory of the action of the former be correct, it would also be indirectly nutritious, by retarding waste of tissue.

---

* I think Johnstone's " Chemistry of Common Life."

Many medicinal plants grow in Paraguay, and the natives have an idea that every herb and flower is a "remedio" for some malady or the other; and as they care little for their own beautiful wild flowers, although they highly prize roses, carnations, pansies, and other exotics, they came to the conclusion, whenever they saw me gathering them, that I was collecting simples. One day I was picking some superb scarlet verbenas which were growing by the roadside, when a country girl came up laden with sugar cane, and, after watching me for some minutes, said, shyly, "For what disease is that a remedy?" "For none, I believe." "Then why do you gather it?" asked she, with wondering eyes. "Because, like you, it is bright and pretty." "Nei-nah, che carai!" (Don't tease me, sir), said she, turning away pettishly, for she thought I was laughing at her.

The Paraguayans had most singular ideas about geography, which was, of course, principally owing to so few of them ever having left their own country, and they could never understand a map. The representation of a large extent of country on a small piece of paper was as inconceivable to them as an abstract quantity is to a rustic. Indeed, drawings generally, except pictures of saints, are scarcely comprehended by them. A priest was once watching me with great attention finishing a view in oil colours of Mount Lambarè, in which two small figures appeared in the foreground; he pronounced it "muy linda" (very pretty), and then asked in some perplexity what saints they were, and why I had painted them so small. The Paraguay is the standard for position and distance, and all countries were either "above or below the river." They imagined that it reached to Europe, and that Francia, Inglaterra, Alemania, Rusia, and so on, were placed as towns, now on this side of it, now on that; they could never realize the existence of another continent with an ocean rolling between. An old native once asked me the very frequent question, if I were far from my own land. I told him yes, more than two thousand leagues. "Que barbaridad!" cried he, as if the earth were a cruel mother to separate her children so far. They always confounded London with England; and even Father Romàn, who had quite an extensive library for that part of the world, I should think nearly twenty volumes, and whom I found reading a Spanish translation of the life of Cardinal Wiseman, asked me, with a most puzzled expression of face, if Lòndres were in Inglaterra, or Inglaterra in Lòndres, and if the latter really adjoined France! From their isolation, they had very naturally formed, also, a very high opinion of the greatness of their country, and the vast political importance it must possess amongst nations; and their hatred of, and contempt for, foreigners was intensified by the fact of, what seemed to them, the enormous pay we received, and that we had come so far to take service with the government of the republic.

No newspapers printed in Spanish, except the government organ "El Semanario," were allowed to enter the country, and in the latter foreigners were often spoken of as robbers and unbelievers, and every pains taken to make them appear ridiculous in the eyes of the natives.

Amongst such a people the arts and sciences would necessarily be in a very primitive condition, those belonging to agriculture and domestic manufactures especially. The loose, sandy soil demands little dressing, and is merely scratched superficially with the rudest of ploughs, simply the thick bough of a tree, with two diverging branches, cut about three feet long, pointed with an axe, and hardened by burning, the two arms sloping upwards and backwards serving as handles. A couple of oxen are yoked in front by ropes of untanned hide fastened to a bar lashed to their horns, and the implement is complete. When worn out, it is easily replaced from the nearest tree growing in the right shape. The use of manure is quite unknown; in the capital the refuse was carefully collected in the *plazas*, but only to be thrown into the river.

The spinning of the indigenous cotton—probably the most ancient art amongst them—is performed with the distaff, a slender spindle of wood twirled between the finger and thumb of the right hand as the fibre is drawn out from a tuft held in the left; exactly, I should say, as it was done thousands of years ago. I saw the Tartar peasants in the Crimea spinning in precisely the same way, and they showed also the same fondness for making towels with borders and ends of elaborate embroidery.* But the Tartars chose simple patterns, executed in silk and wool dyed vividly, and the Paraguayans most intricate lace and needlework, unrelieved by colour. The thread thus manufactured is remarkably fine, even, and strong. It is made into cloth in a style equally patriarchal; weavers travel about the country, carrying their simple loom on their shoulders, and I have seen it set up, and the operator busy at work, under an orange tree by the wayside, the warp-roller suspended from a bough, and balanced beneath by stones, which also, hanging from strips of hide, raised the treddles. There, seated perhaps on a horse's scull, he would produce a fabric as beautiful as it was durable. The thick woollen ponchos and saddle cloths are made even more simply still; the warp is wound over a wooden frame a little larger than the poncho, and a rude boat-shaped shuttle passed in and out amid the threads. They weave in this way most effective patterns, generally in black and white, or a fine blue obtained from the native indigo.

Besides spinning and embroidery, the principal work of the women is cigar making, in which they are great adepts. The cigars, with the exception of those smoked by the makers themselves, are much smaller than those seen in Europe, the "fuertes" are about the diameter of a pencil, and the tobacco is prized in proportion to its strength. One kind, obtained by stripping off the lower leaves of the plant, and only leaving a few of the finest to mature, is called "parà hobì," or spotted leaf, and is worth five or six times the price of the ordinary. I

* The Paraguayan lace is extremely beautiful, and of marvellous delicacy; the patterns were generally drawn by men: I have often seen *billets-doux*, containing but two or three verses of poetry, and the rest of the paper occupie with elaborate designs, generally of full size, for *tupois*, or towels. It sells for a very high price, £15 to £20 was a common one for a handsome towel. Its manufacture was introduced by the Spanish wives of the early settlers, and was, I have no doubt, derived from the Moors.

have seen alarming symptoms of congestion of the brain produced from its use by those unaccustomed to it.

The sugar-cane grows freely, but like all else is sadly mis-
managed. The stools are planted too close together, in fact, I
have seen it growing as densely as corn in England ; as a result,
the juice is very poor in sugar. It is crushed also in a most in-
effective manner. The mill is simply a massive upright frame of
timber, with two vertical rollers of hard wood geared together with
wooden cogs; the axis of one projects above, and to it is fastened
a long pole by strips of hide, and the other end to the horns of a
yoke of oxen ; they walk round in a circle, and thus turn the rollers; the canes are passed between these a few at a time, and as they
have no adjustment, and no other support than the roughly cut
holes in which they turn, of course scarcely a third of the juice
is expressed. The product is strained through a coarse cloth,
and then evaporated in a deep copper pan, set over an open fire
made on the ground, and without a chimney. The use of lime
for clarifying is quite unknown, and as the juice is generally
acid and heated for a long time, nearly all the sugar becomes
uncrystallizable, and the result is very delicious, but rather
costly, molasses. This is stored in hide bags, tied up with thongs
of the same at the mouth. Occasionally they get a good granu-
lar brown sugar, but it is quite by accident. Brazilian sugar,
in spite of the long river voyage, often of three months, and a
duty of 20 per cent., is actually cheaper in Paraguay than that
of their own manufacture. The molasses is there called *miel*,
which properly means honey, and this has led Sir Woodbine Parish
into the blunder of writing that, "The principal drink of the
Paraguayans" (I quote from memory) "is made from honey,
which is very plentiful there," which is not the case; honey,
"miel de abeja"* (which, by the way, is collected and stored
there by a true wasp), in Paraguay is very scarce and dear.
Much of the treacle is eaten with bread in place of butter,
which is little used, except as a "remedio" or as a pomatum ;
but the greater part is fermented and distilled for *caña*—a vile

* Bee honey.

spirit when unrectified, which it generally is, of a disgusting smell, and often, from the condenser being made of copper, most dangerously impregnated with that metal, in the form of acetate. The natives, who are generally abstemious, drank it sparingly ; but the English mechanics in Asuncion, with the usual recklessness and improvidence of their class, consumed it in enormous quantities, and the death of nearly half their number could be traced directly or indirectly to its abuse. The stills were generally made of copper, but I saw in the village of San Lorenzo an earthen one, an example of the very infancy of distillation, and which yielded the tiniest rill of strong waters imaginable. It was simply a red clay jar about four feet high, the top closed by a wooden cover ; a tin tube was inserted close to this, and then passed obliquely through a similar jar filled with water. The first contained the wash ; it stood on the ground, and a fire was built up around it. The product, which I tasted, was detestable, and I marvelled that any one could drink it.

One kind, called *sustancia*, is rectified with some droll additions: plucked fowls, back-bones of oxen, and meat are put into the still, " to give the liquor strength," as they say. It is improved, certainly both in strength and flavour, but was often ammoniacal from the burning of the flesh. I used to make capital spirit for my own use, and had a small still mounted in European fashion, with a proper furnace and chimney, and often tried to induce the natives to follow my plan. They admitted that it was " muy lindo, marvilloso,"* but too much trouble for them. A French distiller, named Lasserre, had a good apparatus, and made money by it ; the fuel he saved alone gave him a large profit.

There are many abundant and, to an engineer, most tempting streams suited for driving mills, but there was but one water-wheel in the country, used for working the blast of the smelting furnaces in Ibicui. Some of the old men told me that the Jesuits had machinery driven in that way, but the very recollection of it had almost passed away. The whole of the corn

---

* Very pretty—an epithet which they often apply in the oddest fashion—wonderful.

used for making bread is powdered in wooden mortars by the women; they pound it with thick staves of heavy wood, not made in the usual shape of pestles, two or three working at the same mortar—the stem of a tree hollowed out—striking in rapid succession, and in such good time that I was reminded of the noise of a fulling mill. Long before daylight in the villages the quick thud, thud is heard on all sides, as the women powder the maize for the day's consumption. The coarse heavy flour thus produced is tossed in the air, that the wind may blow the husk away. Two market women will pound an *almūd* (half a cubic foot) of maize for a medio (about twopence-halfpenny).

A beautiful arrowroot was prepared, in an equally simple manner, from the tubers of the *mandioc*, or sweet cassava (Janipha Lœflingii), and formed an important article of diet. Much of it was also used for stiffening linen; the Paraguayans had an extraordinary fondness for making everything which could be starched as rigid as buckram, and I had some trouble to persuade my laundress that I did not wish my handkerchiefs to be quite so stiff as my collars.

CHAPTER VIII.

DURING the year 1864 affairs were outwardly most prosperous
in Asuncion, and the numerous fiestas were so extended that it
seemed almost one long holiday; but the short day of Paraguayan prosperity was already drawing to its close, and the storm
and tempest which were to usher in its long night of utter
desolation were at hand. The sufferings of the people, masked
by a hollow mirth, but here and there half revealed by a sorrow
terrified into silence, had commenced. The prisons were
crowded with members of the best families, and the conscription
was still sweeping away the young men, the strength of the
country, by thousands. It was with a heavy heart that I went
to the brilliant balls given every few weeks in honour of Lopez;
for I knew how many there, who like myself were compelled to
attend, were mourning the loss of those dearest to them, or trying by a fictitious gaiety and simulated devotion to propitiate
the tyrant they regarded with equal dread and detestation.
Amongst them was one I knew well, Doña Dolores Carisimo,
the wife but a few months of Don Bernardo Jovellanos; I saw
her, a gentle, shy little creature, obliged to stand with a row of
shameless courtezans, marshalled by Mrs. Lynch, and sing a
"patriotic hymn" in honour of Lopez, whilst her husband lay
a prisoner and loaded with irons, in the Colegio.

Before, however, commencing the description of the painful
scenes and episodes of the war, I gladly turn for a moment to

speak of some happy days I passed in exploring the forests and passes of the cordilleras.

I had obtained fifteen days' leave of absence, and a special passport requiring the authorities of each town or village I should pass through to furnish me with horses and all else I needed. I took my servant with me, and a German who was going out to buy tobacco accompanied us for some distance, and kindly pointed out the route we had better take. We did not start till late in the afternoon, and it was after sunset before we had passed the limits of my usual rides. The roads were good, but we had to change horses every two leagues at the government post-houses, and thus lost so much time that the short tropical twilight had faded into night when we reached the town of Capietà, a small place, the houses of sun-dried bricks, thatched with reeds, and arranged on three sides of a square, with the church, a barn-like shed with a wooden belfry, on the fourth. We supped with the *comandante*, and I, not liking the close and hot little room he had prepared me, slung my hammock outside, and was soon fast asleep. The bright moonlight awoke me at two a.m., and arousing the men with some difficulty, I had the horses saddled, and after a wash in the brook which brawled through a stony ravine below the town, rode off as fast as the road, there marshy and intersected with deep narrow gulleys, would permit us. At the first post-house, my servant, who carried almost all his worldly possessions in a huge bundle rolled in his poncho round his waist, was badly thrown, but, thanks to the huge "fender" he was swathed in, escaped unhurt.

Although the hot weather had commenced, the night was deliciously cool, and the full moon, shimmering over tree, rock, and moor, gave ample light to enable us to escape the mishap of a slide into the treacherous morass, which, covered with bright green vegetation, stretched on each side of the road; itself, in many places, but a layer of large trunks of trees laid transversely over the oozy ground. Soon, however, we gained a higher level, and rode by endless fields of mandioc, with its beautiful green and pink foliage, and the darker tobacco plantations, until we reached the town of Ituguà just as the *reveillé* was beating. There we changed horses, and after a tumbler of wine and a biscuit, lit our cigars and galloped off again.

At the next post we received the unpleasant news that a flood had carried away part of the old road, and that it would be necessary to make a wide *détour*. For about a league we rode in the bed of a small but rapid stream—rivulets in countries so densely wooded as Paraguay are often the only practicable roads through the forests, where paths are blocked up and overgrown almost as soon as they are made. The water was occasionally up to our saddle-girths, and the trees met so closely overhead that it was like passing through a leafy tunnel; and so narrow and low that often we had to ride for a hundred yards crouching down to our horses' necks, to avoid the low boughs and tangled network of creepers and parasites. The air was close and hot, and almost alive with gorgeous butterflies sailing slowly and languidly in the slanting sunlight, which broke here and there through the matted vegetation, and lit up the sombre forest beyond. Several times our horses stopped and started in terror, as a huge alligator plunged into the water before us, or as a boa thicker than my arm glided swiftly away, with the light glittering on his undulating scales as if of burnished silver.

I was glad enough when we emerged on the broad plains, and about noon reached the town of Caäcupè, like all the rest, a hollow square ; for the plan introduced by the Jesuits in the " Reductions " has been followed universally throughout the country, and when one town has been seen, the rest seem but copies of it. My occupation of sketching the place excited the liveliest curiosity amongst the natives ; they crowded in a wide half circle behind me, peeping furtively over my shoulder, and falling back in great trepidation if I glanced round. I asked one to stand in front, to have his portrait taken, but he looked so desperately frightened that I was obliged to give it up for laughing.

The country, after leaving this place, became very hilly and loaded with fine timber. I saw for the first time the Guaiacum and the Copaiba, fine lofty trees, growing *in situ*. By the road-side sweet oranges were to be picked in abundance; my man added about half a bushel to the load he was already carrying, to eat on the way, and made a capital breakfast off them. As we had diverged from the road, the farmers, whose *ranchos* I passed, supplied me with horses, always politely and willingly, but I had the power to take any I pleased.

It was now an hour past noon, and the cordillera we had to cross was still blue in the distance, so I thought it advisable to get breakfast and a siesta before going farther, the nearly vertical sun making the latter a necessity. The next post-house we reached was invitingly clean, and there we had some excellent *asado* (broiled beef) and mandioc, to which ample justice was done. The old sergeant, to whom the place belonged, watched with a most amusing mixture of respect and curiosity the "foreign lieutenant" eating, waiting upon us most assiduously the while. When the meal was finished, his daughter, a very pretty *rubia*, brought us water and beautifully embroidered towels for washing, and then cigars. Our host and my companions were soon fast asleep, but I passed the time more to my taste in chatting, under difficulties, with the *rubiacèta*. She could not speak Spanish, and I but little Guaranì; and we laughed so much that at last we woke up "taità," who, greatly scandalized, sent her into the house immediately.

The road now lay through the finest camp (which means meadowland in South America) I had ever seen, the grass reaching high above our saddles. I there saw a *tujuju*, a white crane with a black head, nearly five feet high. About four p.m. we commenced the ascent of the Cordillera Azcurra.

It was not nearly so formidable as I expected it would have been, until near the top, where the slope became so steep that it had been cut into ledges, with trunks of trees thrown across, forming a rude stairway. Our horses clambered up without accident; but though there was not more than a hundred feet of it, I was not sorry when we reached the top, for it was decidedly unpleasant to look back. The whole height of the

pass above the valley may have been 1,500 feet, but it is difficult to estimate, by the eye, the altitude of densely wooded hills.

The view from the summit was glorious ; the mountain chain, the distant river, and the far-reaching camp, seen in one magnificent panorama. At our feet was the beautiful lake of Ipacarai, about four leagues in length by one in breadth, its ripples washing the stems of the palms which crowded the shore, and breaking up the deep shadow from their feathery foliage, which, ever restless, swung in the summer breeze. Here and there stood a *rancho*, with its white walls and thatched roof, and beyond rose more palms, then cedras and lofty forest trees, hung with bright-flowered orchids and brown rope-like lianas, wave above wave to the very hill-tops. In the foreground all was a vivid green, fading gradually away with the distance into a soft purple grey, that melted, with scarcely a defined margin, into the cloudy horizon. The pass itself was walled in by tall, channelled *cacti*, bristling with spines, and loaded with delicate pink and white flowers, and euphorbias more formidable still, for their thorny branches poison as well as wound. In place of grass, the wild pine-apple, or *caraguatá*, covered the ground, whilst its serrated prickly leaves, of a bright scarlet in the centre, barred all straggling from the road.*

As we were resting at the summit of the cordillera, and enjoying the cool breeze and beautiful view, the guide came to my side, and told the following legend, which I do not give *exactly* as I heard it.

"Where we now see the great lake, there was, many years ago, a broad and fertile valley ; and when the good fathers, the Jesuits, first planted the Cross in Paraguay, they found there a large Indian village, encompassed with its fields of maize and man-

---

* This latter plant will some day be of great value commercially: its fibre has been used by the natives time out of mind for making fishing-nets and lines, and a coarse, very strong cloth. Captain Page speaks of it in high terms, but in mistake calls it an aloe: it belongs to the Bromeliaceae. Towards the end of the war, the paper on which the "Semanario" was printed was made from it by Mr. von Truenfeld.

out breakfasting, hoping to reach Piribebuy before noon, for it is only seven leagues distant in a direct line. But we lost the road, had to ride many miles out of the way to get fresh horses, and night was falling whilst we were still in the forest. I had ridden fast for eight hours, and fasting also, for, except a few wild oranges, I had eaten nothing that day. At last, getting impatient, and being better mounted than my servant, I pushed on at a gallop in search of a house, where we could get our tired animals exchanged, and a guide, and at last reached a large *rancho*, with several saddled horses outside, and went up without waiting for my man. About a dozen Indian *peons* sat under the wide porch, each armed with a long knife stuck in his girdle, and an ill-looking fellow was smoking in the doorway. I was in private dress, with the exception of a lieutenant's cap, and had left my sword behind me, but had a revolver in my belt. I wished them good evening, which to my surprise was not returned, and then made the mistake of asking for horses, instead of demanding them. No reply but a growl in Guarani. I was hungry, tired, and out of temper, so I drew the attention of the men to my pistol, and said sharply, " Bring me three horses." The change of tone was instantly effectual, and by the time my servant came up I was again in the saddle, and in a few minutes more we were galloping through the darkness. The road was detestable, and the night so cloudy that I could only just see the dark lofty wall of trees on each side of it ; our guide, however, kept ahead at full speed, and we followed as best we could, and in about an hour reached the town of Piribebuy.

The chief of it had never, I should say, seen a foreigner before. He was a very stout man, with a swarthy skin and small, black, bead-like eyes, which he never took off me for a moment, and every now and then repeated, as if he could never get over such an astounding fact, " Your worship is really an Englishman! Maria Santisima ! and in this poor comandancia of mine ! "

The town is large, but wretchedly built on a bare, rocky hill-

side, with sterile fields around it; I should think it is one of the
most desolate spots in Paraguay. A man in the camp who has
but five cows is considered very poor, and none there, the chief
told me, save himself, had so many. A beautiful stream runs
below it, in a bed of schistose rock, an excellent site for a
water-mill. I went to bathe there at daybreak, to the astonishment of the people, who, although they are fond enough of it
in the summer, never think of washing in cold weather. "Que
guapo!" (What a plucky fellow!) said one. "Que loco!"
(What a madman!) replied his neighbour.

The next stage was to Caraguatai—which means, the river of
wild pine-apples. This, a large and then very prosperous
village, was the end of my journey; but, in order to make as
much as possible of my time, I turned to the south, and took a
wide circuit of nearly a hundred miles in returning to the
capital.

From thence the road led me once more through the silent
woods, rich in picturesque beauty, and solemn as a cathedral in
their dimly lighted depths. In England we still have fine tracts
of woodland; many "a monarch of the glade," which was a fine
tree centuries ago, yet commands our admiration; and a stroll in
the mossy woods is a delight to young and old. But in those
illimitable forests of the New World a feeling of awe, almost
reverence, mingles with the pleasure with which we view them.
They are sublime in their boundless extent, almost oppressive in
their hushed stillness. The vast height of the trees is forgotten,
they are so many, so densely crowded; but our attention is
arrested by the huge solid trunks, knotted, contorted and wound
with gigantic climbers to the topmost bough; or else crumbling
in hoar antiquity, but bright with the tender foliage of the parasites clinging to them still. They are strangely beautiful, are
those great cedras and lapachos, but the silence, unbroken,
save by the trembling whistle of the *chicarra*,* or the ring of my
horse's hoofs, impressed me more.

---

* The balm-cricket, the shrill vibratory whistle of which can be heard at an
extraordinary distance.

After leaving the forest the road became very bad, and for more than a league we floundered through mire and water, expecting that every plunge would be the last our tired horses could make, and the heat in the open plains was excessive. I was glad enough when we entered the next town, and rested under the massive vaulted corridor of the old Jesuit college of Yaguaron.

The town is miserable, but the college, now the residence of the comandantè, is a fine place, with large rooms and broad shady cloisters. In the centre of the grassy courtyard stands a stone sun-dial, cunningly carved. The church, one of the few built by the Society yet standing, looks exteriorly like a huge barn ; for the tower has fallen down, and the bells are suspended on a beam in front. The interior is very curious ; the builders evidently wished to produce great effects with small means ; and massive columns and arches in the choir are represented in profile by thin boards, painted in imitation of stone. The roof is coloured gaudily, red and green, but the rafters are hidden by matting beautifully woven, and the pulpit is supported by a carved figure of a woman in a Roman habit, and decorated with small medallion paintings by no mean hand. Round the walls are large rudely executed pictures, representing scriptural subjects on one side, and stories from the lives of the saints on the other. But the greatest skill and labour had been lavished on the altar and the shrines. The former is a vast structure of carved and gilded wood, with a staircase behind it, in order to give access to the rows of candlesticks which rise in tiers almost to the roof. Over the west door is a gallery for singers, and an organ. I was greatly surprised to find such an instrument there, and was anxious to examine it, but the key of the gallery had been lost, and the comandantè told me that it had been silent for a century. He was very proud of his old church, but it was in a miserably neglected and almost ruinous state.

The day after I was amongst the hills again, and recrossed the cordillera by the Paso Iviè (the bad road), which fully deserved its name. I had been told that it was impassable for bullock-carts, and therefore expected one of the very worst kind; for those lumbering waggons, with their huge broad wheels, get over roads which we should deem utterly impracticable.

A narrow precipitous ravine torn by the rains, such was the pass, so steep that looking down it from above—down more than a thousand feet—to descend in any other way than the very summary one of rolling to the bottom, seemed out of the question. The out-cropping sandstone, however, denuded of surface soil by the torrents, had assumed the form of a rough flight of steps, sometimes broad, but generally in thin, almost sharp, layers; and down that slope we had to ride as best we could. I confess I should have liked to dismount, but the guide did not do so, and I followed his example and him; my servant brought up the rear, carrying my gun.

Then there was another long ride through rough copses and meadow-land, around the flanks of the cordillera, till we reached its termination in the Cerro Santo Tomàs, a bold square mountain, almost vertical on its western face. It must have once stood out as a bluff rocky headland, when the waves of the Atlantic rolled over the low sandy plains of La Plata.

The *cerro* is of mica slate, and its name is taken from a little cave or grotto near its summit, in which St. Thomas took up his residence for some time when he made his remarkable journey to America, ages before Christopher Colon pretended to have discovered it, and about which lay historians are so unaccountably silent. The grotto is used as a chapel, and on St. Thomas's Day crowds of people climb up the steep path to hear mass there; the rest of the year it is abandoned to the owls and the bats, hermits not being an institution in Paraguay.

Beneath the shadow of the *cerro* is the village of Paraguari, which was, like Yaguaron, founded by the Jesuits, who built there, also, a college and a church. The latter had become ruinous, and was being rebuilt when I saw it; the former had been turned into a residence for the chief (here a man of some importance, as the place is a military station) and for the priest of the partido.

When I left my hammock early the next morning, I found that the sleepy little village was showing unusual signs of life and activity. The owners of the two general shops, representing the commercial element of the district, were busily unpacking divers light wooden cases, and displaying their contents to a merry group of señoritas, accompanied by two or three old ladies in black, who were examining the bright-coloured stuffs and ribbons, holding them at arm's length or half unrolled from their waists, evidently with a view to new dresses. Some *mozos del campo* were with them, wrapped in chocolate-coloured ponchos, and lounging, cigar in mouth, against the door-post, or walking daintily on their toes, since the huge rowels of their silver spurs deprived them of the use of their heels.* I stood on the opposite side of the plaza, watching them, and wondering what could have sent the girls dress-hunting so early in the morning. At length, one of them, with whom I had taken a cigar the previous evening, beckoned me to join them : I went, and told them of my curiosity. "O señor," cried they altogether, " to-morrow Carlos Fernandez gives a *fiesta*, a ball at his quinta, and we are all going. You will go of course ? " " I should be very glad, but I have not been invited." " Que importa ! No invitation is necessary : you know them; that is enough ; " and as I had had the pleasure of meeting the sister of Don Carlos, Doña Eusebia Fernandez, several times in the capital, I promised to stay a day longer, and go with them.

On the morrow the sun rose as brightly as usual ; but in the afternoon the wind changed to the south, and a drizzling rain and a heavy mist rolling down from the cerro made the forlorn lit le village look more miserable than ever ; however, I went to look up my fair friends. With dejected looks, and sadly disappointed, they told me that it was impossible to go, the weather would not clear up in time ; even their brothers, afraid of wetting their finery, could not be persuaded to go ; so I deter-

---

* I had a pair of these spurs of no unusual dimensions, the rowels of which were fully six inches in diameter ; they weighed eighty ounces altogether!

mined to set out by myself. The *quinta*, or villa, was about three leagues distant, but the road was said to be easy to find. I found it easy to lose, for after riding about an hour all trace of it had disappeared. The ground was rocky and thinly covered with wiry grass, so that the cart-wheels would make no ruts, whilst horsemen had the whole width of the plain to choose for a path. I felt that my journey was likely to be a bootless one, and the fierce gusts of wind sweeping down from the cordillera drove the rain in my face, shut out all view of the cerro, which had hitherto been my landmark, and, except for the direction of the storm, I had lost my bearings altogether. Night was closing in, so I reluctantly determined to return whilst there was light enough to avoid the obstacles in the path.

I had not ridden far, however, when a man came in sight, riding at full speed, his poncho streaming in the wind behind him. "Adonde va usted amigo !" (Where are you going, my friend ?) I shouted. "I am going to the dance," said he. "Will you show me the way ?" "Con mucho gusto, señor ;" and off we cantered together. The sky cleared as the sun went down, and it was quite fine when we reached the house.

It consisted of two ranges of rooms, perhaps thirty feet long, and built at about half that distance apart, and the space between them was roofed over, I suppose as a threshing-floor. One end was temporarily closed by a screen of planks and hides, and this formed the ball-room. A rude wooden chandelier hung from the rafters, and, with the many candles stuck in holders to the walls, gave a bright but unsteady light as it swayed in the wind.

A crowd of people stood without in the open air, watching the dancers, and snapping their fingers in unison with the tinkling guitars and harps, which formed the orchestra. I dismounted, added my saddle to a heap of others piled on one side of the entrance, turned my horse loose, and then, waiting for a pause in the dance, made my way to Doña Eusebia, a tall graceful girl, dressed in a delicate lace *tupoi* and a bright silk skirt; who was looking on, with delighted face, at the gaicty around her.

The entrance of a stranger checked the music in a moment, and many an anxious look was turned to me, for the sight of an " oficial del gobierno " was an unwelcome one ; but my friend at once recognized me, and, holding out both hands in warm welcome, cried, "Ah, Señor Don Federico, this is indeed a surprise ; you complete our happiness." And the dance went on again. She introduced me to her brothers, fine handsome fellows, and brought me her baby niece, in celebration of whose birthday the fiesta was given. We chatted in the *sala* for a few minutes, and then rejoined the dancers.

The scene was a striking one, and, to an Englishman, per-:fectly unique. At the moment of our return about twenty couples were performing " El Cielo," a complicated measure, half minuet, half waltz, like many of the Spanish dances, performed in figures and with stately steps. The dancers sing as they move in time with the music, and the spectators join in the chorus at regular intervals.

The five musicians had, if I remember rightly, two harps and three guitars with double metallic strings, and they played a wild melody, which rose and fell fitfully, like the wind amongst the hills, and changed its key with the various meanings of the words they sang. Now, for instance, wailing sad and low, as they danced slowly and swung their arms in time to the mournful complaint, " Ay Cielo! ay Cielo! este cruel amor," but quickening into a triumphal strain as they joyfully chanted, " Es mia, es mia, Cielo estoy feliz ! " when the slow measure was exchanged for a rapid whirl, and with outstretched arms and snapping fingers, a *valse à deux temps* brought the dance to a close, amid the plaudits of the lookers-on. We had several other dances, the courtly Montenero, the Media caña, the droll Pishèshèshè, where the right foot drawn over the floor produces the sound the name indicates, and so on.

There were about a hundred dancers : all the girls were in native costume—the classic *tupoi* and bright-coloured petticoat

—which has the advantage of always being evening dress, and the deep black or scarlet border to the snowy bodice is remarkably effective, and very becoming to olive skins.

The mestizo Paraguayans have inherited from their Indian mothers slender, lithe figures and a quick, elastic step, making them admirable dancers. It was impossible to watch them moving so lightly, so naturally and unaffectedly, yet with such precision, through the difficult and intricate mazes of the "Cielo" without admiration. They all wore gold combs of native manufacture, and the fingers of some were completely encased in rings, each covering a joint, and set with chrysolites rudely cut. Some had chains and rosaries in many folds round their necks, all of massive gold, and generally representing the whole fortune of the wearers. With the exception of Doña Eusebia and her sisters, none wore shoes, and their bare feet fell noiselessly on the earthen floor. The men wore the usual camp costume— shirts richly embroidered and of spotless whiteness, cherifes, and ponchos wound round the waist, generally crimson or of some other bright colour. Two long benches, nearly the whole length of the floor, were occupied by the girls, who sat, scarcely saying a word to each other, waiting with demure looks and downcast eyes until they should be claimed as partners. There was none of that pleasant gossip and buzz of conversation, which we think so necessary to social enjoyment; they had met to dance, and did nothing else. Presently some more musicians arrived, and in compliment to me they formed a set of quadrilles; but the result was rather bewildering, for within a few yards of us they were still performing the old dances, and two sets of instruments playing different tunes so close to each other were rather destructive of time, and distracting in any attempt to follow the music. So, not daring to try the complicated figures the others were moving through so gracefully, I contented myself with watching them and chatting with my friends.

We had a capital supper in detachments at midnight, and cigars and *caña* were, throughout the evening, at the service of all. They had commenced dancing at sunset, and kept it up till after daylight, plenty of volunteers relieving the musicians, and the dancers were never tired.

Now who were the guests? With the exception of the family and a few from Paraguarì, all were small farmers and herdsmen, with their wives, sisters and daughters; but it was difficult for an Englishman, with his recollection of the manners and customs of the same class at home to believe that such was the case, for their easy politeness and their consideration for each other were admirable. Their host was a man of wealth and position, son of General Fernandez. They talked with him and his sisters respectfully, but without the slightest awkwardness or restraint. The girls moved and danced gracefully, and although the only answer I received to anything I said to them was " Dai quai castellano, caballero " (I don't speak Spanish, sir), had I spoken their own language they would have talked freely and well.

How is it, I thought then and often since, that people in a similar position in England are so hopelessly uncouth and clumsy? Not want of education, in one sense of the word (for even our rustics are superior to the majority of Paraguayans in that respect,) but an utter inability to perceive the ungraciousness of their manners would seem to lie at the root of the matter; and so far, *cæteris paribus*, they will always be behind those of Latin race.

To return to our *bailè*: we danced until six in the morning, when nearly all the guests departed. Matè was then served, and a number of the farm servants came in dressed as *càmbaranghàs*—some as tigers, goats, and tapirs, others as demons. I had never seen, even in dreams, a scene so horribly grotesque.

My horse had escaped, but they lent me a better one, and during the forenoon I returned to Paraguarì. I found the air there quite cold; indeed, they say that it is the coolest town in Paraguay. The south wind is deflected by the lofty and almost vertical sides of the cerro, and sweeps over the place, thus keeping down the temperature. In the evening I went to

Itá, a large place, where the greater part of the rude pottery used in the republic is manufactured from a coarse blue clay. An Englishman who had been a prisoner many years in the time of Francia was then living there ; he was over eighty years of age, but looked extremely hearty and well ; but he died about two years afterwards. I slept, as usual, in the comandancia, and left at three a.m. the next morning, so as to reach Asuncion before noon, when my leave expired.

The result of my trip was that, more delighted than ever with the beautiful country around me, I gave up all intention of returning to England ; little thinking that in a few short months all my hopes would be blasted, and that Paraguay would be the theatre of scenes and sufferings so terrible that the most guarded description of them will seem exaggerated ; and even I, who witnessed them, can scarcely trust my own memory whilst relating them.

CHAPTER IX.

THOSE who believe that the war between the Allies and Paraguay was one of races, or waged by the free will of the Paraguayans as an expression or consequence of national antipathies, would go far back to explain its causes; indeed, to the foundation of the settlements made by the Spaniards and Portuguese in the New World. And if the war had been one between the Argentines or the Orientàles, and Brazilians, it would be necessary to speak of those old quarrels and outrages which have deluged the great southern peninsula in blood, and engendered an intense and lasting hatred between peoples closely allied in origin and language. But this is not the case, and the Paraguayans, as one of the consequences of their long isolation by Francia, had completely forgotten that the Brazilians were their " natural enemies," and even now they are viewed by them with contempt rather than hatred.*

The Paraguayans are entitled to our warmest sympathies as a brave, though unfortunate people; but it must not be forgotten that so far as they are concerned the war is a most unjust and unprovoked one. I shall be able to show, also, that it was essentially a personal war, waged, on the one hand, by Lopez,

---

* The source of this feeling is rather curious as a psychological phenomenon : the one being for whom an Indian has the most unmeasured contempt is the negro; and the latter regards the former with a mixture of aversion and dread which I often saw most ludicrously displayed during the war.

for the purpose of acquiring fame and power, and, on the other, by the Allies for their own preservation, and with the intention of crushing him before he gained the dangerous ascendency he coveted. I believe its origin may be traced to the time when Lopez visited France, namely, in the year, 1854. He, suddenly emerging from the semi-barbarism of a remote and almost unknown republic, was dazzled by the parade and glitter, the false glory and proud memories of wars and warriors he found around him, and was fired with the ambition of making the brave and devoted people he knew he would be one day called upon to rule, a nation to be feared and courted as the dominant power of South America.

The unhappy influence to which he was soon afterwards subjected strengthened and gave form to these ambitious schemes, and he was only waiting for irresponsible power to be placed in his hands by the death of his father to rush into the first war for which he could find a pretext, or create one. With neighbours so quarrelsome as those "distracted republics" to the west and the south of him, the latter was scarcely a necessity; he had but to espouse the cause of any one party amongst them to have a war on his hands immediately.

In spite of the sufferings I have endured, in spite of the terrible cruelties I have seen inflicted on others by Lopez, in spite of these and the hard judgment I have passed upon him, I look back to this period of his life with regret. I can almost pity him. I am certain from what I afterwards saw that if he had only had but one trusted counsellor who would have developed the good that was in him, rather than the evil, he would have made a zealous, but unstable ruler; and the material improvements introduced into Paraguay, during the lifetime of his father, would have been followed by others of equal or greater importance and utility. But such a Mentor was not to be found in Paraguay; his position, the isolation which the Lopez family maintained, would not admit of it. And the friend he chose abroad, the ambitious and unscrupulous woman he made his chief confidant, proved to be his greatest enemy, and her evil counsel made his desire of military glory, which might have been but a passing whim, the ruling passion of his life.

I have alluded to the disturbed condition of the republics of the Plate; indeed, their normal state may be said to be that of revolution, and for the reason, perhaps, that there they are always talking about liberty, patriotism, and progress, without understanding the first, possessing the second, and indebted for the third to aliens, who advance them in spite of themselves. An Englishman would find any attempt to comprehend the principles and working of political parties there as hopeless as it is unprofitable. There are the Blancos and the Colorados— the whites and the reds; the Crudos and the Cocidos—the raw and the cooked; the Confederados and the Unitarios—the confederates and the unitarians: the latter not a religious sect, nor does theology enter into any of their disputes; but they could not detest their adversaries more thoroughly, nor could the majority know less of what they are quarrelling about, if they were the most zealous of Christians, or the most abstract of questions were at issue. In short, they destroyed the despotic rule of Spain before learning how to govern themselves; they won liberty, only to misuse it.

As I have said, Lopez had but to espouse the cause of any one of those unhappy factions to plunge the whole eastern side of South America into war and confusion; for his power was so well known, and he was so heartily hated by all, that his adhesion to one was sufficient to arm the rest against him.

To show that I am not exaggerating the state of affairs in the Plate, I need only refer to the " Cruise of the Beagle," in which Darwin states that when he visited Buenos Ayres, about twenty years ago, ten presidents had been installed and expelled in twelve months; and five revolts and three revolutions occurred during the progress of the war itself. And when we consider that insurgent chiefs there were generally bribed to lay down their arms and disband their followers by the party in power, we cannot wonder at this state of things. It is but offering a premium for insurrection.

There is now, however, good reason to believe that a better state of things has commenced, and that the Plate will soon enjoy the prosperity which it needs only a stable government to secure.

In 1863 the Blancos were in power in Monte Video, the Colorados expelled. The chief of the former was President Berro, and his opponents were only waiting for a favourable moment to oust them and him ; for, although crushed for a time, the Colorados had not lost heart, nor forgotten the terrible massacre of Quinteros, when 500 of their party, who had capitulated on honourable terms, were murdered in cold blood. At that time General Flores was the leader of the Colorados. Not a bad man, nor a bad ruler; however, he was driven out in 1859, when only half his term of office had expired. He took refuge in Buenos Ayres, and entered the military service of that republic, then warring with the Confederados under the leadership of Urquiza.

He remained there almost forgotten until the beginning of the year 1863, when he determined to attack once more his old enemies the Blancos. The time was an opportune one for him; there was a strong feeling against the *de facto* government of Berro, not only on the part of the people he ruled, but in the Plate generally, shared, moreover, by the alien settlers there, and the foreign representatives. It would take too long to explain how and why, but the general insecurity of life and property, and the revolting cruelties practised, almost without check by the authorities, on the Brazilian *estancieros** of the remoter districts, may be named as the principal causes. Some shocking outrages had, especially, been committed on the frontier, in which it is difficult to say if Portuguese or Spaniards displayed the greater barbarity. Some troops belonging to the republic had, however, distinguished themselves in these deeds of infamy, and the Imperial Government demanded immediate redress and satisfaction, which was refused in language alike intemperate and insulting.

* Stock farmers.

In the meantime Flores had been maturing his plans, and on the 19th of April, 1863, he landed on the left bank of the Rio de la Plata, attended by only two followers; but his name was a host in itself, and soon thousands of *gauchos* flocked to his standard.

A *gaucho*, I should premise, is a herdsman or shepherd, of a type, however, quite unknown in Europe. A wild race of half-breeds, gifted with wonderful skill in horsemanship, with a great fondness for roving, gambling, and playing the guitar; having a supreme contempt for all laws, social or moral, and a tendency, one may almost say a predilection, for cutting the throats of their neighbours, or each other, on the slightest provocation. Such are the *gauchos*, the Ishmaels of the New World, and they formed the army of Flores, and soon outnumbered the national *gaucho* troops by many hundreds; but their general seems to have kept a tight hold on them, and restrained their excesses most effectually.

The day he landed the following proclamation appeared in Buenos Ayres, where his intentions were well known:—

" Soldiers of the Army of Liberty!

" The doors of your native land, which tyranny closed, have been opened, and we are going to deliver our fellow-countrymen from their bondage. We are in arms upon her soil to combat the government of despots, who, always vanquished, applauded and repeated the scandals which caused the hecatomb at Quinteros." And so on, in the usual style of such documents, ending: " Viva la Patria! Viva la Libertad!! Viva las Instituciones!!!" and signed, " Venancio Flores, Campamento en marcha."

The government of Uruguay was much alarmed, and that of the Argentine Republic showed great apparent zeal in defence of law and order; forbidding all disaffected Orientàles to leave the country, but leaving them to show their disaffection for *those* orders by getting out of it how or when they pleased.

In August, 1864, fifteen months after the outbreak of the revolution, Brazil sent its minister Saraiva, whose first note, dated the 18th of May of that year, had met with a very unworthy reception, to press the demands of the Imperial Government for redress of the grievances I have mentioned. He was received with rudeness, and his remonstrances were met by language as undiplomatic as that which characterized the despatches of the preceding year.

The result was an ultimatum from the Brazilian plenipotentiary, under date of August 10, 1864. The Oriental Government declared that whilst the republic was engaged in putting down a revolution in which many Brazilians took part, the demands of Brazil were inopportune, and refused it.

These occurrences were carefully watched by Lopez, who sent an offer of his services as a mediator between the contending parties, which was, however, declined very curtly by both, and treated with contempt and ridicule by the Argentine newspapers. So far he did well, and, Brazil having openly espoused the cause of Flores, he directed a protest to the Imperial Government, on the 30th of August, 1864, challenging its right to interfere in the quarrels of the neighbouring powers, and declaring that he would not look calmly on whilst the laws of nations were outraged. This protest shared the fate of the proffered intervention ; it was received with shouts of laughter, and its author was recommended by the colorados to attend to the state of his *tolderia*—his huts, and settle the squabbles of his half-naked squaws at home.

So Brazil, having made an alliance with Flores, commenced the " war of liberation " by bombarding the unfortunate little town of Paysandu. After a protracted siege the garrison, which scarcely amounted to a twentieth of the enemy, surrendered on honourable terms ; but the commandant and two of his officers were murdered immediately afterwards, it is said, by order of the Brazilian general. Monte Video itself was then invested by the imperial fleet, upon which President Aguirre resigned, and left Flores master of the situation. He, however, refused to accept the presidentship until he had been regularly re-elected ; which was done, and he received, at the same time, in consideration of the anomalous state of the country, extraordinary powers.

Supposing Lopez to have been actuated by honourable motives, there can be no doubt that he was badly treated by all at this juncture, and the Orientàles were blind to their own interests in refusing his help. But the fact was, the very name of Paraguay was hateful in the Plate; not a foreigner had ever entered the country who had not been ill-treated. They went there tempted by the chance of making a fortune—some did so, and left only too glad to have escaped; others held on from habit and the difficulty of breaking up their establishments, but sending to their friends down the river dolorous accounts of the inconveniences and hardships they had to submit to, and of their anxiety to get away as soon as possible: by them Lopez was looked upon as a brutal tyrant, and his people as ignorant and submissive savages.

Lopez, however, did not declare war against Brazil; and the "Marques de Olinda," a passenger steamer running between Monte Video and Mato Grosso (a province of the empire on the head waters of the Rio Paraguay), left for the latter place, on her usual monthly trip, in November, 1864. She stopped at Asuncion ; but there was evidently something wrong—none were allowed to land ; but after a few hours she went on her way up the river. Lopez was undecided: he had not declared war, and to seize the vessel now would be but an act of piracy. On the other hand, the temptation was a strong one : the " Marques de Olinda" was a finer vessel than any he possessed ; she had fallen into a trap, and being unarmed would of necessity make no resistance. The same night a gun-boat, the "Tacuari," was sent after her, and she was brought back to the pier of Asuncion. On board was one of the most distinguished men in the Brazilian empire, Camheiro de Campos, who had just been appointed President of Mato Grosso, and a heavy sum of money intended for the payment of the troops in the province, unluckily for Lopez, in treasury notes. The president was made prisoner, and the vessel armed and converted into a gun-boat with all speed. An embargo was laid upon the vessels in the river to prevent the news getting down, and twelve days elapsed before any notice of the affair left Paraguay.

This notable exploit was the first fatal step in the career of Lopez; it raised a storm of indignation against him in the Plate, and thoroughly alienated the few friends he had·there; and his next operation, the invasion of Mato Grosso, where defenceless towns and homesteads were ravaged and burnt with reckless cruelty—perhaps defensible by the ordinary rules of war—was but another proof that no terms could be made with a man capable of such duplicity and useless barbarity.

The province of Mato Grosso was unprepared for defence, the forts were weakly manned and unprovided with guns of heavy metal; and the officers in command seem to have been quite unfitted for the trusts they held.

Immediately after the seizure of the " Marques de Olinda," Lopez sent General Resquin with a large force of cavalry across the river Apa, who, falling upon the peaceful Brazilian settlements, ravaged all before him with fire and sword.

At the same time another force was sent up the river under the command of General Barrios, brother-in-law of Lopez, consisting of about 3,000 men; the " Tacuari," and two smaller boats, carrying two 68-pounder smooth bores, and four 32-pounders; and on the 14th of November the vessels anchored below the fort of Coimbra on the Paraguay, in lat. 19° 50′ S.

The boats lay some distance from the fort, a small place containing a garrison of about 200 men, and mounting six brass 12-pounders and two thirty-twos; and they blazed away at each other for two days, but little damage was done on either side. The troops were then landed, and set to work cutting a road to the fort through the dense undergrowth of cactuses, bromelias, and other thorny plants which surround it. Whilst the besiegers were engaged in this work, a small armed steamer, moored above the works, got their range, and inflicted heavy loss; and when, at length, they reached the walls they were received with such a heavy fire of musquetry and hand grenades

7

that they retreated with a loss of 250 men in killed and wounded. In the evening the Paraguayans commenced, what they ought to have done the day before, getting their guns into position on shore. The enemy, however, saved them the trouble of breaching the walls, by escaping in the night on board the small steamer, in which they left before daylight. They did this so quietly that for some hours the Paraguayans did not find out that the fort was empty. The flight must have been a very hurried one; for they left the guns mounted and unspiked, the magazine well furnished, and some valuable private property, especially the most costly case of surgical instruments I have ever seen.

This affair seems to have completely disheartened the Brazilians (and correspondingly elated their enemies), for they offered scarcely a pretence of resistance at Albuquerque, Curumbà, Dorado, and Miranda, which fell successively into the hands of the Paraguayans. At the latter place they retreated without waiting to fire the guns they had loaded. The behaviour of the Brazilian troops was most disgraceful; the only activity they showed was in running away, and as far and as fast as possible. It must be remembered that General Barrios had only small wooden vessels, and smooth-bore guns, and he was at first as cowardly as his foes. He reached Coimbra so intoxicated that he could give no intelligible orders, and many of his officers were in the same state. The men scrambled up to the fort without order or plan; and a sergeant and seven men actually got over the parapet, but being unsupported were instantly cut to pieces; and others, whom I saw wounded in Asuncion, told how they had been taken prisoners by them, but managed to escape during the confusion reigning within the works during the assault.

At Dorados a serious accident occurred: they were shipping powder when by some accident it exploded, killing about thirty men and Lieut. Herreros, the best officer they had.

The defenceless people were treated with great severity, and the whole country given up to pillage. Some of the rich *estan-*

cieros, who did not yield as much money as Barrios expected, were tied naked on the brass guns and left in the sun for hours; others were shot or flogged for the same reason; and a Paraguayan soldier brought down some dozens of Brazilian ears strung on a thong, and presented them to Lopez. The two sons of the Baron de Villa Maria were executed for trying to escape; their father owed his life to the swiftness of his horse; and after a toilsome journey reached Rio Janeiro in safety, carrying the news that Brazil had lost one of her richest provinces. All the foreigners they could find were brought down as prisoners, after having been stripped of everything they possessed; they were principally Germans, Italians, and Frenchmen. I saw many poor fellows working as labourers or begging in the streets, who, a few weeks before, had been wealthy merchants or landowners. The Paraguayans captured seventy guns, one steamer, five hundred prisoners, and an immense quantity of arms and ammunition.

In the meantime troops were being rapidly concentrated in Cerro Leon and Humaità, and in the beginning of 1865 Lopez had 100,000 men under his command—fine, athletic, hardy fellows, who if they had had good officers would have been second to none in the world. They were at first badly armed, only about one-fifth of the number having percussion guns, about an equal number had old-fashioned flint-locks, and the rest lances and long knives; but the imperial stores of Mato Grosso furnished a considerable quantity of rifles, which were distributed amongst the best marksmen.

It was one of the great mistakes made by Lopez, withdrawing from industrial pursuits so many men at once. The whole population before the war was less than a million, and one-tenth, and that the flower of the males, from producers suddenly became consumers of food; for some time *that* was plentiful enough, as far as beef was concerned, for the cattle throughout the country was seized for the use of the army, but they got nothing else. Now the Paraguayans, unlike the Argentines and Orientàles, are not exclusively carnivorous; in fact, in the in-

terior they ate little meat, consuming in preference maize, mandioc, and oranges.   About 15,000 of these men were sent to Humaità, a damp, malarious place, where they could get scarcely a
particle of vegetable food, and during the cold, wet winter the
results were, as might have been predicted, a most intractable
form of diarrhœa, pneumonia, and enteric fever, and great loss
of life.   The wretched sheds of hospitals were crowded, and soon
became themselves *foci* of disease; and that fine army melted
rapidly and ingloriously away; the gravedigger was soon more
active than the drill-sergeant.   At Cerro Leon, as well as in
Humaità, thousands perished also through over drilling.   The
men were kept at exercise often eight hours a day in the burning sun, in spite of the energetic remonstrances of the English
medical officers.

In the meantime Flores, assisted by his allies the Brazilians,
had been nominated " Director Discrecionario " of the Republic
of Uruguay, and had, in concert with them, declared war against
Paraguay.   Not content with these two powerful enemies, Lopez
determined to quarrel with the Argentines, and therefore demanded permission to march his troops across the province of
Corrientes.   This was of course refused, since the Argentines
were at peace with Brazil, and Lopez immediately occupied the
city of Corrientes, the capital of the province.   It is said that
he was urged to this step by Madame Lynch; for the editor of a
paper there had published a biography of that lady of a somewhat uncomplimentary character, and she, in her blind rage,
persuaded her paramour to this fatal step.   Be that as it may,
on the 14th of April, 1865, Corrientes, without a struggle, submitted to the Paraguayans.   In the harbour lay two small
steamers, the " 25° de Mayo " and the " Gualaguay."   The
crew of the former loaded her two guns, but jumped overboard
without waiting to discharge them; from the shore they fired
a few musket shots, but a shell or two from the invaders
silenced them.   On board this vessel and her consort the Paraguayans found thirteen Englishmen, a captain, engineers, and
firemen, who were sent to Humaità as prisoners.   There they

were invited to enter the service of Lopez; two did so, the rest declined, and were put in the *calabozo* of the capital, where, with the exception of five who survived an imprisonment of more than four years, they died from disease and starvation.

Lopez committed an unfortunate blunder in his precipitate attack on this place. A British steamer, "La Esmerelda," was within two hours' sail of that port, with two thousand stand of arms on board which he had purchased in England; but Lagraña, the governor of Corrientes, hearing that the Paraguayans were coming, boarded her in his flight down the river, and carried her and the stores with him to Buenos Ayres.

Three days afterwards the Argentines declared war, and on the first of the succeeding month the famous "Triple Alianza" was signed by Brazil and the Argentine and Oriental Republics. In the Appendix I give a translation of this document, by which it will be seen that the Allies ostensibly sought only the destruction of Lopez, and the free navigation of the river, guaranteeing at the same time perfect liberty and independence to the Paraguayans.

Two months before, an Extraordinary Congress had met in Asuncion, and Lopez told the members what he had done, and what he intended to do. There was, of course, a great display of patriotism, and the lives of the people and all they possessed were placed in his hands—a somewhat superfluous offer, since he could do as he liked with them already. They gave him the title of field-marshal, and increased his pay to 60,000 dollars a year. Another "patriotic" movement commenced about this time, by order of Madame Lynch, that the women should "offer," for his acceptance, one-tenth part of all the jewellery they had. Woe to her who did not pay it, either in kind or in money, to the uttermost farthing! These "offerings," on various pretexts, were constantly being collected: at one time, it was a statue to his late father, that produced about 30,000 dollars; then a gold sword, a gold case to put it in, jewels to ornament it—none but diamonds were accepted, chrysolites were not good enough, nevertheless they were not returned to their owners; and a gold wreath for his heroic brow, this was late in the war, when he was trembling in a bomb-proof which he never quitted by day. And in addition to this, the poor creatures were obliged to sing patriotic songs, and come in troops before him, decked out in tawdry finery for the delectation of his eyes and ears. I saw many of these painful exhibitions, where members of the best families in Paraguay had to mix with the rabble, and, not daring to show their grief—the use of mourning had been forbidden—sing and dance for the amusement of the mean, selfish tyrant; mean enough to despoil the market girls of their chains and ear-rings, and to pocket trinkets, taken by the police in the name of patriotism and liberty.

On the 8th of June, 1865, he left for Humaità, to assume personally the command of the army, and took with him the whole of the gold coin left in the treasury, in addition to the " offerings " which had then been made to him. Three days afterwards was fought the battle of Riachuelo, the first of a long series of partial defeats and disasters, almost any one of which might have been decisive, but for the mismanagement and misunderstandings of the Allies.

To show that I am speaking advisedly, I quote the following from a despatch of Mr. Gould's to Lord Stanley, dated Sept. 10, 1867 :—

" When Lopez commenced the war he was at the head of a fine army. . . . Since then he must have lost, in one way or the other, upwards of 100,000 men, for 80,000 have died from disease alone.

" It is only owing to the dilatory manner of proceeding of the Allies, and their want of energy, that he is still able to prolong his resistance. Had their fleet taken up in time a position between Paso de la Patria and Itapirù, after the surrender of a part of his troops at Uruguayana, none of the 25,000 men with which he invaded the Argentine province of Corrientes would have been able to recross the Paranà into Paraguay.

" On the 24th of May, 1866, he was repulsed with such fearful loss that the Allies might have entered his entrenched camp the next day with the greatest ease. It took him three days to reorganize any considerable force, as he himself acknowledges. His losses on that occasion amounted to between 12,000 and 15,000 men.

" On the 2nd of September, when the Allies took Curúzú, had they marched at once on Curupaity they would have easily advanced with but comparatively slight resistance. They lost a fortnight, during which he strongly entrenched himself, and were eventually repulsed with immense slaughter. . . . . They have remained stationary for more than six weeks, while by pushing forward a few thousand men on their extreme right they would entirely cut off his communications with the interior, and very soon compel him to surrender at discretion."

I shall presently give a short account of these operations. I am getting in advance of my narrative, but it cannot be too soon nor too strongly impressed upon the reader, that it was the wretched mismanagement of the allied generals alone which prolonged the war. We sometimes thought that it was done intentionally, in order to make it one of utter extermination.

CHAPTER X.

IN June, 1865, the Brazilians blockaded the river with nine
large vessels, two of them plated ; they did not venture to enter
the mouth of the Rio Paraguay, which was only guarded by the
fort of Itapirù, mounting three 82-pounders, but lay in the
Paranà, about three leagues below Corrientes, off a small stream
called Riachuelo.

Lopez determined to attack them there, anticipating an easy
victory. Indeed, his only fear seemed to be that they would
run away before he could get at them. To prevent their escaping he had, however, sent forward a force by land, under the
command of Colonel Bruguez ; and a battery of rifled 12-pound-
ers, six or eight in number, was established at Bella Vista, an
advantageous point some miles below them.

With the same end in view, Captain Meza, who commanded
the Paraguayan fleet, was ordered to run past the enemy without firing, and then turn back and board them as he came up.
This precaution did not seem an unnecessary one after the cowardice shown by the Brazilians in Mato Grosso, and I am quite
sure they would much rather have cut their cables than fought,
if the attacking force had been less disproportionate.

The Paraguayan fleet consisted of eight wooden and iron river
steamers, four of them of from 300 to 600 tons each, the rest of
about the size and build of the passenger boats running between
London Bridge and Westminster. They were as follows : Ta-

cuari, six guns; Marques de Olinda, four guns; Igurey, five guns; Paraguarì, four guns; Salto Orientàl, four guns; Jejuì, two guns; Ypòra, one gun; Pirabebè, one gun; and five *chatas*, flat-bottomed boats, each carrying a 68-pounder, and the most formidable part of the fleet. The guns of the steamers were principally 14-pounders, but there were six 32-pounders amongst them, one of which, however, was disabled after firing a single shot; and they were crowded with troops.

The Brazilian fleet consisted of nine large vessels, two of them plated, and carrying about sixty guns, several of them 70-pounder rifled Whitworths, and two 120-pounders. They were well manned, and had strong and lofty nettings stretched as a precaution against boarding, and which, in fact, saved them from capture.

Early on the morning of the 11th of June, Captain Meza with his little fleet steamed down the river, and shortly before noon was abreast of his formidable antagonists. He could move but slowly, for the *chatas* being in tow retarded the steamers very much; yet the preliminary manœuvre was performed without much damage being sustained. In truth, the Brazilians were then in so desperate a panic, for they had been taken by surprise, and were amazed to see the little vessels going steadily on after receiving their fire, that had an efficient officer been in the place of Meza, the whole of their fleet might have been captured; but he, poor old man, was quite unfit for his post; indeed, I was assured by the English engineer of his boat that he lost his head completely as soon as the firing began, and did not issue a single order afterwards. An excellent plan was suggested to him by Mr. Watts, the engineer of the " Tacuari," namely, to sink two of his smaller vessels below the fleet, and then attack it with the heavy guns of the *chatas*, until there was time to get a battery established on shore above the Brazilian position. There can be no doubt that it would have been a successful one; but Meza was then too bewildered to understand anything, and the golden opportunity was lost. Many of the officers were intoxicated, the men fought as they pleased, or as they could, and the movements of the vessels were really directed by the English engineers on board of them.

After firing in a disorderly way for some time, and inflicting considerable damage on the Brazilians, the Paraguayans came up again, still towing the *chatas*, and desperate efforts were made by the men to board their gigantic opponents. The "Tacuari" ran alongside the plated "Paranahyba." The top of her paddle-box was on a level with the rail of the latter; a sergeant and about a dozen men cut through the boarding netting with their long knives, and leaped upon the deck. It was cleared without striking a blow! The crew, officers, and all, ran below without staying to see how few were their enemies, or perceiving that their boat, having forged ahead, had left them without support. The vessel would have been taken if the delighted Paraguayans had only secured the hatches; but the sergeant, in his exultation, amused himself by marching up and down the deck, beating the *réveillé* on a drum which he found there. The sound seemed to act as an invocation. A crowd of marines, with fixed bayonets, suddenly rushed up the hatchways, and charged the invaders; they, seeing that discretion would then counsel a retreat, jumped overboard, and swam to the shore. The sergeant was under my care some time afterwards, and I have often heard him tell the story, and of the shouts of laughter with which his companions saluted the terrified *cambas*,* as they tumbled over each other in their eagerness to get below.

This temporary success was the only one of the day; the Brazilians soon ceased firing, and ran full speed into the light vessels of the Paraguayans, and crushed all they could reach with ease.

The "Tacuari" had passed before this manœuvre was tried, and the "Igurey," although towing the disabled "Ypòra," managed to escape. The "Yberà," fortunately for her crew, had not passed the enemy's fleet, owing to her machinery temporarily

---

* Blacks, in Guarani, but during the war only used to signify Brazilians.

giving way, and three of her consorts joining her, they slowly and in a half-sinking state steamed up the river.

The Brazilians were only too glad to see their daring little adversaries disappearing in the distance, and made no attempt to stop or follow them. The story of the rest is soon told. The "Marques de Olinda," a fine handsomely fitted vessel, having water-tight compartments did not sink, but, falling on her side, drifted down with the current, and grounded at length, a worthless wreck, off the Chaco shore. The "Salto Orientàl" went down immediately, but the water was so shallow that part of her works remained above it. Her commander was then lying mortally wounded on the cabin table, the rest of the officers had been killed, and her partly submerged deck was covered with dead and dying men. The "Belmonte," which had crushed her, was bearing down again, when Mr. Gibson, her English engineer, mounted on the bridge, and shouted to her crew not to fire. An officer came forward, and told him to haul down his flag : he obeyed, and boats were sent by the Brazilians to take off the wounded, the few others were told to remain where they were. The "Paraguari" grounded in shallow water, and then having been set on fire by the Brazilians all but her hull and machinery was destroyed. The "Jejui" was completely smashed.

The Paraguayans admitted a loss of 750 men, but they really lost double that number, and two of the English engineers perished. The Brazilian loss was very heavy, 500 to 800 in men, and their vessels were severely handled. In running past Bruguez's battery the "Iaquitinhoua" received several balls, and was, in trying to get out of range, run ashore ; the Brazilians made several attempts to get her off, but were unable to do so, and abandoned her without firing the magazine or even spiking the guns, and the latter were carried off by the Paraguayans soon afterwards.

Such was the end of the battle of Riachuelo, and it is not too much to say, that that battle of four hours and a half really decided the war, for it gave the Allies the command of the river. If those nine vessels had been captured, I am certain that Lopez would have been victorious, for he would have instantly appeared before Buenos Ayres or Monte Video, and, by threatening a bombardment, compelled them to make terms with him. The fort of Martin Garcia would not have deterred or stopped a man who had dared to attack such a fleet with a force so disproportionate.

Mr. Gibson remained on the wreck till night; and then as no help was sent to him, he set to work with a few Paraguayans who remained, constructed a raft, got them on it, and drifting down in the darkness, landed on the right bank. With great difficulty they made their way up by land to Paso la Patria, a good-natured *estanciero* having supplied them with food when they were nearly perishing for want of it, and thence to Humaità. There he was at once put into prison as a traitor for hauling down his flag, in place of being rewarded for saving the lives of the remnant of the crew by his presence of mind. He remained in irons about three months, and was then set at liberty, but died soon afterwards.

Captain Meza was severely wounded, a musket ball passed through his shoulder and right lung. He arrived in Humaità in a dying state. Lopez sent to tell him that if he survived he should shoot him for cowardice. He never rallied, and died eight days afterwards.

On that eventful 11th of June I called upon General Barrios, a brother-in-law of Lopez, who had just been gazetted Minister for War and Marine, to congratulate him on his appointment. Whilst I was having a cigar with him a telegram came in, announcing that a great victory had been gained.* This was about eleven a.m., and it must have been sent off before the battle began. He was greatly elated, and preparations were made for a ball in the evening; but as no confirmation of the message was received they were suspended, and the next morning some inkling of the truth was known, and those who had relatives in the fleet were sad with anxious foreboding.

---

* I should have mentioned before that an electric telegraph had been erected between the capital and Humaità, by two German engineers, Mr. von Truenfeld and Mr. Fischer

In Humaità every one acquainted with the true state of affairs felt the greatest anxiety whilst the battle was known to be going on. Early in the afternoon a boat, one of the reserve, came up, bringing the news of a complete victory, and arrangements were commenced for receiving the conquerors. But hour after hour passed away, and their anticipations of a serious disaster became almost a certainty; but the truth was not generally known till the next morning, when the half-sinking ships came in. The day broke cold and wet, yet the river bank was crowded by men and officers, few of whom had slept that night; a dense fog over-shadowed the river, and the men, clustered about the batteries and the capstans for tightening the chains, were shivering in the damp air, as with gloomy faces they tried to peer through the dull grey curtain before them. Presently the masts of the steamers were seen, with cut cordage and disordered rigging hanging from the splintered yards. A few from amongst the eager crowd hurried down the slippery stairs, much whispering went on, for it was as much as a man's life was worth to spread bad news, and then as the dead and wounded were brought on shore the truth was known. The tide had turned, such easy prizes as the " Marques de Olinda" and the riverine towns were to be gained no more, and from that day forward, although there were occasional slight successes, and the Allies paid a full price for the blood they shed, it was evident that the sun of Lopez was setting, amid storm and tempest, for ever.

I mentioned that a battery had been posted at Bella Vista, another was established by Major Cabral, at Cuevos, six leagues below it. The Brazilians remained a month at Riachuelo repairing damages, and then ran the gauntlet of the batteries. All the men, except those at the wheel, kept below, and so lost but few men, it is said. As soon as they had gone the Para-guayans came down, tried to get off the stranded iron-clad, but not succeeding, carried off her guns and part of her engines; the battery of Col. Bruguez had prevented the Brazilians doing so. They also raised the shell of the " Paraguari," which had been built in England for Lopez only a few months before, at a cost of £50,000, and towed it up to Asuncion, with the intention of refitting it, which was, however, never done.

About a third of the army had been concentrated in Argentine territory by this time, under the command of General Roblès, and in August a corps of twelve thousand men was detached, under the orders of Colonel Estigarribia, and composed of the finest troops Lopez possessed, and well armed, the majority with Minié rifles. His intention was to march them to Monte Video itself, through Argentine, Brazilian, and Orientàl territory. And, if audacity could always command success, Lopez ought certainly to have succeeded in the enterprise.

This small force, unprotected on its line of march, with no means even of guarding its rear or keeping open its communications with head-quarters, and unprovided with food, beyond a small herd of cattle, enough for a few days' consumption, and then depending upon what could be found on the road, was to fight its way if attacked, or, at the best, march through an enemy's country for a distance of nearly eight hundred miles, when I doubt if a man amongst them could understand a map or knew whither their road would lead them.

But the fate of the expedition was soon decided. After passing San Borja, on the left of the Rio Uruguay, in Brazilian territory, they were met by the Imperial troops, commanded by the Emperor in person, and in such strength that Estigarribia must either retreat or capitulate. It is possible that Lopez, believing that troops were being massed there, but underrating their strength, had sent him with a small force, expecting to easily rout them, and that the "march to the sea" was but an idle flourish of trumpets. But, on either supposition, there was already no hope for Estigarribia; his men were in a starving state, and whether conquerors or conquered the result would be the same. The village of Uruguayana had been taken and rudely fortified by the Paraguayans, and some attempt made to more regularly entrench it; but on a flag of truce being sent in negotiations were commenced, and the Paraguayans capitulated on the 17th of September.

Some of the prisoners made their escape, and after weeks of wandering found their way back to Humaitâ, and brought the news of this fresh disaster, but, for a fortnight after it was generally known, no notice of it appeared in the " Semanario," and even then it was dangerous to speak of it.

Lopez was furious ; for days no one dared to speak to him, and the name of Estigarribia could only be uttered in the most cautious of whispers. And when at length the " Semanario" spoke of his capitulation, it was only to revile him as the most infamous of traitors. It was declared that he had been bought with Brazilian gold ; that his army had superabundance of food, that the men were burning to attack their foes, but he prevented them ; and so on, in wearying reiteration of miserable falsehoods and groundless calumnies.

The fidelity of General Roblès was then suspected, but I cannot believe on good grounds, although he was a bad, cruel man, and bribes were the weapons the Brazilians were most used to fighting with. But the story of letters from them being found hidden under stones near his quarters, and directed to him, is itself a very suspicious one. I doubt the man, but I doubt the evidence still more. However, it was deemed sufficient by Lopez, and he was arrested.

General Barrios was sent to bring him back to Humaitâ, and he treated his fallen comrade, and once intimate friend, with every indignity. He even made him, a fat, clumsy man, walk two leagues in the sun, at his horse's heels, to the place of embarkation.

On his arrival at Humaitâ he was put in irons, tried, condemned, and, four months afterwards, shot. This long interval between condemnation and execution must not be regarded as an indication of mercy ; indeed, practically it was the reverse of humane ; it is but the old Spanish style of treating criminals. Prisoners used to be put to the question *fort et dure*, to make them confess their own guilt, or frequently to feign themselves guilty, and then tortured again to induce them to give up the names of their accomplices. So, in Paraguay, men who had been condemned to death were kept in irons for months, in the hope that they would implicate some one as yet unsuspected. It is needless to add, that numbers of innocent people were accused in this way by unfortunate creatures suffering every misery, and yet clinging frantically to any means of prolonging life. Roblès was not shot till the 8th of January, 1866.

Shortly after the disaster in Uruguayana I spent three weeks in Humaità, and, on the occasion of some national holiday, I attended a *beso manos*, a levée of the President's, when he delivered a speech, which few who heard it are likely to forget. The bishop addressed him, not, as was customary, the minister of war, and after the usual string of fulsome compliments, he spoke, hesitatingly, of the desertion and treason of Estigarribia and Roblès. Lopez heard him, impatiently, to the end, but hardly waiting to acknowledge the beginning of the bishop's speech, burst out in a torrent of invective and passionate complaint, concluding in a loud tone, very different to his ordinary delivery: "I am working for my country, for the good and honour of you all, and none help me. I stand alone—I have confidence in none of you—I cannot trust one amongst you." And then striding forward, and raising his clenched hand, trembling with passion, he cried, "Cuidado! But take care! Hitherto I have pardoned offences, taken pleasure in pardoning, but now, from this day, I pardon no one." And the expression of his face gave double power to his words.

As I looked round on the wide circle of officers, bowing low as he left the room, I saw many a blanched face amongst them, for they knew that he would keep his word.

He then commenced a system of punishing the relatives of all real or supposed deserters, which soon spread misery and ruin widely through the country. Hundreds of perfectly innocent people, principally women, suffered thus vicariously for the faults or misfortunes of their sons, husbands, or brothers.

There was one family, one of the first which thus expiated a fault committed by a relative hundreds of miles away, I was very intimate with. It consisted of a widow and several children. She was named Doña Oliva Corbalàn, of pure Spanish blood, and very proud of it, somewhat haughty to strangers, but genial and kind-hearted to her friends, pious, but not bigoted, generous and charitable to a fault. As they lived generally in their handsome *quinta* some distance from the city, the señora had gone to the expense of getting out a carriage from England; but the grim old president sent to tell her that he and his family were alone to enjoy that luxury; it was not for " republicanas," and she had to put it down.

She was sister of the Padre Corbalàn I mentioned in chapter VI.; for it is one of the curious customs of the country that married ladies retain as a prenomen, and widows resume, their maiden names. Her husband was named Garcia, and so were her children called, but she Corbalàn, as before her marriage.

When her brother was arrested, she purchased a large house in the capital, which had been built for Madame Lynch, who declined to occupy it, however, because the shrieks of the prisoners being punished in the *calaboza* behind it disturbed her. Its position was its recommendation to the señora, because, by sitting constantly in a balcony at the back, she could sometimes catch a glimpse of her unfortunate brother, and assure herself that he still lived.

She had five sons. Jaimè, the eldest, an idle, dissipated fellow, lived in the city; the next was being educated in Paris; and the younger, bright-eyed, delicate boys of eight, ten, and twelve years of age respectively, were at home with her. There were also four daughters, two of them grown up, pretty, gentle girls. Shortly after the war commenced, Jaimè, then about twenty-two, was sent as a sailor on board the "Tacuari," and Fraylan, the next, into the army.

About six months later, a sister of Doña Oliva's, then recently a widow, was arrested for having, it was said, spoken disrespectfully of Lopez. I knew her well, a quiet, timid woman, who would, I am sure, have done nothing of the kind. She was condemned, of course, and was put into a little room at the rear of the Ministerio de Hacienda, which Mr. Skinner had been using as a dog-kennel for some time, and there she, a young, delicate woman, remained for six weeks, with a sentry standing day and night at the open door.

During the year 1866 Lopez was very busy laying torpedoes in the river, which were made by an American, who had suggested the plan to him. When this man died the work was continued by a Polish refugee, named Michkoffsky, who had settled in the country, and married a native lady. He used to take the torpedoes down the river in a canoe, rowed by four boys; one of them, named Gonzales, was a nephew of the Minister of Agriculture, and Jaimè was ordered to assist him.

One morning in September Michkoffsky started as usual with a torpedo, but he had not gone far down the river when he found that something had been forgotten; so he told Jaimè to put him on shore and await his return. Waiting, however, only until his superior was out of sight, young Corbalàn told the boys to row on; and, as they were below the batteries, escape was easy, and they gave themselves up to the Brazilians, torpedo and all.

When Michkoffsky came back, he searched in vain for the missing canoe, and then, returning to head-quarters, reported what had happened. He was at once arrested, charged with having connived at the desertion, put in double irons, afterwards reduced to the ranks—he had held the rank of captain, was sent to the front, and soon afterwards killed.

I was greatly distressed when this news reached Asuncion, for I knew that the relatives of the deserters would be severely punished, and they were all intimate friends of mine; nor were they long left in suspense. Two days afterwards Señora Corbalàn was in the hands of the police, the whole of her large real and personal property was confiscated, and she and her daughters were exiled to the village of Caàguazù, an Indian settlement in the great forest of that name, a hundred and fifty miles from their once happy home. They were stripped of all they possessed, even to the ear-rings and ornaments of the children, and to the dresses they were wearing. Some cast-off clothes were thrown to them, and barefoot they made that long and weary journey.

I have since heard that Doña Oliva is dead, her eldest daughter insane, the rest penniless orphans. The third son had already been killed. His brothers were at once sent to the front; one died from cholera; the other, a shy little fellow, a great favourite of mine, perished on the battle-field. One of my colleagues saw him brought to the rear mortally wounded; the poor child knew him, but could not speak, yet, turning as he heard his voice, died, with the glad smile of recognition on his lips.

The families of the others fared the same. The mother and sisters of Gonzales were sent to a *guardia* in the Gran Chaco, a pestilential swamp, where only the heron and the rattlesnake can thrive, and where they died soon afterwards.

His uncle, the minister, a white-haired old gentleman, was imprisoned for more than two years, and was then executed.

Before these events, several other desertions had occurred, but the relatives of the culprits were allowed to shield themselves by publishing anathemas against them in the "Semanario," and disowning all relationship with them. I have a number of these miserable letters lying before me. In one, a mother bitterly curses her son; in another, a man heaps imprecations on the head of his brother; a wife disclaims and vituperates her husband, who had not, by the way, deserted at all, but died a prisoner of war in Corrientes. I saw this lady a few days after the letter appeared, and, as I knew her intimately, ventured to ask her how she could have written it. " To save my children," said she, the merriest little woman I have ever met with. " It is all false; you know that I love my husband dearly; but, señor, what would you ? " I do not know if I can present a more shocking picture of the state of affairs in Paraguay than one such letter reveals. And yet this " Semanario," every article in which was submitted to Lopez before printing, and filled with such free expressions of popular opinion as the above letters, has been received in Europe as a just exponent of the Paraguayan question; "communications to the editor," signed by English workmen, in its pages have been accepted as proofs that no British subjects wished to leave that house of bondage, and it has been quoted as a record of popular sentiments!

Another victim, who suffered later in the same year, was Señor Acuña, a tall white-haired man about seventy-two years of age. He had been for many years postmaster in Asuncion, and from his kindly and courteous manners was a general favourite. He was born in the province of Tucuman, but had lived long in Paraguay, and had married a native lady, a Recaldè, one of the best but most unfortunate families in the country. He had been ordered to detain all letters addressed to certain suspected persons in 1864, and lock them up; three years later he was charged by Lopez with having guiltily concealed them, and thrown into prison. Shortly afterwards his wife, an aged woman, shared the same fate, but not the cell of her husband. They remained in solitary confinement seven months, and were released in a dying state. They expired, within a few days of each other, shortly after they were set at liberty.

CHAPTER XI.

As a relief to these painful narratives, I recall a few reminiscences of my happier years in Asuncion.

As soon as I had mastered Spanish I was appointed Professor of Materia Medica and Chemistry, and had a class of about forty *practicantès* (medical students) in the General Military Hospital. They were selected from amongst the most promising scholars in the College of Asuncion by the Principal Medical Officer, and when the war commenced we had a numerous staff of native assistants. But to teach them was disheartening work; they seemed to remember so little, and would never think for themselves, never try to go through any process of reasoning. If they once got a wrong idea into their heads nothing could remove it; like the Indians of Central America, who, having confounded *envierno* (winter) with *infierno* (hell) could never after be persuaded by the Jesuits that the latter was hot!

Soon after the blockade our stock of medicines was almost exhausted, and my efforts were principally directed to finding native substitutes for them. There was plenty of astringents amongst the mimosas, carminatives enough, euphorbial purgatives, and I made absorbent mixtures in a roundabout way from the mountain limestone; for quinine we gave arsenic, calomel we manufactured; but opium, which we needed more than all, was not to be replaced. I had planted a quantity of poppy plants, but they were all destroyed by the cattle one unlucky night.   The castor-oil plant grows wild everywhere in the country; it is called in Guarani *mbaicibó*, but, singularly enough, the natives, although they used its seeds as a violent and dangerous purgative, had no idea that the oil, which they got at a high price from Buenos Ayres, could be made from it.

I have not yet, I think, said anything about the way in which we lived there, or what we ate.   Fermented bread is very little used: it could be bought in Asuncion, but the natives prefer *chipa*, which is made from mandioc or cassava starch, known in England as Brazilian arrowroot, and in a manufactured form as tapioca.   The starch is kneaded with new cheese, melted fat, salt, water, and a little coriander seed, and baked in one of the earthen ovens, resembling huge ant-hills, seen at the rear of every house.   It is usually formed into long cylindrical rolls; but for presents they make it all sorts of grotesque shapes.   It is white, rather close, and when new, very pleasantly tasted, but it will not keep.   If a little bone-earth were added, it would be just such a bread as a chemist would devise: a perfect food.

Maize is extensively used, and the golden yellow cakes made from its coarse flour are very nice.   The seeds of the Victoria Regia, there called *abati-irupé*, or water-maize, are sometimes used in the same way; they make capital crisp cakes.

The ordinary cookery is simple and good; they broil steaks to perfection, or rather roast them in front of a fire made on the ground; and mandioc is an excellent accompaniment, though not equal to good potatoes, which, by the way, are tubers hardly larger than chestnuts in their native country.

Their grand dishes, however, I do not like, with the exception of *carne con cuero*, beef roasted or baked in a piece of its own hide big enough to enwrap it, which is delicious.   Their *pastéles* and so on always reminded me unpleasantly of that "Banquet in the style of the Ancients," described in "Peregrine Pickle."   There is one abomination they are very fond of, which must have been esteemed in England in the time of

Charles the Second, namely, *fœtal* calf, for Shadwell, in his "Woman Captain," amongst other strange luxuries speaks of

"Fawns out of their dams' bellies ript."

They are very partial to preserves, *dulces*, as they call them, and make excellent guava jam (not jelly) and candied fruits.

They use an excessive quantity of fat in cookery; and are fond of it, also, in the most readily obtainable form, as a pomatum. During the fêtes I once came on a pretty "little golden comb" seated on the door-step to catch the last of the fading sunlight, and dressing her long rippled tresses with the aid of a looking-glass propped up by a stone, a comb in one hand and—ought I to tell it ?—a candle in the other, and passing them alternately through her glossy wealth of hair, before plaiting it into a coronet, black as a raven's wing ; the rose, massive ear-rings, and jewelled *peynè*, lying on the threshold beside her. It was pleasant to catch a glance from the pair of roguish eyes, raised quickly from the sloping mirror as I passed.

In their toilettes, a rose, placed over the left ear, was never forgotten, for they are all, gentle and simple, extremely fond of flowers, and one could never be sure of retaining a blossom with propriety for many minutes. If you should have a bouquet on your table, and visitors call, some at least of the flowers must be offered and accepted ; and should you ride off with some, and make a second visit, they must be given, or at least, exchanged, before you leave. If they should be more than ordinarily beautiful, the gift may be regarded as more than a compliment. One day a friend of mine was presented with some lovely camellias by a señorita, whom I afterwards saw a wife, a mother, and a widow within a year, and not wishing to lose them, tied them to his saddle-bow before paying the next visit. As he was bidding a Doña Juanita adieu, however, she unluckily caught sight of the treasure, and with many apologies for his *forgetfulness*, he begged her, of course, to do him the favour to accept them. She admired them very much, asked carelessly who gave them to him, and then with the sunniest of smiles again wished him good-bye. He rode off; but finding that he had dropped a glove, returned and ran hastily into the house, and there saw his fair friend tearing up the unfortunate flowers into the smallest of pieces, and stamping on them, with an expression of face far from angelic.

I had a photographic apparatus with me, and, wishing to get the portraits of some of the Payaguà Indians, I asked the *cicique*, the chief, who used to sell me ostrich feathers, carved gourds, etc., to let me take his, but he replied that he was not going to have his ugly face copied for white men to laugh at, and stalked angrily away. But not to be beaten, I went down to Captain Meza, who was then captain of the port, and asked him if he could send me up two or three of the men. He was greatly amused at the idea of taking the portraits of Indians, but promised me as many as I liked. On the morrow he sent a few soldiers to the Chaco, and brought over the entire tribe, men, women, and children; and to make sure that they did not run away, rode up himself at the head of them.

I took several portraits easily enough; for they stood as fixedly as if they had been carved out of wood, staring affright-edly at the camera. Amongst them was an old woman, said to be more than a hundred years old, a dreadful old woman, with a scarcely human face, long white hair hanging down to her waist, and withered, fleshless limbs. I have never seen such an object as she looked, upside down, in the focusing-glass.

When I had finished, I gave them two bottles of rum. There was a general fight, and the old woman to whom I had handed one of the bottles took too much, I fear, before she parted with it; for whilst the others were quarrelling over the residue she kissed my hands rapturously, and then, to my horror and con-fusion, threw off her blanket, and danced round and round the camera in a state of absolute nudity.

Shortly after the capitulation of Estigarribia I went down to Humaità to inspect the hospital and field boticas, but I saw very little of the formidable batteries which have made it so famous. It is a dreary place, flat and marshy, the soil a retentive clay, so that a heavy rain-fall makes a lake of it. On all sides stretch the dismal *esteros*, the interminable marshes, which were, however, the strongest defences of the place, with narrow, bad roads winding through them. A little raised above the general surface would be a few neglected fields, a grove of ragged old orange trees, and a poor rancho ; nothing else between the low parapet on the land side and the distant hills, a blue line on the horizon. Within the works there were long ranges of barracks, mere sheds built of *adobès* and thatched with reeds, a single-storied brick house, where the President resided, he at one end, the Bishop at the other, and Madame Lynch between them, and a few squares of tiled rooms for the officers. The church, rather a favourable specimen of native architecture, was gaily painted outside, and had a double row of life-sized wooden saints within. The tower had been built so badly that they dared not suspend the bells within it, so they hung from a beam at its base. The batteries were hidden by a belt of trees from the lines, and none but those having business there were allowed to go near them. They were principally earthworks, but there was one brick casemate, called the London Battery. They mounted then about 200 guns, mostly thirty-twos.

On the land side there was only a single parapet and ditch, with re-entering angles, commanded by field-pieces, mounted *en barbette*, and bastions at long intervals, with four heavier guns in each. But when Mr. Gould, Her Majesty's Chargé d'Affaires, visited it in September, 1867, it had been greatly strengthened, and was a most formidable place. He reports as follows :—

"The river-side batteries of Humaità at present mount only forty-six guns, namely, one 80-pounder, four 68-pounders, eight 32-pounders, the rest are of different calibres. The battery of Curapaity, towards the river, mounts thirty 32-pounders (this was an outwork to the south-west of Humaità).

"The centre is defended by about a hundred guns. On the left are 117 guns, including four 68-pounders, one 40-pounder rifled Whitworth (recovered from the wreck of the Brazilian iron-clad after the battle of Riachuelo), one 13-in. mortar; fourteen 32-pounders, and many rifled 12-pounders.

"Humaità, on the land side, is protected by three lines of earthworks, on the innermost of which eighty-seven guns are mounted. Total on the left, 204 guns. The grand total is, therefore, 380 guns."

The hospitals were placed far from the barracks, and in the rear of the batteries, so that they were tolerably certain to come in for a good share of the shot aimed at them, and such proved to be the case; casualties in the wards were very frequent, and on one occasion a single ball killed thirteen men as they lay in their beds.

I heard in the marshes surrounding three sides of the fortress the "blacksmith" frog for the first time. The noise it makes is most extraordinary, exactly imitating the sound made by hammering a thin plate of iron. The batrachians of the tropics are as noisy as they are hideous, and they have a most singular way of expressing their feelings; I have often stopped in the *esteros* to listen to them croaking in chorus. One would commence in a loud solemn tone, and then hundreds would join in, until the very ground seemed to vibrate with the deep guttural bass of the marshy choir. There would succeed a moment's silence, and then some Lablache, in a yellow waistcoat, would growl out his awful solo, and the chorus would swell and boom until the noise was almost deafening. On the evenings succeeding a storm, when the frogs were always noisiest, the marshes would be glittering with the smaller fire-fly (*Lampyris occidentalis*), which emits a yellow intermittent light of great brilliancy; and as it was never seen but over wet ground, the noise and the light served as beacons and bell-buoys, as it were, and often warned me of bad places in the road when riding home at night.

On those still, humid evenings, when the air is almost saturated with moisture, the activity and brightness of these glittering insects is most remarkable. In the latter, however, they are greatly exceeded by the large fire-fly, or *lucerna*

(Pyrophorus luminosus), which gives a steady green light of great beauty, which it can brighten or almost extinguish at pleasure. I regret that I did not examine this phenomenon more closely. Under the microscope the illuminators have the appearance of conglomerate glands, a number of pear-shaped sacs traversed by large tracheæ with several branches. And I should say that the amount of light is regulated by the graduated admission of air through these tubes; it is certainly not a vital process, for I ascertained that it continued to be evolved long after death, and even after the organ had been separated from the head.

There is another light-bearer of even greater beauty, the *larva* of a beetle, a grey ungainly worm by day, but at night a bracelet for Titania herself, a double chain of living emeralds, with a clasp of a single ruby.

To return to the fortress : I had intended to have stopped for a week, but was detained nearly three, and for a reason so absurd that I cannot recall it without laughing.

President Lopez had ordered from Paris a peep-show, such as one sees at fairs in England, but on a very grand scale, and a phantasmagoria lantern. They arrived safely shortly before the river was blockaded, but unfortunately the printed directions for setting them up were mislaid, so his Excellency ordered Captain (now Lieut.-Colonel) Thompson and me to arrange and exhibit them. We were not very well pleased with such a task, but of course obeyed.

When ready for display, Lopez, accompanied by the bishop and three or four generals, made the tour of the exhibition to the sound of martial music, and attended by us as showmen. We had great difficulty in preserving our gravity; the childish delight and misconceptions of our fat patron were so absurd as he stood on tiptoe to gaze through the bulls-eyes at " The Bay of Naples by moonlight," or a " Chasseur d'Afrique engaging ten Arabs at once."

The magic-lantern scene was more ridiculous still; a wide passage, or *zaguan*, connecting two courtyards, was closed with curtains at one end and by the screen at the other; the machine was placed within, and chairs arranged in a semicircle for the President and his *suite*, whilst the soldiers for whose amusement the exhibition was principally intended, it was said, found standing room without.

Most of the slides represented battle scenes from the Franco-Italian campaign; these did not excite much enthusiasm, but the comic pictures were received with roars of laughter, and the bishop was very nearly the death of us. There was light enough reflected from the screen to see him distinctly, and his contortions, as he tried with handkerchief stuffed into his mouth to stifle his laughter, were excruciatingly diverting. He dared not laugh out, yet his delight at the figures, especially at one, where the nose of a dwarf gradually reached portentous dimensions, was utterly beyond his control.

This was good fun for one night; but we had succeeded so well that the performance was to be continued till further orders, and that was no joke; however, I was taken ill a few days afterwards, and was allowed to return to the capital.

I kept my bed for nearly a week after my arrival there. Whilst I was still ill, Mr. Atherton, an English merchant, who had been grossly misused by Lopez, and robbed of a large sum of money, on the pretext that he had had dealings of an illegal character with Don Carlos Sagier, a wealthy Paraguayan, who, having obtained permission to visit Corrientes wisely declined to return to his native land, died suddenly, not without strong suspicions of poison.

Mons. Cochelet, the French consul, took up his case strongly, as he had previously that of some of the arsenal men, who had been ill-treated by the police, and he incurred the lasting hatred of Lopez in consequence. This gentleman is entitled to the warmest gratitude of the Englishmen in Paraguay, for the disinterested zeal and activity he showed whenever his official position enabled him to serve them. Her Majesty has had no consul in that country since 1859.

Shortly before, Mr. Whytehead, the chief engineer, died, to

the deep regret of his friends, and the serious loss of the Paraguayans. He was a man of remarkable skill, and had raised the arsenal to a state of great efficiency.

When I returned to Asuncion, a great many wounded had been sent to the General Hospital. The poor fellows were crowded two in a bed and between them in the wards, and hundreds of others were lying outside under the colonnades, in the miserably cold and wet winter weather. There was only Dr. Rhind and Mr. Fox to attend them, the native assistant surgeons could not be trusted to act by themselves, for excepting a little instruction from the latter gentleman in anatomy, and some teaching from me in Materia Medica, they had learnt absolutely nothing. So I wrote to Dr. Stewart, the surgeon-major, offering to do what I could to help them. He mentioned the subject to Lopez, who at once appointed me *Cirujano del* 2do *clase*, that is, assistant military-surgeon; and I commenced my duties by amputating a leg above the knee, ten minutes after my commission reached me.

The sick were sent to Cerro-Leon, and generally but to die. It was not medicine, but proper food, they wanted; and dysenteric patients fed exclusively upon boiled meat were not very likely to recover. This was represented to Lopez; but he only said, with a sneer, "If you have no better advice, as a medico, to give than that, do not come to me again."

The unfortunate Paraguayans suffered successively, epidemic attacks of measles, pneumonia, small-pox, and cholera, the latter of the Asiatic type. The mortality from each was appalling; before any serious battle was fought on land they had lost 50,000 men in the hospitals! They were sent up, poor fellows, in the half-crippled steamers, from the front—for the hospitals at head-quarters were full to overflowing,—a journey of three or four days, and as a rule did not get a morsel of food on the way; from a third to the half usually died and were thrown overboard. The condition in which the survivors arrived was shocking beyond expression, and I saw their sufferings with an indignant pity, which frequently overpowered me

completely. Almost or quite naked, with their wounds untended, dirty and famished, and so emaciated that when dead
they dried up without decomposition,—they were carried up
from the pier to the hospitals ; and then had to lie, perhaps for
a week or till they died, on the ground ; but one never heard a
word of complaint : they bore all with a silent heroism, which
won them our heartiest sympathies.

The General Hospital is, as I have said, built on a low hill
to the west of the town, and was constructed, I believe, by
Francia ; it was, at least, used as a cavalry barrack, and part of
it as a residence by him, during his days of gloomy tyranny ;
and my quarters were the very rooms, distinguished by wooden
ceilings, which he occupied. It is a large building of a single
floor, but rather lofty, and forming two complete and one unfinished squares. In front is a long piazza of heavy stucco
columns, in the centre a chapel, at one end a guard-room, and
at the other the officers' quarters. The wards are mostly large
lofty rooms, but badly lighted.

My day's work was as follows : Before breakfast I went over
to the *Botica*, or Dispensary, where I usually heard a sound of
tinkling guitars and shuffling feet, rapidly exchanged for vigorous
pounding in empty mortars when the assistants heard me un-
locking the door of my office. I had become too well accustomed to the native indisposition to work to notice *that*, so I
arranged their duties for the day, examined any preparations
which were being made under my personal superintendence, and
signed the requisitions awaiting that formality. When I had
breakfasted, I commenced the tour of the wards. At my door
I found, if the weather were fine, a group of laughing and
smoking señoritas, the lady nurses, who were anxious to show
their patriotism by tending the wounded, or, in other words, had
been ordered by the police to do so. I had set my face strongly
against this movement from the first : it was most disagreeable
work for the poor girls ; we did not need them, and excepting
that they amused the wounded, they did no good ; and their
flirtations, carried on with the medical students and pet patients,

wasted much valuable time, and led to several lamentable scandals. Therefore I declined their services with many thanks, a rapid shake of their hands, and the advice, "Do whatever you please, but pray do not touch the wounded." It will not be imagined that I object to good female hospital nurses; they are of course incomparably better than men; but I do object to amateurs in that capacity, and to pretty girls of sixteen being so employed, very strongly.

I enter a lofty room, about a hundred feet long and twenty wide, the roof of palm trunks and bamboos under the massive tiles, and black with the smoke and dirt of fifty years. The floor is of tiles, damp and uneven. The low narrow windows are all on one side of the ward, and the ends are in gloomy shadow, so deep that the festoons of dusty cobwebs seem part of the solid walls. The whole space is filled with rough bedsteads—rude wooden frames with a netting of strips of hide stretched across them—placed as closely as possible, only leaving a narrow pathway between them; for, although the hospital should have but three hundred men in it, nearly thrice that number are now crowded within its walls.*

In each narrow bed lies a wounded man, some on bags of sacking stuffed with moss, others on the bare thongs, which emboss themselves deeply in their flesh. Most of them are nearly naked, save for the bandages over their wounds and shattered limbs, or else a poor thin rag of a sheet is all they have; there are no blankets, although the weather is cold and damp; and the air is so close and fetid—for the poor shivering wretches *will* close the shutters of the unglazed windows at night—that a stranger can hardly breathe it, and yet it is full of visitors, almost all women.

Around one bed is a group of them, talking eagerly to a wounded son or brother, his lately dim eyes now flashing back the happiness beaming from theirs; for has not the doctor told him that he will be a cripple for life, and will never be taken away from them more? They are very affectionate, and to leave

* At one time we had nearly 1,000 wounded there.

home is the greatest of misfortunes to them. A little farther on, a thoughtful mother has brought the well-thumbed guitar with its slender tinkling strings, and her son has raised himself on her arm, and is rattling out the "Media Caña," which his sister and a boyish *practicanté* are gaily dancing, his attention divided between admiration of his pretty partner and fear lest I should surprise him there ; and an old man, with fluttering pulse which will soon beat no more, on the bed beside them, nods his head feebly to the half-heard, but unforgotten melody. Nearer the window a priest with bowed head is listening to a whispered confession. Let the absolution be quickly given, O Padre ! no penance can be needed; he has passed through a very purgatory of suffering already !

Farther yet, in the shadow of a recess, is a still sadder group. A wife in tearless agony is supporting the head of her dying husband. The chill hue of death is whitening his pinched features ; it needs no practised eye to tell her there is no hope now. The little present of chipa and cigars, she has journeyed so many weary leagues on foot to bring him, has fallen unheeded on the ground, and she is muttering Ave Marias with frantic haste, as she tries to force a piece of orange between his clenched teeth. But they cannot stay his fleeting spirit, and the little tired child, who has fallen into so deep a sleep beside him, will wake an orphan.

I picture no imaginary scene. Day after day the actors changed, some few restored to health, some to a life of crippled helplessness, others, and they more numerous than all, passed to the bare cemetery on the hill ; but the same sad drama went on; not a bed was untenanted for many hours.

I am waiting at the door, watching, half envying, the dancers, till the idle *practicanté* catches sight of me, and hurriedly commences a pretençe of doing something, and then, with a sheepish face, brings me the list of those who have entered since yesterday. And a general chorus of "Buenos dias mi padre, we are all quite well this morning," greets me from the patients.

And now I commence my daily work. The new comers are

first examined carefully, and then the rest, as I pass quickly between the lines of beds, only pausing by those severely wounded; for, with four hundred or more on my hands, little time can be given to the rest.

Here and there a man holds out his arm, and begs me to feel his pulse. They seemed to regard it as a sort of charm, and always thanked me gratefully if I acceded. Others would feebly beckon me, and motion me to bend down to their lips, to hear the whispered, "Oh! my father, I am weak, very weak," almost their only complaint. But they are very quiet and patient; a groan or cry is rarely heard, although I am making no idle rounds. If to the frequent question, "Shall I get better?" I could give no hopeful answer, they would but reply, "Está bien" (it is well), in a tone of sad, but uncomplaining resignation.

The morning soon passes. I rest from noon till two o'clock, and then to work again. In the afternoon I perform such operations as cannot be done in the wards, or assist Dr. Rhind, my skilful and kind-hearted colleague, with his. It is often long after sunset before the last case is done with, and almost too tired to eat my dinner, far too tired to enjoy the ride which used to be my chief pleasure, I go early to bed, for I can scarcely hope for an undisturbed rest, since I take the night duty of the whole hospital.

CHAPTER XII.

BATTLES OF THE BANK, PASO LA PATRIA, BELLACO, AND CURUPAITY.
NEGOTIATIONS AND DIPLOMACY.

SUCH was my daily life for some months, and in narrating it I have passed over the invasion of Paraguay by the Allies, which did not take place till the 17th of April, 1866, or about seventeen months after the first blow was struck by Lopez by the seizure of the "Marques de Olinda."

I may mention here, that the stock of powder Lopez had collected was enormous, and in addition to that stored by his father, and two thousand barrels which arrived a few days before the blockade of the river, he captured a good deal in Mato Grosso. But there was a reserve store of about twenty tons of saltpetre and sulphur for the manufacture of more in a magazine near my quarters. One evening, by some accident, it ignited, and as the combustible and the supporter of combustion were warehoused in the same building, the fury and rapidity of the conflagration may be imagined. It raged and roared like a volcano for two hours; and not a pound of the whole was saved. He afterwards tried to make gunpowder with nitrate of soda, which is found sparingly in Paraguay; but, of course, unsuccessfully.

The official paper stated several times that large deposits of saltpetre had been found, but such was not the case. During the lifetime of Don Carlos I made an extensive series of analyses, by his orders, of samples of soils brought from all parts of the country to determine this very point; and I then reported that nitrate of potash did not occur in any one of them, and that there was no probability of its being found in Paraguay, an opinion which was confirmed by the reports of Mr. Twite, a mining engineer, who afterwards surveyed the country. This was one of the many *canards* spread by Lopez concerning the " inexhaustible resources of the country," and elaborated to mislead the enemy and public opinion abroad.

After the capitulation of Estigarribia in September, 1865, the Allies marched their forces into Corrientes, and with a little severe fighting drove the Paraguayans out of that province. A Provisional Government had been installed there by order of Lopez, who stated that he had only occupied the territory for the purpose of rescuing the people from tyranny! However, it soon came to an end, and order was once more re-established.

The Paraguayans retreated, and crossed the Paranà without molestation, the commanders of the Brazilian squadron allowing them to pass, almost under the guns of the fleet, with 80,000 head of cattle, stolen from the Corrientinos, to Paso la Patria, when they could have been cut off with the utmost ease; and in October, 1865, the army of Lopez was concentrated in Paso Pucù (*the long pass*), a strip of dry land bounded by the impassable *estero* of Nembucù on the east, and the river Paraguay on the west.

The allied forces encamped on the northern frontier of Corrientes, opposite Paso la Patria. They numbered sixty-two thousand men of all arms ; namely, 40,000 Brazilians, 18,000 Argentines, and 4,000 Orientàles, with two hundred guns. They remained there inactive six months, and although six ironclads, carrying heavy rifled guns, had been added to the fleet, it dared not pass the little battery of Itapirù, mounting three guns, I believe 32-pounders, but certainly not heavier than 68-pounders. The monitors exchanged shots with it at a long range for three months, and the result was the dismounting of one gun in the fort.

Active operations were again initiated by Lopez, who had arranged a plan for the surprise and capture of the batteries established on a long, low island, opposite the embouchure of the Rio Paraguay.   He intended to fall upon them at night, the Paraguayans were to drop silently down the stream in large flat, punt-like canoes, and slaughter the sleeping garrison.

There is little doubt that such a scheme would have succeeded, but, fortunately for their intended victims, the Paraguayans are the most dilatory of men, " *Espera hasta mañana* " (Wait till to-morrow), is their motto, as it is of most South Americans ;   and day was breaking when they reached the low grassy shore of the island.   Eight hundred men were in the canoes (a reserve of half that number remaining on the mainland to assist them if necessary, and a few hours afterwards they were almost all that were left of the expeditionary force), and at first success seemed a certainty ; for with a frantic yell the half-naked Paraguayans threw themselves, sword or knife in hand, on the startled Brazilians, who recoiled in disorder beyond their second lines ; but there a storm of grape and canister, poured almost into the teeth of their pursuers, checked their advance, and gave time for the garrison to reform their disordered ranks, and prepare for the second assault of the enemy ; who, baffled but undaunted, came on again with a spring like a panther, again to be mowed down by the pitiless iron hail ; a third and a fourth time, and then the shot whistled harmlessly through the trampled reeds : there were but dead or dying strewn beneath them.

A few managed to swim across the stream, a few were brought off by the canoes which had escaped the shot of the iron-clads, which soon afterwards added their fire to that of the batteries, but above five hundred men were left dead by noon.   The Brazilians lost nearly double that number in killed and wounded.

This took place on the 10th of April, 1866 ; and a week afterwards the allied army crossed the Paraná, and encamped on its banks, having the Estero Bellaco, as the southern border of the great marsh of Nembucù is called, on their right, and the river itself on the left.   There an entrenched camp was formed, defended by batteries of great strength.

The Paraguayans attacked them in force, on the 24th of May,

and again carried, in the furious rush in which they threw
themselves upon them, the most formidable of the defences;
but, undisciplined and commanded by officers who knew little
of their duty, who drove them on, never led them, they then
got into confusion, and fled, a disorderly mob. They suffered
fearfully in their flight; the guns which they had captured, but
had not attempted to disable, were turned upon them, and
nearly fifteen thousand dead and dying strewed the plain in
front.

That battle of the Bellaco may be said to have annihilated the
Spanish race in Paraguay. In the front ranks were the males
of all the best families in the country, and they were killed
almost to a man; hundreds of families, in the capital especially,
had not a husband, father, son, or brother left. Old men who
had been left in Humaità, Indians, slaves, and boys now filled
the attenuated ranks of the national army.

The Allies made no attempt to follow up their success, but
only too thankful that they had not been swept into the river,
hoped that Lopez would now sue for peace. But he was not a
man to be disheartened, even by so crushing a defeat, and at
once set to work fortifying his position, and in all haste collected
the few men who had hitherto escaped the conscription. He
drew a triple line of parapets and stockaded ditches across the
narrow strip of land he held between the Rio Paraguay and the
marshes which protected his left; and threw up a strong earth-
work at Curùzù, on his extreme right overlooking the river.

The Allies did nothing for nearly four months afterwards, when
assured of the trustworthiness of their iron-clads, they moved
them up the river, destroyed the little battery of Itapirù and captured Curùzù, after a severe struggle, on the 2nd of September,
and again sat down to congratulate themselves, to rest and be
thankful.

They gave Lopez a fortnight to reorganize his forces and
strengthen the already formidable lines of Curupaitỳ, which
would have been formidable to the best troops in the world, and
much more so to men commanded by a general so utterly incom-

petent as Caxias; who now had not his usual excuse of want of information to offer; for the Paraguayan position was not only examined in the ordinary way, but a balloon was called into requisition, and from that aërial point of vantage the lines were repeatedly reconnoitred.

However, on the 22nd of September, 1866, the Allies stormed the lines, but were repulsed with great slaughter. It was the story of the Bellaco over again, only changing sides. The Brazilians carried the first two lines, but at the third wavered, turned and fled, and were terribly cut up before they could get out of range.

If Lopez could have left the shelter of his works, he might then have finished the war; but he dared not trust such an army as he then had in the open field. His best men had all perished, his forces had melted to a fourth of their original strength, although the conscription had been sending recruits faster than he could find arms—on the battle-field—for them. All within the ages of ten and sixty years had been taken; the teeth of the rake were set closer at every sweep, and nearly *two hundred thousand* males had been drawn from a total population of less than a million !   And of this multitude scarcely twenty thousand remained: 80,000 men died in the hospitals from disease, or rather from bad and scanty food and want of the commonest necessaries of life; 12,000 were lost through the unfortunate expedition of Estigarribia; the rest had perished in battle, or had been taken prisoners. The Allies tried to utilize the latter by forming a Paraguayan Legion, incorporated with the Argentine forces; and it is stated, I fear truthfully, that they shot many who did not " volunteer" to fight against their own people. Be that as it may, the result was a very unsatisfactory one, the Paraguayans took every opportunity of deserting; for, as I have said, love of home and of country is a passion with them. In a skirmish near Estero Bellaco, the advance guard consisted of 700 of their new allies, a portion of the forces of Estigarribia, and they went over to a man, taking their arms with them, directly they caught sight of their own flag. Lopez repaid their devotion by shooting all the more respectable amongst them, for not returning sooner.

On the 3rd of November a desperate attempt was made to destroy the magazines of the Allies at a place called Paso-Chanàr, then their head-quarters. In the grey of the morning a force of 8,000 Paraguayans fell upon the camp, so suddenly that the drowsy sentinels were bayoneted at their posts, and their foes were burning the stores of the Argentines before an alarm had been sounded. Fortunately for the Allies, however, the starving Paraguayans came upon some suttlers' huts, and stopped to plunder them ; this gave the Brazilians time to come up ; they fell upon the now disorderly crowd of marauders, and routed them with immense loss. The Paraguayans left 3,000 dead on the field, but the singularity of the affair is, that although routed they managed to capture some of the field-pieces of the conquerors. The Hon. Mr. Pakenham writes to Lord Stanley :—
" A curious incident connected with the recent engagement is, that the vanquished seized, and were able to carry off several pieces of artillery belonging to the victors; a proceeding unusual, I believe, in modern military annals."

Although hard and obstinate fighting had been the rule, diplomacy was not forgotten. The Brazilians had tried theirs, characteristically, by offering large rewards to deserters, and Lopez retaliated by putting their captured officers to the front to persuade *their* men to run away. A wretched little Brazilian lieutenant, who had distinguished himself in this way, and was set at liberty in the capital to watch Mr. Washburn as a reward for his services, told me, with many contortions of countenance, how his eloquence was stimulated on these occasions by a bayonet in the rear. " Habla, hombre ! speak up, man ! shout to the cambàs !" the delighted Paraguayans used to cry to the unhappy wretch on the parapet before them, prodding his legs at every word.

In September, 1866, after the capture of Curùzù, Lopez tried negotiations of a more regular character, and proposed a personal conference between himself and President Mitrè,

Generalissimo of the allied army ; which was acceded to, and the meeting, which promised the happiest results, took place on the 2nd of that month.   But no good came of it.   Lopez consented to treat on the basis that the Allies should withdraw from Paraguay, he doing the same from Mato Grosso, and that the question of boundaries should be settled by arbitration.   These conditions were at once rejected, the Allies insisting, as a *sine qua non*, that Lopez should resign the presidentship, and leave Paraguay.   The next day he wrote that the people would not allow him to accept such terms, that he could not abandon a country which he loved so dearly, and so on, and the correspondence was broken off.   After the disaster of Curupaitÿ, of course any hope of an arrangement was impossible ; the pride of the Brazilians and Argentines had been too deeply wounded.

The " Semanario " was filled for weeks afterwards with patriotic addresses and laudations of the President, praising him especially for the generosity and humanity he had shown in offering terms of peace to his demoralized and perishing enemies, and declaring that they (the Paraguayans) would all die ere he should leave their fatherland, of which he was the glory and the saviour.   Unwittingly they spoke the truth.

These addresses served as a pretext for demanding fresh contributions, and the women were stripped of the little jewelry they still possessed, for making the massive gold covers of an album, containing the signatures of those whose sentiments were supposed to be recorded in them.   At the same time two flags richly embroidered in gold and with stars of brilliants and other precious stones in the centres ; a sword of honour, in a jewelled case, both of massive gold ; and a wreath of the same precious metal, were also made for him.   A large sum of money remained in hand, and this was intended for the purchase of a tiara and a marshal's staff in Europe ; but it was sent to Paris when Mons. Cuverville left the country.   When finished, six of the most prominent men left in the capital went down to the Paso Pucù to present it, and their fate must have encouraged the others.

Two of them were shot for "want of patriotism" within a week of their arrival, one was left in irons, one died from cholera, and two returned.*

The story of the fall of these men is so characteristic that it is worth telling. Each of them read a written speech which had been carefully prepared for him; but, even with the paper in their hands, they had so completely lost their self-possession that they stumbled and hesitated like schoolboys over their task; this put Lopez greatly out of temper, and one of them, named Urbieta, a simple old country gentleman, tried an improvised cheer to mend matters; but, thinking principally of what he ought to avoid, he shouted lustily, " Viva Don Pedro !" (the Emperor of Brazil) instead of "Don Francisco Solano." He was instantly arrested, and was executed a few days afterwards as a traitor.

The Allies were so disheartened by the repulse from Curupaity that they confined themselves to a strict blockade of the river, and a feeble and badly directed fire from the iron-clads, until the 15th of August, 1867, when ten monitors passed the batteries of that place, and anchored about a mile below Humaità, which they did not venture to pass in turn until after the usual six months' rest and consideration.

In the August of 1866, an American, named Manlove, and late a Confederate major of cavalry, presented himself to Lopez as a volunteer ; but he met with a chilling reception, for his history had preceded him. Lopez, it seems, had friends in the camp of the Allies. Newspapers were pretty regularly conveyed to him, and one printed in Buenos Ayres spoke of Major Manlove as a crack shot in the Argentine service, who was going to pick off Paraguayan officers. He laid, however, an ingenious scheme before Lopez, which, if adopted, might even then have changed very materially the aspect of the war. He asked a commission to fit out privateers in the Antilles to prey

* They were Don Satunino Bedoya, Paymaster-General (a brother-in-law of Lopez), Don Venancio Urbieta, Chief of Yaguaron; Don Pedro Barrios (brother of the General), and three others whose names I have forgotten.

upon the Allies, attacking in preference merchant vessels. He did not ask money, or only sufficient to take him home *viá* Bolivia and Panama, and one or more Paraguayan officers might accompany him as subordinate commanders. He stated that he had two vessels ready, and they would start as soon as he had letters of marque to distinguish him from unauthorized pirates.

Lopez, however, would not trust him. He was looked upon as a spy, kept in prison for some time, then liberated and sent to the capital, where he received pay for a few months from the Government; but in 1868 he was again arrested, and was shot towards the close of the year.

I may remark that a general distrust of those around him, even of those who were most strongly bound to him by ties of blood or self-interest, was a distinguishing feature in the character of Lopez, and one which materially hastened, if it did not occasion, his downfall. If, before beginning the war, he had frankly stated to the chief engineer, Mr. Whytehead, that such an event would take place, and asked his aid, I am certain that he would have received most valuable assistance. The country, strongly protected by nature, might have been made almost impregnable ; and the terrible mortality which almost destroyed the army before it took the field would have been prevented if the aid of the medical officers had been sought, and their advice taken. But " the gods first make mad those they would destroy," and the punishment of his crimes seemed but the shadow of them.

From the first, the most important and zealous help was given him by the English engineers in his service; for, although we all heartily disliked Lopez, the Paraguayans, as a people, could but claim both our aid and our sympathies, from their bravery, their devotion, and their cheerful obedience. It was one example of the perplexing state of " those distracted countries " that the very help we gave our friends was the cruellest wrong we could do them ; for a crushing defeat at the beginning of the war would have been an incalculable advantage to them.

One of the oldest defences of Humaità was a chain stretched across the river, many years before, by Don Carlos Lopez. When hostilities commenced two others were added, and the three were supported by lighters, and strained taut by capstans on shore. The lighters also served as floating prisons, and in one of them Padre Corbelàn was immured. Rows of piles were also added ; but the latter generally failed from the necessity of fishing them when the river was high. A large number of torpedoes were laid down, some of most formidable dimensions ; but the greater number were exploded by drift-wood brought down by the floods, or perhaps by inquisitive alligators.

When the war commenced the heaviest guns in Paraguay were 68-pounder smooth bores ; but some excellent rifled guns were made in the arsenal by the English workmen, especially a 150-pounder Whitworth, cast from the metal of the church bells. The Brazilians furnished them with shot ; but thousands of pounds' worth of costly machinery was melted down for missiles, nevertheless.

CHAPTER XIII.

OUR work meanwhile went on as usual. The hospital at Asuncion
was ever overcrowded, in spite of the fearful mortality, which
our utmost efforts seemed powerless to check, and my own
health was giving way, through the excessive strain upon my
bodily and mental powers, and for several days at a time I had
to keep my bed from utter exhaustion. In addition to my
hospital duties, I had lately taken charge of the English women,
the wives of the mechanics, and their children. The costliness
and scarcity of food was beginning to tell upon them, also, and
many were seriously ill.

The month of October, 1866, had commenced, and we were
looking forward with anxiety to the probable effect of the hot
weather on the inmates of the already pestilential wards, little
thinking that we should soon have to leave them, almost unaided,
to their fate. On the 8th of that month I had been out for a
short ride, a luxury I could then rarely indulge in, and on my
return found Dr. Rhind in a state of considerable uneasiness.

A telegram had been received from Paso Pucù, ordering him
and Mr. Fox to visit the Lady President together at seven p.m.
The order arrived only shortly before that hour, and Dr. Rhind
went immediately in search of his colleague, but could not find
him until half-past eight o'clock. They then went down to her
house; but the old lady was in a very bad humour, and refused
to see them. The next morning they went again, but with the

same result. Shortly afterwards an order came from Surgeon-Major Stewart, written by command of the President, requiring them to state severally why they were absent from duty, and what they were doing the previous afternoon. They did so, but the answer of Mr. Fox was considered so unsatisfactory that Lopez sent an order to Mayor-de-Plaza Gomez to put them both under arrest. Poor Rhind, who was consumptive and then very weak and ill, came to me in great distress, and told me that the major had sent for him, and added, " I am certain they are going to put me in prison. I cannot bear it. I shall never come out alive." I tried to cheer him up, not very successfully, for I was as anxious as he, and feared the worst.

All day I worked as usual, but my thoughts were with my absent friend. In the evening his adjutant came up to tell me that he was a prisoner, and that I was to take charge of the Hospital General, which then contained eight hundred wounded ; whilst Teniente Ortellado, an old native practitioner, completely ignorant of surgery, and indeed of almost all else, was left in charge of the Estanco and San Francisco hospitals in the city. Altogether, more than fifteen hundred wounded, including convalescents, were left in our care and of a few *practicantès*, native medical students. The next morning I received an open note from Mr. Fox, asking me to go down to see him and take charge of his keys. I went immediately, saw the Mayor-de-Plaza, who told me very gruffly that they were " *incomunicablè*," that is, not permitted to be seen. I begged him to endeavour to obtain an exception in my favour, and he promised to do so. Dr. Rhind had accidentally taken with him a knife of mine which I wanted for an operation ; I availed myself of this as an excuse to send, through the Minister of War, a letter (open, of course, and in Spanish), asking for it, but really to assure him that I would send him all he needed, and serve him in any possible way.

A fortnight passed away ; I worked literally day and night, for I had a presentiment that I should soon follow my colleagues, and was anxious to leave as little to be done as possible ; and I performed more serious operations in that time than I had ever hoped to have the good fortune to meet with in the whole of my life. It was well for me that I had so much to engross my attention; for when I saw the misery around me, and reflected how much of it would have been relieved but for the arrest of my friends, I was scarcely able to restrain the expression of my indignation, an exhibition of which would have been as dangerous to them as to me. I was always thinking of Dr. Rhind, however, and of the wretchedness he must be enduring.

On the morning of the 22nd, my friend Mons. Laurent-Cochelet, the French consul, sent me a packet of letters, which had been sent through the lines by the Imperial Chargé d'Affaires to Paso Pucù, and which he had brought up with him to Asuncion. Two were for me, the rest for Dr. Rhind. I was delighted with my own, for two years had elapsed since I had last heard from home, and also with the thought of how cheered and amused my old friend would be if he could only get his. So I buckled on my sword, and went down directly to the Mayoria. The great man was engaged, the adjutant said; I must wait. I waited for two hours in the sun, vexed at the loss of so much valuable time, and then found that he was simply engaged watching the game of *sortijà*. He was seated with the chief of police and another officer, when I went up to him, and asked if he had yet received an answer to my application, through him, for permission to visit my friend. " No," said he; " why are you so anxious to see him? " " Because I hear he is ill, and he is, I know, anxious to see me." I then went on to say that I had received, through the French consul, a packet of letters from his family for him, and was most desirous to deliver them personally. I knew that unless I did so he would not receive them. " Give those letters to me," the mayor said, sternly. " Señor," I replied, quietly, " I cannot do that, they are private letters, unless I get an order from him to do so." " Teriho " (go), said he, in an angry tone, " and do not trouble me again." I told him that it was the last favour I should ask of him, and went. But the danger of my position did not for a moment occur to me.

In the evening I rode over to the consulate, to tell M. Cochelet what had happened; but he was at dinner, so saying that I would return later, I went on to visit a native friend. On the road an officer met me, and, with great politeness, said the Mayor-de-Plaza wished to see me, and that I was to take the letters. I went directly, thinking that permission had arrived for visiting Dr. Rhind, but soon found how grievously I had mistaken.* As soon as Gomez saw me he shouted, "I order you under arrest." "Indeed, señor," said I; "why? and until when?" "That you will know to-morrow. Have you the letters?" I assented. "Take care of them." A squad of men, with fixed bayonets, came to the door, and I was marched off between them, through the guard-room, across the great courtyard, and through a narrow passage into a cell, on the floor of which a candle was burning. And then the full horror of my position burst upon me: I was a prisoner.

I sat down and asked the officer who brought me in for a cigar, which he gave me. I told him I was hungry, not having dined, and he promised that some food should be sent for. I then, as far as the dim light of the candle allowed me, examined my dungeon. It was about twelve feet by eight, the walls of rough brickwork; from a heavy column in the centre of the wall sprung two arches, and above them the roof at a considerable height, of palm trunks, and tiles laid in earth. The floor was of mud, full of hollows, cold and wet. The only furniture, a *catrè*, that is, a hide stretched on a wooden frame, and a broken chair.

I had been up all the night before with a difficult surgical case, and when I had eaten my supper I threw myself on the rude bed, in my clothes, and was soon soundly sleeping.

I was awakened in the morning by the band playing the *réveillé*, as usual, at four o'clock. I lay awake some hours : I could hear that it was raining heavily outside, but no daylight appeared. In truth, as I soon found, my prison was so situated that, except in bright weather, I should live almost in darkness. The large door was wide open; but as it looked only into a long arched

* People were rarely arrested publicly.

passage connecting the two courtyards of the Colegio (for I was within the old Jesuit college), all the light I could get would be that reflected from the wall. There had once been a window, but it was now jealously blocked up; the ledge, however, remained, and made me a very useful shelf.

About ten in the morning a sergeant came in, and ordered me to follow him. I did so, and was taken to a small room, in the front of the building. I found there Capt. Silva, an alferez,* a sergeant, and Señor Ortellado, a notary. By the former I was sworn on a sword, and then examined very tediously by the latter for several hours. Written questions were read to me; my answers were taken down on loose sheets, and then copied on stamped paper. I was first asked a number of formal questions about my name, age, birthplace, religion, and so on, and then if I knew why I had been arrested. No. Did I not know that it was the first duty of a soldier to obey his superiors? Yes, certainly; but I was not a soldier, my rank being honorary. Was I in the service of the republic? Yes, but without a contract, and in a non-military capacity. Did I not know that it was forbidden by law to deliver letters which had not passed through the post-office? No, I had never seen or heard of such a law, nor had I even infringed it, since I had not delivered the letters. Would send them there, if permitted, and would, of course, pay the postage. He then asked me if I had the letters, and ordered me to give them up. I demurred, questioning their right to deprive me of them, as they had not shown me by what authority they were acting. Capt. Silva told the sergeant to put a set of *grillos* (fetters) on the table. Taking the hint, for, of course resistance was out of the question, I gave up the letters. I was then examined, at great length, about my private correspondence, the people I wrote to, where they lived, and so on. Why did I refuse to obey the orders of the Mayor-de Plaza? Because I considered that he had no right to deprive me of private letters, and because, if I had done so, he would not have given them to the owner; for he had already taken

* An ensign.

one letter of mine, with a distinct promise that he would deliver it to Dr. Rhind, and had not done so. How did I know
that ? Because it urgently needed an answer, which he had not
sent, and his servant, who saw him every day, told me that he
had not had it.

I was sent back to my prison until the evening, when, the
said servant having been examined, and denying that he had
said anything to me about the letter (he was afraid to speak the
truth), I was called again.

Ortellado asked me how I dared give false evidence. I replied that Englishmen were not in the habit of doing so, and that
my word was surely more credible than that of a servant. But,
not wishing to involve the man in any difficulty, for that would
inconvenience Dr. Rhind himself, I said that as he spoke but little
Spanish, and I still less Guarani, I might have mistaken him.

The day was almost spent, and I passed from the ruddy sunset into utter darkness when I returned to my cell; shortly
afterwards, however, they brought me a candle set in a little
earthen cup, and I then found that some bedding had been sent
me from my quarters, with a basin, a water jar, and a chair. I
soon went to bed, but not to sleep, the physical fatigue had passed
off, the mental only excited me, and I then discovered a source
of wretchedness, which to this day I cannot think of without horror, but which I had been too weary to notice the night before.

Near the threshold, but in the passage, stood, day and night,
a sentry armed with musket and bayonet, and relieved every
two hours; a more effectual guard than bolts or bars. He
stood facing me, and about eight feet from my bed; and from
nine o'clock at night until the *réveillé* sounded the next morning,
every quarter of an hour, shouted, " *Sentinela alerta!*" at the
top of his voice, to show that he was not sleeping. This startling cry was taken up in succession by the others, in the chain of
sentries, within and without the prison, and by the time the last
had finished the first began again. It was terrible! To be
thus awakened by a sudden yell, all hope of sound and peaceful
sleep destroyed, and the painful consciousness that I was a pri

soner perpetually forced upon me, was a cruel torture.   Never shall I be able to efface it from my memory.

Often have I passed the whole night pacing wearily the short length of my prison, or lying with my fingers firmly pressed up my ears, lest I should fall asleep but to be awakened by that dreaded cry.   For months I only slept every third night.

To return to my examination.   The next day I was called to hear the evidence read over to me from beginning to end. When it was being taken I noticed that Captain Silva and the notary frequently left the room with the papers, and I now found why they had done so.   My replies, nominally copied from the loose sheets, had been grossly distorted; all that tended to exculpate me was omitted ; and they had inserted a fictitious confession of guilt, that I had asked pardon for my offences, and that I had stated that I was willing to bear any punishment awarded me !

I need scarcely say that I had neither confessed nor said anything of the kind, for it was contrary to the whole tenor of my replies and to the truth.   I protested in the strongest language against these misstatements and the unworthy treatment I was enduring after my long and zealous services; and said, that instead of fairly examining me, they had only sought to find me guilty.

I told them that I was aware that ignorance of a law did not excuse its evasion, but I neither knew that there was any such regulation concerning the delivery of letters, nor had I even broken it.   I had not delivered the letters to Dr. Rhind, and I considered that I had a perfect right to receive them from M. Cochelet; for they had been sent to him under a flag of truce with despatches by the French secretary of legation, and brought from Paso Pucù by the consul himself; and under such circumstances I considered that they need not to have been sent to the office ; if, however, they ought to have been, it was clear that the consul should have sent them, and not I.

Moreover, I had received many letters, official and private, from Humaità and Paso Pucù, many forwarded by the Mayor-de-Plaza himself, others by the captain of the port, and none of them had ever passed through the post-office or been stamped. I knew perfectly well, when I made this defence, that it was useless, in so far as preventing my condemnation was concerned; but I hoped that one of them—Captain Silva especially, who seemed greatly struck by my argument—would report it to Lopez, and that the injustice with which I was being treated would be brought home to him. For, up to that time, I had received no ill-treatment from him, and thought that, as an Englishman, and one who had faithfully served him several years, I should be soon set at liberty. Without a reply Ortellado told me to sign the depositions. I declined to do so, saying that they knew that they were falsified and unjust to me. He called my attention to the irons again, and at the same time assured me that if I would give them no further trouble I should be set at liberty in a few days. Seeing that it was useless to resist, and dreading the severities to which I should have been exposed had I been put in irons—deprived of bed and chair, and with only a hide on the ground to sit or lie upon—I reluctantly signed the papers.

I have much pleasure in adding, that Captain Silva treated me with uniform politeness and consideration, evidently obeying the instructions he had received unwillingly. He promptly checked the insolence with which the ensign began to treat me, said how pleased he had been with my kindness to the sick, gave me some cigars, and shook hands with me warmly as I left,—never to see him again. He died from cholera, poor fellow, shortly afterwards.

I knew at the time of my arrest that this affair of the letters was but a pretext for punishing me, for I had been warned by an influential friend that I had fallen into disgrace, and that an opportunity to do so was alone waited for; he dared not, however, write me what my offence really was, and it is only since my return to England that I have learnt how I had incurred the anger of Lopez. I have mentioned that the sudden death of Mr. Atherton was regarded with great suspicion; indeed, at the time it was very generally believed by the natives that he had been poisoned by order of the Dictator.   How this rumour commenced I cannot tell, but I am certain that I had no part in originating it ; however, I got the credit of having done so, and Lopez never forgave me for it.   Moreover, my intimacy with the French Consul, and especially with the Corbalàn family, was an offence in his eyes.

And now the weary monotonous life of a prisoner was before me.   At first I regarded it with a dread and horror that did not allow me to think what it might be and how long it should last; but I never gave way to despair : I tried to view it as a phase of my life that, like sickness or a broken limb, must needs be borne ; and except when incipient delirium from low fever and nervous exhaustion made me almost frantic for a few hours, I suffered with a patience and calmness I had scarcely hoped for.   I gradually became accustomed to the dim light reflected from the wall of the passage, and in clear weather could see to read for several hours a day.   But when the sky was overcast, and until the sun was high, I was in a gloom so deep that, to any one entering from without it would have seemed total darkness. My only fear was that the damp would affect my health ; for the mud floor was beneath the level of the courtyard, and the walls, the beams, and even my mattress on its under side, were covered with fungoid growths, green and slimy with mouldiness, and with an odour so earthy that I could but think of those to whom it had probably been both a prison and a grave. It was miserably cold, but they would not let me have a blanket from my quarters, and sent only a tattered piece of red baize, which had long done duty as a table-cover, in place of it.

My companions in misfortune were lodged in the courtyard beyond me.   Mr. Fox had quite a cheerful room outside, he told me afterwards, where he could see the señoritas going to church, and sometimes even a handkerchief waved towards him. Dr. Rhind was nearer to me, but in more lightsome quarters. He heard from a sentry of my imprisonment, and one Sunday morning chanted Jackson's "Te Deum" right through, to let me know of his whereabouts.

Next to my cell was an open corridor, where a great many prisoners were confined in chains, which all day long clanked dismally, and often in the night I heard them clash suddenly when the *presos* were startled in their sleep by the cry of the sentries. Now and then I caught sight of them through a chink in the thick boards which covered the window, and sometimes they passed to the great quadrangle through the passage in front of my door. They were of all ages, some very old men, others but boys, but all reduced to the last stage of emaciation, mere brown skin and bone. All had one pair of heavy fetters rivetted on their ankles, rough with callosities and cicatrices of old wounds, several two; and one man bore on his skeleton-like legs three heavy bars, which swung creaking backwards and forwards as he slowly shuffled along. Yet they were not half so wretched as one would have thought; they used to laugh and sing, and have clattering, staggering races in their narrow den.

One of them—I think it must have been he with the triple *grillos*, for he had such a droll face—used to tell endless stories (I could faintly hear the murmur of the words through the thick walls), which were received with bursts of laughter and a rattling of fetters, which reminded me of that terrible scene in "Les Misérables," where the "chain" in their mad desperation make the early morning hideous with shouts and clashing irons. They were allowed to do this by the sentries, who enjoyed the stories and jokes as much as they, and gave them notice when an officer was coming. One day, however, they were all so interested in some story of great facetiousness that they did not hear the usual "*charqué*" (look out!) and the grim old comandantè himself came upon them whilst they were all screaming with laughter at the climax. They were silent in a moment! A hushed stillness succeeded to the uproar, and I could almost feel that they were pale with terror. The comandantè said not a word, but walked back, and soon returned with a squad of soldiers. The unfortunate story-teller was thrown on the ground, and flogged severely; his yells made the place ring again : and two or three of his most vehement applauders shared the same fate. They were as still as mice for days afterwards.

Every week or so, one and another of them would be taken out to the *patio* to be flogged. These were sad days for me, I dreaded their coming, and did not recover from the pain they occasioned me for many hours afterwards. I think the fact of hearing, without being able to see the infliction of their punishments, made them more terrible. To hear the dull, heavy thud of the stick wielded by those stalwart, pitiless corporals, and to know that it was descending on living flesh quivering in agony, made me faint and sick with horror. As a surgeon I was, they told me, one of the coolest of operators, and yet these sounds used to unnerve me completely the whole day through. I then little thought that I should one day have to suffer a worse punishment!

I was not quite alone in my dungeon, but my companions were of a class I would have gladly dispensed with. Centipedes, scorpions, and toads; the latter so big, so cold and hideous, that the strongest minded of women might have screamed at them without a blush. Personally, I do not object to toads, and often laughed heartily enough at the fright I have given my native friends, who believe in the old-world error that they are venomous, by tenderly handling specimens I could scarcely put in my hat for obesity. But to put the naked foot upon one in searching for a slipper in the dark is not agreeable, and the extraordinary sounds they emit in the dead of night do not tend to make them pleasant companions. The first I have named, however, were far worse: to centipedes and scorpions I have an intense aversion, and the fact of catching three fine examples of the latter interesting creatures *on my bed* in one week did not reduce it. I found, moreover, that I was not alone in my dread of them. One afternoon I saw a dozen or more cockroaches hurrying in evident terror out of a hole in the wall; they tumbled out in the most reckless way in the very best lighted part of the place;

and I despatched them as fast as they sprawled on the floor—
for next to a centipede I think I detest a cockroach, and they
are one of the plagues of South America—wondering greatly
what would follow, expecting a snake, when out came a pair
of large scorpions, male and female, with stings erect, and
looking the most vicious creatures imaginable. I inserted my
cigar deftly into the hole to bar their retreat, and then watched
their proceedings. They stopped for a moment near the edge
of it, and then hastily and in some amazement searched in a
wide circle round it for the routed cockroaches. Not finding
their prey, they in turn became frightened, and tried to escape,
but retributive Justice, represented by my slipper, descended
and crushed them to atoms.

I was surprised to see that a spider, which had established
herself in a hole in a post near my bed, was more than a match
for them, and how readily the strong-jointed, sting-bearing tail
was bound down, harmless and motionless. Several small
scorpions, and one large one, were destroyed by my watchful
ally. She afterwards took to laying; and, wishing to test the
fecundity of spiders, I several times removed the ball of eggs
(almost as large as herself) as soon as it was finished, and six
times was it replaced in a few weeks. Her relatives were
numerous in my gloomy lodging; in fact, looking at the condition of the massive beams and rafters overhead (a long chink
under the eaves permitted a straggling gleam of daylight to fall
upon them, and show me how thickly they were draped with
the dingiest of cobwebs) and the rough walls covered with a
threadbare tapestry of their weaving, I could almost say that I
lived in one huge cobweb, with a most thriving and industrious
family of spinners around me. They did not all spin, but, like
the great hairy *nyandè*,* a spider which looks more than a match

* *Aranea avicularia*, of which it used to be said that it caught small birds in
its huge webs and fed upon them. The fact is, however, that it does not spin
any web at all, but, as stated in the text, catches its prey by suddenly springing
upon it; its venom is very powerful, and will produce considerable inflammation
in the human subject.

for a linnet, there were several which depended upon their address and agility for securing a meal; and they fell upon their prey so suddenly that they seemed to have leaped into existence at the very spot where they were first seen. One especially, a grey, flattened spider, with a body as large and scarcely thicker than a shilling, and with striped limbs, also compressed vertically, moved with a celerity which was really marvellous, and could shoot into cracks so narrow that it seemed to sink into the wall itself. I found, however, that by bringing my finger down slowly and perpendicularly I could pinion it, and one very large one, which I thus caught several times in the same long afternoon, at length ceased to struggle, and let me stroke it, I think, with positive pleasure. Its apparently rough body, which I imagined to be covered with cartilaginous plates, was really as soft as velvet, the attachments of the *septa* which preserved its curiously compressed form caused the allusion. But the proceedings of a smaller kind, not larger indeed than a grain of rape seed, amused me the most. They wove little silky webs over every minute depression in the wall, with an oval opening on each side, through which they sprang out if anything touched the threads. They used, when game was scarce, to run around the outsides of their lodgings, and make visits to, or rather precipitate descents upon, each other; one starting out of its hole, and the intruder taking its place, to be rapidly ejected in turn. This diversion they would keep up for hours at a time. I fancy it was a sort of flirtation with serious intentions, but whether of a matrimonial or cibarious character, I never ascertained.

I lived in constant dread of being bitten or stung by some of these venomous creatures; but except those of the genus *cimex*, not one during those many months molested me. The place was too damp for fleas to exist in, so I escaped one of the plagues of the torrid zone.

CHAPTER XIV.

AT first I saw no one but the sergeant and a felon who brought me my daily meals. They never spoke to me, and when I asked for anything I needed, intimated compliance or the reverse by a nod or a shake of the head. One day, about a month after my arrest, a soldier came in place of the convict, a fact I ascertained by the absence of the clank of irons as he entered, for it was too dark then to see much of their dress or features. The next day the same man made his appearance, and the weather being then fine and bright, I recognized, to my great joy, my old servant Tomàs. He was greatly affected at the sight of me ; the plates clattered together as he set them out on my bed, which served me as a table as well ; and in a husky whisper he asked, " Como está usted, mi señor ? " " Quite well, Tomàs, thank you." I should have added more, and longed—how eagerly !—to ask about my friends ; but the sergeant growlingly told him to begone, and not talk to me. He came, however, every day afterwards, often groping his way in with outstretched hand, after leaving the bright sunlight, whilst I, accustomed to the darkness, could see the mice playing even in the farthest corner. We were sometimes allowed to speak a few words, or rather he might answer me, never venturing a question himself ; the sergeant, meanwhile, standing with a drawn sword between us, to prevent any closer communication.

He was a faithful servant, and greatly attached to me, always speaking of me as "taità" (father), and, except in the case of sugar—which no Indian can resist pilfering—honest enough; he took great care of my personal property, and was furious because the comandantè used to ride my horse.

Shortly afterwards another boon was accorded me. Major Gomez came to inspect me officially, and I begged him to let me have books and wine. The long days would be greatly shortened if I could only study, or even pore aimlessly over a well-known page, and I was getting so weak and emaciated that the latter was imperatively necessary. He granted both. I had plenty of books and a fair stock of wine, and I got them, grudgingly at first, afterwards without difficulty.

So I used to lie in bed till noon, and read and doze alternately; for my nights were often sleepless, and it was only in the morning that I could hope for a few hours' undisturbed rest. Singularly enough, my dreams were never, or very rarely, of the scenes around me; I half heard the noise of relieving guards, and the busy hum and hammering in the workshops above me; but they took other tones, and called up strange associations, usually of my former life, and far away home; I often awoke laughing at some droll absurdity my vagrant fancy had conjured up, and then how blankly terrible the weary day and restless night would seem before me! Breakfast arrived about eight o'clock; but I kept in bed, and read, if there were sufficient light, till twelve. Then I had a "tub" under difficulties, for my bath was too big for the cell, and would have used too much water; and I had only a basin—luckily not a French one—and a *cantarillo*, a globular water-jar with two necks, holding but a small supply. This operation was an endless source of wonderment to the sentries and passers-by. A prisoner washing! Why, they would have as soon thought of bathing when sick, when the most ignorant of them knew perfectly well that it would be certain death to wet but the finger-tips under such circumstances !*

* By the way, when I was coming up the river the first time in the Para-

I had dinner about two, it was often a good one, for a native family I had been intimate with most generously and courageously cooked for me, and did a thousand other little acts of kindness ; and then I smoked two cigars, and read again till dusk.

When tired of reading, and during the long interval between the close of my day and the arrival of the lantern, which announced the beginning of the outer night, I used to pace from end to end of my prison, and I formed thus a broad beaten path. The sentries were greatly amused at my restlessness, for a native would never think of making any exertion merely to pass time away ; if he could not get a cigar, he would lie down, and sleep like a dormouse : so they cried out to passers-by, " *Mirè que quartì*, what a racoon that fellow is ! never still ; he prowls about half the night."

Whilst walking thus backwards and forwards, I amused myself by delivering, in silence, peripatetic lectures on social and scientific subjects, to an imaginary audience, alternately in Spanish and in English. But I found that this mental exercise excited me too much, so much so that even when the much-hoped-for third night had come I was unable to sleep, and lay wearily tossing from side to side, and listening every quarter during those long hours for the dreaded " Sentinela alerta " of the sentries, not half so wakeful as I. So I gave up my ghostly professorship, finding that the best plan to obtain sleep was to walk slowly, and let my thoughts ramble as they would. But when the low fever I was suffering from (when I had been a prisoner six months) had greatly weakened me, even with this precaution I could get no rest, and used to pace the whole night away, weary and worn out, but unable to remain still a moment.

Sometimes, when I saw the pale moonlight shining on the

guayan steamer, I found but one basin and two towels for all the thirty passengers—and even those I had to myself. The others looked on, first speculating if I were suffering from some malady necessitating frequent ablutions, but at length coming to the conclusion that I must be a very dirty animal, since I needed so much washing. It is said that Lopez, wishing the first passenger steamer to be fitted up in the English fashion, ordered a comb and a tooth-brush to be placed in every berth.

wall of the passage, and silvering one side of the wide quadrangle—I could catch a glimpse of it through the chink in the window-shutter—and the old cloisters beyond, half veiled in the black shadow, I felt as if I must go mad; the contrast was so painful between the calm beauty of the scene without and the sordid wretchedness within.

In the inner courtyard were several political prisoners, all men well known to me. One, an Argentine, named Capdevila, I saw pass my door several times; he had been a merchant of some wealth in Asuncion, and when war was declared against the Confederation he remained, hoping, as a quiet and inoffensive man, to escape persecution; but he was soon sent down to Humaità as a prisoner, simply from his nationality. His wife, however, bribed Madame Lynch to intercede for him, and he, with one or two others, was set at liberty; and pitying his countrymen who were still in captivity, he sent them food and clothes several times; but this act of charity was construed into an offence against the Government, and he was sent to the Colegio, and put in irons. About a month after his arrest I saw the poor old man marched off (to the Policia, I suppose), and return with two pairs of *grillos* on his legs; they took away also the hide he had been allowed for sleeping on, and left him to lie on the bare ground. Three weeks afterwards he again passed more slowly and feebly, and returned some hours later with three bars. He caught sight of me as he went by, and, in raising his hat, stumbled and fell, and only with great difficulty scrambled up again. His cup of misery was not yet full: after a shorter interval he was once more marched out, and, as several hours passed away, I made sure that he had been set at liberty, but to my grief and horror he returned late at night in a far worse plight than before. He still wore three bars, but so thick and long that he staggered under their weight, and was more than half an hour crossing the court inch by inch, and at length he crawled by my door on his hands and knees. Yet he did not die, but several months afterwards was shot at San Fernando.

This was not the worst. I often saw respectably dressed men taken into that dreaded courtyard, followed by a group of ruffianly policemen ; and, knowing what was coming, I closed my ears with my fingers, or buried my head beneath the bed-clothes to exclude the agonizing shrieks and groans which, after a shorter or longer time would tell of the hellish deeds of the executioners. Sometimes I heard blows, but frequently the cries of the victim alone told how they were torturing him. One afternoon a poor fellow was *estacado*—horizontally crucified just beneath my window.· Never shall I forget what I endured that day in listening to his moans and occasional frantic yells and prayers for mercy, and in picturing to myself what he was suffering. After hours of such torments I would see them sometimes led, sometimes carried back again, pale and bleeding, a piteous spectacle.

Several times, also, prisoners were brought there to undergo the punishment of running the gauntlet ; a double line of soldiers was formed,—one day I counted four hundred of them as they marched by the door of my cell—and each was armed with a stick ; the offender was stripped naked and had to run a certain number of times between their ranks, receiving a blow from each as he passed. The drums were kept rolling to drown his cries, but I could often hear a piercing shriek in spite of them.

It may be asked, did I never form any plans of escape ? Often enough, but I knew it was hopeless to try them ; and as I had, as is usual there, not been told my sentence, I thought that every day would be, perhaps, my last, and that on the morrow I should be free. At first sight, escape seemed easy enough : the door of my dungeon was wide open, and the sentry was often a mere child who could hardly shoulder his musket, and many times was soundly sleeping across the threshold ; but the walls of the courtyard were high, there was another sentry at the end of the passage, and the only means of egress was through the guard-room, always full of men. But even had these difficulties been evaded, one had but passed from a small prison into a larger one—the whole country was one huge cage. The Allies were two hundred miles off, the river was guarded at short intervals by small bodies of men perched on platforms elevated about thirty feet above the banks, and to travel by land was impossible. My dress, my skin, my language, or my silence, would have betrayed me in a moment, and there was not a native who would not have denounced me, had I met him; for his own safety would imperatively demand it. To get food, to cross the dreary swamps, swarming with rattlesnakes and jaguars, on foot, to pass over the open pampas and the grassy hills without detection, would have been all but impracticable. And the most conclusive answer to this very natural question is, that not a single prisoner *did* escape, nor, as far as I could learn, with the exception of a few Guicurù Indians, even make any attempt to escape, of the hundreds who were captive there. I doubt if Baron Trenck himself could have succeeded.

The sentries envied me sometimes, I think, for the vaulted passage in which they stood was a terribly cold and draughty place. At night they often crept furtively into the dungeon itself, and lay there, shivering in their thin and scanty ponchos, in many cases their only covering, save poor cotton drawers. Lying awake at night, I have heard the younger ones, perhaps ten or twelve years of age, crying bitterly, from terror at being left alone in the dark, gloomy vault, or from the cold, perhaps, hunger. Once I saw a chubby, flaxen-haired boy, who held his musket like a pole before him, the tears running down his cheeks, trying to weep silently, but a sob shook him at intervals. I asked him in a whisper what was the matter. "I want to go home to my mother," he whimpered most unheroically, "and I am afraid of the dark." Poor little fellow, I thought, you are even more miserable than I.

During the day many people were constantly passing, and I occasionally saw some of my old patients, stumping along, perhaps, with a wooden leg, to the workshops within. One of them always nodded to me if he could do so unobserved, or expressed pantomimically his pity, and he showed his esteem for me in such a singular way that I must tell his story. He came up from Paso Pucù, shortly after I had been appointed assistant-surgeon, severely wounded, and so reduced by starvation that I had little hope of saving him ; he was, also, and had been for some years, insane. I fed him well, and then amputated one of his legs below the knee, extracted a ball from the opposite hip, and patched up divers sword cuts about the trunk. To my surprise, he recovered very quickly, and became so sleek and fat that I could never look at him without laughing ; for, perched on his single leg, he looked like a huge top : and whenever I passed his bed he used to cry, " *Che-nesi-eté, taitá*" (Quite well, father !) and pop his head beneath his poncho to escape examination. Shortly after my arrest he was sent to the Colegio to work as a shoemaker. One night I heard some one murmuring in a low voice at the door of my cell, but the light from the lantern was so feeble that I could not make out who it was ; a few nights afterwards the same occurred again; I sat up in bed, and saw that it was my mad patient. The sentry was fast asleep, and he had crept to the threshold, and knelt there, with upraised hands, praying for me—" for his dear father, the good doctor," as he called me, and beseeching the Holy Virgin to protect and deliver me. I was greatly touched by this expression of the poor fellow's gratitude and commiseration.

My health at length gave way, low fever prostrated me completely, so much so that my jailors became alarmed lest they should kill me without orders ; and Ortellado, the native doctor of the San Francisco hospital, was sent to see me. I told him what I wanted—stimulants and tonics ; he had never heard of such remedies for fever, he answered, and could only prescribe purgatives and various decoctions of herbs, which I declined, preferring to die naturally ; and Lopez spread a report at the time that I had asked for poison to kill myself! Fortunately I received three or four bottles of brandy, when I most needed it, from my good friend M. Narcisse Lasserre, a French distiller in Asuncion, and that, I believe, under God, saved my life. For my throat was so swollen and relaxed from the dampness of the place that I durst not lie down for fear of suffocation ; and had it not been for the opportune arrival of the brandy, I have little doubt I should have sunk and died ; because, although I knew I needed it, I had become so listless and " sick from hope deferred " that I allowed day after day to pass without telling Tomàs to bring it.

My colleagues were imprisoned for nearly three months, and then, early one morning, set at liberty. Both had suffered greatly. The health of Mr. Fox was most seriously injured. Dr. Rhind's disease had made great progress, and he never recovered from the shock his arrest occasioned him ; he lived, however, more than twelve months afterwards, and died peaceably in his own house. To say that he lived universally esteemed, and died deeply regretted, would seem but the repetition of a hackneyed phrase ; in his case, it expresses but a simple truth : he was a man who won friends without an effort, and never lost one he had gained. My servant came with a radiant face to tell me the news, hoping that my own release would follow, little thinking that I had eight months more to suffer.

It is useless to prolong this tale. I remained there, in that horrible place, in a dim twilight or total darkness, a fetid atmosphere, surrounded by prisoners dying from Asiatic cholera, and without once leaving it or seeing sunlight, for ELEVEN MONTHS. I left it sick, weak, and half blind, and so changed in appearance that my most intimate friends scarcely knew me. On the evening of the 22nd of September, 1867, a sergeant told me to get ready, for I was to see the Mayor-de-Plaza ; and about half an hour afterwards I was taken across the great *patio*, at almost the same hour at which I had entered it so long before. The sun had set, and candles were to be already seen in the officers' quarters ; but to me the light was brighter than my eyes could bear, and in a dazed and half-dreamy state, doubting the reality of what I saw, I walked slowly through the guard-room. There all the officers had collected ; they expected, I suppose, to have had the gratification of seeing me pass them humbly and bareheaded, as is the fashion there; if so, they were disappointed.

With the Mayor-de-Plaza I found Señor Ortellado, who read to me the order of release, with a proviso, however, that I should not pass beyond the city; so I was still but a prisoner at large. I signed it, and then Gomez paused, evidently for the customary thanks and expressions of gratitude to the President. But I disdained to express a thankfulness I could not feel, and astonished him by saying that he had treated me with injustice and cruelty; and then, bowing coldly to both, I left the room.

They allowed me to have four soldiers to carry my bed, etc.; and, as my servant had not arrived, and I did not know where Dr. Rhind was living, I went to the house of the nearest Englishman, Mr. Taylor, the master builder.

I found him and his family at supper, sitting with the door open. I knocked and walked in. They started from the table in affright when they caught sight of me (I did the same when, shortly afterwards, I saw myself in a looking-glass). A more spectral figure is scarcely imaginable: my face was almost fleshless, and as colourless as that of a corpse; indeed, I resembled one more than a living man. My hair, uncut for thirteen months, hung over my shoulders and mingled with my beard, both quite grey; whilst my eyes, with the pupils widely dilated by the darkness, seemed to have concentrated within themselves the life which had deserted the rest of my body. No wonder I startled them, and that the children were petrified with terror.

At first I was unable to speak, from agitation and the fatigue of walking. Mr. Taylor, however, came forward and said, hastily, " *Que quiere usted, señor ?* " (What do'you want, sir ?) " Why, Taylor," I replied, " don't you know me ? " " Good God ! " cried he, trembling ; " it is Mr. Masterman." The tears stood in his eyes as he shook hands with me. They were all greatly affected, and the pity they felt for me seemed for a time to make congratulations out of place.

The news of my release spread rapidly over the town. Dr.

Rhind, who had no words to express his gladness, carried me off to his home; and the American minister, the French consul, and a large number of my friends, native and foreign, called to tell me how happy they were to have me once more amongst them.

I found that Dr. Rhind and Mr. Fox were still in the service of Lopez, not being able to help themselves, and that the latter had been sent to Humaità. I was undecided what to do: I was most anxious to aid the poor fellows in the hospital, but, at the same time, felt the greatest aversion to serve a man who had treated me so infamously, and who had stated, moreover, that the reason why I was imprisoned so long was, that I had refused to cure the sick and wounded. I thought I might get over the difficulty by applying for permission to commence private practice, but my application was refused; and, of course, to re-enter the service of the republic was then out of the question.

CHAPTER XV.

I FOUND that I was principally indebted for my liberation to
the good offices of the Hon. Chas. A. Washburn, United States
Minister. He wished me to attend Mrs. Washburn in her
approaching *accouchement*, and had applied persistently for my
" pardon " until he obtained it, and he now offered me the post
of private surgeon, to be exchanged for Surgeon to the Legation
if the Paraguayan Government should show any intention of
molesting me. I accepted this offer with pleasure ; for, although
but an honorary one, I hoped that I should have been safe from
any further persecution, and that an opportunity would soon
present itself for leaving the country, even if the war should
not be speedily terminated, as we expected.

I found him located in a large house in the Plaza Vieja (Old
Square) of Asuncion, a place big enough for a barrack ; in fact,
at one time fifty people were living comfortably in it, and the
rooms of his secretary and myself would have accommodated as
many more in an emergency. It occupied almost all one side
of the square, had a large garden in the centre, with a huge
algibe, or tank, and warehouses of immense capacity. It had
been offered to him rent free by Don Luis Jàra, to whom it
belonged (that is to say, the latter had been ordered by Lopez
to vacate it for Mr. Washburn's accommodation) ; and he continued to occupy it—on the same easy terms—as long as he
remained in the country.

I used to ride about a good deal within the town, but constantly followed and watched by the police; and I finished several paintings I had commenced long before. Time passed thus very pleasantly, and still more so when Mrs. Washburn and her infant, needing change of air, removed for three months to the *quinta* (country villa) of Señor Bedoya at La Trinidad, about two leagues out of town. It was a handsome house, built and furnished by the late President for his own use; at his death it became the property of Doña Rafaela, his youngest daughter, who afterwards married Don Saturnino Bedoya, Paymaster-General.

With some difficulty permission was obtained for me to visit my patients there twice a week, but Mr. Washburn stated that he should decline the invitation to occupy the *quinta* unless it were given. The Lady President was most anxious that he should go there, for an advance on the part of the Allies was daily expected, and she knew that his presence would protect her and her personal property. So the poor old Vice-President Sanchez gave orders to the pickets to let me pass, on his own responsibility. He was anxious to serve the Señora Presidenta, the mother of the Marshal, but at the same time desperately afraid of offending Lopez himself; and my indisposition to re-enter the Government service had so enraged the latter, that Señor Sanchez, a mere cipher, durst not mention even my name to him. I record this otherwise trifling circumstance because of the use which was made of it afterwards.

I had applied, in proper form, for permission to practice medicine as a private surgeon, and Dr. Rhind strongly supported my application. It was refused, however, as was also a petition subsequently presented by the English mechanics, praying that I might be allowed to attend them at their own expense. I should remark that this petition was written without my knowledge, and I only heard of it on the morning of its presentation. The Vice-President said that he vetoed it because I had refused to serve the Republic, and that I had not attended Mrs. Washburn, although I had been liberated for that purpose.

On hearing this, I asked Mr. Washburn to write me a letter, testifying that I had done so, which he did.*

Asiatic cholera had appeared in Paraguay, in April, 1867, but it was principally felt by the army; wherein the deaths from this cause alone were from forty to sixty a day. Lopez, ever watchful for an opportunity to calumniate his enemies, stated that men had been sent over in women's clothing to convey the infection; and, afterwards, that the springs had been poisoned by emissaries of the Brazilians, and that what the doctors called cholera was really caused by drinking the water from them. And one day a small balloon, which had been sent up to try the direction of the wind, came over from the allied camp; it was picked up by two soldiers, and shown by them to several officers. They were all arrested, and sent to a wretched hut without a roof, on the outside of the lines, where no one was allowed to go near them but a boy who carried a little beef and water twice a day. Lopez said that the balloon contained the poison, and that he feared these men would extend the effects of it; but his fear really was that it carried papers of a revolutionary character—the "poison" he most dreaded.

At the beginning of the year, the hot season in South America, it broke out in the capital, and committed terrible ravages. At first very few cases recovered; they were taken up to the hospital but to die; fully one-fourth of the people in Asuncion, then principally women and children, perished. We soon had it in the Legation; Basilio, a native servant of Mr.

---

* Mr. G. F. Masterman.

Dear Sir,—In reply to your request that I should give you a certificate in regard to your attendance on Mrs. Washburn, I will state that you were her sole medical attendant during her illness; I say not only this, but that you gave entire satisfaction, and that the Vice-President, in stating anything to the contrary, must have been misinformed.

Very respectfully,
Your obedient servant,

(Signed)   Chas. A. Washburn.

United States Legation,
     Asuncion, May 10th, 1868.

Washburn's was first attacked, and I had an opportunity of treating a case of the disease of the worst Asiatic type, and the great satisfaction of saving him.

I had no little difficulty in carrying out the necessary treatment, for his mother, an old Payaguà, did all she could to thwart my efforts. In Paraguay they have but one name for sickness—fever; and but one way of treating it, *dieta*, starvation, emetics, and purgatives. I well remember the astonishment of the native wife of poor Michkoffsky, when I gave her child, who was sinking from typhus fever, a glass of wine, and told her to give him as much of that, and beef tea, as he could swallow. "But, señor, he has fever," said she, with startled eyes, and hastily arresting my hand. And only because the Italian *curandero*, who had been starving the poor child for a week, said he must die, would she try a treatment which seemed so extraordinary to her. If an intelligent woman of the better class thought thus, it may be imagined what trouble I had with an obstinate Indiana. A dreadful old woman too, scarcely more than four feet in height, a dark-brown shrivelled creature, with a most witch-like face. She would mount on a chair by Basilio's bedside, gaze eagerly in his face, and a ghastly object he was, by the way, and then utter the most fearful howls imaginable. She loved him passionately, poor creature, with the fierce, jealous love which Indian women have for their young children, and "he was her only son, and she was a widow." She had, I think, some vague idea that I was experimenting upon him, and that my remedies were unholy and poisonous, and hence her distrust of me.

During Basilio's convalescence, my friend Mons. Lasserre was attacked with the same terrible disease. I was anxious to attend him, but it was running a great risk, for the police had received orders to watch me so closely, to prevent me practising medicine, since I would not re-enter the service, that I scarcely dared to leave the Legation ; however, I owed so much to him and his kind-hearted family, for their attention to me when I was a prisoner, that it was clearly my duty to help him now,

and I did so. It was another bad case, and I could not leave
him for many hours.

On the evening of the second day, when I was completely
exhausted with want of rest and anxiety, for two other members
of the family were attacked, Major Manlove came over to tell
me, through some misconception, that the police were waiting
outside to arrest me, and that I must not leave the house till
Mr. Washburn, who was then absent, could convoy me over.
Madame Lasserre, imperfectly understanding what was said,
thought from my concerned expression of face that her husband's case was hopeless, became almost frantic in spite of all
I could say to reassure her, and at length fainted.

I was returning to the bedside of my patient, when a Scotch
servant of Mr. Washburn's ran in, crying out that Basilio was
dead, that everybody else was mad, he thought, and that I must
go over to the Legation directly. I went: it was a false alarm
about the police ; but I certainly agreed in the servant's opinion
when I entered the courtyard, for the confusion there was
almost indescribable. A crowd of native women were clustered
about Basilio's room, howling for the dead, the yells of his
mother heard above them all. Mrs. Washburn was standing,
frightened and crying, under the piazza, vainly asking what was
the matter. Her maid was in hysterics on the floor in one
room, and a young native lady, who was on a visit there, had
swooned in another ! I sent Mrs. Washburn back to her bed ;
and, when I had stopped the noise opposite, found, as I expected, that Basilio was not dead, nor likely to die. He had
got out of bed, against positive orders, fallen from weakness,
and his head striking a chair he lay stunned and insensible.
His mother, who was a spy of the police, had just returned from
a visit to the Policia, and found him lying as I have described.
She came at once to the conclusion that he was dead, hastily
collected all the women she could find to howl over his remains,
and hence the tumult.

I had an opportunity of punishing her a little while afterwards. I collected a quantity of paper collars, and one day,

when she had been begging me to let her show how grateful she was for the recovery of Basilio, I gave them to her with express directions to wash them very carefully; and sat at the door of my room to see the result. She brought a large pan of water, and seating herself on the grass in the courtyard, began to wash them vigorously. I shall never forget the expression of her face as she gazed in fear and astonishment at the tattered mass of rags in her hands! She got up slowly, with her mouth and eyes wide open, and brought the fragments to me, actually trembling with fear. I tried in vain to look serious, and at last burst into uncontrollable laughter; she gave one glance at me, and then went off in a furious rage, kicked over her pan of water, and to my great satisfaction did not speak to me for a month afterwards.

Mons. Lasserre recovered, as did his brother and a servant who had a slight attack; but I could wish they had all died, for a few months afterwards they were arrested, sent to San Fernando, on that utterly unfounded charge of conspiracy, that miserable fabrication, which caused the death of so many innocent people; and poor Madame Lasserre, a young, pretty, and remarkably clever and engaging woman, was left an orphan and a widow: her father, husband, and brother were shot.

There was one little incident connected with this case which showed how futile was any attempt at concealment. Mons. Lasserre suffered greatly from cramps during the attack, and a number of his countrymen came in to rub the knotted muscles. One of them, a carpenter, rubbed with such zeal that he nearly stripped the skin off. A few days afterwards the Lady Presidenta came to visit the Minister, and I was presented to her. We had a long talk together, and presently she said, " O señor doctòr, tell me, is it true that the big carpenter rubbed all the skin off Don Narciso ? " I was startled, but replied cautiously, " It may be so, señora; but Dr. Rhind attended him." Which, fortunately for me, was the case; for he, although then too ill himself for work, stayed some hours in the house with him, and greatly aided me with his advice.

When I was released from the Colegio, I was most anxious to know what had been done in my absence. Many of my friends were dead, I found; but, with the exception of the return of Mr. Washburn, there was little change in the state of affairs. The Allies had really done nothing but batter Humaità from a safe distance, and the end of the war seemed as far off as ever. The Minister had had great difficulty in returning to Paraguay, the Brazilians at first refused to let the U. S. gunboat appointed to take him and family up the river pass the blockading squadron, and he was detained in Corrientes more than six months. Whilst there he visited the camp of the Allies, and was received in a very flattering manner by President Mitre; and the Marquis de Caxias sent an officer to him to say that as he was detained by the imperial fleet it was but just that Brazil should bear his expenses. This was but an oblique way of offering a bribe.

Mr. Washburn tried in vain by remonstrance to induce the Brazilians to let him pass, and at length in a despatch directed to Admiral Ignacio, he stated that it was his intention to force the blockade. A few days afterwards the gunboat steamed through the fleet, which, as might have been expected, did not oppose her passage, the admiral saying, courteously, that they could not afford to quarrel with their good friends of the north.

Mr. Washburn presented his credentials to Lopez as Minister Resident (he had before held the position of Commissioner of the United States in Paraguay), and at once tendered his good offices as mediator.

Lopez adhered with wonderful tenacity to his old conditions, but he was willing to make a visit of one or two years' duration to Europe, as a compromise, which the Allies would not listen to. Mr. Washburn then, I think most unwarrantably, constituted himself his advocate, knowing perfectly well the character of the man, and the frightful atrocities he had committed, and wrote a despatch to the Brazilian minister, which was published in the "Semanario," in which he asks him what the Brazilians would think if Marshal Lopez, as a preliminary to a truce, should demand the abdication of the Emperor ? This was, of course, mere special pleading. He knew why the war was commenced, how it had been carried on, and the hopelessness of the struggle on the part of Paraguay. He also knew that the resignation of Lopez would at once put an end to it ; and if *his* professions were to be believed, that he fought only for the honour and glory of his people, it is evident that he ought to gladly sacrifice his power and position to their good. He knew that Lopez would have been perfectly content if the whole of his people were destroyed (with the exception of a sufficient number to labour and tend, making the country one huge estate of his), could he but retain his hold of it. Long before the war the title-deeds of all the larger estates were ordered to be deposited in his hands, and the property of all political prisoners, all deserters, real or surmised, and, in many cases, of their relatives, was forfeited to the State—that is, to himself. All title-deeds which were not *en régle* were destroyed, and the property reverted to the " State." *

* The way in which they were tested may be judged of from the following anecdote, which I can vouch to be authentic. Don Carlos Lopez wished to buy some property belonging to a wealthy native, named Recalde, living in the Calle Comercio, but which the owner declined to sell, so he was ordered to bring the title-deeds of the house he occupied for verification. They were handed to a Juez de Paz, a civil judge, who reported that they were perfectly correct. The President told the judge sternly to begone; and sending for another, said to him, " I gave these papers for examination to Jeuz Fulano, and the fool reports that they are ' conformé '; examine them minutely, and tell me if they are so." It is needless to add that the owner, whom I knew well, remained but a short time in possession of his house, and that the coveted property was quietly given up. And I could cite numerous other instances of people who were compelled to sell their property to the President, or members of his family, for a tithe of its value, and did not always get that: one may suffice. An old man named Pereira, who lived in the Calle del Sol, near the Aduana, wished, as he was pressed for money, to sell his house, and offered it to Madame Lynch for a very low sum. She bought it, but did not, as is the custom there, pay the purchase money before receiving the title-deeds, and the seller was afraid to ask her for it. She told him, however, to ask Caminos, the President's secretary, for it, who replied that he knew nothing about the transaction; and poor Pereira actually lost both his house and his money, and died in Paso Pucù from starvation.

This despatch of Mr. Washburn's did, moreover, a great deal of harm. People in Europe, who could gain but little information about the real state of affairs in the Plate, and naturally felt great sympathy for a little republic bullied, in appearance, by two larger ones, and Brazil to boot, thought that a man who was thus openly supported by the American minister must be in the right, and the shocking stories of his cruelty, which occasionally reached them, must be fabricated or greatly exaggerated. However, it led to no practical result, and the " *distinguido amigo del Paraguay y la Libertad*" was soon forgotten by the " Semanario."

In the month of August, 1867, Mr. Gould, Her Majesty's Chargé d'Affaires, visited Paraguay for the purpose of obtaining the liberation of the many British subjects then virtually prisoners of Lopez. He did not succeed, except in the case of three widows and their five children, who were given up; but I am glad to say that he was not cajoled either by the flattery or the falsehoods of Lopez; and when his letters to Mr. Buckley Mathew, our Minister Plenipotentiary to the Argentine Republic, were published by command, the first clear and reliable account of the state of affairs there was given to the world. These letters are so graphic, and confirm so exactly my own statement, that I give the following extracts from them :—*

" Paraguayan Head-quarters. Paso Pucù, August 22, 1867.

" The very evening of my arrival " (*the* 18*th instant*) " I was informed by the President's secretary that his Excellency would receive me privately, and I had therefore the honour of

---

* How the Foreign Office could have remained indifferent to the fate of British subjects in Paraguay, after the publication of these despatches, it is difficult to understand; and these letters were kept back lest public opinion should compel some measures to be undertaken for our rescue. The inertness of our Government was freely discussed in Paraguay, and I have often heard the natives express the greatest contempt for it. A friendly sergeant said to me one day when I was a prisoner, "Our President and we don't care a *real* for you of England; but the North Americans! *Caramba!* that is another matter! What gun: and what men they have got!"

spending a couple of hours with the President, who assumed towards me an extremely frank and cordial manner.

"After reminding me that this was not an official interview, and inquiring the object of my visit to his camp, his Excellency said that he deeply regretted that I should have been charged with such a mission, as he could not, under the circumstances, possibly dispense with the services of the British subjects in Paraguay, who were all in his employment, and bound by contracts. His Excellency moreover added that he could not allow any foreigners, at the present crisis, to quit the country, or even return from the camp to the capital. Should permission to leave be granted to one, his Excellency observed, the rest would, in all probability, wish to follow. He had, therefore, been obliged to refuse a private and most pressing appeal, which Mr. Washburn, the United States minister at Asuncion, had addressed to him on behalf of an American citizen." This citizen was Major Manlove.

"Mr. Bèrges, his minister for foreign affairs, had in consequence only recently notified publicly that no foreigner would, in the actual critical state of affairs, be permitted to withdraw from the republic." So recently, that this notice only appeared when Bèrges had received the notice of Mr. Buckley Mathew, stating that the object of Mr. Gould's visit was "to facilitate the departure of such British subjects as were desirous to leave Paraguay."

"His Excellency dwelt at considerable length on the partiality which he had at all times shown for Englishmen, whom he had exclusively employed ; on the great benefits he had conferred on some of them." This was very far from being true. Our pay seemed handsome on paper, but as half was paid in *billets* at par, when they were at from 20 to 80 per cent. discount, and the gold at a premium of 20 per cent., it really amounted to but a moderate sum. And the value of the cattle taken by Lopez, without a farthing of compensation, or even a pretence of paying for it, from Dr. Stewart's estates, would itself have paid the salaries of one half of us. We were certainly allowed much more liberty than the natives were, and as we received part of our pay whilst they got none at all, we were more liberally treated; but it is idle to say that any benefits had been conferred upon us.

"His Excellency further assured me that none of them had the slightest cause of complaint; on the contrary, they were one and all perfectly happy and contented. None of them, to his knowledge, desired to leave the country, and all had engagements, which they were gladly fulfilling to his entire satisfaction. I should have every opportunity of conversing with the few British subjects in his camp, who would fully corroborate all he had stated."*

Now, what are the facts? With two or three exceptions, the contracts of all of us had long since expired, and we were most anxious to leave the country, but dared not even say so. Mr. Gould was kept under most careful surveillance,† and "the few British subjects in the camp" were afraid to be seen speaking with him; and on the morning after this interview Lopez sent for Dr. Stewart, as the Englishman holding the highest rank in his service, and said to him, "*Cuidado! Si yo sepa que algun Ingles diga que quiere salir del pais.*" [Take care! If I should (only) know that any Englishman says that he wishes to leave the country]. Those only who know Lopez can understand the full force of this sentence.

"His Excellency proceeded to complain of the want of sympathy evinced by Her Majesty's Government towards Paraguay; of his desire to cultivate more friendly and intimate relations with Great Britain not having been reciprocated; of the way in which his policy had been misconstrued in England; and finally, of the breaches of neutrality committed by Her Majesty Government during the present war. He had, unfortunately, no one to advocate his cause, and he was shut out from the rest of the

---

* *Vide* evidence of Mr. Eden and Mr. Newton in the Appendix.

† Colonel Thompson states that "he was placed in the centre of the room in a long hut; the partitions were only of reeds, and anyone in the others could see and hear all that was going on."

world. He considered it very unfair on the part of Her Majesty's Government to call upon him to give up the small number of British subjects, who had freely entered his service" (but not to fight, however); "while no notice seemed to be taken of the loans, ships, and arms obtained by his adversaries in Great Britain, and of the hundreds of Englishmen fighting against him in their ranks.

"With regard to the despatch addressed by you (Mr. Buckley Mathew) to his minister for foreign affairs, his Excellency stated *that he could not be expected to take any official notice of it, as you have not yet presented your letters of credence, which can only be done personally.*" (The italics are mine.) "He therefore considered he would have been fully justified in refusing to listen to any request I might be instructed to make on behalf of the British subjects in Paraguay, *as I was unprovided with any direct communication from Her Majesty's Government to that of the republic.*" Mr. Gould had neither an armed force to support his demand, nor even a right to make it. "Nevertheless, to prove his anxious desire to meet the views of Her Majesty's Government, he would overlook these diplomatic informalities, and endeavour to make some exceptional concession in its favour without prejudicing his position, which had become exceedingly delicate, in regard to other neutral powers, since the publication of the notification he had previously alluded to.

"His Excellency concluded by making some highly flattering remarks about me, and saying that such was the sympathy he felt for me, that out of personal regard he would wish to see my mission brought to a successful termination."

It is impossible not to admire the skill Lopez displayed in this interview; the wily savage was fully a match for his antagonist, fettered as the latter was by the fear of injuring the men he had been sent to save, through any remark which might show that he was acquainted with the facts of the case ; and the ingenuity with which he makes it appear that giving up three widows and their children was proof of his friendly feeling towards England, and a compliment to Mr. Gould, who continues : "I began by endeavouring to convince the President that the object of my mission was not to complain of the treatment of British subjects in the republic, but simply to request his Excellency to allow those amongst them who might desire to leave Paraguay to avail themselves of the facilities for doing so placed at their disposal by Her Majesty's Government. I added that this friendly request was based on a positive international right, and that a refusal on his part to comply with it would be not only highly impolitic, but inhuman. If these British subjects were all, as he asserted, happy and contented, the number of those wishing to leave would be so insignificant as to cause his Government no embarrassment, while he would thus, by a very small sacrifice, gain over to his side, not only Her Majesty's Government, but public opinion in the United Kingdom, which had become interested in their fate. The arrival of Her Majesty's gunboat in the Paraguayan waters had placed my countrymen in an exceptional position, and rendered the notification he had referred to inapplicable to them. I would not take upon myself to call in question his Excellency's assertions, but I had good reason to believe that the contracts of most of the Englishmen in his service had long since expired, and that some, at least, of them were anxious to return to their homes. I would not, however, attempt to ascertain their real feelings on the subject until his Excellency had consented to their departure. I should, by doing so, merely place them in a false and painful position.

"I concluded by assuring his Excellency that I would, through you, call the attention of Her Majesty's Government to the various causes of complaint he had considered himself justified in pointing out to me. I moreover undertook fully to inform you of the peculiar and critical position in which he now finds himself.

"Paraguay has for many years past almost exclusively employed Englishmen. The medical service of its army is entrusted to four English surgeons and an English apothecary. The works in its arsenal are carried on by a small number of

English draughtsmen and mechanics. English engineers have charge of its steamers. Its railway, many of the public buildings, and the formidable system of defensive works which has so long set at defiance the allied armies, have been constructed under the supervision of three English civil engineers." This last statement is not quite correct: the river batteries at Humaità were built by Capt. Morice, R.N., who had left Paraguay before I reached it, and Col. Weisner, an Austrian. The new works were designed by the latter and by Mr. (now Lieut.-Col.) Thompson, who was a civil engineer, and the only Englishman who, at that date, had entered the military service of Lopez. "Finally, its mines are worked by an English mining engineer. It is mainly owing to the exertions of this handful of Englishmen that Paraguay, reduced to its own limited resources, has, under the direction of President Lopez, thus far been enabled to prolong the desperate struggle in which it has been engaged for upwards of two years. Hence the natural reluctance of his Excellency to part with men whose services are invaluable to him, and whom he cannot possibly hope to replace under present circumstances.

"At a subsequent interview President Lopez said he would, in the absence of his minister for foreign affairs at Asuncion, and on account of the difficulties of communicating with that capital, prefer that I should remain at his head-quarters ; and he would therefore name his secretary to treat me officially. Should I persist in carrying out my instructions literally, he would be under the painful necessity of bringing the negotiations to an abrupt and disagreeable termination. However, if I would agree to be satisfied with the women and children, whom he was willing to give up on grounds of humanity, and represent to Her Majesty's Government that this was the only concession he was in a position to make at the present moment, he would most gladly consent to their departure, provided measures were taken to prevent their communicating to his adversaries any information which would be injurious to his cause.

"I partially agreed to his terms, observing, however, that I could not take upon myself to guarantee that Her Majesty's Government would be satisfied with such a partial measure; but that of course it would materially lessen the unfavourable impression which an unconditional refusal would be certain to produce.

"I have made up my mind to proceed with the greatest caution and moderation; and if I find it eventually impossible to obtain the release of those I have been commissioned to bring away, I will accept the compromise his Excellency has prepared, leaving it entirely open to Her Majesty's Government to take whatever further steps may be deemed most advisable to effect the deliverance of the British subjects who may still remain at Paraguay. With this object I will not hurry on the negotiations, as, although I shall thereby expose myself to some danger and great personal discomfort, I feel convinced my countrymen will be in comparative safety so long as I remain amongst them."

Mr. Gould then received a note from Gen. Barrios, minister of war and marine, stating that Major Caminos had been appointed officially to treat with him, and that the negotiations were to be carried on in writing. He wrote in French, knowing that the secretary was but a cipher, and that he was really treating with Lopez, who speaks that language well. But he goes on to say, "Before replying to my note the President expressed a desire to see me." Mr. Gould was, however, unwell, and several days passed before he could visit him; then, " in the presence of Señor Caminos, he read over the note, and kindly pointed out what he considered a grammatical error, which I at once gladly corrected. He then proceeded to make another more important alteration, which I did not feel myself at liberty to consent to; but I finally agreed to take back the note for reconsideration, in order to avoid what I feared might end in an unpleasant discussion, which I had every reason to be anxious to avoid.

" His Excellency actually proposed to me so to alter the wording of the note as to make it appear that the only object of

Her Majesty's Government in sending the 'Doterel' to Paraguay was to facilitate the departure of the few English women whom his Excellency felt disposed to give up.

"I explained that although these women had undoubtedly a prior claim, and Her Majesty's Government would be grateful for the exception made in their favour, still it did not in any way invalidate the claim of the other British subjects in his dominions to the consideration of their Government. I would, however, take time to reflect on his proposal, but I feared I was so bound by your instructions as to preclude the possibility of my complying with it.

"The next morning I handed back to Señor Caminos the note in question, after having substituted the words '*et surtout*' for '*en outre*' at the beginning of the sentence which refers specially to the English women in Paraguay."*

Several notes followed this, but led to nothing, as might have been expected. Mr. Gould says, "The only remarks I will venture to make with regard to Señor Caminos' note of the 23rd of August are, that he avoids the main question; first, by speciously endeavouring to make it appear as if there were no British subjects in Paraguay desirous of leaving it; secondly, he does not see fit to give them an opportunity to express their wishes on the subject; thirdly, I regret to say he was perfectly aware at the time that several of them made no secret of their wish to quit Paraguay, though he was to a certain extent justified in asserting that none of them had officially applied for permission to leave; finally, he admits that they would not in any case be permitted to take their departure.

"I may as well, before proceeding any farther, point out to you the peculiar position occupied by British subjects in this remote republic. They are all, with one single exception, I believe, in the Government service." With the exception of three it should have been. "Their contracts were made in

---

* "En outre (et surtout) il y a des femmes et des veuves d'anglais, chargées d'enfants, qui ne doivent continuer à rester sans but exposées aux périls de la guerre."

England, and afterwards renewed in this country ; but most of these contracts have expired since the beginning of the war. Thus many, who might now desire to return home, were not at liberty to do so when the Doterel last visited Asuncion. Her stay was but short, and the object of her presence not generally known. These British subjects have in general been very well treated by the President, and their salaries are regularly paid even now. However, on the one hand, owing to the depreciation of the paper currency, in which they receive one half of their wages, they have to submit to a loss of nearly forty per cent.; while, on the other, they have to pay exorbitant prices for whatever they require, in consequence of the rigorous blockade which has excluded Paraguay from the rest of the world for upwards of two years. President Lopez treats them very much as if they were a more valuable class of his own subjects ; never consults their wishes, and employs them in any way that suits his purpose, without their daring to offer the slightest objection. In this way he may safely say that he has never used compulsion towards them, as his wishes are no sooner conveyed to them than they are, in appearance at least, willingly complied with. On their side, the dread of incurring his displeasure is so great that they would hardly be likely to make any imprudent request, which would in all probability not be granted, and might entail upon them the most serious consequences.

"The case of Mr. Henry Valpy is the most unjustifiable of any. This gentleman is a civil engineer, who came out specially from England with Mr. Burrell to make a railway. Mr. Valpy's contract, though once renewed, has long since expired, and the railway works are suspended in consequence of the war. This gentleman was indirectly asked to accept military service, but he had the strength of mind to refuse, and offered to give up his salary, as his services were no longer available. He was, however, induced by the President to continue drawing one half of his pay, and since then he has made himself as useful as he could in the capital. Ten or eleven months ago he was called to the Government-house, and told to prepare to proceed to this camp.

He objected, but was informed that it was the President's order, and consequently he would have to go. On his arrival in camp his Excellency presented him with a sword, and requested him to get a military uniform, although he gave his Excellency to understand he had conscientious scruples, which prevented him from accepting military service. He has hitherto resisted putting on military uniform, and has only been employed in making surveys at a distance from the enemy's positions; but, even so, shells have exploded in his immediate neighbourhood. He is treated very much as a prisoner at large, and the President is so incensed at his passive resistance, and at his having, through me, privately expressed a wish to leave, that I have, with reason, the greatest fears for his personal safety. The very fact of his often having been seen with me will, I apprehend, tell against him.

"Mr. Fox is also most anxious to leave. He is not bound by any contract, or even verbal engagement, and moreover he is in rather delicate health. I incidentally mentioned his name, without, however, compromising him.

"Others would, I know, gladly do the same, but, fearing the consequences, wisely refrained from expressing to me their ardent wishes on the subject. President Lopez, in an unguarded moment, acknowledged to me that he considered he had a perfect right to treat Englishmen in his service (and he does not give them the option of retiring from it) just in the same way as he would his own subjects. The men in the arsenal, for the most trivial offences, are at once locked up, or put on board the steamers, where they have very hard work, and are continually exposed to the fire of the Brazilian iron-clad squadron below Hamaità.

"*Such is the terror inspired by President Lopez that, fearing the information I had might be attributed to the unfortunate British subjects in the camp, I avoided, for their sakes, taking any notice of the case of a young English apothecary, who, for a slight breach of discipline, has been under arrest in the capital for the last nine or ten months.* The position of British subjects in Paraguay was, up to the commencement of the present war, a very good one ; but since then it has materially changed, as I believe I have succeeded in proving, and may yet, I fear, become still more precarious." Mr. Gould concludes : "During my prolonged stay in this camp my unfortunate countrymen have happily been in comparative safety, although my position was both irksome in the extreme, and not altogether unattended with danger from various quarters. The whole camp is now more or less within range of the enemy's guns, and President Lopez's violence is such that I was repeatedly warned to be most guarded in my intercourse with him."

Mr. Gould left, taking the women and children in question with him ; but, notwithstanding his representations of Lopez's lawlessness, and the dangerous position in which our countrymen remained, little or nothing was done for their relief. It is true that a gunboat has been twice sent up the river to repeat the farce of asking for the release of British subjects. The answer returned to the first application was that none wished to leave, and a foreman in the arsenal went on board and stated that such was the case ; but Mr. Nesbit, the man in question, was accompanied by Levalle, a Paraguayan, who speaks English very well, and if he had stated the truth he would have imperilled the safety of his wife and children, who were then on board. It was on this occasion that Mr. Fox, through an order given by Lopez when he was so intoxicated that he did not know what he was doing, was lucky enough to make his escape. And I believe a third has been sent, since Lopez retreated to the cordillera, with a despatch from the admiral, to which, we are informed by General McMahon, Lopez declined to reply.

Another letter of Mr. Gould's, dated September 16, 1867, should be noticed as exemplifying the cunning of Lopez. He states that, finding that any further negotiations were useless he determined to leave, and goes on : " The state of my health was also such as to necessitate an immediate change of air, and to cause serious alarm to the English medical men in the camp, from whom, at considerable risk to themselves, I experienced the greatest kindness.

"To my surprise, late in the afternoon, Lieutenant-Commander Michell suddenly appeared, accompanied by three of the President's aides-de-camp. He informed me he had been spending an hour alone with his Excellency, who had treated him with the most marked kindness and condescension, and made many inquiries about what was passing outside his camp. This was the first notice I had received of the arrival of the gunboat, although Curupaitỹ is in telegraphic communication with Paso Pucù. When Commander Michell had left me to return to head-quarters, a horse was brought up by a soldier; but I refused to leave until the President should have signified, in a becoming manner, that I was at liberty to re-embark. Shortly afterwards two of his officers were sent to accompany me, and I then proceeded to Curupaitỹ, where I was detained fully an hour, waiting for Commander Michell and his party.

"While there, one or two shells were fired in that direction by the Brazilian iron-clads below Humaitả; Commander Michell was, I believe, covered with sand by the explosion of one of them. This mistake, unintentional on the part of the Brazilians, can only be attributed to the British ensign having, for some reason or the other, been lowered by the Paraguayans from the flag-staff at Curupaitỹ long before Commander Michell and I re-embarked. Owing to these delays night had closed in before Her Majesty's gunboat was able to return to her former position in the rear of the Brazilian squadron off Curùzù."

I should have greatly enjoyed the chance of hearing the kind and condescending conversation Lopez held with the gallant and gratified officer. It provided Madame Lynch with excellent after-dinner jokes for some time afterwards.

There can be no doubt that the British ensign was lowered by command of Lopez. Mr. Gould had shown a most unwelcome pertinacity in trying to carry out his instructions, and had gleaned a few facts which it was most inconvenient to let the outside world know anything of; therefore it was hoped that a Brazilian shell would have silenced him for ever, and we see how nearly this ingenious scheme succeeded.

In the letter of the 10th there was enclosed the following excellent *résumé* of the information Mr. Gould had been able to collect :—" Since the commencement of this protracted war, but little, if any, reliable information has been received as to the actual position of this country. The Allies themselves, strange to say, seem to be as much in the dark as the rest of the world. Though the opportunities of ascertaining the true state of affairs have been extremely limited since my arrival here, still I have succeeded in collecting information of some interest.

" The whole country is ruined, and all but depopulated. Everything is seized for the use of the Government. The cattle on most of the estates have entirely disappeared. All the horses, and even the mares, have been taken away. The slaves, of whom there were 40,000 or 50,000, have been emancipated ; the males sent to the army, and the females, with other women, forced to work in gangs for the Government. Many estates have been altogether abandoned. The scanty crops raised by the women are monopolized for the supply of the troops. The women have been obliged to part with all their jewels and gold ornaments, though this extreme measure has been called a patriotic offering on their part.

" Three epidemics, measles, small-pox, and cholera, besides privations of all sorts, have reduced the population of this unfortunate country by more than a third. It is variously estimated to have never exceeded 700,000 or 800,000 ; but on this point I have not been able to obtain any reliable data. The mortality among children has been dreadful, and both scurvy and itch are very prevalent. The trade with Bolivia is insignificant, owing to the almost insuperable difficulties of communication.

" When the war first commenced President Lopez was at the head of a fine army of nearly 100,000 men, and he had immense supplies of arms and ammunition, which his father and he had been carefully accumulating for years previously. His fleet consisted, however, of only twelve or fifteen river steamers of light construction.

"Since then he must have lost, in one way or other, upwards of 100,000 men, for 80,000 have died from disease alone. Many of his steamers have been captured or destroyed, and he may yet have eight or nine, only two of which are, however, in a good serviceable state.

"It is only owing to the dilatory manner of proceeding of the Allies, and their want of energy, that he is still able to prolong his resistance. Had their fleet taken up in time a position between Paso la Patria and Itapirù, after the surrender of a part of his troops at Uruguayana, none of the 25,000 men with whom he invaded the Argentine province of Corrientes would have been able to recross the Paranà into Paraguay. On the 24th of May, 1866, he was repulsed with such fearful loss that the Allies might have entered his entrenched camp the next day with the greatest ease. It took him three days to reorganize any considerable force, as he himself acknowledges. His losses on that occasion amounted to between 12,000 and 15,000 men. On the 2nd of September, 1866, when the Allies took Curùzù, had they marched at once on Curupaitỳ they would easily have advanced with but comparatively slight resistance. They lost a fortnight, during which he strongly entrenched himself, and were eventually repulsed with immense slaughter. Again, when they advanced lately to Tuyùcuè, he was not prepared to resist a determined attack. He has, however, since strengthened his works on that side. There they have remained stationary for more than six weeks, while by pushing forward a few thousand men on their extreme right they would entirely cut off his communications with the interior, and very soon compel him to surrender at discretion; for he has no longer a sufficient force to venture upon a serious attack.

"The allied forces now amount to 48,000 men in the field, and from 5,000 to 6,000 in hospital. Of these, 45,000 are Brazilians, 7,000 or 8,000 Argentines, and 1,000 Orientàles. Since my last visit, in April, the Brazilian army has been rejoined by the 2nd corps, which held Curùzù, and the 3rd under General Osario, which was at that time somewhere in the Misiones. Moreover, large reinforcements have arrived direct from Brazil, and the Imperial Government has engaged to send out 2,000 men per month to keep up the army to its present strength. President Mitrè has also returned with a part of the forces lately employed in quelling the insurrection in the Argentine Provinces. They are fully supplied with every requisite for a campaign. Of the above amount, fully 8,000 are cavalry, and well mounted; besides, fresh horses are daily arriving in large numbers. The army is likewise provided with a great many field-pieces.

"The Brazilian iron-clad squadron consists of ten vessels, which easily forced their way past the batteries at Curupaity. There are, it seems, two deep-water channels in front of these formidable works. The farthest from them is defended by three lines of stockades, to which torpedoes are attached. Admiral Ignacio, however, took the fleet up the nearest channel, and by shutting his ports, and keeping close under the cliffs on which the guns are mounted, avoided in great measure their fire, as they could not be sufficiently depressed, and he thus lost but a few men. Only one of the iron-clads was disabled, by a shot striking the condenser, and was exposed to a very heavy fire until another vessel came to its assistance, and, lashed to its side, towed it up past the batteries. The squadron is at present stationed a little more than a mile below Humaità, into which its shells fall, as well as into the rear of Curupaity. The communication with the squadron of wooden vessels, seven in number, stationed opposite Curùzù and below Curupaity, is easily maintained by means of a road four miles long, through the Chaco, defended by three redoubts and 1,400 men.

"Thus the whole of the river front, or right of the Paraguayan camp, is exposed to the fire of the fleet.

*   *   *   *   *

"The Paraguayan forces amount altogether to about 20,000 men, of these 10,000 or 12,000 at most are good troops, the rest mere boys from twelve to fourteen years of age, old men and cripples, besides from 2,000 to 3,000 sick and wounded. The men are worn out with exposure, fatigue, and privations. They are actually dropping down from inanition. They have been reduced for the last six months to meat alone, and that of a very inferior quality. They may once in a way get a little Indian corn; but that, mandioc, and especially salt, are so very scarce, they are, I fully believe, only served out to the sick. In the whole camp there is absolutely nothing for sale. There must be, from what I saw, a great scarcity of drugs and medicines, if not a total want of them, for the sick, whose number is rapidly increasing. Few recover, as may be naturally expected, under such circumstances. Cholera and small-pox, which exist to a certain extent in the allied camp, are spreading very much among the Paraguayans. The horses have nearly all died off, and the few hundreds which yet remain are so weak and emaciated they can scarcely carry their riders. The last 800 or 900 mares in the whole country have, however, just been brought in. The draught oxen are in a dreadful state, and cannot last much longer. The cattle in the camp, some 15,000 or 20,000 head, are dying very fast for want of pasture. Fresh cattle are occasionally brought in at night; but they are also generally in poor condition. Large herds are said to be kept near Humaitá, in some marshy place near the river, which is very difficult of access to the Allies. The few steamers still plying between the capital and the camp can only land their cargoes at night, as they have to come within the range of the Brazilian iron-clads below Humaitá. Many of the soldiers are in a state bordering on nudity, having only a piece of tanned leather round their loins, a ragged shirt, and a poncho made of vegetable fibre. They all wear clumsy-looking leather caps. A great part of them are still armed with flint guns, though in the course of the war many Minié rifles have been captured from the Allies.

"The Paraguayans are a fine, brave, hardy, patient, and obedient race of men; but they are beginning to be dispirited, judging from what I have seen on the one side, and the accounts

I have heard on the other. They neither give nor accept quarter, even when wounded. Paraguayan wounded have been seen, when lying on the field almost in the agonies of death, to stab any wounded enemy within reach."

I may add that the little boys who were made into soldiers were ordered to cut the throats of any wounded they saw on the ground; and a sergeant, one of my patients, told me, with some pride, that he had "degollado" several of his own wounded men, to prevent their falling into the hands of the enemy. "Others, again, especially of late, throw themselves on the ground at the approach of the foe, without offering the slightest resistance, but refuse pertinaciously to surrender, and have to be run through as they lie."

I expect the truth is, that the poor fellows, not understanding a word of any other language than Guarani, threw themselves on the ground to show that they *did* surrender; they were, however, systematically taught that the Brazilians always slaughtered their prisoners; and after the rout of Lopez at Lomas Valentinos, a friend of mine actually saw them bayoneting the wounded as they lay in long lines under the trees. We know that a cowardly enemy is always the most merciless.

"The garrison of Humaitá consists of five battalions, of which three are composed of old soldiers, one of boys and convalescents, and one of wounded men returned to duty; in all about 3,000 men. 6,000 are stationed along the left from Humaità to the Angulo, and 5,000 from thence to Curupaitỳ. The reserves, consisting of three battalions of infantry, and four or five weak dismounted cavalry regiments, numbering altogether from 2,000 to 2,500 men, are stationed at Paso Pucù, the most central position in the camp, and the head-quarters of President Lopez. Among all these troops there are probably not 10,000 able-bodied men."

Yet, in spite of this weakness, starvation, and misery, the Paraguayans held their position for nearly eighteen months longer, and were then conquered, not by the Allies, but by mightier foes—hunger and disease.

CHAPTER XVI.

WHILST the allied army was lying idle at Tujutì, skirmishes took
place between the Paraguayan and Brazilian cavalry very frequently ; by Lopez they were magnified into great battles, and
were invariably victories ; the loss on the part of the enemy
was usually 5,000 men, whilst their own, the " Semanario "
stated, was two or three killed and a few wounded ; nevertheless, some scores of the latter always reached the hospitals a few
days afterwards.

In 1866 a road—a mere bridle-path—was made through the
woods from the eastern side of Bolivia to the head waters of
the Paraguay, and a few traders came down it, and realized
enormous profits by the sale of the flimsiest of prints, with
more dressing than cotton in them, at a dollar a yard ; chocolate
at five shillings a pound, and salt at thirty-five pesos (about
forty shillings) the arroba of twenty-five pounds. Some of
them left with their money, but the rest were pounced upon
by Lopez as " conspirators," and lost both their gains and
their lives.

Lopez took advantage of the arrival of these Bolivians to
issue a pompous decree in the Government organ for the
regulation of the trade between the two countries, for the purpose of making the Allies believe that an important commerce
had been initiated between them. Copies of this decree and

similar documents used to be dropped by the Paraguayans between the lines of the two armies.

Speaking of salt reminds me of an amusing blunder I saw in an American illustrated paper, " Leslie's Weekly." The writer, Lieutenant Holmes, of the "Wasp," sent his journal and sketches to that paper, and they are editorially introduced as scenes " described with the simplicity and conscientiousness of an observant sailor." After giving his impressions of the river, and getting quite enthusiastic in his admiration of it, and the " beautiful parasites growing in the water," and wondering at the strange animals called " Kapurchas (carpinchas), and looking like tapirs " (!) he speaks of Mount Lambarai (Lambarè) as " a mount of three hundred and fifty feet high, and is said to be composed entirely of rock salt; therefore of great value to the country, where that condiment is so very scarce." It does not seem to have struck this observant sailor that salt, in a country where such a mass of it existed above ground, must have been about as " scarce " as it is in the ocean. Lambarè is really of basaltic rock, and I suppose having heard that, he thought that the word was but another name for rock salt. His sketches are also as divertingly unlike the places they are supposed to represent as can well be imagined.

One of the Bolivians, Dr. Rocas, started a small weekly paper, called " La Centinela "; and another, the " Cacique de Lambarè," was printed by the Government, in the Guarani. I give in the Appendix a specimen of this scurrilous print.

In the beginning of this year (1868) several regiments of women were actually formed. They volunteered their services, of course, but the reader need not be reminded what the voluntary offering of the Paraguayans meant; and for some time it was expected that they would be sent to the front, but after they had been drilled for a few weeks the idea was abandoned. This fact has been several times commented upon, and as often denied, but I can vouch for the truth of it. I have before me a printed list of names, sixty in number, commencing with that of Juana Tomasa Frutos, and ending with that of Brigida Chaves, and headed, " Lista nominal de las señoritas que se ofrecen para tomar las armas."*   Doña Carolina Gill, an old friend of mine, was " capitana " of one company ; and I several times saw the girls going off to be drilled, their hair dressed with tricoloured ribbons.   One day they were reviewed by the Lady President at La Trinidad.

During the months of December and January the river had risen to an extraordinary height, and most of the dreaded torpedoes being twenty feet or more under water, the Brazilian ironclads ventured close to Humaità ; and on the morning of the 19th of February it was seen that one of the lighters, which supported the chains, had capsized, and that these impediments, in consequence, had been got rid of.   For the first time, perhaps, during the war the enemy showed some daring, and three monitors ran past the *ribéra* batteries, and, without receiving any serious damage, anchored above the forts.   On the 21st the news reached Asuncion, and it was ordered to be evacuated within twenty-four hours.   I can scarcely say if the order were received with greater consternation or joy.   With the exception of the police and the scanty garrison, none but women and children remained of the native population, with a few hundred foreigners ; the former were terrified at the idea of leaving their homes, but at the same time they hoped that at last the weary war was at an end.   Don José Berges, the minister for foreign affairs, informed Mr. Washburn of the order, and that the capital would be temporarily removed to Luquè, a village about twelve miles in the interior.   The latter refused, however, to leave ; for he hoped that the Brazilians would occupy the capital at once, and that we should be rescued.   But he had grievously mistaken.   The same day, Doctor Don Antonio de las Carreras, ex-prime minister of Monte Video, and Señor Rodriguez, ex-secretary of the Legacion Oriental, asked permission to stay with him ; and when a number of the English mechanics, whose contracts had expired, begged for shelter there, he told them that if the vice-president would give them

---

* List of the names of the young ladies who offer to take arms.

permission to stay they might occupy some spare rooms in the building. They went down to the Government-house, and saw Col. Fernandez, the commandant, who said that if they did not go into the streets unnecessarily they might stop in the Legation; and accordingly six or eight, with their wives and children, twenty-two in all, took up their quarters with us.

The next day the city was completely deserted; and when two of the monitors made their appearance on the 24th, except for a stray dog, no signs of life were visible. Mr. Washburn, the French consul and I watched their approach from the roof of the consulate with great interest, expecting that they would take up a position in front of the city; for the battery at Tacumbù had only one heavy gun and a few field-pieces. But they stopped and engaged this work at almost the verge of their range. The shots flew far wide of their mark, the greater number fell harmlessly into the river and a few into the city, the only damage being the destruction of a balcony of the President's palace, a slice off the front of a house, and the demolition of a couple of dogs in the market-place.

I regret that I have not the official (Brazilian) account of this operation to quote from, for it gives one an excellent idea of the trustworthiness of the accounts transmitted by the Allies to Europe.* Any one reading it would imagine that a severe action had been fought; the vice-admiral talks of "having severely chastised the insolence of the Paraguayans in firing upon him," and the damage inflicted, when I can state positively

---

* To those who, like myself, are fully acquainted with the state of affairs in the River Plate, the utter untrustworthiness of the accounts transmitted to, and published in, the English newspapers is astonishing. And, especially, the way in which mere hearsay statements are received and quoted even by men who could, without the slightest trouble, test the truth of the stories they repeat. In Commander Kennedy's recent account of his visit to Paraguay, for instance he states that President Lopez was educated in the École Polytechnique of Paris, and also served in the British army in the Crimea. Now Lopez was in his 29th year when he visited Paris, and he went there as Minister Plenipotentiary to negotiate a treaty of peace and commerce between Paraguay and France and England; and he reached no nearer point to the Crimea than Marseilles, where he landed in 1854.

that not a single shot struck them at all. After firing about four hours, the iron-clads returned down the river, and we heard no more of them. The people, however, suffered severely, though indirectly, from this futile attack. They were driven out into the small villages to the north-east of Asuncion, where there were not houses enough to shelter one-fourth of their number; they encamped under the trees, or in the open air, during that month of heavy rains—seven or eight inches sometimes falling in the day—and endured every form of misery; food was excessively scarce and dear, all trades and occupations were at an end, they were dying by hundreds from disease and famine, and nearly all were attacked by intermittent fever.

The appearance of the town during and after the evacuation was indescribably wretched; long before daylight I was awakened by the creaking of the wheels of the heavy bullock-carts on their wooden axles, and I saw long lines of those primitive vehicles laden with household goods, followed by their owners on foot, and by the poorer people, both nearly all women, bending under the heavy burdens they carried on their shoulders. They all appeared frightened; and, with the red eyes of those who have passed a sleepless night, looked sadly on the homes the greater number of them were never to see again. When the last stragglers had passed, the silent streets glowing in the hot sunlight seemed as if they had been untenanted for a century, save by the vultures which wheeled slowly in narrowing circles overhead.

It would have been imagined that the Brazilians would have completely commanded the river now that they had passed the chain, for Lopez had only five or six small wooden steamers left, and they had fifty-four large steamers, several of them plated, eleven small, and forty-eight sailing vessels. Nothing of the kind! They blockaded Humaitá from above, after a fashion; that is to say, supplies could not be thrown in by day, but at night the Paraguayans seemed to do as they pleased. And on the 21st of March Lopez actually crossed the river to the Gran Chaco side, and made his way unmolested to San Fernando, about fifteen leagues above his former position, and still on the left bank, with three-fourths of his army and many of his heavy guns.

It was an extraordinary feat, and was most admirably planned and carried out; although the loss in men and guns, from the badness of the road, was considerable. An English artisan was a prisoner at the time in Humaità, and he afterwards gave me some very painful details of his sufferings, and those of others on the road, a mere cart-track, through the swampy woods. The men were often up to their middles in mire and water, numbers of the sick, old, and weakly were drowned, and many of the guns, after almost superhuman efforts to drag them through, had to be abandoned. A clever *ruse de guerre* had enabled the Paraguayans to mislead the enemy, and the lines of Curupaitỳ were abandoned for more than a month before the Allies found out that the birds had flown. The guns were gradually removed from the embrasures, and " quakers " (logs of wood) put in their place; the troops, meanwhile, were constantly massed in the front, leading the enemy to expect that an attack in force would be made upon them, and taking off their attention from Humaità itself, whence the artillery was being sent across the river in large flat-bottomed boats at night. When all was ready the men silently retreated from Curupaitỳ to Humaità, leaving numbers of dummies, made of sacking and reeds, standing by the wooden guns, and a few soldiers to fire volleys occasionally, to keep up the deception.

Before leaving Lopez committed an act of atrocious cruelty. He had many prisoners of war; it would encumber him too much to take them on to San Fernando, and the scanty force left in Humaità could scarcely guard them, so he ordered the whole of them, except the officers, to be slaughtered in cold blood; and on that summer's afternoon several hundred men were mercilessly butchered. The morning after this fearful scene he commenced his retreat, and in three days reached San Fernando, a place just above the embouchure of the river Tebiquari, with about 8,000 men. The movement was so cleverly managed that the Allies were completely thrown off the scent, and some weeks elapsed before they discovered where the Paraguayans had gone.

A force of about 3,000 men was left to guard Humaità, and they held it until the 24th of July, in spite of ten iron-clads, and in the face of 80,000 of the enemy, provided with abundance of arms, ammunition, and food.

A second *ruse* was tried successfully by the scanty garrison; great activity was shown near the river, boats and canoes full of men were seen passing in the dusk and early morning; the fire had slackened, at last ceased, and not a man or sign of life was to be seen within the works; it was evident that the garrison had " stole away." So thought the Brazilians; but to make sure, the iron-clads were moved closer, and, aided by the land batteries, poured a tremendous fire into the devoted place, from sunrise till night, on the 15th of July. Not a gun was heard in reply, and, expecting to march into deserted batteries as they did at Curupaitÿ, the next morning a general advance was ordered, and 6,000 men moved rapidly over the open ground towards the empty embrasures. About 200 yards in front they found a redoubt, from whence a few musket shots were fired by a small party of Paraguayans, who immediately retreated. The dense columns, in wonderfully good humour, and a little disordered, I expect, by this time, entered the battery, which was empty, and then pressed on to the main works in front of them. Five minutes more, and the green and yellow ensign will wave over the last stronghold of the tyrant! The foremost men were breaking into a run to be the first to enter, when—a yell of " Muerto à los cambàs! " rose high above the noise of the exulting throng, the loaded guns were run out, and a moment afterwards poured a storm of grape and shell into the disordered crowd; there was a fearful carnage, an instant of terrified indecision, and then a disordered flight.

A victory! and the victors were but a throng of famine-and-fever-stricken men. Lopez, once out of the way of danger, seems to have left them to their fate; the few cattle they had

when he left had by this time all but disappeared, great numbers
were killed during the bombardment of the 15th, and no new
supplies were sent to them, although the road through the Chaco
was open. On the 19th Col. Alèn sent to tell him that they
were eating the last of their stores. His answer was, "Hold
out for five days more, and then retreat." They obeyed, although they were starving even then, and trying to support life
by cutting the hides of the slaughtered cattle into strips and
boiling them for food; and their commander was so maddened
by the misery around him that he tried to commit suicide ; but
the pistol ball, with which he would have taken his life, only
destroyed one of his eyes. At length the appointed day came
round; they crossed the river, but not without discovery, and
many of the boats were sunk by the enemy's fire, and a serious
disaster happened as they were preparing to embark. A large
quantity of powder and shell had been brought down to the
shore, and a crowd of women and children stood around, waiting to carry it to the boats under cover of the night, when
a shell fell in their midst: there was a sudden flash, a heavy
report, and the poor creatures were hurled in all directions,
blackened corpses.

So on the 24th of July, 1868, all who could had crossed the
river, and Humaità was abandoned to the dying and the dead.

But the fugitives found themselves, to their dismay, completely cut off from the road they were to travel ; the river was
unusually high, and had converted the low marshy ground they
had reached into an island. Col. Alèn and a few of the stronger
men overcame this difficulty, and reached San Fernando, where
he was, shortly afterwards, put in irons, tortured most barbarously, and, after months of unspeakable suffering, shot as a
traitor. The weaker, the wounded, and the women and children
remained with Col. Martinez, the second in command, in blank
despair. They were soon discovered by the Brazilians, and
summoned to surrender. Their commandant refused. The
iron-clads came up, completely surrounded them, and they were
again ordered to surrender. In their desperate misery the

Paraguayans fired on the flag of truce; and then day after day shot and shell was poured into the unresisting crowd, and still the same answer. Their aimless, useless obstinacy is terrible to think of, yet it was almost sublime in its silent heroism and self-abnegation. Too feeble to fight, too worn out to hope to escape, they refused all mercy, and died as they lay. At length, after six days' carnage, a priest induced Col. Martinez to yield, and the scanty remnant capitulated at his orders. Lopez treated this surrender as a dereliction of duty, and added one more to the terrible list of his crimes, by *shooting the mother and wife of Col. Martinez for his so-called desertion!*

A great many of the officers, being better fed than the men, were able to escape with Col. Alèn; but they were all treated as criminals on their arrival at San Fernando. An article appeared in the " Semanario " a week or two afterwards, stating that the information that they were out of provisions was false, and that the garrison was amply provided with food when Alèn and Martinez traitorously gave up the place to the Brazilians. Most of these unfortunate men were executed. The fact of the prolonged resistance made by the fugitives after leaving the fortress, and that the Allies found it absolutely bare of all stores, is a sufficient answer to the charge.

CHAPTER XVII.

MR. WASHBURN and his family returned from La Trinidad in the
beginning of February, 1868; in fact, the Lady President had
received orders to request him to leave her house, for he had
by this time fallen from grace. Lopez, disappointed that the
proffered mediation, which promised so much, had come to naught,
vented his wrath upon the man who had attempted it; and the
refusal of Mr. Washburn to leave the city on the approach of
the Brazilians was an offence he only waited for an opportunity
to punish.

And he gave new offence to Lopez in April by an act of
great imprudence. We had been ordered not to go into the
streets; but Major Manlove used to take his cows to water, and
hitherto had not been interfered with. One day, however, he
was returning, and galloped half across the square in front of
the Legation. To do this was interdicted by a municipal ordi-
nance; he was unfortunately seen by the police, and was commanded to present himself at the bureau, where he was detained
for some hours. When Mr. Washburn heard of this he went
down to the Policia, and seeing Manlove sitting on a bench
outside, and guarded by two or three men, he lost his temper,
and thrusting the policemen on one side, put him on his horse,
and sent him back to the Legation.

An angry note came from the foreign office the next day,
complaining of the outrage, and when Mr. Washburn shortly

afterwards went down to San Fernando to see the President, it was evident that his devotion to his cause had been forgotten, and that he had fallen into disgrace. Within a few weeks he quarrelled with Major Manlove, and, knowing that he would be immediately arrested, ordered him to leave the Legation ; he did so, removing to the empty house of my old friend Mons. Lasserre, of which he had the keys and permission to make use. He was once more seized by the police, put in prison, sent to Villeta, and afterwards shot.

Mr. Bliss, another American, came over from a cottage he occupied, and took possession of the empty room, for he was no longer considered safe where he was. This man's name has, I am sorry to say, appeared so frequently coupled with mine that I ought to say a few words about him. He is the son of a Baptist missionary labouring amongst the North American Indians, and as he had an extraordinary talent for acquiring languages he was recommended to the Argentine Government, then in search of some one to treat with the Indians occupying the vast plains between their territory and that of Bolivia, as a fit person for this post; he went, and, I believe, carried out his mission successfully ; but on his return down the river Vermejo he fell into the hands of Lopez. He was then engaged by the latter to write a history of Paraguay from *his* point of view, and on the strength of his promise he had free quarters and rations from the Government. He wrote, also, articles for the " Semanario," patriotic speeches to be delivered by outraged women, and curses on deserters, real or supposed, at a very reasonable price indeed, considering the bitterness of them.

He is a clever man, but a thorough Yankee ; in person and address exactly realizing Dickens' Uriah Heep, and I disliked him intensely from his vulgar and dirty habits, *à la Amèricain.* However, except at table, where I could not refuse to meet him, I saw very little of him.

All went on as usual for some time. My valued friend, Mons. Cochelet, the French consul, and his family got safely out of the country, although Lopez, who detested him, tried

the same scheme for destroying him as he had in the case of
Mr. Gould; and more pertinaciously, for he kept him, his wife,
and four children more than a week in Humaità, in the line of
fire; and used to laugh heartily after dinner at the "gran susto"
(the fright) they would get before they could leave. I am glad
to say that, although several shells burst near them, none of the
family received any hurt.

His successor, who was a very different man, went in for
popularity strongly, as that word was understood by the *putas
de la capitàl*. He soon became one of the most intimate friends
of Madame Lynch, and distinguished himself by making patriotic speeches on every possible occasion in favour of Lopez,
in which he lavished the most extravagant praise upon him,
speaking of him as the most famous of living generals, and one
who was destined to occupy the brightest page in history as the
saviour and idol of his country; whilst to me he declared, with
the most sibilant of expletives, that he was the meanest tyrant
in the world. Shortly after his arrival he dedicated a silk flag to
Santo Tomàs, with the arms of France on one side and the
name and titles of Lopez on the other, and placed it with much
ceremony in that saint's grotto. I think he also "assisted,"
as he would say, at a visit to the Virgin de Milagros of Cāācupè,
made by Madame Lynch. This virgin deserves a passing
notice. It is a wooden image, in the church of that village,
which bows its head in a gracious and, of course, supernatural
manner, if the petition, offered before the shrine containing it,
is to be granted. But in order that the virgin—I know not if
the celestial or the wooden one be meant—should not be troubled
with improper prayers, the suppliant must previously submit
the favour to be asked to the priest, and pay the sum of one
dollar; then, if he approve, they repair to the church together,
and offer up their petition, in the temple of God, to the tinselled
idol standing there, and its head bows, of course, at the right
moment.

On this occasion religion and business were combined, for
Madame brought an order from Lopez directing the priest

to deliver to her all the jewels and offerings of value in the chapel; and she took them away with her.

We soon found that we were prisoners in the Legation, and dared not even venture into the street; only Mr. Washburn, his secretary, and a native servant being allowed to leave the house. The English mechanics, also, were in a very unhealthy state, from change of diet and want of exercise. They had made a most unfortunate mistake in entering the Legation, their money rapidly melted away, for the provisions Basilio was allowed to buy for them were very dear; and they incurred the anger of Lopez by refusing to work in the Arsenal, where they were greatly needed; and, therefore, Mr. Watts, the leader as he was believed to be of them, was afterwards shot at Villeta.

On the same 16th of June, when the Allies suffered their severe repulse from Humaità, we were surprised by the sudden appearance of Señor and Señora Leite-Pereira in the Legation; they came in hastily, and begged Mr. Washburn to protect them. It seems his *exequatur* as Portuguese consul had been that day withdrawn, and fearing that his arrest would follow, he sought shelter under the American flag. His offence was, that he had supplied such of his countrymen as were prisoners of war with food and money, which bare act of charity was construed by Lopez into sympathy with his enemies.

The next day a letter came from the Foreign Office to Mr. Washburn, asking if the fugitives were in his house. He replied in the affirmative. On the 20th the Paraguayan Secretary for Foreign Affairs, Don Gumesindo Benitez, demanded to know why the consul was allowed to remain in the Legation. Mr. Washburn replied that he was not obliged to answer a demand of that kind, but that Señor Leite-Pereira was his guest. On the 23rd another despatch came of a very serious tenor. It demanded from Mr. Washburn a packet of papers left with him by José Bèrges, ex-Minister for Foreign Affairs, who was then a prisoner at San Fernando on a charge of conspiracy and treason. Mr. Washburn replied energetically that he had never received any but official papers from Bèrges, and that he had no private documents of his in his possession. In a few days the demand was repeated, and a letter from Don José himself, or rather signed by him in a trembling hand, was enclosed, in which he was made to say, that his treason being discovered concealment was now useless, and he begged Mr. Washburn to give up the two packets of letters and papers, one marked "Papeles de Bèrges," and the other with the name of his brother, which he had confided to him. In the same letter was a most minute account of their last interview, after which the papers were said to have been brought away by Mr. Washburn, the position of the furniture in the room, the desk from which they were taken, the conversation they had had, evidently veracious as far as the conversation was concerned, for it was exactly in the style in which the minister conversed; and the description of the meeting between him and Bèrges, the room in which they met, the precautions they used in hiding the papers, and so on,—so circumstantial and minute that I had great difficulty in believing that they had never been placed in his hands.

The despatch went on to say that Mr. Washburn had dismounted in the courtyard of his house—shut in by the front rooms from the street—carrying the papers in a small valise; had taken that into the dining-room, then into his office, and had placed the packets in an iron safe there. It was evident that we had a spy in the house; I had long suspected something of the kind; for I had frequently seen Basilio's old mother peering at dusk about the door of the *sala*, especially if any visitors were there, and then leaving the house, often, for hours at a time. But we used to laugh at her, for there was no treason to spy out. On the day mentioned in the letter, some weeks before, Mr. Washburn really had gone to visit Señor Bèrges, then seriously ill, carrying the valise they described so minutely, and afterwards visited the Lady President, or as she was now called, Doña Juana Carillo, her maiden name, for she was, also, in disgrace—as they truthfully recorded ; and afterwards Señor Leite-Pereira. From him Mr. Washburn carried the packets in question, not of letters, but "billetès," paper money. On the 10th of July another long despatch came, demanding that not only Señor Leite-Pereira, but Dr. Carreras and Señor Rodriguez, should be expelled from the Legation, to be tried for conspiring against the government of Paraguay.

This was the first official notice we had received of the discovery of a conspiracy against the President, although we had heard rumours that such was the case, and that great numbers of both natives and foreigners had been arrested for complicity in it.

I never believed the story of the plot for a moment, for the Paraguayans have so little trust in each other that a conspiracy amongst them was impossible, indeed this had been the strongest safeguard of Lopez ; and as for the foreigners, they were only too fearful of the police to attempt anything of the kind.

The request had been previously made, but without mentioning any specific charge against them. Mr. Washburn refused to entertain it for a moment, and told the Paraguayans that so long as these gentlemen pleased to remain they should have all the protection his house afforded. That, however, amounted to very little ; it was only the respect which Lopez would feel for his ministerial privileges, and the fear that any outrage might lead to hostilities, which could make them secure there. It was also evident that any futile resistance on the part of the accused would but increase their punishment ; and, as Mr. Washburn declined to promise that he would stay till the end of the war, they, confiding in their perfect innocence, resolved to give themselves up and meet the charges made against them. I felt the utmost sympathy for them, although I was only intimate with Señor Rodriguez ; for a fear, I could never trace to its source, of some trouble with the government had prevented me even talking with the others, except when they required medical advice.

Dr. Carreras was a short, slender man, of about fifty years of age, with a good head and delicate features, and an extremely nervous manner, owing probably to years of ill-health, and a very rapid speaker. Rodriguez was a young and handsome fellow, of remarkably pleasing manners and polished address; he had read much, spoke French well, and was learning English. Leite-Pereira was a Portuguese, of good figure, but with the characteristic ugliness of his race—the worst in that, and other respects, in Europe. His señora, a Paraguayan, a tall, handsome, and very pleasing woman, had crossed the Atlantic, and lived some years in Lisbon before her marriage. She was an excellent example of what the natives might be made by education.

At noon, on the 12th of July, we exchanged our sad and last *adios.* As soon as they left the porte-cochère they were seized by the police, who had been watching the house for more than a month, night and day, and at once marched down to the Policia. There they were put in irons, and sent down in a boat to San Fernando. The same day all the English, except myself, left also. Col. Fernandez promised Mr. Washburn that they should not be molested; but they were kept as prisoners in the railway station for some time, and then sent into the country. Five were arrested, and one, Mr. Watts, was shot, leaving a wife and several children.

Whilst they were in the station a train came in one night, laden with prisoners. They could not see the poor fellows, for no lights were allowed, but they heard their groans and sighs, and the clanking of their irons. They comprised nearly all the male population of Luquè. In fact, only three officials were left, Sanabria, the chief of police, Col. Fernandez, and Gumesindo Benitez. About eighty Italians were taken, twenty Frenchmen, all the Bolivians, and several others of different nationalities.

On the 13th of the same month another demand came. Mr. Bliss and myself were to be expelled; and, on the Minister stating that we were members of his *suite* and, therefore, entitled to equal immunities with himself, three days afterwards Bliss was charged with the same crimes as Dr. Carreras had been, and

I with "having committed others of equal gravity." Scarcely had Mr. Washburn replied to this demand, when another despatch arrived, filling some thirty pages of foolscap, and being the "confessions" of Carreras, Bèrges, and Capt. Fidanza, the latter an Italian, an intimate friend of Mr. Washburn's. They charged him with being the chief of a secret revolutionary committee, of which they were members, their object being the destruction of Lopez and the rendition of the country to the Allies. He was said to have received a large sum of money from Don Benigno Lopez (the President's brother) for distribution amongst them and the rest of the conspirators, and that he had, stored in an iron safe in his office, the minutes of their meetings, and various letters, sent by Caxias, arranging a plan of co-operation and mutual assistance.

Mr. Washburn, I say it with all deference, made the great mistake of replying *seriatim* to these charges, argued the points with the Paraguayan minister, and in most undiplomatic language ; and assumed that Carreras and Rodriguez really had made these charges against him.

I watched with great pain the course he was adopting, and ventured to suggest a more dignified mode of proceeding, and a less colloquial style of writing. My suggestions, however, were received so ungraciously that it was impossible for me to offer my aid a second time ; and letters were sent which only furnished grounds for fresh accusations, and by their want of dignity degraded him in the eyes of Lopez.

Every ten or twelve days a voluminous despatch in reply was received from Señor Benitez ; most politely worded, ever professing the utmost respect for Mr. Washburn, often admirably arranged, and always well written ; yet full of the most serious charges against him, and so well argued, so clearly supported, and with such a mass of evidence to back them, that I could hardly hold unshaken my certain conviction that they were false, base fabrications from beginning to end.

Not content with writing, late one night Señor Benitez came in person, to urge Mr. Washburn to give up the papers of

Bèrges, and supply the conclusive evidence against the conspirators, which was still wanting. Unfortunately, his Excellency has a very imperfect knowledge of the Spanish language; and, as they were alone, the full force of what the secretary said will never be known; and I could gather from Mr. Washburn little more than a summary of the matters discussed. However, Benitez said to him, "All is discovered—you must confess;" which, as I shall tell presently, led to his own arrest and execution. About a week afterwards Madame Lynch came on the same errand. She told him, also, that he must confess; that Bèrges had stated positively that the papers had been deposited with Mr. Washburn; and that he ought to give them up, and "trust to the mercy and generosity of the Marshal, who took pleasure in pardoning penitent offenders."

On her return to San Fernando she publicly repeated at the table of Lopez all she had said to him; and added, that Mrs. Washburn had called her aside and, with tears, implored her to intercede on her husband's behalf. "That," said she, "is a convincing proof of his guilt;" and she urged Lopez, and was supported in her advice by the bishop, to have Mr. Washburn brought down a prisoner to San Fernando.

In the next letter the Minister repeated the phrase that Benitez had used, and also that he had spoken in a former despatch of the conspiracy breaking out on the President's birthday. In the succeeding one Benitez denied that he had used those words; and went on, "It was not I, Señor Ministro, who spoke of the revolution breaking out on the day you have mentioned, but I thank your Excellency for the information." Mr. Washburn was furious, and for days after was continually repeating, "No fuí yo, Señor Ministro, que hablé," etc. He might have borne the insult with patience; for it was the last letter the secretary wrote: a few days after he was in irons, was put to the torture, and his evidence added to the mass he had been quoting from. I came in for my share of abuse: I was described as a needy mendicant, who had come to Paraguay begging my bread. My contract I signed in London! I had also "been plotting treason for months before I entered the Legation." It must have been when I was in solitary confinement then. And I had been "expelled from the army in disgrace;" when my impression is, that I had never been in it, and that I had refused to re-enter the service of Lopez. However, I bore it all very coolly, and set to work studying French and Spanish novels with great industry. By the way, in the latter, the polite villain or the brutal ruffian, as the case may be, is always an Englishman! And I read, to my great amusement, in one of them that a member of Parliament, who had brought in a bill for the destruction of Roman Catholics, had a number of statues of different sizes (*varios estatuas de diferentes tamañas*) erected in his honour by his admiring colleagues!

To anyone from without it would have seemed that the people within the Legation must be some of the most formidable ruffians in existence; for, under the pretext that we intended to escape, and that we still—in some very mysterious way—carried on communications with the enemy 250 miles distant, a strong body of troops surrounded us day and night; pickets of a dozen men were placed at the four corners of the square, and sentries with fixed bayonets at every door, whilst others incessantly patrolled the streets.

In the beginning of August the whole of the correspondence was published in the "Semanario," with the exception of two of Mr. Washburn's letters, which contained statements too dangerous for publicity. In one of them he spoke of Mr. Bliss and myself in high terms; him as a literary man of great talent, and me as a "recluse devoted to science," and the most unlikely person in the world to meddle with plots and revolutions.

Benitez very acutely replied, "Your Excellency spoke in the same high terms of Carreras, Rodriguez, and the other confessed criminals (*reos confesados*) before they were taken prisoners, and now they are liars and perjurers;" showing how great an error Mr. Washburn had committed, in admitting that they might have given voluntary evidence against him, when he knew perfectly well that it was impossible they could have done so. It was evident that torture had been applied, or that the words had been put into their mouths. One document, purporting to be the evidence of Don Benigno Lopez, was quite a curiosity in its way. It described with wonderful minuteness a visit he had paid to Mr. Washburn, how they talked together, where they sat, of the interruption to their conference by the entrance of " Cati " (Kate, Mrs. Washburn's maid) with a tray of glasses with brandy and water, of the gold he then paid to him, and the two clothes-basketsful of paper money his slaves afterwards brought up for distribution amongst the conspirators, and so on. All, except the payment of the money and part of the conversation, was true without doubt ; for Mr. Washburn did talk most imprudently. Amongst ourselves it was all very well to say what we thought of the war and the character of Lopez ; but he used to tell things to natives—to this very Don Benigno, to Bèrges, to many others, and especially to a smooth-spoken, flattering Italian, named Parodi, who " Your Excellency "-ed him into the most perilous of confidences, and then betrayed all to Mrs. Lynch—which, perfectly right in themselves as mere personal opinions, became treason and conspiracy if the point of view were shifted a little.

And he had placed himself in a false position from the first. None knew better than he the character of Lopez ; that he was ', cruel, selfish, unscrupulous tyrant, who, sooner or later, by slow degrees, or some great calamity, would inflict unspeakable misery upon the people he ruled ; for was he not writing a book on Paraguay at which the world was to wonder and shudder ? And yet he could write such a despatch as the one I have quoted to the Brazilian Minister, and could return to Paraguay, after once leaving it in safety, and by his very presence give a moral support to Lopez, which was of incalculable value to him.

And he made his position worse by those unfortunate letters, which served no useful purpose. We should not have been arrested one day the sooner if he had not written one of them. He was perfectly innocent of having conspired against Lopez, of course ; for there was not, and never had been, any conspiracy ;

but his love of trading, his want of dignity and independence, his frequent sinning against those subtle laws, "the habits of good society," and of which the Paraguayans, with their grave, formal, Spanish politeness, think so much, were really the sources of all his trouble; and his helping a man whom he could not conscientiously support, was the error they punished. The dread he showed of any examination being made of his papers puzzled me for a time, until I found that it was the manuscript of his "History" which imperilled him. But the very fiscàles, the native prosecutors, began at last to believe from his manner that the story they had themselves concocted was true, and that the "papèles de Bèrges," which had never existed, were actually hidden in the iron safe.

In the midst of all this writing, war had not been forgotten. Lopez, finding his position at San Fernando a bad one, fell back and marched forty leagues higher up the river to Villeta, and threw up a strong battery two leagues below, at Angustura (the narrows), to command the river, on the very spot where Sebastian Gabot, in 1568, had his first fight with the Indians of Paraguay. The Brazilians followed him, landed on the right bank of the river below Angustura, and then, making a road through the Chaco marshes—a work of immense labour and difficulty—marched up above him, the Argentines remaining at Palmas, a few miles below. We could plainly hear the firing in Asuncion, and hoped, though against hope, that the Allies would at last show some activity, and release us from our dangerous position.

Lopez, at this period, was seized with a sudden fit of devotion; he had a chapel built in front of his quarters at San Fernando, and attended mass there daily at noon, and, in addition, he would sometimes remain on his knees for two or three hours at a time, motionless and silent before the altar.

His hut was partly underground, and, with the chapel, protected by an immense mound of earth, and he rarely moved, except at night, beyond the shelter of it. He seemed to have abandoned the army to its fate after the retreat from Humaità;

and devoted the whole of his attention to the reports of the tribunals appointed to try the prisoners, and in inventing new punishments for them. He had always been in the habit of drinking freely, and now did so to excess, passing his time in alternate fits of intoxication and devotion.

Ever since the arrest of Carreras the Legation had been completely invested; as I have said, there was a picket of a dozen men at each corner of the house, and a chain of sentries around it from sunset to sunrise, but the native servants used to talk with the men, and we learnt in this way what was going outside our little world. One day the former told us that a "cañonero Americano" had arrived; and sure enough, on the 29th of August, Mr. Washburn received a letter from the commander of the "Wasp," United States gunboat.

He was overjoyed, and well he might be; for it was very doubtful how much longer he would have been personally unmolested; and at once demanded his passports, which were not sent, however, until the 8th of September, and then we learnt that our fate was sealed. "The criminals, Bliss and Masterman, must remain to be tried by the tribunal of the country," said the letter enclosing the passports for the rest.

I passed the morning of the last day in writing letters to my friends in England (for although I had a strong presentiment that my life would be spared, yet I felt that the chance was a desperate one), and in hiding a little quinine and opium in the seams of my coat.

In the afternoon, Señora Leite-Pereira, who had been permitted to stay after the arrest of her husband, left to return to the house of her mother, a few miles from the capital. I have not heard what became of her afterwards.

We went to bed soon. I slept but little, and was dressed by daybreak, then had a glass of milk and a biscuit, and waited for the end. The French and Italian consuls came early; to the latter Mr. Washburn left the care of the large amount of personal property belonging to foreigners, who had sent it there for safety, but to fall, however, the more readily into the hands of Lopez, and which he did not make the slightest effort to save.

Mons. Cuverville told me of his own apprehensions ; that his chancellor, Mons. de Libertad, had been denounced, and was expecting arrest every hour; and also confirmed the story that every foreigner in Luquè had been arrested.

In order to spare the feelings of Mrs. Washburn, it was arranged that she should leave the Legation escorted by Mr. Meinke, the secretary, and her two English servants ; and that the rest should not start till she was out of sight. As I accompanied her to the porte-cochère the police made a rush at me, but I disappointed them for a moment.

I shook hands with the native servants, not forgetting my particular friend, Basilio's mother, who gave me her blessing, and then waited till Mr. Washburn was ready.

At the last moment he repeated what he had said more in detail the night before, that we were at liberty to accuse him of any crime, if, by doing so, we could secure our own safety ; for he had heard from the servants that all the prisoners had been tortured, and expected that we should have to pass through the same terrible ordeal.

CHAPTER XVIII.

WE left the house together, but Mr. Washburn walked so
rapidly that the consuls and ourselves could scarcely keep up
with him, and he was a few yards ahead when we reached the
end of the colonnade. There the police, who had been closing
around us, simultaneously drew their swords, rushed forwards,
and roughly separated us from the consuls. I raised my hat,
and said, loudly and cheerfully, " Good-bye, Mr. Washburn;
don't forget us.'' He half turned his face, which was deathly
pale, made a deprecative gesture with his hand, and hurried
away. We—that is, Mr. Bliss, the negro Baltazar,* and myself
—were surrounded by about thirty policemen (the rest taking
charge of the Legation), who, with shouts and yells, ordered
us to march down to the Policia. I had burdened myself with
a travelling-bag filled with linen, a water-proof sheet, and a
thin light mattress; but I might have spared myself the trouble,
for they were all taken from me. When we reached the office
we were halted in the road, and kept standing there about an
hour; then the negro was taken within, after some time Mr.
Bliss, and lastly myself. When my turn came I found the
chief of police seated in the corridor, with a group of his savage
myrmidons around him; he looked at me in silence for some
minutes, and then by a gesture ordered me to be stripped. My

* A servant of Dr. Carreras.

clothes were most strictly and systematically examined, the lining torn out, and every fold ripped up ; my little packets of quinine and opium were of course discovered, pounced upon with a shout of triumph by the men, and put carefully on one side. My handkerchief, cravat, and money were taken from me, the rest returned. I was then told to sit down, that fetters might be rivetted on my ankles, and afterwards taken through a side court, and thrust into a cell. The door was secured, there was no window, and I was left in total darkness to my bitter reflections.

I rolled up my poncho for a pillow, lay down on the ground, for there was not even a stool in the dungeon, and tried to sleep; but in vain : so I passed the time by carefully reviewing the events of the past six months, so as to fix them clearly in my memory, and I did the same systematically every day afterwards ; for I had a firm presentiment that, although I should have to suffer much and long, my life would be preserved, and that I should some day tell the story as I am now relating it.

About seven o'clock in the evening the door opened; a sergeant and two men entered with a lantern : one carried a hammer and a small anvil, the other a set of irons. I rose as they came in, but the sergeant motioned me to lie down again. The fetters I was wearing were removed, and the massive bar the man bore on his shoulder was rivetted in their place. Two rough iron loops, with eyes at their extremities, were first placed over my ankles ; then the bar, which was about eighteen inches long, and two in diameter, was thrust through the eyes, and an iron wedge, with many a blow of the heavy hammer, rivetted firmly at one end, whilst a broad head secured it at the other. Thus fettered, it was with the greatest difficulty that I staggered to my feet, and then sat down again scarcely able to bear the weight. I had previously heard the clang of the hammer as they were rivetting similar irons on my companions.

A short time afterwards the sergeant reappeared, and motioned me in silence to follow him. I did so. He led me to the front of the Policia, where, by the light of some lanterns, I saw Mr.

Bliss and Baltazar mounted sideways on mules, and another waiting for me.

I was lifted into the saddle, for the thirty or more pounds' weight of my fetters prevented me even raising a foot from the ground. The group of brutal policemen wished us, amid shouts of laughter, *buenos noches* and a pleasant journey, and we started, guarded by a sergeant and two men armed to the teeth. I recognized in the former an old patient of mine; and he must have been a good-natured fellow, for as soon as we were out of sight of the Policia he stopped us, dismounted, and tied the strap of the off-stirrups to the bar of our fetters, and showed us that we could thus support them with our hands; but my wrists were nearly dislocated by their weight before we reached the end of our journey. I thought at first from the direction that we were only going to the railway station; but I soon found to my dismay that Villeta was our destination, a distance of thirty-five miles.

The journey, apart from the pain I was suffering, was one of inexpressible sadness to me, as the road lay for many miles through the beautiful lanes, bordered with cedras and bitter orange trees, where I used to ride almost daily, and in which I had botanized and sketched a hundred times. There was no moon, but the stars were shining brightly in the cloudless sky; and every copse, every dell, where the ferns and tall arums grew, was visible in their yellow light. And the white *quintas*, shaded with trellised vines and climbing roses, where I had passed so many happy hours, and the familiar gardens and fields around them, called up scenes and reminiscences I would gladly have forgotten till better days. The houses were empty, many already falling to decay; their owners were dead, or prisoners like myself; the fences destroyed, and the gardens trampled by straying cattle. Destruction and desolation, war, pestilence, and famine had swept all trace of gladness from the land, leaving only bitter memories and vain regrets.

I begged the sergeant to let us travel as slowly as possible; for at every step the heavy bar swung backwards and forwards, and a jolt was agonizing. He did so ; but once, in descending a steep slope, the mules broke into a trot; in trying to steady the bar I lost my balance, and fell to the ground. I was tied to the girths, and, unable to extricate myself, was dragged for some distance head downwards, the mule kicking viciously the while. Fortunately, the only damage was a deep cut in the ankle and a few bruises. The sergeant kindly let me lie on the grass a little while, and then we went on again. The road soon became very bad ; and in a deep miry ravine my companions were both thrown, but were only slightly hurt. At each guardia we stopped a few minutes, and I could get a draught of water to relieve the burning thirst I suffered ; for the rough blistered iron soon cut through trousers, boots, and socks, and swung on the bare flesh whenever my tired arms forced me to let it fall. The pain fevered me ; indeed, it was sometimes so intense that the dread of a broken leg alone kept me from fainting.

The path often took us near the river, and I saw distinctly the lights of the steamer which was carrying Mr. Washburn and his family down to the gunboat at Angustura. Sometimes we had difficulty in proceeding through the deep ruts and marshy ground ; but we had light enough to find our way, for the night was, as I have said, a most beautiful one, still and warm, the air fragrant with the perfume of the orange blossoms and the flowering orchids which hung in festoons from the wayside trees, and brightened by the fire-flies sparkling and flashing amid their branches.

At length that long night passed away ; the stars one by one sunk beneath the western ridge, the air grew colder, and the grey dawn broke as we neared the basaltic hill of Ypanè, but still many miles from our destination. A few men and girls bearing baskets on their heads passed us occasionally on their way to the encampment ; some did not raise their eyes from the ground, others looked at us pityingly ; but the spectacle of prisoners passing in chains was too common to excite either surprise or comment. I was greatly exhausted with pain and hunger, and, seeing a girl carrying a basket of bread, I begged the sergeant to give us a morsel to eat; he kindly bought a little cake of baked cassava meal, and, looking round cautiously to make sure that none were watching, divided it amongst us; it was but a mouthful, but as I had taken nothing but a glass of milk the day before I was glad enough of it. He had been very considerate with us during the whole of the journey; but now, as people were about, and an officer might pass at any moment, he dared not show us any more kindness; he spoke roughly, and urged us on at a quicker pace. We went over hill after hill, or rather swelling uplands covered with coarse grass and low shrubs, and at length surmounted that overlooking the little village of Villeta; there we halted before a group of officers; my feet were untied, and I fell exhausted, and more dead than alive, on the ground.

An *alferez* harshly told me to stand up. I tried, but the weight of my irons threw me on my face, but at length, by a violent effort, I staggered to my feet. A few paces off was a square space, enclosed with hide ropes; I was told to go within it, and then, too fatigued to notice the poor wretches, my fellow-prisoners, I threw myself on the bare ground, and fell almost immediately into a deep sleep. Late in the afternoon I was awakened by a blow with a stick, and told to rise and march towards a little grove of orange trees about half a mile off. Aching in every limb, I obeyed, and, supporting my fetters with a strip of hide, moved with pain and difficulty in the direction indicated, as fast as my bruised and bleeding feet would carry me. A *carbo*, or corporal, followed, armed with a bayonet and a stick. "Go faster!" he shouted every moment. I tried, but in vain, to do so. He thrashed me savagely with his stick over my shoulders and arms, knocked me down, and beat me more cruelly for falling. At last, bruised and breathless, I reached a group of little huts, made of branches and reeds, and placed in two rows. I saw Mr. Bliss and Baltazar taken separately on one side; I went to the other, and entered the farthest hut. Within it was seated an old captain, named Falcòn, and a priest, whom I afterwards found acted as secretary.

The former signed me to enter, and, after scrutinizing me for a few minutes, said, "Ah ! we have got you at last. Now, confess that Washburn is the chief of the conspirators, and that you took refuge in the Legation for the purpose of plotting against the Government." I replied that I had no confession to make, that I had never plotted against the Government, but had done all that lay in my power to serve the Paraguayans, that I was sure that Mr. Washburn was quite innocent of the crimes alleged against him ; and I explained in a few words under what circumstances I had entered his service. He heard me with many marks of impatience to the end, and then said, "You will not confess?" "I have no confession to make." "Confess," he repeated, "or I will see if we cannot make you." Then turning to the priest he told him to take me out and put me in the rack (*potro*). He took me behind the hut, but close to it, so that Falcòn within could hear all that passed. I prayed silently for strength to bear this great trial, and then looked round for the implements of torture ; but found that these savages, like those in "The Last of the Mohicans," ought to have expressed regret that their means of inflicting pain were so primitive. The priest again urged me to confess, but I replied, as before, that I was not a conspirator, and had no confession to make. He then said something to the corporal, in Guarani, who shouted out, "Bring the *uruguayana* here !" At his call two soldiers came forward, carrying a bundle of muskets, and ropes made of strips of hide. I was told to seat myself on the ground, with my knees raised ; I did so, and was again asked, "Will you confess?" "No ; I am innocent."

One of the men tied my arms tightly behind me, the other passed a musket under my knees, and then putting his foot between my shoulders forced my head down until my throat rested on the lower musket ; a second was put over the back of my neck, and they were firmly lashed together. They left me so for some time, striking the butt-ends of the fire-locks occasionally with a mallet ; the priest meanwhile, in a monotonous voice, as if he were repeating a formula he had often gone through, urged me to confess and "receive the mercy of the kind and generous Marshal Lopez." I made no reply, but suffered the intense pain they were inflicting in silence. At length they unbound me, and I was asked once more, "Will you confess?" I replied in the negative. They bound me up as before, but with two muskets at the back of my neck. As they were tightening the cords I threw my head forward to avoid the pressure on my throat, and my lips were badly cut and bruised against the lower musket; the blood almost choked me, and I fainted from the excruciating pain.

When I recovered I was lying on the grass utterly exhausted, and felt that I could bear no more; that it would be far preferable to make a pretended confession, and be shot, than suffer such cruel torture. So as they were about to again apply the *uruguayana*, as it is called by them, I said, "I am guilty; I will confess:" and they immediately unbound me. The priest said, "Why were you such an obstinate fool? Your companion Bliss was only threatened with the torture, and confessed at once." This was the case, as he told me himself afterwards. I had heard poor Baltazar loudly praying for mercy several times, and now the sounds of heavy blows, each followed by a shriek from him, proved how much more they were prepared to inflict upon us: they were flogging him most cruelly, and afterwards crushed his fingers with a mallet. I pitied him very much; for he knew nothing whatever about the pretended plot, nor the charges against his master, and could not save himself, even by protesting that he was guilty.

I drank some water, and tried to eat a little meat they offered me, but could not. And then, returning within the hut, I told, as well as I could remember it, part of the same story which had been wrested from Carreras, Bèrges, Benigno Lopez, and the rest, whose depositions I had read with Mr. Washburn. There was no help for it, but God knows with what agony and shame I repeated that wretched tissue of fables and misrepresentations. But it must be remembered that for three months I had suffered great anxiety, daily expecting to be arrested;

that I knew how mercilessly those who refused to confess were
mangled before execution ; that I had had a long and painful
journey ; and that I had been without food for two days. On
the other hand, I could do but little wrong to the accused. Mr.
Washburn was safe on board the "Wasp" ; Rodriguez, Gomez
(late the Mayor-de-Plaza), Bedoya, Barrios, and Gonzales, had
already been shot or had died ; and as to the others, I could
only repeat as such what I had read of their own depositions.

I had had also the express permission of Mr. Washburn to
say anything against him I pleased. He says in his evidence
before a Committee of Congress, in answer to Mr. Willard—

"I said to Bliss and Masterman you may say anything about me
that you think may help you. You may say that you saw me steal
sheep, or commit burglary, if you think you can thereby prolong
your lives." *Washington, U.S., March* 30, 1869.)

My belief from the first was, that they wanted me simply as
a deponent, and such was really the case; and if I had not
given the false testimony they required it would have been
forged, and I should have been shot to prevent its contradiction.*
However, I made a very lame story of it, although it was easy
to so represent the words and actions of Mr. Washburn as to
make his opinions appear overt acts of conspiracy. As for the
rest, I declared, truthfully enough, that they had never talked
with me on the subject. Falcòn, and especially the priest, got
out of all patience with me ; twenty times they threatened to
put me in the *potro* again, and twice were on the point of doing
so, when I luckily remembered something Mr. Washburn had
said against Lopez. I think the old captain was not a bad
fellow, and he helped me whenever he could by leading questions, and elaborated my scanty evidence into quite an imposing
deposition ; but, of course, he stood himself on the edge of a
precipice, and had he shown any open sympathy for me his life

* In the "depositions" not a word had been said by any one against me, and
this increased my difficulties, for I did not know what they expected me to
accuse myself of.

would not have been worth an hour's purchase. The priest, on
the contrary, exhibited the most venomous spite against me,
sneered at my " half revelations," and urged Falcòn over and
over again to "put that obstinate devil (myself) in the *uruguayana*, and make an end of him."

During my examination several officers came in, Major Aveiro,
Capt. Jàra, Col. Serrano, and others. Jàra was the son and
heir of Don Luis Jàra, the late owner of the house Mr. Washburn occupied, and for which, relying on his privilege as a
minister, he most unwisely refused to pay any rent; he was very
anxious to know what had been said on the subject. I told him,
and answered the questions of the others as vaguely as I could.

From the conversation and questions of these men I gathered
several valuable hints as to the course I had best adopt, and I
also ascertained, incidentally that Mr. Washburn was then on
board the " Wasp," and that I could not therefore endanger his
safety by anything I should say against him.

Late at night a priest named Romàn came in, and asked for
my depositions. Falcòn, who was evidently in great awe of
him, handed over the papers. He read them through, was
about to tear them in pieces, but restrained himself, and threw
them contemptuously on the table, saying, " *Que miserables dis-
parátes!*" (What wretched trash!) Then turning to me, " Are
these your revelations? Now, look you, I go for a short ride,
and if on my return I do not find that you have confessed
clearly that the great beast *(gran bestia)* Washburn is the chief
conspirator, that he was in treaty with Caxias, and that he
received money and letters from the enemy, *and that you knew
it*, I will put you in the *uruguayana*, and keep you there till
you do." Captain Falcòn seemed to draw a long breath when
his terrible colleague had withdrawn. I begged for a little time
to arrange my thoughts, promising to then tell them all I knew.
I might well ask it : I had been under examination fully six
hours, and was utterly worn out. At this moment, as I pause
to recollect what I said, how vividly the whole scene comes
before me! The little hut, about ten feet by six, made of hur-

dles covered with reeds, and lighted fitfully by two flaring tallow candles as their flame sways in the wind. In the centre is a table with three sound legs, and the broken fourth lengthened with a stout piece of sugar-cane tied to it with a strip of hide. On it are the candles guttering into their rude holders of sun-dried clay, and lighting strongly the face of the low-browed priest; a mean, crafty face, furrowed with wrinkles, which make him look double his age, and not improved by the rough stubble which covers his lean angular jaws—he has not shaved for a week ; and the tonsure on his occiput looks like a weedy clear-ing. He is biting his ragged nails, and watching the face of the captain with a weary, impatient look, which changes to one of fawning humility if their glances meet.

His companion has gladly given me the time I asked for ; he is tired and perplexed himself, and is smoking his cigar without enjoyment, chewing rather than burning it. He is a short, stout man, with a bald head, and now that he has taken off his huge silver-rimmed spectacles, he wears an air of *bonhomie* strangely at variance with his present employment. He is seated on a box filled with piles of manuscript, the depositions of the accused : never, perhaps, in the history of the world, have so many lies been crammed into so small a space ! Be-yond is his bed, a raw hide laid on a few bundles of long grass —no bedclothes ; he will roll himself in his poncho presently, and sleep as he is—turn in all standing, as a sailor would say. Above hangs his sword, a pistol, and his horse gear, and that is all. I am seated near the door on a low stool, the top made like the inverted ridge of a house. Outside, the guards, three men, are lying asleep on the ground, one is grasping his musket in his brown sinewy hand, those of the others are leaning against the hut.

The clanking of my irons, as I move uneasily on the hard seat, calls the attention of the "fiscal" to the business in hand. "Come, Masterman," he says, not unkindly, "let us have the whole of the story ; tell us how the great beast intended to destroy us all." He puts on his spectacles again, and writes down my words in a condensed form on a spare piece of paper, for he likes to amplify them himself, without any particular attention to what I did say; but I am too tired to object and protest as I did at first, and am not sure but that it is better to let him do as he likes. "The criminal, having confessed freely and voluntarily his guilt," he begins to dictate to his secretary, the awkward subject of torture being kept in the shade, "and having been solemnly admonished by the Señores Fiscàles to tell the whole of the truth, now, in order to relieve his burdened conscience, deposes that Washburn was the originator and chief mover in the plot," and so on through two sheets of closely written foolscap. I got on swimmingly for a time, but presently I was asked how much money Washburn had paid me. "Not a rial," I answered, stoutly, and truly enough. "How much were you offered?" asked the priest. "Nothing: he never offered me money, for I might have accepted it." "Señor Capitan," said he, turning impatiently to his companion, and pointing a trembling finger at me, "put this *añariù*, this son of the fiend, in the *potro;* crush him at once; he is misleading us with lies."

I protested earnestly that I had told the truth, and whilst talking was racking my wits for some plan by which I might reconcile my admission of guilt with the statement I had made, that I had never been one of the conspirators, my great dread being that they should demand evidence against the Ballesteros, Lasserres, and others—my personal friends many of them, others known only to me by name—who had been arrested some months before, but might be still in existence; and I would have died under the torture rather than have done so. I rapidly arranged a plan which served my purpose, and enabled me to put on one side many perilous questions. Thus: I had had many disputes with Mr. Washburn on political and literary subjects; he, a democrat of ultra red-republican principles, and extremely liable to forget, in the heat of argument, the amenities of civilized society, and detesting England most heartily, was not very likely to agree with me on these points; and we had many wordy differences. I magnified these into quarrels; and put it to them, as reasonable men, if it were likely that a person who regarded me as an enemy, and who only retained me in the house because he needed my professional services, would place his life in my hands by confiding such a secret fully to my keeping? and, told them that, in my opinion, I had only received the partial initiation which constituted my guilt, because he feared that I should by some accident discover what was going on, and in revenge denounce him. Whereas, by telling me part of the plans he would secure my silence as an accomplice, and moreover make it a point of honour with me to guard a secret which had been so generously confided to me by a man who hated and had ill-treated me. My story, plausible enough in itself, had just enough truth in it to make them readily receive it.

Falcòn listened to this with every sign of approval; and as it was now nearly midnight he told me I could lie down on the sand and sleep, a little way from the hut, whilst my evidence was clean copied. I could not sleep, and lay in the dark, for the night was stormy, and black clouds swept across the angry sky, revolving the trying events of the day. More than an hour passed; I was then recalled, and my "first deposition" read over to and signed by me. As I was leaving the hut the old captain gave me half a loaf of *chipa*, for which I warmly thanked him; and he promised that on the morrow my heavy fetters should be exchanged for lighter ones. The soldiers were awakened, and I was marched back to the *guardia;* my feet were firmly tied to a hide rope. I wrapped my poncho, a thick railway-rug, around me, and was soon soundly sleeping.

When I awoke in the morning I found I was wet through, and lying in a pool of water (heavy rain had fallen, and the wind was bitterly cold), and that it is indeed true that misfortune makes us acquainted with strange bed-fellows. On one side of me was bound Don Antonio de las Carreras still sleeping, and the corpse of Lieut.-Colonel Campos on the other. The latter had died unheeded and untended during the night, and lay there staring blankly with open eyes at the rising sun.

About seven o'clock in the morning the end of the hide rope was untied, the sleepers awakened by a shower of blows, and we in turn freed ourselves from the knotted loops round our ankles. The corpse was thrown into a hide, and dragged away; the officer in command of the guard remarking, " What, only one this morning!" and thrown into the river. We were then placed about ten feet apart, and I was warned not to speak to my companions; so I sat down in the driest spot I could find within my limits, and looked wearily around me. What a scene of misery!

Within a space on the gently sloping hill-side, which had been roughly cleared from brushwood, and about a hundred feet square, lay forty prisoners; and on all sides, as far as I could see, were similar enclosures tenanted in the same way. The nearest was somewhat luxurious, for each prisoner had a little straw kennel to lie down in; and there I saw Don Venancio, the President's eldest brother, and Captain Fidanza, an old friend of Mr. Washburn's; the rest were officers, some of high rank. I have said that Dr. Carreras lay next to me during the night: I was removed some distance from him in the morning; but he had time to whisper, "Has Mr. Washburn gone ?" " Yes." He was about to ask other questions when a sentry noticed us, and growled, " Hold your tongue." He was a pitiable object ; indeed, so changed that I could scarcely recognize him. Emaciated, travel and blood-stained, he was but a shadow of his former self, and for two months he had been lying, as I saw him, in the open air, with no shelter from sun or rain but a blanket. He had rolled this up for a seat, and was furtively trying to question me by the motion of his lips. His hands were covered with dirty rags; he unrolled them, and showed me his mutilated fingers, a sickening sight; but the greater part of the day he sat motionless, with sunken eyes bent on the ground, and his scanty grey hair blowing unheeded over his face. His servant, poor Baltazar, in the farthest corner, had thrown himself face downwards on the earth, and lay there, refusing all food, until he died a few days afterwards.

The only other man I knew in our sad company was Mr. Taylor, the master-builder; he was not in irons, but looked sadly ill and worn. He was with a group of Italians, as I judged from their accent, who were somewhat privileged; they had made a little tent by stretching a sheet over four sticks about two feet high driven into the ground, and were allowed to talk together; they had some yerba, and now were boiling water in a tin pot over a fire in their midst, for they, with the exception of one of their number, who seemed to be sick, had crept from under their scanty covering, and sat in a circle outside; for want of a *mate*, the tea was brewed in a cow's horn, and sucked in turn through a tin *bombilla*. Taylor looked at me, and raised his hands with a gesture of commiseration, but did not dare to give any other sign of recognition. In the centre of the prison encampment, or guardia, as the natives termed it, was a row of priests, I think eight in number; they were all in irons, and must have been recently brought in, for their long cloth cloaks were little worn: then some prisoners of war—there was a major and three captains amongst them, as I learnt when our names were called over; they were not fettered, but were in the last stage of misery, almost, some quite, naked, covered with wounds, and the majority too feeble to walk; and lastly, a group of felons, distinguished by a single iron ring on the right ankle; these looked scarcely human, were without a rag of clothing, and generally lay together in a huddled heap on the ground. From the latter classes a certain number was selected every day to sweep out the guardia, and bring wood and water for themselves and the rest; blows, kicks, and the vilest abuse being showered upon them by the soldiers at every step.

In our rear was the kitchen; that is, a large iron pot set over a fire in the open air; there a stalwart negro, assisted by several prisoners, prepared the food for all the guardias around, and little enough it was; a small allowance of boiled meat and broth in the morning, and at night a handful of parched maize and the bones and scraps left by the soldiers. I saw Carreras, once the most influential man in Uruguay, an ex-prime minister, eagerly gnawing the gristle from a few well-picked bones contemptuously thrown him by a passer-by. Can I give a more vivid picture of our miserable condition? The meat, when cooked, was put into little wooden troughs, and then distributed amongst the prisoners. They were arranged in groups of five, and a trough placed in their midst; some had horn spoons, others pieces of orange peel or broken gourds, and with these they drank the broth, and then divided the meat and bones. The horn spoons were coveted treasures, I found; and when a prisoner died who had had one, there used to be a furious contention amongst the survivors for its possession, often leading to a severe thrashing administered indiscriminately to all within reach. As I had only just been sent there, nothing was given to me until late, when the negro cook came by with a piece of roast meat he was eating, and gave me part of it. This was the third day I had fasted, but for the *chipa* I had had the night before; but I had no wish to eat. I only begged for water, and that they would not give me.

In the afternoon I was again called before the fiscales, and my examination continued, this time conducted by Father Romàn himself. The same old story was gone over; I repeated every conversation I could remember of Mr. Washburn's, in which Lopez was abused or laughed at, keeping always in view the tale I had told the day before, and declaring, whenever the subject was mentioned, that I knew nothing whatever of the conspiracy, but that it had existed, and the few particulars I could glean from the depositions of Bèrges and Carreras. Padre Romàn was more easily satisfied than I had expected, and dismissed me about eight o'clock at night. I was taken a short distance to another hut, where I found Major Aveiro (a negro) and Lieut. Levalle, a Paraguayan, who had been educated in England, and spoke English and French very fairly. They had learnt, from Mr. Bliss, that I had written home by Mr. Washburn; but he told them that the letter was to my mother, saying nothing about the other one to *The Times*. I, by a fortunate coincidence, said the same ; for I should have had little chance of saving my life if the latter had been known to exist. I was now ordered to write another letter, which Aveiro dictated in Spanish—my version was, of course, in English—in which I was made to say that I was guilty of the crime of conspiring against Lopez, that I had freely and voluntarily confessed it and the guilt of Mr. Washburn, and had thrown myself upon the mercy of the President, who would, I hoped, spare my life. This was most carefully examined by Levalle, word by word, and explained to Aveiro and another officer who was present. One phrase puzzled them : I had written, " Mr. Washburn conspired against H. E. the President and the Government of Paraguay." Aveiro said, " But his Excellency *is* the Government—there can be no other ruler here ;" utterly unable to conceive the idea of a constitutional administration. Father Romàn came in afterwards, and I reminded him of the promise that my fetters should be exchanged. He told me that on the morrow it should be done, and that I should have better food and treatment ; I expect, in consequence of a letter which Mr. Washburn had sent to Lopez, in which he protested against the outrage of detaining forcibly two members of his *suite*, reminding him that seizing us in the street in his presence was as great an insult to the American flag as if we had been taken in the Legation itself, and that the Government of his country would certainly avenge it. Mr. Bliss was then brought in, and he was asked if his former statement about the letter was true ; he replied ; " Yes ;" and to prevent any dangerous cross-examination I told him rapidly what I had said and written. I was further ordered to write another letter, to the fiscàles themselves, which was dictated to me by Romàn. In it I humbly asked permission to write the letter " as a relief to my burdened conscience, and to further the ends of justice" !

I afterwards found that Mr. Bliss had already written a long letter to Mr. Washburn, in which he says : " Finding myself at length released from the restraint which your Excellency has so long exercised over my will, I cannot do less than confess freely and spontaneously the important part Y. E. has taken in the revolution, in which you have involved many persons, and among them myself. I have declared (feeling deeply, because I would like to avoid such a scandal to Y. E., but following out the truth) that your Excellency has been the soul of the revolution ; and if this deed now appears in the light of heaven, confessed to by all its accomplices, to whom does it owe its existence, save to Y. E., who has continued its direction up to a very recent period? I consider myself therefore completely absolved from the promise which Y. E. extorted from me yesterday, in your office, not to reveal your proceedings, old or new." This is continued for some time, and ends, after asking him to send back his letters : " The truth having been fully displayed, these letters cannot serve your Excellency for any object, and since they are false, it suits me no longer to keep the mystery of hypocrisy," etc. . . . " I advise you as a friend not to attempt to fight against the evidence given by infinite witnesses."

Except in saying that I believed in the existence of a plot, that Mr. Washburn was the chief of it, and that I had been invited to join it, the whole of my evidence was perfectly true. For, fortunately for me, Mr. Washburn had been so hearty in his detestation and abuse of Lopez, in which I thoroughly agreed with him, and had expressed his feelings so incautiously, that I had no difficulty in satisfying the 'fiscàles (within the limits my primary story prescribed), and without even betraying a confidence, since Mr. Washburn had given me express permission to say anything I liked against him.

To return to my narrative : the next morning my irons were exchanged for lighter ones, and we each received a little cake of cassava meal, and boiled meat, which was afterwards continued twice a day.

When it arrived I noticed one trait in the character of Dr. Carreras I liked very much. It is the custom in South America for slaves to bear the same surnames as their masters, and when the *comandanté* said that he had orders to give Carreras better food, the doctor cried eagerly, " There are two of that name here; there is the other," pointing to his dying servant, "surely we are both to have it."

That day and the succeeding were most wretched ones for us; the rain fell in torrents, and we had to sit or lie literally in a pool of water. But I soon found that even sitting unsheltered in a drenching rain was preferable to exposure to the burning sun, which I afterwards endured hour after hour, prone on the cracked and scorched ground. The thirst I suffered the deepest draught could not have assuaged, much less the two hornfuls of water a day, all they gave us. If I, with a thick blanket to shelter my head, felt the torrid sun so much, what must the many naked captives beside me have suffered?

Some of them were natives, some Brazilian negroes; they could bear it without much inconvenience; but the majority were foreigners, and it was pitiable to see the expression of mute agony their faces bore, and the frantic eagerness with which they drained the horn, when at length it came round, to the last drop of the muddy, tepid water. The prisoners of war and the felons were better off than the rest in this respect; they went twice a day to the pits into which the surface water drained, and served as wells; they could there drink their fill, and bring back as much as their vessels would hold. Some had horns or tin pots, others gourds or pieces of hide formed into a bag. One happy man—for, with my parched throat, I looked upon his treasure with bitter envy—had a Wellington boot in place of a pitcher. He was a Brazilian major—a ragged, dusty scarecrow; but as he passed, bearing carefully, by a stick inserted through the straps, that dripping bootful of dirty water, he was looked upon with angry, blood-shot eyes, fierce in their expression of intense longing to change places with him. For how selfish, how brutally callous, we all became in our misery! how enviously we gazed at a man less heavily ironed than ourselves, and almost cursed the poor wretch who had crept into the shade of a bush on the edge of the clearing! One day, as the long straggling line returned from the pits, an Italian, his eyes glazed with fever, rose on his elbow as he heard the clink of the tins, and in feeble tones begged but for a drop of water, groping blindly for a steadying hand the while; the man he asked, himself tottering on the verge of the grave, repulsed him with a muttered imprecation, and the poor wretch fell back, half turned, and died. Thus day by day were our ranks thinned; by twos and threes they passed away and were at rest. Did I pity them? Ah, no! I would then have welcomed death with a sense of as glad relief as a tired child seeks its mother's arms.

About a week afterwards I was removed a few yards to the rear with Dr. Carreras, and we each crept beneath a little hut of reeds about three feet high. Mine had been built over a bed of wild pine-apple, which, with reckless carelessness, or perhaps intentionally, had been left *in situ*. How thankful I felt for the shade! and even for the occupation the uprooting of the *caraguatá* gave me; I set to work with a pointed stick to dig down to the tough roots, but my hour's labour was scarcely finished when the order came to march. We were turned out into the sun, and had to wait for some time, for we were at the head of the sad procession and the hundreds of prisoners; and the lines of the guard and men carrying the cooking pots and troughs were marshalled with difficulty, blows and curses being showered mercilessly on the sick and loiterers.

From one of the hovels near me crept out on all-fours Don Benigno Lopez, the President's youngest brother; he was well dressed, but heavily ironed; and from another, a spectral old man I was long in recognizing as the ex-minister for foreign affairs, Don José Bèrges. He was leaning feebly on a hedge-stake, and was followed by his successor, Don Gumisindo Benitez, bareheaded and with naked fettered feet. Then two very old men, evidently in their second childhood; they were without a rag to cover them; one was in irons, and could only crawl tremblingly on his hands and knees; the other looked round with a timid smile on his silly face, pleased with the bustle around him, and evidently but faintly conscious of what was going on. Can any stronger proof be asked of the ferocious cruelty of Lopez ?   Great-grandfathers in irons !   Men who had long since ceased to be responsible beings, who were no more to be feared than newly-born children, who were indeed in their life's revolution returning to helpless infancy ; such poor, shuddering, creaking wrecks of mortality to pass the remnant of their days as prisoners !   And what would their offence be ? A wailing complaint for the loss of their few comforts, a passionate lament for the death of their sons or grandchildren ; an idle word spoken in garrulous old age, and construed into treason, or perhaps simply the fact of their relationship to some poor wretch who had died in the rack or on the scaffold.

At length we set off in an easterly direction, skirting the base of the hills, through a narrow defile, and then into a pathless wood.   In the former we got into some confusion ; the prisoners were huddled together and separated a little from the soldiers who, with fixed bayonets or drawn swords, were guarding them. It was an opportunity I had long been waiting for ; for some minutes I was at the side of Dr. Carreras ; he asked me again, in an eager whisper, if Mr. Washburn had gone.   "Yes, he is safe," I replied in the same cautious tone, and then went on to ask him if there were any truth in his depositions.   "*No, no— lies, all lies, from beginning to end !*"   "Why did you tell them ?" I asked somewhat unnecessarily.   "That terrible Father Maiz," said he, " tortured me in the *uruguayana* on three successive days, and then smashed my fingers with a mallet."   He looked at me with an expression of utter wretchedness on his worn face, and held out his maimed hands as a testimony. Then after a pause he asked me, "Have you confessed ?" " Yes," I answered, sadly.   " You have done well ; they would have compelled you to do so : God help us !"   I told him about a difficulty I had had in not being able to say how much money Mr. Washburn was said to have received from the Brazilians, although the sum had been mentioned several times in the " depositions," and asked how much I should say.   "Fifteen thousand ounces, I told him," he replied ; " lies, false, false !" Rodriguez he had not seen for many weeks, and believed he was dead. He asked me then about the fate of his servant, who had attended him since he was a child; he had disappeared two days before, dead without doubt.

In the forest a wide clearing was soon made, for it was principally of young timber, the blackened stumps still remaining showing how the old trees had been destroyed: it was too great a mercy to expect any shade to be left for us; in fact, the clearing was so wide that the heat was as great as on the hill-side. The two old men being found too feeble to walk were each put in a hide, and carried with a pole by two soldiers; they were tumbled out on the ground when we halted, close to me, yet thanked their bearers with "God reward you, my sons, God reward you!" But the next day they were denied this favour, and were thrashed most horribly by the corporals to make them go faster; it was heart-rending to hear them, in weak treble tones, praying for mercy, and to see them arrive an hour after the rest,* covered with dust and blood; for they had crawled on their hands and knees nearly a mile. Several women were brought in that day, all but one strangers to me, but evidently belonging to the better class of natives; two or three had the little huts I have mentioned, others had formed a screen of a shawl or two strained over a few sticks; and I saw one poor girl, about sixteen years of age, crouched under a hide propped against her shoulders; she never moved save to turn her screen as the sun wested, and sat with her eyes bent to the earth, and tears often stealing silently down her cheeks. One night the soldiers told them to sing; they murmured faintly a "tristè," one of those melancholy love songs the Paraguayans are so fond of. As I listened to its wailing tones, scarcely louder than the night breeze, I thought I had never heard so piteously sad a strain.

Soon after our arrival there, Don Benigno, Bèrges, and Carreras were sent away, and I was put apart from the rest, and received better food than they; in fact, if I had only had shelter from the sun and enough water I could have patiently

---

* Our camp had been shifted further into the wood.

waited for the end—whether death, to which I had been condemned, or liberation. My sufferings from thirst were intense: my lips were cracked, and my tongue as dry and leathery as one in typhus fever ; and, to make the cruelty the worse, a spring ran close to us. All day long, whenever an officer passed, a feeble cry of " Agua, señor, por el amor de Dios, un poco de agua ! " (A little water, sir, for God's sake !) came in humble, supplicating tones from the parched throats around me. At the word, the sleepers, who, as I often did, were dreaming of cool streams and dripping fountains, would start up eagerly, thinking the time for the water-jar to go round had come, and then with a groan sink on the ground again in bitter disappointment. Yet five minutes of time, and but trifling labour, would have given us the boon we begged so vainly.

I remained there four days ; and one afternoon, as I was viewing the shocking spectacle of a prisoner being tortured in our midst, a guard came and took Mr. Bliss and myself away with them, I fully expected, to be shot, but it was to rejoin our late companions. They were located in a rocky cleft in the hills, far from the others. I found there Leite-Pereira, Captain Fidanza, Bèrges, Don Benigno, and Don Venancio Lopez—the latter a colonel and the President's eldest brother,—Benitez, and Carreras, each in a hovel apart. We were placed with them, with some boughs of trees as a temporary shelter, and, better than all, the sergeant brought me a large gourd full of clear cold water ; but we had scarcely rested when the order came to march once more. Without a thought of complaint, I got up from the ground, tied a leather thong to the bar of my fetters, and set out. We walked in line about half a mile, then were halted, and by a mounted officer, who arrived at that moment, sent back again to the huts. After a delay of ten minutes we started once more, at, I should think, five o'clock in the evening. Our way was for some distance by a narrow deep path over the sandy hills, so narrow that my *grillos* were often fixed across it, and it was difficult to free them without falling in the effort to extricate myself. We marched or shuffled slowly in single file, with a soldier between every two prisoners, and the colonel at our head. He walked with an angry, impatient expression of face, frequently looking back at his brother, who, heavily ironed, could move but slowly. In front of me was Carreras, also fettered, and so feeble that he threw himself on the ground in utter exhaustion whenever we stopped to rest. The guns of the enemy were thundering away quite close to us, and I several times heard the sharp report of exploding shells; in fact, the sudden advance of the Brazilians had caused our removal. How delighted we should have been had they appeared in front of us! although I have little doubt that such an event would have led to our instant execution; indeed, I have since learnt that it was a favourite trick of Lopez's to send a group of prisoners, against whom nothing had been proved, to the front, and then express his regret that an unexpected movement of the Allies had compelled him to order them to be shot, to prevent them falling into their hands. Several prominent men were murdered in this way.

After journeying about two hours we joined the great body of the prisoners, extending in a vast crowd over the dusty plains. "Here comes another drove of beasts!" shouted the soldiers, as we came up; and, in fact, most of the captives looked scarcely human. It is said they were then six hundred in number; but I think there must have been very many, perhaps twice as many, more. Men, women, and children, in three divisions, were hemmed in by soldiers on foot and on horseback, fully armed and with sticks in their hands, with which they thrashed those outside and those that fell from exhaustion; whilst the officers, with drawn swords, rode amongst them, dealing out blows right and left in wanton cruelty. The spectacle was rather one which Dante might imagine as a scene in the lower Inferno than an episode of modern times, and witnessed by me, a living man.

When first caught sight of we were on a hill, they in the plain beneath; little could be seen clearly; there was a dense cloud of dust, and a heaving tumultuous throng, swaying from side to side, and slowly creeping towards the hills in the distance. The red rays of the setting sun flashed now and then from whirling sword blades within it, and more constantly from the line of bayonets without; small groups were detached in the rear, from which the horrible din, in the distance a confused roar, swelled loudest; heavy blows, dull thuds, or quick incisive lashes resounded on all sides, with an incessant clanking of fetters, groans, shouts, cries, and curses; it reminded me of the close of a battle, when there were but the helpless fugitives to slaughter. The savage passions of our own guards seemed to be aroused by the sight: they urged us on faster, no longer allowing us to rest, and poor Carreras was beaten several times with the flat of the sword for falling as he staggered along.

Mrs. Lynch passed soon after, in a carriage and pair; she bowed with a gracious smile; we took off our caps to her, all well knowing that a word from her could send us to the scaffold, or worse, on the morrow. I have since learnt that she took every opportunity of talking about the conspiracy, and abusing Mr. Washburn and his friends to Lopez, incessantly harping upon his generosity as a ruler, and their base ingratitude. " Oh, how your Excellency has sacrificed yourself for the sake of your country !" she would say to the fat, drunken sensualist after dinner; " and these wicked men have conspired against you ! Es muy tristè, señor—Oh, very sad indeed !" Not, I believe, from any desire to destroy us, but simply for her own safety's sake. She could be sure that a man who had imprisoned his brothers, flogged his sisters, shot their husbands, and threatened his mother, would scarcely respect any other tie.

Before night the crowd being entangled in a narrow defile, we overtook it, and the scene was horrible beyond description. The poor fellows had not rested as we had done on the way, and were more exhausted by starvation, and fell at every step; crowded together, they were half choked by heat and dust, and their bleeding limbs showed how fearfully they had been goaded on their way. Close to me I saw a tall, thin old man, a well-dressed foreigner, stumble and fall; in a few moments he was stripped, and two corporals were thrashing him mercilessly; he staggered to his feet, and blindly hurried forward as fast as his fetters would permit, and again fell; the same dreadful scene was repeated, and an officer, after striking him several times with a sword, stamped on his head till his white hair was dabbled in blood. An empty bullock-cart passed at this moment; he was taken up insensible, and thrown like a log into it. I prayed then, I hope still, that consciousness never returned to him.

I met with but one mishap—falling into a hole, and only received a few blows, to encourage me, as I scrambled out. When we reached the open country once more we turned from the road, and in almost total darkness made our way through the dried-up marshes. The ground was covered with hummocks of tall coarse grass as thick as reeds, with a narrow tortuous path between. The natives found their way easily enough, for they have a most cat-like clearness of vision at night, but we foreigners got on very badly; the hummocks were too high to step over, even if we had been unfettered, and too dense to force one's way through. I kept close to the soldier in front of me, and did pretty well; but Carreras, with his usual ill luck, stumbled through or over the mounds every minute, and cut his face and hands badly, till at last the officer, tired of thrashing him, told two of the men to seize his arms, and they dragged him by main force for the rest of the way. How long we were scrambling through it I cannot tell, nor how far we travelled— not more than four miles, I should think; but it was late at night ere we halted. I was completely worn out, and almost breathless with the exertion I had made; water was, however, near at hand—we each took a deep draught; stakes were driven into the ground, the hide ropes stretched, and we were secured as usual, but before they had finished tying me down I was sound asleep.

I thought we should have continued our journey on the morrow, imagining that the cordillera of Paraguari, which we saw in the purple distance, was our destination ; but this was to be my last encamping ground, and the grave of all, save two, of my companions.

We were in a district called Pikysyri, close to the spot where Lopez was routed three months afterwards. It was, as I have said, a dried-up *estero*, not a very pleasant place, as the heavy rains, we might expect soon, would speedily convert the whole into a swamp again. The next day the wind charged to the south, and we had a furious "pampero," which smothered us in dust, and made us shiver with cold, and at night the rain came down in torrents. I lay awake, for my ankles were badly cut, and had swollen to such an extent that the fetters hurt me too much for rest. I was under the lee of a tall hummock, and protected from the cutting wind, but was, of course, soon wet through. It was a wretched sensation to lie on the ground firmly tied—I could only half turn over under ordinary circumstances, but now the pain was too great to think of moving my tumid ankles—and feel the rain beating down, and, worse than all, the cold water slowly stealing higher and higher up my back, and to know that it had to be endured for fourteen hours in that one position, and perhaps as many more, huddled under a saturated blanket. Every afternoon at four o'clock those detestable hide ropes were sent to the pit, from which our drinking water was drawn, to be soaked, in order to make them tolerably pliable ; then one end was tied to a stake firmly driven into the ground, and, a series of loops being formed, the ankles of those not in irons were slipped through them and firmly secured by a knot above the loop, and drawn tight by the whole force of two men. If the knot should slip, as it often did, the pain it occasioned was excruciating. Those in irons were better off at night, for the rope was fastened around the ends of the bar, and they could turn from side to side. In addition to this precaution, which one would have thought sufficient, the sentries were doubled at sunset.

In two or three days they had built us kennels of the old pattern, not high enough to sit in ; but as I got nearly half as much as I could have eaten, had shelter from the sun, but not from the rain, which came through as through a sieve, could I only have escaped fresh examinations, I should have looked upon myself, all things considered, as a very lucky fellow; and, in fact, they did leave me to myself for so long that I began to hope that I was forgotten. My companions were less fortunate; every day, and sometimes twice or thrice a day, were they marched off beyond a grove of orange trees (the very name of that tree has become hateful to me, and I have not tasted one of the fruit since I left Paraguay; whenever I see it a smell as of blood fills my nostrils), and did not return for hours, and then looking jaded and more sorrowful than ever.

On the 23rd of September Don Benigno Lopez was put to the torture; he had been taken away early in the morning, and did not return till after noon, when he shuffled slowly into his hut, which nearly faced mine, and shortly afterwards an officer, with three men carrying the well-remembered bundle of muskets and cords, came up. Don Benigno turned pale, and rose tremblingly as they came near him, thinking probably of his brother-in-law, Don Saturnino Bedoya, who died under its infliction some months before, and followed them, at a signal from the officer, behind a copse of trees near at hand. About an hour passed away, several officers, including Major Aveiro, went to see him, and at length he was led back, unable to stand, and with his face frightfully distorted by the agony he had suffered.

I lay awake all that night, wondering what could have been their motive, when he had already made such a full confession, and thinking that perhaps I should have to undergo that terrible ordeal again. To my horror, the next afternoon I was sent for by Father Roman. I found him installed in a comfortable rancho behind the orange trees; he was writing as I entered, and as for some time he went on with it, taking no apparent notice of me, I had an opportunity of studying his appearance at leisure, and I am not likely to forget it. He was, as an army chaplain, dressed in lieutenant's uniform, and wore a sword; all that pointed out his clerical character being a small red cross on his left breast, and the little stubbly tonsure on his crown. He would have made an admirable study for Torquemada. A stout, handsome figure and of commanding height, but with a cruel, sensual face, and a merciless, thin-lipped mouth.

At length he pushed his papers from him, and stared at me as I stood holding up my fetters with one hand and my hat in the other. " Well, how do you feel ? " said he. " I am ill and weak." " Bah ! It is your conscience which troubles you. Confess your crimes, confess what that beast Washburn did. Look," said he, pointing to a group of soldiers outside ; " I have the *uru-guayana* ready for you, and you will be shot afterwards." I told him I had nothing new to confess, he could not extort anything more. " Well," said he, " I give you one more chance ; tell me now all you have told, and then make an end of the story." I went over it, dwelling especially upon my quarrels with Mr. Washburn, and the consequent improbability that I could know much of his secrets, and pleading that never imagining the plot would be discovered I had not noted, nor tried to remember, any particulars concerning it. " But you must have had many conversations with him on the subject." " Scarcely any ; he did not trust me ; and guilty men do not like to speak of their evil deeds." He saw that I was only fencing with him, and got out of all patience, and told me that Bliss, who, it seems, was confessing and denouncing vigorously, had already filled many sheets of closely written foolscap with his revelations, and that if I did not imitate him, the *potro* (the rack) should make me regret my obstinate reticence.

Whilst he was talking, another native, habited like himself, came in ; a fine, tall, soldierly looking fellow, about thirty years of age, with an extremely good head and handsome features. I did not notice the little red cross, and had no idea at the time that he was a priest. He sat watching me without speaking till Romàn had concluded, and then said, " Why, Mastermàn " (as the natives always accented my name), " your hair is quite grey although you are much younger than I ; how is that ? " " Señor," I replied, " I was eleven months in prison ; it is

not my age which makes me grey." "Eleven months! that
is a trifle; I was a prisoner more than three years." "Indeed! I am sorry for you; what is your name?" Or,
in the formal Spanish, "What is the grace of your worship?" He laughed, and said he would not tell me then; but
later I found to my surprise that he was "the terrible Father
Maiz" of Carreras. I had expected to see a very different man.

They consulted together in an undertone for some time, and then
Padre Maiz went to a hut a little way off, and soon returned,
bringing Mr. Bliss with him. I had not till then pictured to
myself how miserable my own appearance must have been; but
the most abject wretch I had ever imagined was exceeded in the
reality by him as he approached; any manliness he had ever
possessed seemed to have been completely crushed out of him;
and, dirty and famished, ragged and untrimmed as I was, I
shrank from contact with him.

I was directed to tell him what I had confessed. I did so,
and he fully confirmed all I had said about my differences with
Mr. Washburn, and then—as he told me afterwards, to let me
know how I could best please my interrogators—went on to tell
some scandalous stories of the minister. I hastily interrupted
him, and begged the *fiscales* not to go into such matters. They
told me to make myself easy, that they were fully known, and
had been placed upon record by Bliss and other witnesses.

When he had gone, Father Romàn settled himself luxuriously
in his chair, and, with eager eyes and pendent lip, prepared to
listen to the tales he had heard, and yet of which he would have
enjoyed the repetition so much. I had infinite pleasure in disappointing him, and with passionate earnestness urged reasons
touching his national pride so closely, and especially appealed so
successfully to that of Father Maiz, that they let me go, and I
returned with a thankful heart to my wretched hut in the *estero*.

As soon as I reached Pikysỳrì I had made myself a calendar
with rings of grass, adding one link to the brittle chain every
morning, and a larger one on Sundays, I had previously kept
mental count of the day of the month and week, but I found I

was forgetting ; so I asked a good-natured sergeant one day to adjust my reckoning, and then commenced my mensual chains, which took the place of the short and long scratches with which I used to record the flight of time on the walls of my former dungeon.

On the 27th of September a guard, with fixed bayonets, led off Dr. Carreras and Don Gumisindo Benitez to the little copse where Don Benigno had been taken four days before; a couple of priests and some men with spades went with them. I prayed that they might soon be despatched, and their sorrows be ended, but I now know that a more terrible fate was in store for them; they were inhumanly tortured for a long time before their execution. I waited with feverish anxiety for the end; but it was late ere a volley of musquetry and a thin cloud of smoke rising over the bushes told that all was over, and that "the wicked had ceased from troubling, and the weary were at rest."

Dr. Don Antonio de las Carreras was a man of capacity and attainments superior to the generality of his countrymen, of polished manners and extensive reading, a scholar and a gentleman. For a time he had wielded immense power—it was said cruelly; but the severity with which he put down the revolution in Saltos was, I believe, justifiable; in fact, the want of similar firmness has been the strongest incentive to revolt in his own and the neighbouring unhappy republics, and has made them the scenes of perpetual anarchy and bloodshed. He was foully murdered in the country where he had hoped to find a safe asylum, and by the very man who ought to have been his staunchest friend, in whose defence he had perilled his own life, and forfeited reputation, wealth, and position.

Don Gumisindo Benitez was but an average Paraguayan, one who could make a sounding speech and write as he was bidden. He lost his life by over zeal : trying to encompass Mr. Washburn in the net of lies he was weaving, he fell blindly into the very pit to which he would have dragged him. Seeking by letter, and afterwards by a personal appeal, to induce him to avow his guiltiness of a crime which had never been committed, telling him that he might thus extricate himself from his dangerous position by the certain destruction of the rest, he used the unfortunate phrase, "All is discovered! you must confess," when Lopez had *not* discovered all he professed it was necessary he should know. He therefore came to the conclusion that Benitez must be himself a conspirator, since he spoke of a perfect knowledge which the fiscàles disclaimed.* He was at once arrested and put to the torture, told the same story of falsehood and infamy about which he had written so glibly, and, after infinite suffering, died a shameful death.

* This information was given me incidentally by Lieut. Levalle. The mention of this officer's name reminds me that he was a good illustration of the uncivilizable nature of the Indio-Spaniards. He had been sent to England when quite a youth, and to a school in Richmond (Dr. Kenny's), where he remained for some years, and learnt to speak English pretty well, and French very much better, but he acquired little else ; especially I noticed that he had been quite unable to get over the arithmetical difficulties which beset his race, he could not manage the simplest sum in compound multiplication. The great advancement of England, the convenience of our homes, the comforts of our social life, our streets and buildings, seem to have made no impression on him.

He was fond of talking with me, and I tried to learn what effect European life had had upon him; but a feeling of bitter resentment against his schoolfellows who had teazed him at Richmond—and that I learnt more from the angry fire which burnt in his eyes and swarthy cheeks when he spoke of it, than from anything he said—seemed to be his chief reminiscence.

CHAPTER XIX.

THE next day a great many prisoners were shot, close to where I was lying; they were principally native officers, the late occupants of the second guardia. All the afternoon the butchery went on ; some forty or fifty must have fallen. At one time the firing was so heavy that a sentry near me asked the sergeant if the "cambàs" (the Brazilians) were upon them. "No," said he, carelessly ; "they are only shooting *presos*." Day after day the same atrocities were committed. A clattering of irons would be heard in the distance, a ragged, wild-eyed wretch would shuffle by, and often did not return—why, a spluttering volley told.

Sometimes, however, it was but a visit of greater or less duration to the rancho behind the orange trees. There one or other of my companions went every day ; lean, haggard Don José Bèrges and Don Benigno most frequently. One day I saw the former kneeling in the mud at the feet of Major Caminos ; a drizzling rain was falling, and there was the ex-minister, who had held that post for more than twelve years, and had been sent on a special mission to England and the United States—in his feeble old age, his thin grey hair falling wet and tangled on his shoulders, with clasped and trembling hands imploring mercy from a brutal soldier, who but two years before would have crouched bareheaded in his presence. But Lopez hated and, I think, feared him ; for when his own election was talked of, the people whispered, and in no very cautious tones, that Don José would be the man of their choice, if they could but have one; and he was watched and suspected from the very beginning of the war.

The month of September passed away, and the succeeding one, with little change. The weather became hotter; but I no longer suffered from thirst; for a kind-hearted *comandante* had given me a *cantarillo*, a little two-necked earthen bottle, holding about a quart, which was filled every morning; and my greatest daily anxiety was lest it should be broken when sent to be re-charged from the skin of muddy water brought for our use. I used to keep a number of pieces of charcoal in it, which improved its flavour wonderfully; I saved them from the live coals they brought me to light my cigars; for I then enjoyed the rare luxury of smoking. One evening an officer came round with a number of little boxes, containing gifts from Madame Lynch, to be divided amongst those mentioned in a list he held in his hand, from which I learnt, by the way, that Major Manlove was still living. I received some cigars, sugar, yerba, and a bottle of rum; and, after living upon scanty meals of boiled meat, often without salt, for two months, it may be imagined with what satisfaction I discussed them. I had often watched with hungry envy the many "encomiendas" (gifts of eatables, etc.) the two brothers of the President received, and longed to share them, especially the bread, which arrived new nearly every morning from their mother's house; only a man who has lived on meat alone for weeks, and very little of that, can know how delicious bread or biscuit is.

My examinations were resumed at intervals; sometimes I was sent for in the middle of the night, or at early dawn, and kept for eight or ten hours under interrogation. I often wonder now how I managed to talk so much and tell so little, and am not at all surprised that Father Román was always threatening to shoot me or send me to the *potro*—his patience was tried to the uttermost. But I believe that I had a secret friend in Father Maiz; he was always eager for information, and used to have long conversations with me on subjects as far as possible removed from the conspiracy, to the great disgust of his irascible colleague. I also offered to make a minute plan of the Legation from memory, and intentionally spoilt two I drew; but Romàn punished me for that, by keeping me up the whole of one night to replace them; my object being to escape the searching cross-examinations I dreaded, for one single slip would have been fatal to me, by proving that I was not so guilty as I pretended to be. One day I hesitated at calling myself *reo confesado* (a confessed criminal); Romàn pounced upon me instantly. "What! are not you a criminal? Must I send you to the rack to confess over again? That beast (Washburn) is not a conspirator either, I suppose?" I protested that he had mistaken me, that I was the guiltiest of men. "Ah," rejoined he, "you will find that out when you are sent to be shot." Which was consolatory.

One afternoon I saw them about to put a foreigner in the *uruguayana.* I only saw his face for a moment; he was deathly pale, and was holding out his hands as if praying for mercy. I have not been able to ascertain who it was, but I am certain it was not a Paraguayan.

Just in the rear of my hut the two sisters of Lopez, Doña Inocencia de Barrios and Doña Rafaela de Bedoya, were imprisoned, each in a covered bullock-cart, or *carreta,* about seven feet long, four wide, and five high. They remained, poor ladies, shut up in these moveable prisons for more than five months; I often saw them wheeled past on their way to the *fiscales:* the front and the windows had been blocked up, and the door behind was secured with a padlock; but an opening had been made in front, about six inches high, through which I suppose their food, etc., would be handed into them. Many times I heard young children crying there, but I do not know if they were theirs. The sufferings they endured almost exceed belief. About December, 1867, their husbands incurred the displeasure of Lopez, it is said, because the speeches they made on the occasion of the presentation of the sword of honour were not sufficiently . "patriotic," and they were detained, and their families ordered down to San Fernando. Early in the succeeding year they were put under arrest. Don Saturnino Bedoya was at first charged with having robbed the Treasury (he was Tesorero-General), and afterwards with complicity in the pretended plot; he protested his innocence, but was put to the torture, which was applied so severely that they dislocated his spine, and he died in intense agony. General Barrios, in order to escape so terrible a fate, tried to commit suicide by cutting his throat, but the wound, although deep, was not sufficiently so to prove fatal; it was dressed, and the day afterwards he was shot. His wife and her sister were taken from their prison, and they were compelled to witness his execution. They, very naturally, poor women, in their grief and despair, expressed their detestation of the barbarous and unnatural cruelty of their ferocious brother; this was reported to him, and he ordered them to be flogged in a manner outraging decency and all feelings of humanity, which was at once carried out. Not content with this, he sent them back to their prisons, and forced them by threats of worse treatment to depose falsely against their murdered husbands; and in December, 1868, he compelled his mother to leave her house at La Trinidad, where she had remained virtually a prisoner for nearly two years, and go to Luquè, the temporary capital, and there, before the altar of the church, swear that she recognized Francisco Solano alone as her child, and cursed the rest as rebels and traitors. She piteously pleaded her advanced age (she is over seventy) and disease of the heart as excuses for not complying; but the officer charged to see that her son's orders were carried out told her she must obey or die, and she went. I think the whole sad history of human crime cannot show one record exceeding this in heartless cruelty. A widowed mother, who had seen her youngest son and her two sons-in-law executed as criminals; of her remaining sons, one a prisoner, and the other loathed and cursed by thousands as a very fiend incarnate; her daughters outraged and caged like wild beasts; and she, in her helpless old age, compelled on pain of death to mumble imprecations on the dead and living of those dearest to her, and at the command, too, of her eldest born, the child she had once so tenderly nourished. Better that she had died then, but better, a thousand times, that he had never been born.

About the middle of November the chancellor of the French consulate, Mons. de Libertad, arrived in Pikysỹrỳ. Before I was arrested the consul told me that he had been charged as an accomplice; but I scarcely thought that Lopez would have ventured on such a step, but the fact that he did so proved how reckless he had become. He looked weary and frightened when he arrived at the encampment, and ate scarcely anything for several days. He was put in the hut next to mine, was not in irons, but was tied in the stocks *(cepo de lazo)* every night like the rest of us; the two brothers of Lopez alone escaped this. He was examined several times, and at great length, always returning with the haggard look of a man who had been almost harassed to death. He had been very intimate with Don Benigno, and from that and his official position his evidence was regarded as of great value, as a means of blinding the people of Paraguay and the outside world to the utter lawlessness of these proceedings. But they got, I believe, very little out of him, until at last Mr. Bliss (who by this time had become a great pet of Father Roman's) was sent for to tell him what he should say. Mons. de Libertad naturally revolted from the idea of telling such baseless lies, and at last, in sheer desperation, said, "Tell me what you want me to depose, and I will say it." Mr. Bliss is my informant, and he told me with great glee of the wretched falsehoods he made him swear to at last; of the meetings the conspirators had had in the house of Don José Bèrges, their plans, the very documents they drew up, and the names of the committee, of which Bliss himself was secretary! I believe I am right in saying that the latter had not even entered the house of Don José, and, of course, the minister had never condescended to any intimacy with such a man. However, Mons. de Libertad was more fortunate than the rest of us; for the French minister in Buenos Ayres sent up a gunboat to look after the consul as soon as Mr. Washburn notified him of the dangerous position in which he was placed; and on its arrival M. de Libertad was sent on board as a prisoner. I am informed that he has since been dismissed from the diplomatic service; not, however, because it was believed that a conspiracy existed in which he had taken part, but because he had not supported in a becoming manner the dignity of his office. He used, I know, to talk very imprudently with Don Benigno of the sufferings of the people, and the uselessness, indeed, folly, of continuing a hopeless struggle; but as to these complaints, opinions, and lamentations taking the form of a conspiracy, I do not believe it for a moment. I was never intimate with him, nor with Don Benigno, but I was with several of the others, said to be their accomplices; and I am perfectly sure that if anything of the kind had been set on foot I should have known of it. The admission of Carreras, however, is conclusive on this point; and the earnestness with which he whispered the words, "Lies, all lies, from beginning to end," carried full conviction with them. I cannot doubt their perfect innocence.

One day, about this time, the fiscàles sent for me, and Father Romàn favoured me with a long exhortation, to the effect that I ought not to feel the slightest gratitude to Mr. Washburn for obtaining my release in 1867, and that no motives of friendship should deter me from telling all the truth about him, and so on. He continued for some time in this strain, and then informed me that Mr. Bliss was writing a history of the conspiracy, and asked me if I would do the same. Of course I said yes; and he told me that if my performance were satisfactory, *perhaps* my life would be spared; for although they believed my statement that I had not joined the conspiracy, still the knowledge of its existence, which I had "confessed," was itself punishable by death, and I had, as I knew, been left for execution.

Under these inspiriting influences I commenced writing my first work. My hut was raised and enlarged to enable me to sit upon the ground, and I was furnished with a box as a table; two sheets of paper at a time, an ink bottle and a pen, which were all taken away before sunset, lest I should attempt any surreptitious writing. I set to work with pleasure; for I hoped to put into the mouth of Mr. Washburn opinions and remarks I dared not write as from myself, and thus open the eyes of the people to the true state of affairs; but at the same time I determined to say nothing about the plot. I commenced with a description, in a few words, of the prosperity and happiness of the country when I first reached it; then I repeated many conversations I had had with Washburn, in which he spoke of Lopez as a cruel, avaricious tyrant, and an incompetent general; of the folly and hopelessness of struggling against the Allies, whose strength and resources I exaggerated; the certainty that the Government of the United States would resent the insult offered to Mr. Washburn, and the immense power he would wield as soon as he reached Washington. In order to conceal my real object, the whole was interspersed with ridicule of him and his friends the "macacos" and "cambàs" (the baboons and "niggers" of Brazil), and laudation so fulsome of Lopez, that he would indeed be a blind man who did not see through it directly. I did not say one word about the plot; but a paragraph, of a few lines only, was inserted by Father Roman, stating that Washburn was the chief of the conspirators, and that I had been invited to join them by Carreras. The whole formed a pamphlet of about a dozen octavo pages.*

They were very dissatisfied with my performance, and told me that I had shown so little zeal that I should probably be shot after all; and no wonder, when it was compared with that of Mr. Bliss, who actually wrote a book of 323 pages, a copy of which is now *lying* before me, in a double sense. It contains a pretended life of Mr. Washburn, who is accused of every species of rascality, from stealing spoons at school, to an intention to assassinate Lopez himself; with a full account of the plot, the plans of the conspirators, and the form of government they intended to introduce. Mons. Laurent-Cochelet, the late French

---

* I believe, however, it was not printed, for I have never heard of a copy of it having been seen.

consul, a man most highly and deservedly respected, figures as
one of their agents, and the evidence against the rest of the
" traitors " is completed in every respect. I had wondered why
my companions were so frequently sent for by the fiscàles ; but
I found afterwards that they were re-examined, and forced to
swear to the truth of all the stories forged by him. I had a narrow
escape myself; one day I was sent for in a great hurry, and told
that I had once attended a meeting, in the house of Bliss, of a
revolutionary committee, and I was required to state what had
occurred on that occasion. The names of those present were
read over ; but nearly all were strange to me, and I could swear
most positively that I had never met them, and knew nothing
about them. Fortunately for me, Captain Falcòn was the
examiner, and he was convinced by my earnestness that I was
speaking the truth ; had it been Romàn, I should have been put
to the torture without doubt.

I had been a prisoner about eleven weeks when, early one
morning, the colonel was removed to a better hut, and his place
was occupied by the most deplorable object I had ever seen in
human shape ; two soldiers came staggering along, bearing in a
hide suspended from a bamboo a man, nearly naked, and with
his head resting on his knees ; I should have thought him dead
but for the groan he uttered as they threw their burden on the
ground. I saw his haggard face for a moment as they dragged
him along to the hut, but did not recognize him ; his huge joints
showed that he had once been a tall, stout man, but he was now
so emaciated that the sharp bony ridges seemed cutting through
the skin, and he remained doubled up as when I first caught
sight of him ; yet, helpless cripple as he was, he wore double
irons. During the siesta a good-natured sergeant, who often
came to speak to me when the officer was asleep, crept into my
hut, and I asked him who the new arrival was. " Col. Alèn,"
said he ; " poor fellow, they have so crushed him in the *uruguayana* that he will never stand again." This officer had been
private secretary to Lopez before the war, and afterwards had
command at Humaità. He was then a fine, handsome fellow,

with frank and jovial manners; and I well remember seeing him one day leading a band of music, accompanied by a crowd of dancing women, around the camp, and bringing them up to "*saludar*" Dr. Rhind and myself, and making a speech in our honour. He was accused of treason after the fall of Humaitâ, arrested, flogged, tortured most inhumanly, and afterwards shot.

Later, a scheme for justifying their treatment of me was arranged by the fiscáles. They stated that I had never been pardoned for my former offence, and I had only been conditionally liberated. I might attend Mrs. Washburn; but I could not practise medicine; I had, however, done so, and gone to La Trinidad *without leave*, therefore I had been again arrested. They told me that Mr. Washburn had lied to me in saying that the Vice-President had ordered the pickets to let me pass. (I not only know that the permission was given, but also that Col. Don Venancio Lopez, the President's brother, himself came to tell Mr. Washburn that I could go whenever I pleased!) I was glad to hear this story; for it proved that some stir was being made about me; and, in truth, the news that an American gunboat was on its way had set their ingenuity to work.

On the morning of the 3rd of December I was sent for, and found Father Maiz seated alone under a tree; the soldiers who guarded me were sent to a little distance, and he gave me a long lecture on the subject of consistency, that I must always tell the same story as that which I had told them, in all places and under all circumstances, and that it was my duty to denounce Mr. Washburn as a conspirator all over the world. I could scarcely conceal my joy, for I knew that help had come; but I replied, submissively, that what was written was written; that which I had said I could never unsay. He smiled approvingly; for anything in the shape of an aphorism delighted him greatly. He went on to tell me that a new minister had arrived from the United States, and that the President had commuted my sentence of death to banishment for life, and he trusted that I would employ the rest of my days in praising the clemency of the Marshal,

and denouncing the wickedness of Washburn. I promised that
I would make the truth fully known : and now I am fulfilling
that promise. A blacksmith was called, the rivets were cut off,
and my irons fell clanking to the ground ; but even then I
could scarcely believe in my good fortune. I had so long lived
in hourly expectation of death, that I could not be sure that
Padre Maiz was not mocking me when he said that in a few
days I should leave the country. However, I thanked him unaffectedly for the kindness he had shown me, and for the good
news he gave me ; but he said that my thanks were due to the
President, and that I ought to write a letter to his Excellency,
expressing my gratitude. I excused myself, saying that he
could express it verbally so much better than I could in my
imperfect Spanish ; so I would leave it in his hands. A smile
flitted across his grave face as he told me I could return to my
hut ; I suspect he had made a shrewd guess as to what was
passing in my mind at the moment.

It was with a strange sense of relief and exultation I walked
quickly back to the *guardia ;* as I passed my companions in misfortune, they turned towards me weary, listless faces, mutely
asking what the change might mean ; for themselves, they had
lost all hope, and death was the only release they looked for ;
and for all, save two of them, it came within a fortnight of that
day.

In the evening an officer brought me some tea, biscuit, and
cigars, and, better than all, some coarse but clean linen. Two
days afterwards I was again ordered to go to the hut of the
judges. On my way I met Father Maiz, who repeated the sub-
stance of what he had told me before, and reminded me that
my life depended on my discretion. He told me, also, that two
American officers were then waiting to hear me declare that my
written statements were true, and that I must satisfy them that
such was the case. I bitterly felt the false position in which I
was placed, but I never for a moment doubted that they were
aware of my innocence, and would therefore take all I said at
its true value.

As I neared their quarters I saw at a glance that some pains had been taken to improve the outward state of affairs. The old crumbling rancho had been furbished up, the ground around it neatly swept, not a trace was to be seen of chains or thongs, and the sandy soil showed no evidence of the blood which had been spilt around it; whilst the grove of orange trees, and the thick undergrowth beneath them, did not allow a glimpse of the prisoners to be seen. Near the door was a table, with a bottle of rum and some glasses; beside it stood Lieutenant Kirkland, and within the cottage sat Captain Ramsay, both of the United States navy.

As I approached, Mr. Bliss crept slowly out, bowing profoundly, and smiling deprecatively to Father Maiz, who hastily told the soldiers to take him away; and I can almost excuse the treatment I received from his countrymen when I recall his air and figure.*

In passing Captain Ramsay I whispered to him, "I hoped to have been spared this degradation; but don't judge me now." I dared not say more; for Levallè and another Paraguayan, who also spoke French and English, immediately followed me. Seated within the room I found Father Romàn, another priest as secretary, and Major Aveiro. My depositions were read over in Spanish, the two Americans understanding that language, and at the end of each sheet I was asked, "*Està conforme, y es esta la firma de usted?*" (Is this correct, and is that your signature?) I replied, of course, in the affirmative. When the one was read in which I was made to say that I was guilty, and that I knew that a conspiracy existed, Captain Ramsay asked me, with a perplexed air, "But is this really true?" I hesitated, and for a moment was inclined to risk all, and say boldly, "No, utterly false;" but, thinking that in a few hours I could

---

* Lopez sent him a free pardon, and told him that, in consideration of his earnest repentance, and the zeal he had shown in atoning for his crimes, he might keep the 15,000 dollars which he swore he had received from the Brazilians, and transmitted to Buenos Ayres by the hands of Mr. Washburn; and he trusted, he added, he would make good use of the money! We often hear of one being paid in his own coin, but we rarely see it done so literally.

set myself right, and that it would be the height of folly to peril my life in mere bravado, I replied, in English, "I beg you will ask me no questions." "What does he say?" asked Father Romàn, suspiciously, in Guaranì; and Levallè translated my answer to him. He paused a few moments, and then, rising, requested the officers to take a glass of rum with him. They went out together, but he returned immediately, and asked, whilst an angry frown darkened his face, "Why do you not wish to be asked any questions?" I told him that I was ill and weak—truly enough, and that I was anxious to return to my hut, which satisfied him, but at the same time showed in what jeopardy a single incautious word of mine might place me.

The two officers were on the most friendly terms with the Paraguayans, and intensely enjoyed their abuse of Mr. Washburn. They had breakfasted with Lopez and Madame Lynch, and seemed to have been fully persuaded that I was really as criminal as I appeared to be. The advocacy of the cause of Lopez by their late minister had excited such indignation in Buenos Ayres, that I can scarcely wonder that they were prepared to believe any charges made against him, and if he were guilty of conspiracy, they would assume that I was also.

I was sent back to my hut when they left, and passed a wretched night; for the *comandantè*, desirous that I should appreciate liberty when I obtained it, tied me so tightly with the leather thongs that I could not sleep for an instant through the pain they inflicted. Five days passed away. I came to the conclusion that I had been deceived, after all, and that my unwilling corroboration of the so-called depositions would be made a pretext for detaining me, and that, as an Englishman, I could not expect that, after I had been abandoned by my own Government, Americans would trouble themselves about me. But the delay was caused by Admiral Davis falling into the same unfortunate error as our own officers had done. Misled by his prejudices against Mr. Washburn, and allowing them to be strengthened by the specious cunning of Lopez and his mistress, he departed from his instructions, and tried diplomacy—

without success; the odds against him had decided before the game began; so he consented to receive us as prisoners, that we should be so treated during the voyage, and that we should be sent to Washington for trial. Even this did not satisfy Lopez, or rather he dreaded the disclosures we should inevitably make, so he tried to keep us after all; and it was only when the admiral threatened to fire on the batteries that he would let us go. Of course, I knew nothing about this till afterwards; and every day seemed longer and more hopeless than the last; but on the evening of the 10th of December, three months to a day after my arrest, I was sent for for the last time. I had been two hours in the *cepo*, and bound with such cruel severity that I could scarcely stand when they loosened the thongs.

At the old place I was met by Father Maiz; he shook me warmly by the hand, brought me out a chair, and, in a cautious tone, congratulated me on my escape. His colleague sat within the rancho, examining a pile of freshly-printed papers, and favoured me only with a jealous scowl as I passed; I think he must have felt as a hungry spider would which had seen a fly escape, after being half entangled in his web. I joyfully divided the residue of my cigars and biscuit amongst the men who were guarding me, and begged the good-natured sergeant to let Colonel Alen have my water-jar; he was delighted also, and promised to give it to him. But I had still long to wait, for Lopez was unwilling that any of the troops should see us going away, and it was quite dark when we started; and we were mounted on such wretched horses that it was past midnight ere we reached Angustura, where the gunboat was lying.

The officer in command of our party was very anxious to enter into conversation with me, and his voice sounded strangely familiar, but it was so dark that I could not distinguish his features; I found afterwards that he was Don Eduardo Aramburu, an old friend of mine. On the way I had ample proof how carefully the approaches to the camp were guarded, and how impossible escape would have been; every ten minutes or so we were stopped in silence by levelled muskets; sometimes there would be a dozen men, at others two or three only, lying down in the long grass, and so completely hidden that they seemed to spring from the earth at our horses' feet. The road over the swampy moorland was detestable, so that we could only move at a foot pace, every now and then we plunged into the reedy pools, and it was with the utmost difficulty that the starving brutes we were mounted on struggled through them. I was glad enough when at length we reached the batteries, and could see the bright light of the steamers reflected in trembling lines far up the river. We dismounted, Don Eduardo shook hands with me, and, as the bank was steep and slippery and I was too weak to walk more than a few paces, he lifted me in his strong arms into the canoe, whispering in my ear, " Oh, my friend, how I envy you! " and soon the paddles, aided by the strong current, brought us alongside the " Wasp."

I had expected the same warm welcome as I should have received on board an English vessel under the same circumstances, but Kirkland, the commander, called the master-at-arms and said, " Take these men forward, and put a sentry over them." I was thunderstruck. Mr. Bliss was fawning, as usual, hat in hand ; I told him angrily to put it on, and said, " You surely will not send us forward ? Mr. Bliss is the son of a Baptist minister, and I have held the rank of lieutenant in Her Majesty's service, and here for several years. When you saw us last we were treated as criminals, I hope you do not consider us so." He replied, " I receive you as criminals and shall treat you as criminals till you are proved to be innocent." Admiral Davis expressed to me afterwards his regret at the unworthy treatment I had received, which was, he assured me, contrary to his express orders ; and when I afterwards found that Kirkland had treated Mrs. Washburn with the grossest rudeness in his own ship, only because he had quarrelled with her husband, I ceased to feel surprised at his brutality to me.

I passed the greater part of the night comparing notes with Mr. Bliss, and was intensely disgusted with the statements he told me he had made ; I could have excused him readily enough for some of the things he had said, had he not exulted at the mischief he had done ; but he told me gleefully how he had completed the evidence in every particular against the prisoners who had not yet been executed, and was absolutely proud of the infamous part he had played. For the rest of the voyage I kept out of his way as much as possible.

We lay off Angustura for three days for the purpose of landing General McMahon the new American Minister, and his baggage, and then steamed down the river. We passed the ruins of Humaitá on the afternoon of the 15th ; it had been crumbled almost to the earth ; the only conspicuous object was a mound of rubbish crowned by the tottering remains of the twin towers, showing here and there traces of colour and ornament, which marked the site of the church. The quarters of Lopez had entirely disappeared, and the greater part of the low barrack sheds also ; as for the batteries, I tried in vain to find an embrasure or a parapet which would tell me where they had been. A little to the south of the old *place d'armes* a mushroom village of suttlers' wooden huts had sprung up, reminding me strongly of the Crimea ; the shanties of wood and canvas were almost the same, and bore the well remembered signs, "Hôtel de France" and "Café d'Alliance" painted in great sprawling letters across the front, or fluttering on the tattered flags above them. But the trim order in which Humaitá had been kept under the old *régime* had been forgotten, and a dirtier or more disreputable-looking place it was impossible to imagine. The river was crowded with shipping ; I counted more than fifty vessels flying the Brazilian flag between Humaitá and Tres Bocas.

As soon as we anchored off Monte Video we were transferred to the flag-ship "Guerrière," and as I was still kept under surveillance, although not under arrest, I wrote, on the 26th of December, under flying seal, to Her Majesty's Chargé d'Affaires there, describing the indignities to which I was exposed, and begging him to interfere. He replied that as I had, he understood, claimed the protection of the United States, he could not do so ; but he advised me to apply personally to Admiral Davis.

I did so, and had a most satisfactory interview with him. He professed ignorance of the fact that I had been treated as a prisoner on board his vessel, but said that he had promised Lopez that I should not be allowed to communicate with the shore in Brazilian waters ; he explained to me all he had done, and appeared not a little astonished at the information I gave him concerning affairs in Paraguay. I offered my parole, which he at once accepted ; he desired the officers to treat me as his guest, and all restrictions on my movements were removed.

We lay off Monte Video for a week, and then left for Rio Janeiro. The day after our arrival there the British Minister, Mr. Buckley Mathew, came off; I was presented by the Admiral, and had long and interesting conversation with him ; he had heard of the treatment I received from Kirkland, and expected I should have complained of it to him, indeed he privately blamed me in that I had not done so ; but after the frank explanation and expressions of regret of the Admiral, and taking into consideration that he had saved my life, I felt it would be ungenerous to enter into the question, and therefore said nothing about it.

On the 25th of January I was transferred to the "Mississippi" mail-steamer, and left for New York. On my way I had the pleasure of catching a glimpse—it was little more—of the scenery of the Amazon, for we went up as far as Mariñon to embark a few passengers and some tons of India-rubber. We reached our destination without any incident worth notice ; and I at once reported my arrival to Mr. Seward, who replied as follows :—

DEPARTMENT OF STATE.
Washington, Feb. 24th, 1869.

Sir,—

I have received your letter of the 21st instant, reporting your arrival at New York, in obedience to the orders of Rear-Admiral Davis, South Atlantic Squadron.

In reply I have to inform you that the Executive Government of the United States does not claim any jurisdiction over you on account of the orders referred to, especially as it is understood that you are not only a British subject, but also an officer now, or lately were so, in the Paraguayan service.

This Department, however, would be gratified to receive from you, in writing, or orally, any statement which you may think proper to make in regard to the interesting proceedings in Paraguay with which your name has recently been connected.

I am, sir, your obedient servant,

(Signed) WILLIAM H. SEWARD.

To Mr. G. F. Masterman,
     Late Assistant-Surgeon, Paraguayan Service.

I accordingly went on to Washington, had the pleasure of half-an-hour's conversation with Mr. Seward, and gave all the information which I imagined would interest him; then returning to New York, I at once left for England.

I may mention, by the way, that in the latter city I went through the curious process called "interviewing." A reporter from the *Tribune* called upon me, and politely begged that I would furnish him verbally with full particulars of my life in Paraguay. I felt strongly tempted to laugh several times during the interview, knowing the use which would be made of it, but a deep sense of how much I owed to the Americans kept my risible muscles in order. The next day three columns of the *Tribune* were devoted to a full report of my conversation, remarks, personal appearance, and so on.

CHAPTER XIX.

MR. TAYLOR AND CAPTAIN SAGUIER'S NARRATIVES.

THROUGH the courtesy of Mr. Russell Shaw, C.E., I am enabled
to give the following narrative of the sufferings of one of my
fellow-prisoners, written by that gentleman from the dictation of
Alonzo Taylor himself, shortly after his release and arrival in
Asuncion. He says :—

"My name is Alonzo Taylor. I was born in Chelsea, and I
am a stonemason and builder by trade.

"In November, 1858, I made an engagement, through Messrs.
Blyth, of Limehouse, to serve Lopez in Paraguay, for a period
of three years, and teach the natives my business.

"I am a married man, but I thought I would go alone, and see
what the country was like. In 1861 my wife and my children
came out to me, and we lived in a house near the Aduana. To
our parlour I built a fireplace and a chimney, the first made in
the country.

"I got good pay and not too much to do, and the President (he
was only General then) treated me very kindly, so I made a new
contract soon after my wife came out, for four years more.

" The war with Brazil and the Argentine Confederation commenced in 1865 ; but it made little difference to me, except that
the paper money was depreciated, and, therefore, we got less
pay. So, when my contract was finished, I asked the Government to let me make a new one ; but they said at the Ministerio

that they were too busy to attend to such matters, but that if we worked as usual we should be liberally treated. I heard no more of the matter till December, 1867, when Major Fernandez, the chief clerk in the War Office, told me that if we liked, we—that is, the Arsenal men—could make new engagements, and might state our wishes.

"About this time I returned to Asuncion from the interior, where I had been building furnaces for distilling sulphur, on a plan I arranged with Mr. Masterman for making powder.

"Although I was disgusted, by this time, with the war, and the change in the country consequent thereon, still I did not see my way clear, or how I was to get my wife and children out of the country; for Lopez never gave us the option of leaving : so I made a contract for another year. Many Englishmen in the employment of the Government refused to make fresh contracts, and I wish I had acted in the same manner.

"During my stay in Paraguay I attended to the practical carrying on of many works, such as the mould-loft, the new foundry, and fixing machinery in the Arsenal; railway stations and bridges, the new mole, and President Lopez's fine new palace. A grand palace it is—all of stone and solid brickwork, not of mud bricks, as they generally use there ; but he never occupied it, and I hope never will. I used also to draw the pay of some of my countrymen when they were away, and keep it for them; and I looked after the widows and poor little orphan children. We had plenty of them ; for many of our men drank themselves to death.

"I say all this to explain why I went to Paraguay, and why I remained there ; and now I will tell of my sufferings during five months' cruel captivity. But being more accustomed to work with chisel and trowel, and with compass and drawing pen, I scarcely know how to describe in adequate language the horrors I have witnessed ; so I will confine myself to the exact truth as a plain man ; but I wish I could picture these scenes as some could do it, that their full agony and misery could be brought before the reader, and that he could fancy he heard, as I do even now, the shrieks and groans of the poor helpless creatures being tortured to death.

"This was how it commenced. On the 21st of July, 1868, after working hard at the soap works at Luquè, I returned to my house at ten o'clock at night. Shortly afterwards a cavalry soldier knocked, and told me through the door that I was ordered into the capital by the Minister of War and Marine, but he could not tell me why. But I knew that it was useless to resist; so I mounted my horse, and went with the soldier, who, when we passed the Ministerio, told me that he had orders to conduct me to the captain of the port; so we rode on to the river bank, where I found a crowd of men. I dismounted, and was immediately, despite my remonstrances, put in irons, and placed with eight or nine other prisoners until the morning, and then we were put on board the "Salto de Guayrà" steamer. Mrs. Lynch and her eldest son, Francisco, came on board with some officers about eleven, before we started down the river. As she left the steamer, Mrs. Lynch looked, but she took no apparent notice of me, although she used to be very kind to me, and my daughter was often in her house. I had asked an officer who was on board, and used to be very intimate with me, if he would let me speak to her; but he said that being a prisoner I could speak to no one, much less to her. He abused me, and seemed to delight in my misfortune.

"At this time President Lopez had his head-quarters on the Tebicuari, a large river which runs into the Paraguay. We got there about four o'clock in the morning, disembarked, and had to march to the camp, a distance of six miles, in irons, and it was then our sufferings commenced. Our party consisted of an old man named Sortera (he was very ill, and was not in irons, because he was unable to walk; he was the father of the 2do captain of the port); two Orientàles, six Italians, a Corrientino, three Spaniards, one Paraguayan, and myself; eleven in all. With the exception of two, all wore one set of irons, and some two—thick bars and rings, weighing from twenty to thirty pounds. A six-mile walk in Paraguay at any time would try a good pedestrian; but with heavy fetters on both ankles, in which one could only slowly shuffle along, it was dreadful work. Besides that, we had to carry two of our sick companions, old Sortera and an Italian. They were put in hammocks, and carried slung on a pole. We had a strong guard with us, and they accelerated our march by an unsparing use of the point of the bayonet, and flogged those who lagged behind with thongs of raw hide.

"Poor old Sortero got by far the worst of it, for he was almost imbecile; and, in addition to constant complaints of his hard fate in being, at his advanced age, treated so cruelly, he used very bad language, and they thrashed him without mercy to keep him quiet.

"That dreadful journey made a stronger impression on me than anything I suffered afterwards; for it was all new to me, and I was in robust health. Afterwards, when I was reduced in health and strength, I became stolid and listless, and suffered much less, both morally and physically.

"After hours of incessant toil we arrived at San Fernando, a place never to be forgotten in the history of Paraguay; for it was there that nearly all the victims of Lopez perished, and under tortures, too, inflicted with fiendish ingenuity.

"Daily I saw men tortured in the *cepo de uruguayana*, of which more hereafter; others and women flogged, many of them to death, or shot or bayonetted in the most cruel way, during the months of July, August, and September; all of them charged with treason and rebellion, but quite innocent of those crimes. More than seven hundred of them were slaughtered altogether.

"On arriving there I saw Mr. Stark, a kind old gentleman and a British merchant. He had resided in Asuncion many years, and was greatly esteemed and respected. He looked very ill and dejected. I was not allowed to speak to him, but I saw him flogged, and often treated very brutally in other ways. He was shot, with a batch of other prisoners, about the beginning of September. John Watts, another Englishman, who was chief engineer to one of the gunboats, and Manlove, an

American, were shot on the same day. To the best of my knowledge, only two Englishmen were shot by Lopez ; the other died from starvation and exposure, as did one of my companions the day after our arrival. Poor Mr. Neuman was flogged horribly ; his cries could be heard all over the encampment, and he expired undér the lash.

"Old Sortera held out through months of starvation and suffering, but died eventually at Villeta, of ague.

"At San Fernando were hundreds of other prisoners in the same deplorable condition as ourselves ; but as we were not allowed to speak to each other, we could not compare notes, and it was only after my release that I learnt that they were all charged with treason.

"Our so-called prison was only a piece of ground about twenty yards square, staked out, and with the sky for a roof. The mode of securing us was equally simple, but dreadfully painful. To one of the stakes a hide rope was made fast ; prisoner No. 1 lay down on his back, and loops were knotted fast round both ankles ; then No. 2 lay down two yards off, and was tied to the same rope. This was repeated until the row was full ; then another was commenced in the same way, and so on. The ends of the ropes were secured to other stakes, and they were stretched by the full strength of two or three men, until they were as taut as harp strings. We suffered terribly ; my ankles were soon covered with sores, and almost dislocated by the strain on them. In each prison space lay about fifty men. This mode of securing prisoners is called " *el cepo de lazo*," or rope stocks. Thus we lay night and day, with the exception of a short time in the morning, when we were marched into the woods under a strong guard. Sometimes those who tied us up were more merciful than others, and did not strain the rope so tight ; but frequently the agony was dreadful beyond expression.

"A chain of sentries surrounded us, who used to kick and thrash us as they pleased. They had orders to shoot or bayonet any who tried to escape. A request but for a little water was often answered by a severe flogging.

" There we lay exposed to the burning sun, to the rain and storm, and almost maddened by the biting and crawling of the thousand insect plagues of the tropics, with very little food, and that only the offal of the beasts killed for the troops. We got no salt and no tobacco, the latter was the greatest privation of all.

" Of the prisoners, many were taken out to be examined or tortured, others to be shot. I seldom saw anyone undergo the torture; for it was inflicted behind the bushes, or in the huts of the judges.

" I saw an Argentine officer taken away one day, and when he returned the whole of his body was raw. The next morning, when we were loosened, I pointed to his back, but did not speak; he let his head fall on his breast, and with a stick wrote in the sand 100. From that I gathered he had received a hundred lashes with a cow hide, or else with one of the creeping plants (I think they call them lianas) which grew in plenty on the trees around us. That afternoon he was sent for again, and when he came back he wrote 200. The next day he was shot.

" The prisoners were of all nationalities, and of all grades and positions ; but with the heat, wear and tear, the rain and wind, they were soon all alike, nearly naked. And our guards used to offer us pieces of bread, or a few spikes of maize for our clothes : and, suffering from hunger as we did, we were glad to purchase a day's life at the price of a coat or a shirt. Amongst them were many women, some of them belonging to the best families in the country ; some quite old and grey-headed, others young and pretty, especially Dolores Recaldè, a tall and beautiful girl, and Josefa Requelmè, a handsome woman, with very fine eyes. They suffered much, poor creatures, though they had little Λ-shaped straw huts to shelter them (as did some few of the other prisoners of the highest class) and used to weep piteously over their miserable fate.

" Before giving an account of the examination and torture I was subjected to, besides that I daily suffered in the *cepo de lazo*, I must go back to a circumstance which occurred some time before, and which, as will appear in the account of the interrogatories, gave me the clue to the cause of my arrest.

"Two or three years before, an Italian, named Tubo, arrived in Asuncion, and opened a school; he was an agreeable and plausible man, but I did not like him. However, I sent one of my boys to his school for a short time. Signor Tubo made this a pretext for occasionally borrowing money of me. Subsequently I received a message from him, requesting my attendance at a meeting at his house with the object of initiating me into the mysteries of freemasonry.

"Having heard that it was a good thing to become a mason, especially if abroad, and also out of curiosity to know their secrets, I went, but found it was only a miserable attempt to extort money. All I got was a little apron, a sight of some pretended cabalistic characters, with which the room was adorned by the mountebank Tubo, and a lot of mystical rubbish I could not understand. I said nothing the whole time I was there, and left as soon as I could, taking the little apron with me, that I might have something for my money, though it was too small to be of any use to me.

"The next day I wrote to Mr. Watts, one of the steamboat engineers, about it, and he replied that it was all nonsense, and no freemasonry at all; upon which I told Tubo that I would have nothing more to do with him.

"Whether the freemasonry was connected with the so-called conspiracy or not, I cannot say. For my part, I do not believe that there was any conspiracy at all, unless on the part of the President himself and some of his tools, to rob foreigners of their money.

"But to return to San Fernando. One day, when I was tied up as usual, I saw Major Serrano go past; so I called out to him, for I used to know him very well, and take *maté* with him nearly every day, 'Major Serrano, do you know Thompson?' (Mr. Thompson was a civil engineer who took military service under Lopez, and distinguished himself very much, afterwards being made a Lieut.-Colonel.) Serrano replied, 'He has no power here.' This was said politely, but in a tone which showed that I could expect no kind offices from him. I told him I only wanted to send for some clothes, and get something to eat.

"Serrano did not answer, but ordered the corporal of the guard to untie me, and then, taking me on one side, the following conversation took place:—

"'Do you know why you are here?' 'No, I do not, and wish I did.'

"'There are several charges against you; the first, that you are fully acquainted with the name of the proposed new president; the second, that you have received a sum of money from Captain Fidanza; and Tubo has confessed, and divulged that you are one of his accomplices.'

"I replied that the charges were all false, and that both he and Tubo knew that they were.

"Serrano went on: 'Well, I give you until to-morrow to reflect; and if you then make a clean breast of it, the President will be merciful, and your life will be spared.'

"I replied that I had nothing to confess, either the next day or at any other time, and my position and character were too high to fear accusations; my countrymen and the Government had always had confidence in me.

"Serrano said, 'Yes, you once had clean hands; but things have changed, and you have become as dirty as the rest.' He then ordered me to be tied down as before.

"The next day Serrano came again, and asked me if I had considered the matter, and if I would confess all I knew. I replied that I knew nothing, and requested that I might be confronted with my so-called accomplices.

"Serrano became furious, and at once ordered the officer of the guard to put me into the *uruguayana*. It is said this torture was invented in the days of Bolivar, the South American liberator, and hence its old name of 'Cepo Boliviano,' changed by Lopez to 'Cepo Uruguayana,' after the surrender of Estigarribia there in 1865.

"The torture is as follows, and this is how I suffered it: I sat on the ground with my knees up, my legs were first tied tightly together, and then my hands behind me, with the palms outwards. A musket was then fastened under my knees ; six more of them, tied together in a bundle, were then put on my shoulders, and they were looped together with hide ropes at one end ; they then made a running loop on the other side, from the lower musket to the other ; and two soldiers hauling on the end of it, forced my face down to my knees, and secured it so.

" The effect was as follows : First, the feet went to sleep, then a tingling commenced in the toes, gradually extending to the knees, and the same in the hands and arms, and increased until the agony was unbearable. My tongue swelled up, and I thought that my jaws would have been displaced ; I lost all feeling in one side of my face for a fortnight afterwards. The suffering was dreadful ; I should certainly have confessed if I had had anything to confess, and I have no doubt many would acknowledge or invent anything to escape bearing the horrible agony of this torment. I remained two hours as I have described, and I considered myself fortunate in escaping then ; for many were put in the *uruguayana* twice, and others six times, and with eight muskets on the nape of the neck.

" Señora Martinez was tortured six times in this horrible way, besides being flogged and beaten with sticks until she had not an inch of skin free from wounds.

" At the expiration of two hours I was released ; Serrano came to me, and asked if I would now acknowledge who was to be the new president. I was unable to speak, and he went on to say that I had only been kept in the *cepo* a short time, owing to the clemency of his Excellency Marshal Lopez, and that if I did not then divulge it I should have three sets of irons put upon me, eight muskets in place of six, and kept in much longer. I was so utterly exhausted and so faint at the time that his threats made no impression on me. Afterwards I was taken back to the guardia, and as a great favour I was not tied down that night.

" The next day, July 25th, Serrano again called me up, and

asked me who authorized me to mine the railway bridge at Ibicuỳ, a rivulet about three miles out of Asuncion. I replied that I had never heard of the bridge being mined, and that I knew nothing of such falsehoods.

"On the 26th, Serrano came again, accompanied by an officer named Aveiros. The latter asked me what masonic grade I had. I replied that I was not a mason, but that on one occasion I went to the house of an Italian named Tubo, who was endeavouring to establish a lodge on false pretences and mere moonshine.

"Aveiros said, 'Do you know that we have Tubo here?' 'No; how should I?' Serrano said, 'We will have you face to face;' and Tubo was brought to the hut. The examination was conducted by a young Paraguayan lawyer, who had been some years in England, named Centurion. He asked me, pointing to Tubo, 'Do you know that man? do you know that he hates you?' He repeated the words, 'Do you know that he hates you?' in English, as I did not understand it when said in Spanish. I said, 'I wish to explain in English, as you (Centurion) understand it perfectly.' He said, 'There is no need to grant your request, as you speak both Spanish and Guarani sufficiently well.' I said that I certainly ought to hate Tubo; for he had got a good deal of money out of me on false pretences, and had cheated me in the masonic business.

"Tubo then said that I had signed a paper consenting to form one of his masonic society. This I denied, and then Centurion asked Tubo if I had signed such a paper. Tubo hesitated, and said, 'I think he did.' Centurion said angrily, 'Your thinking is of no use; did or did not Alonzo Taylor sign the paper?'

"Tubo became more embarrassed, and could give no answer; so I told them that the whole affair was an imposition. He was dismissed, and I never saw him again, and heard that he was shot.

"After Tubo left, Centurion questioned me about my countrymen, and why some of them would not sign fresh contracts. I replied in Spanish, ' *Cada barril tiene su asiento, y cada per-*

sona conoce sus intereses,' (that is, every man knows his own interests best). Serrano and Aveiros together: 'No, no, Alonzo, that won't do. You know why they will not renew their contracts.' I replied, 'I do not, but I do know that we Englishmen are heartily tired of war, and the reason why we went to the American Legation was, because there being no English consul in Asuncion, we thought that we might get protection there until we could leave for England. My other object in going there was in order that Mrs. Taylor, who was near her confinement, might have the benefit of Mr. Masterman's assistance, as there was no other medical man in Asuncion; besides, I knew Mr. Masterman.'

"Centurion: 'Indeed! then it is your opinion that the 'niggers' will take the town, and that you may be able to serve them.'

"I replied, 'No; I have always been faithful to his Excellency, and we have all done our duty, but are sick of the war, and want to leave the country.'

"Serrano: 'You were once a good servant, Alonzo, but for some months you have behaved very badly.'

"I was then taken back to the guardia, and put in the lashings as usual, with strict orders to speak to no one.

"It is useless to attempt to describe the miseries of our daily life in San Fernando, one unvarying round of privations, fresh prisoners, punishment, and executions. Not a day passed but some of us were taken out to be beaten, tortured, or shot. The cries of those being flogged were heart-rending. Two Orientàles I saw flogged to death; and when young Capdavilla was shot, he was black and blue from head to foot from the blows inflicted on him.

"There were several ladies amongst the prisoners; they were flogged in the huts, but we could hear their cries.

"Some few of us were lucky enough to get a piece of hide to lie on at night, and make a shelter of by day. Only those who have lived in a tropical country can understand how trying it is to lie in the burning sun unsheltered.

"We had very little food, and that chiefly offal; when it rained, which it did very often, we got none whatever, and I was always hungry.

"I had managed to preserve a stump of a lead pencil, and with it I made dots in the lining of my hat to record the flight of time, and I marked the executions down in the same way, long marks for men in important positions, and shorter ones for the rest. But the lining of my hat got loose, and I lost it and the pencil, on the march from San Fernando to Lomas Valentinas, and thus perished the only memorandum I had of the number of executions. But I am sure I am below the mark in stating that three hundred and fifty prisoners were shot during our stay at San Fernando.*

"There were several guardias besides the one I was in, and there was one devoted to condemned prisoners ; it was next to mine, and I could plainly see how many were taken out for execution, and who they were. I saw Watts and Mr. Stark taken out about the end of August or beginning of September.

"The first execution I have any record of occurred on the fourth of August, when about forty-five were shot. Amongst them the two Susinis, and another Italian named Rebaudi. Those who could not walk were taken in carts, the others marched down two by two in irons. Then a volley and a few straggling shots gave us food for meditation. If the victims had good clothes on, we saw the guard and the lower grade of officers come back wearing them.

"I found the want of tobacco a great privation ; but one day I picked up a piece of clay, out of which I fashioned a pipe, which afterwards served for all hands on our way to Villeta : tobacco I used to look for, when we were set loose in the morning, by the paths and wayside. The exposure to wet we suffered, and want of food, brought on rheumatism, ague, and dysentery, of which many died ; indeed, it seems almost a miracle to me that any survived such privations.

"I cannot recollect the date when the army commenced their

* Nearly double that number really perished there.

retreat to Villeta, but it was in September; but I shall never forget what we suffered on the way.

"To give an idea of it, I should tell something about the country there. It is, like all on the western side of Paraguay nearly as far as Asuncion, very flat and marshy, covered either with impenetrable woods or immense lagoons, and everywhere intersected by rivers; it is, I should say, almost equally divided between land and water. The roads, or rather paths, are, therefore, never direct, but follow the edges of the woods, and go from one piece of high land to another, winding three or four miles to make one. The woods are so matted together by creepers that they look like scaffoldings covered with ropes, and the lagoons, when shallow, are full of a close grass, or reed, five or six feet high, and with rough saw edges which cut like a knife. In other places the palms seem to have killed all other vegetation, and extend for leagues and leagues; but it is worse walking there, for the fallen leaves and branches are covered with long sharp spines.

"Before starting our irons were taken off, but we carried them with us, and we were allowed to talk together on the march; at night we were put in the *cepo de lazo* as usual. I counted about 260 prisoners, fourteen of them foreigners, the rest Paraguayans. Amongst the former I remember

"Señor Cauturo, an Argentine and a great friend of Stark's.

"Fülger, a German watchmaker.

"Harmann, also German, and married to a Paraguayan.

"Lieut. Romero, an Argentine.

"Capt. Fidanza, Italian.

"Leite-Pereira, Portuguese.

"Segundo Bello, Argentine.

"Batolomé Quintara, ditto.

"Amongst the latter were four ladies: Doña Juliana Martinez, wife of Col. Martinez, who, after the evacuation of Humaità, surrendered to the enemy with his 500 men reduced to skeletons by fatigue and want of food.

"Doña Dolòres Recaldè.

" The Señoritas de Egusquiza, two aged spinster ladies, sisters of Egusquiza, formerly Lopez's agent in Buenos Ayres.

" Two bullock-carts were dragged with us, supposed to contain the sisters of Lopez.

" The first day we marched three leagues, and were terribly cut about by the thorns and long grass. On the evening of the second day we reached the edge of a large *estero* or shallow lake, and the guides said we ought to wait for daylight to cross it; but when the officer in command was appealed to, he said, ' Prisoners to go forward at once, their march to be accelerated by the bayonet if necessary.' Which was done, nor was the latter used sparingly. We waded in up to our middles, exhausted by our day's march, and without food; yet we had to struggle through for five weary hours as best we could, and when we reached the other side we got nothing to eat; but they let us make fires to warm ourselves, for the nights were bitterly cold.

" We finished our journey of 100 miles, in spite of the difficulties of the road and our exhausted condition, in seven days; I mean as many of us as survived. Señora Martinez walked the whole distance, although her body was covered with wounds, her face blackened and distorted, and with a raw place on the back of her neck the size of the palm of my hand; for this poor lady had been put six times in the *uruguayana*, as I have said. She was, until her arrest, most intimate with Madame Lynch; but she was then selfishly abandoned by her once affectionate friend, and left to her dreadful fate. When I first saw her she was an extremely pretty young woman, and had reached but her twenty-fourth year when executed. She often spoke to me on the march, for companionship in misfortune makes us all equal and confidential, and Doña Juliana told me all her sorrows. She was very anxious to know if a large black mark she had over one of her eyes would disappear, or if it would disfigure her for life. The latter was the case; for when I saw her led out to execution on the 16th or 17th of December, the mark was still there. Her only crime being the fact that she was the wife of a gallant officer, who had been abandoned by Lopez, and was compelled to surrender through starvation!

" We got very little food on the road ; for it was only when we had to get out of the way, to let the troops pass, that we could find time enough to cook the wretched meat they gave us.

" I well remember one awful *estero* we had to go through ; it is called the Estero Ypoa, and the bottom is of deep and stiff clay. We reached it late at night, and came out early in the morning; but not nearly all those who went in, for the weak and sickly, and the old men, could not toil through it, and were either drowned or bayonetted. I saw two old men stuck fast in the mire, and left there to die of starvation or to be devoured by the vultures, which were already flying around them.

" We arrived at Villeta early in September, and there we were placed as before in the open air and in the stocks. One day I saw Mr. Masterman brought in as a prisoner in irons, and an American named Bliss with him ; but they did not remain long in the same guardia. I did not dare to speak to him ; and I saw him one day with his face bloody, so I suppose he had been tortured.

" Only three executions took place there before December. Dr. Carreras, late prime minister in Monte Video, was the first to suffer; to this man can be traced the origin of this disastrous war (?) He was brought in a cart from San Fernando with Don Benigno Lopez, the President's youngest brother, and Leite-Pereira, the Portuguese consul. Then several priests were executed, with Cautura, and a great many officers, I should say fifty, were shot on that occasion.

" To add to our miseries, cholera broke out amongst us, and our camp was shifted about four hundred yards up the hill. Afterwards we were again removed to a greater distance.

" About the 7th of December the Paraguayans had lost, I expect, a great many men; for sixteen officers were taken from amongst the prisoners, and released. At the same time, about thirty foreigners, who had been brought from Cerro Leon, and many natives who had been imprisoned on various charges, some for three or four years, were executed. I saw them all confessed before being shot. The priests brought chairs, and the condemned knelt in front of them in turn. Amongst those shot on this occasion I saw Fülger and Gustav Harmann, Germans, and the Argentine lieutenant, Romero.

" Soon afterwards Mr. Treuenfeld, the German telegraph engineer, was brought in a prisoner. He did not seem to recognize me ; but at night we lay near each other, and he said, ' I shall have plenty to tell you about Washburn (the American minister) and the English gunboats ; but I cannot do so now, for I am not allowed to talk.'

" On the 16th or 17th of December Col. Marco, formerly chief of police, rode up to the guardia with several other officers, and he read the following names from a piece of paper :—

" ' Sosa. (A priest.)

" ' Juliana Martinez. (Poor lady ! she could scarcely stand, she was so emaciated and weak.)

" ' Dolòres Recaldè . (A tall and once a very beautiful girl.)

" ' Luisa Egusquiza. (This poor old lady must have been sixty years of age, with grey hair, and a very benign and venerable look. Her sister had already died, alone in her wretched hut.)

" ' Benigno Lopez. (Brother of the President.)

" ' José Bèrges. (Formerly Minister for Foreign Affairs.)

" ' —— Bogado. (Dean of the Cathedral of Asuncion.)

" ' Colonel Alèn. (One of the commanders of Humaità. He had lost an eye in trying to commit suicide.)

" ' Simon Fidanza. (An Italian merchant captain, who sold his ship to Lopez, and was not afterwards allowed to leave the country.)

" ' Leite-Pereira. (Portuguese consul).'

" Each answered to his or her name by walking forward and standing in front, until a line had been formed and the list gone through ; then they were marched off with a strong guard in front and rear. The sad procession was closed by three priests carrying chairs, who would confess the condemned at the place of execution. We never saw them again. At the expiration of about an hour a volley was heard, then a dropping shot, and all was over. The guard came back, one old soldier wearing Captain Fidanza's surtout, and the officer the uniform coat of Leite-Pereira, with its gilt buttons.

" Perhaps some of these men may have deserved death. Captain Fidanza was said to have denounced the rest, but that was after he had been tortured, and he soon became insane. But surely there can be no excuse for such a revolting crime as shooting defenceless and innocent women for the faults, real or pretended, of their husbands, brothers, and lovers. Whether there was a conspiracy, time will show; but if the so-called conspirators were convicted on no better evidence than that on which I was kept a prisoner for five months, they must be regarded only as victims and martyrs. The truth will out some day, and then President Lopez will take his proper place in history, as a hero or a fiend.

" On the 21st of December we were released from the stocks, as usual, at 6.30, but at once tied down again, because the Brazilians had got our range, and shell was flying over and close to us, and the Paraguayans hoped to see us thus got rid of. But I felt no fear, and was quite resigned; for the shocking misery I had suffered for five months had blunted, indeed nearly obliterated, all feelings, moral and physical.

" Four days afterwards Lopez and Mrs. Lynch rode through the guardia, with several officers, and I think she drew his attention to us. We were ordered to stand in a row, and he came up to us, and asked, ' Are you all prisoners?' We replied, ' Yes.' And then Mr. von Treuenfeld appealed to his Excellency, who asked him why he was there. Mr. Treuenfeld said he did not know, and the President told him he was at liberty, and might retire. I then approached, and said I should be very grateful for the same mercy. Lopez asked me who I was, and affected great surprise when he heard my name, and said, 'What do you do here ? You are at liberty.' Then the other prisoners, ten in number, came up and received the same answer. We remained with the officer, but without a guard, until the 27th of December, when, at five o'clock in the morning, heavy firing commenced, round shot and shell flew amongst us, and shortly afterwards we were charged by the Brazilian cavalry. I was slightly wounded by a rifle-ball in the shoulder, but succeeded in escaping to the woods, accompanied by two Argentine gentlemen. But many of the prisoners were too weak to move, and they were all killed.*

" Later in the day we fell into the hands of some Brazilian soldiers, who took us before the Marquis de Caxias. He questioned me, and then told me to go where I pleased. I said I was too weak to walk, and one of his officers, Colonel G———,† who had been a medical man, was kind enough to take care of me. I cannot express how much I owe to him.

" I was a miserable object, reduced to a skeleton, and enfeebled to the last degree. When I was at Luquè I weighed 178 pounds ; and when I went on board the gunboat ' Cracker,' only 98 pounds.

" After recruiting my strength for four days at Lomas, I left on horseback for Asuncion. I suffered terribly on the road ; for I had scarcely any flesh on my bones, and had not strength enough to keep myself in the saddle.

" There I arrived at last, but so ill that I could not speak for some days ; but another Brazilian officer was very kind to me, and also Major Fitzmaurice, an English officer in the Argentine service.

" The next day I went on board the ' Cracker,' where I was most kindly received by Commander Hawksworth Fowke, and found myself at last, thank God ! safe under the British flag. Everybody on board did all they could for me ; but it was some days before I could speak plainly, and could only lie huddled up on the deck.

---

* Only five escaped, Mr. Taylor wrote subsequently.

† The name of this officer is unfortunately illegible.—G. F. M.

" My wife and children I have not yet seen ; but the French consul told me that they were in the cordilleras, alive and well. I am daily getting stronger and gaining flesh, but I look like a man just recovering from yellow fever ; and as I dictate this to Mr. Shaw, my memory sometimes seems to leave me ; I cannot fix my attention ; but I hope I shall soon recover my health, both of mind and body.

" Asuncion, *Jan.* 20*th*, 1869. "

At the end of this painful narrative Mr. Taylor gives an anxious account of the money entrusted to his care by his fellow-workmen, all of which was, of course, lost.

The following narrative appeared in " La Nacion Argentina," a newspaper published in Buenos Ayres, on January 15, 1869. I knew the author of it, Captain Saguier, very well, and as one of my fellow-sufferers, his testimony is most interesting to me, especially as it also confirms many of my own statements.

I saw a very bad translation of it in an English newspaper shortly after my return from the Plate ; but I cannot now lay my hand upon it. In the following version I have adhered as closely as possible to the text of the original.

The editor of " La Nacion " says :—

" Captain Don Adolfo Saguier has furnished us with the following details relating to the acts of barbarity perpetrated by Lopez.

" He (Lopez) caused the prisoners to receive five hundred, a thousand, and even two thousand lashes before shooting them.

" Dr. Carreras was flogged thus most barbarously. Captain Saguier, who was placed within sight of Dr. Carreras, and, like him, in fetters for five months, saw the punishment inflicted, and speaks of his shrieks wrung from him by the blows inflicted with a hide rope and with sticks.

" Berges was also flogged before being shot. Don Benigno Lopez (the President's younger brother) before execution was almost cut to pieces. Captain Saguier saw it done, and knows the executioner who flogged him; he is named Aveiro, and was formerly a secretary in the Inland Revenue Office.

" The Marquis de Caxias holds as prisoner a captain of cavalry, named Matias Goigurù. It was he who commanded at the execution of Benigno Lopez, General Barrios, the bishop, Dean Bogado, the wife of Colonel Martinez, Doña Mercedes Egusquiza, Doña Dolòres Recaldè, and others, whose names he does not remember.

" This took place on the 21st of December, 1868, and their execution was witnessed, by order of Lopez, by his two sisters, Inocencia, wife of General Barrios, and Rafaela, widow of Don Saturnino Bedoya (who had been put to death, as Lopez had directed, by the prolonged infliction of the torture called the 'Cepo Uruguayana'), and his brother Venancio. They were, after the execution was over, shut up in a large bullock-cart and sent away, but he does not know whither.

" The greater number of the prisoners suffered tortures of all kinds before being made away with, such as the *Cepo Uruguayana*, flogging, and hunger. Many of those unhappy men, who had been put to the torture, died, sometimes five or six a day, from the agony or from starvation.

" All these almost unheard-of scenes of horror were shown a few steps from, or in the presence of, Don Adolfo Saguier, who was also put in the *Cepo Uruguayana*. His fetters weighed, moreover, forty-five pounds, and he lay in the stocks for five months, exposed to the sun and rain, as were all his companions in misfortune. This gentleman does not know why he was imprisoned; nevertheless, he imagines that having been named *fiscàl* to examine, in the style of Lopez, more than twenty poor fellows, and having questioned them without putting them to the torture or flogging them, and being unable to find any fault in them, he was, for that reason, immediately added to the crowd of victims to suffer the same fate as they. He considers that his life has been most providentially preserved, that he might tell to the world the horrible deeds of that monster *(para relatar al mundo los horrores de ese malvado)*.

" He suffered the torture of the *cepo Uruguayana*, which, according to him, is a thousand times worse than those invented by the Inquisition in the time of Torquemada. When he suffered it, he fainted after a short time ; on his recovery he found that he had been taken back to his old place, and lay once more in fetters, and in the stocks *(cepo de lazo)*.

" He made the march on foot from San Fernando to Villeta, his feet swollen, and his body emaciated by the sufferings he had undergone. He performed impassively this terrible journey of forty leagues over almost impracticable roads ; for orders had been given to bayonet all those, without distinction, whose strength gave out. There were generals, commanders, officers, soldiers, felons, priests, women, children, old men—in short, people of all kinds—who made the journey ; as might be expected many of these poor creatures fell to the ground exhausted, praying to God, and in a loud voice to their guards, that they would give them but a moment to rest, and then to go on again. But the orders of the monster were peremptory, and those who fell were executed without pity by Hilario Marco, formerly chief of police in Asuncion, who commanded.

" It is useless to attempt to write the deeds of that monster Lopez ; for the language has not yet been invented in which one could narrate such unheard of horrors as he has committed, and that, too, in this age of civilization. Cruelties which were perpetrated in the most barbarous times cannot equal, nor even be compared to those which this barbarian has committed, almost in our sight. From the 21st to the 27th of December, almost all his men fell, and those who escaped with him were nearly all wounded, and were without supplies and ammunition. There only remain three or four little steamers hidden in the branches of the Upper Paraguay ; and the small force he can get together will soon be destroyed by the expedition sent in search of him.

" Amongst the executioners in the service of the tyrant we may mention the following as the most infamous, leaving the rest for another occasion :—

" General Resquin.

" Lieut.-Colonel German Serrano.

" The priests Maiz and Romàn.   Maiz is he who was a prisoner for three years, accused as a conspirator ; afterwards he unsaid all *(se desdijo de todo)*, and became, on coming out of prison, one of the most barbarous and cruel instruments of Lopez.

" Luis Carminos was another of the executioners who condemned and murdered on his account. Also one Beron, and Aveiro, whom we have named before.

" Amongst the foreigners who have suffered were those of all nationalities : Englishmen, Frenchmen, North Americans, Spaniards, Italians, Portuguese, and Germans.   It is useless to speak of the Argentines, Orientàles and Brazilians, who have been sacrificed in crowds.

" Amongst them we may mention several Frenchmen who were flogged to death, as were Messrs. Anglade and Filisbert.   It should be noticed that even the chancellor of the French consulate (Mons. de Libertad) scarcely escaped from the clutches of the *sbirros* of the tyrant.   He has now gone to Europe in the gunboat ' Decidée,' and, by order of Lopez, as a prisoner.

" Of Italians : Fidanza (the captain of a barque), the two brothers, Susini, Rebaudi, and many more.

" Of Englishmen : Stark and others, whose names we have not now before us, but those who are inquisitive or interested in these matters can learn them from Dr. Stewart, who is accessible to all.

" Of Germans: Neumann, Gustave Harmann, and others.

" Of Spaniards : Galarraga, Elordoi, Uribe, and many others.

" Of Portuguese : The Consul of H. P. Majesty, Leite-Pereira, the Vice-Consul Vasconcellas, and others.

" We have mentioned that the Argentines, Brazilians, and Orientàles were sacrificed *en masse*.

" There was one circumstance, perhaps unparalleled in history, attending the execution of Colonel Laguna.   He received the fire of the platoon, and was pierced by four balls ; in spite of this he rose from the ground to a sitting posture, and begged them to finish him ; a second time he received their fire, and again sat up, although his chest appeared torn to pieces. They again fired, and once more he raised himself ; and this terrible scene lasted until he had received the fifth volley, when he expired.

" The Bolivians who entered Paraguay by way of Santo Corazon, to trade with the tyrant, were, without exception, sacrificed, in company with all the commanders and officers sent to him by General Saa de Pocito, by way of Bolivia.

" Gaspar Campos and Telmo Lopez were amongst those who perished from hunger ; for they were in the rear of the immense crowd of prisoners, very near to Senor Saguier : and the negro who divided the rations, consisting of a little piece of meat at ten and four, was, without doubt, rather carnivorous, and only when he was himself well filled did he attend to the poor hungry wretches at the times indicated, and frequently there was not enough for all. In such a state of affairs the weak and the sickly would perish first ; and thus died every day six, eight, or ten prisoners.

" It is incredible that in the present age, when the telegraph presents such a facile mode of communication between distant countries, and when even in barbarous regions manners have softened and improved, such atrocities should have been committed so close to us, and in the presence of several (diplomatic) agents from foreign countries, who have to a certain extent authorized them by their presence. These agents, moreover, had frequent communication (with their Governments) by means of vessels of war, and yet have not protested, nor even, if they had not courage enough to do that, tried to escape, that they might demand, in the name of justice, protection for, and endeavour to save, some few of the many innocent people who have fallen victims to the ferocity of the savage Lopez. Far from this, they have remained quietly there, embarking the treasure which he has stolen from foreigners, and from the Treasury of Paraguay."

The last paragraph alludes to the French and Italian consuls, who were living on the most intimate and friendly terms with Lopez, receiving presents from him and Madame Lynch, making speeches in his favour at the public entertainments, and dining *tête-à-tête* with him and his mistress, whilst their countrymen, whom they had been sent to protect, were being put to death, day by day, after suffering the most appalling tortures and misery; none knowing better than Mons. Cuverville that all these unhappy men, women, and children were perfectly innocent of the crimes they were charged with and suffered for; and he alone holding the key to the mystery; the means of proving conclusively that the charges against them were baseless fabrications.

The treasure, mentioned above, was that contained in several boxes marked as belonging to Madame Lynch, and received on board the Italian and French gunboats. I doubted this story at first; but my friend Lieut.-Col. Thompson, who was in command of the battery from whence the boxes were shipped, confirms it in his "War in Paraguay," where he says (p. 290), "Some of these steamers took away a number of heavy cases, each of which required from six to eight men to lift it; they probably contained some of the ladies' jewellery which had been collected in 1867, as well as doubloons."

CHAPTER XX.

WHILST I was still a prisoner I could hear, day after day, the
heavy reverberations of the Brazilian guns, and occasionally the
sharper report of an exploding shell, but no progress seemed to
be made; indeed I had long ceased to look for help from the
Allies; but they were not entirely idle. On the 1st of October
four iron-clads passed the batteries at Angustura; they hoped to
steal by at night in the shadow of the woods on the opposite
shore, but were discovered by their unsleeping foes, and received
several shots; " every ball striking their armour," says Thompson, " gave out a bright flash" (a good illustration of the con-
version of motion into heat and light); and fragments of splintered wood floating down the stream at daybreak showed that
they had not passed unscathed. By the middle of the next
month several other vessels joined these unhurt, for a long arm
of the river, following the erratic course of streams flowing
through sandy formations, had gradually deepened its channel,
and that which the year before had been but a shallow brook
covered with water lilies, was now a canal deep enough for the
passage of sloops of war, and with an island in front of it to
screen them from the Paraguayans. The iron-clads passed
through and anchored off Villeta; but there they had a hard
time of it, for a number of riflemen were hidden in the brushwood on the left bank, and every Brazilian head shown above
the bulwarks was the target for a dozen balls.

Caxias had by this time come to the conclusion that following Lopez up the country and leaving the whole breadth of it open for his escape was not the best way of finishing the war; and he had conceived the plan of making a road through the Gran Chaco, and attacking him in the rear of his position. The work was a long and difficult one, although the distance was but three or four miles, for every foot of the road had to be built on a swamp densely covered with trees, and intersected by a hundred streams. However, the trees were cut down and their stems laid side by side, and supplemented by palm trunks, formed it; several bridges were constructed in the same way, and towards the end of November it was ready for the passage of the army.

The Argentines remained at Palmas a few miles below Angustura, but the Brazilians numbering 32,000 of all arms moved up on the 25th of that month, embarked in the iron-clads at the northern end of the road, and landed at San Antonio, a village four or five miles above Villeta. They were allowed to land without molestation, and from my hut I could plainly see the long lines of tents they occupied.

Between their position and that of Lopez was a deep, narrow stream called Ytòròrò (roaring water), which fell in foaming rapids into the Paraguay; it was crossed by a bridge on the high road to the south, and, with the ever-recurring marshy woods, protected the northern flanks of the Paraguayans. This bridge was the key of the position, and Lopez sent General Caballero to defend it with 5,000 men and twelve guns. The enemy with their whole force attacked him on the 5th of December. The army was separated into three divisions; Osorio, in command of the 3rd brigade, marched early in the day up the stream, in the hope of finding a ford, with the intention of outflanking the Paraguayans; but the ground was so difficult that he only succeeded in getting far enough to place it out of his power to render the other divisions the slightest assistance during the fight. To General Orgollo was given the command of the centre, with orders to carry the bridge; whilst Caxias remained with the reserve on the right. About 10 a.m. Orgollo gallantly led his men to the attack, and, in spite of a terrible fire from the Paraguayan artillery, crossed the bridge with the head of his column and charged Caballero, but after a severe hand to hand fight was forced to retreat. The Brazilian field guns now came up and cleared the bridge, and Orgollo again charged, but was once more beaten with great slaughter, and even after a third attempt the Paraguayans remained in possession, but the crimsoned torrent showed how dear it had cost them. The enemy, beaten and disheartened, fell back, and it was only when Caxias with the whole of the reserves fell upon the decimated Paraguayans, that they abandoned the post they had defended so stoutly, and retreated with half their guns, leaving 3,000 Brazilians dead on the field.

The position of Caxias was now a very critical one. Supplies were sent up with difficulty, Lopez harassed his outposts incessantly, and cut off several herds of cattle on their way through the Chaco; and victories bought so dearly as the last would soon compel him to retreat; so, nerved with the courage of despair, he again moved forward, and, after a pretty severe skirmish with the vanguard of the Paraguayans at Avaỳ,* again met Caballero, who had been reinforced, and now commanded 4,000 men and twelve guns. The Brazilians had 24,000, and literally surrounded their foes; but these, as usual, fought so desperately that they were cut down almost to a man before they would yield. Caballero was dragged from his horse and robbed of his massive silver spurs, but as, luckily for him, gold lace had by this time become very scarce, he was dressed so plainly that the *cambàs* had no idea how redoubtable a soldier had fallen into their hands, and he actually made his escape, with a few of his best men, from the midst of them. The Brazilian loss was again very heavy, 4,000 men *hors de combat*, and Osorio, who commanded, was severely wounded.

Lopez was now seriously alarmed, and in all haste commenced entrenching his position at Ità-Yvatè, and, anxious as

* A stream, so named after Ava, a famous chief of the Gauranis : y means water, and also a river.

ever to keep as far as possible from where fighting was going on, ordered the lines to be extended so far that he had not the means of manning them, and his rear was left quite open. " This, however," writes Colonel Thompson, who made them, " did not signify with a general like Caxias, who was certain to find out the strongest part, and attack there," as proved to be the case.

But as a general Lopez was even worse than he. It was the desperate courage of his men, not any talent of his own, which had preserved him so long. And there can be little doubt that if he had had the battalions so uselessly slaughtered at Ytòròrò and Ypanè behind the lines of Ità-Yvatè, he might even then have defeated the Brazilians, and, afterwards falling upon the Argentines, have retrieved his position when it seemed most desperate.

It is difficult to give a clear description of the position of the Paraguayans without a plan ; but it may be sufficient to say that there was an unfinished star-fort on the crest of a low hill, a ditch and parapet at some distance in front towards the river, and, to the south, much stronger lines resting at one extremity on the river, and on the other on the marsh of the Pikysyrì. The latter were garrisoned by 1,500 men and boys, and mounted forty guns. About 3,000 of the best men, with fourteen guns, occupied the star-fort, and a thousand more were scattered along the outer parapet.

On the 17th of December the Brazilians made a cavalry *reconnaissance*, and, surprising the 45th Regiment of Lancers, killed all save the commander and three men ; and on the 21st the whole army, now reduced to 25,000 men, took up a position in front of the Paraguayan lines. A division was detached, under General Barreto, with a battery of field artillery, which attacked the trenches of Pikysyrì, and carried them, killing 700 of the defenders and taking 200 prisoners, amongst whom were many women and children. Shortly after noon, the main *corps d'armée* choosing, as had been anticipated, the only point where they could meet with serious resistance, attacked the centre of

the Paraguayan lines, and captured them after a most unnecessary loss of life ; drove the men from their guns, but they were
driven back in turn from the higher fort, the donjon of the field,
and they lost 3,500 in killed and wounded before sunset. Lopez
during the night recalled the few men he had sent on to Cerro
Leon and Caäpucù, and about 600 were added during the next
two days to his scanty forces ; but it was evident that in a
speedy retreat to the cordilleras lay his only hope of safety.

The Brazilians were waiting for the Argentines to join them,
and for the arrival of part of their artillery which had been left
at Palmas, and thus gave him an excellent opportunity to
escape without risking another engagement on the plains ; but
he did not do so, expecting, probably, that with their usual
procrastination the Allies would leave him unmolested for some
weeks to come.

On the 24th the Argentines came up, and on the morning of
Christmas-day the Allied Generals sent a demand to Lopez to
lay down his arms within twelve hours, reminding him of the
amount of blood which had been shed, and begging that he
would, by immediate submission, save the lives of the few of his
people who were yet left. His answer was a remarkable one.
I regret that I have not a copy in the original language, for the
only English translation I have seen is so poor and incorrect
that it gives but a sorry idea of the spirit of the original. I
suspect it must have been written by Father Maiz ; but whoever was the author it does infinite credit to his ability. Lopez
writes, or is made to write, as if he were doing honour to the
allied commanders in noticing their letter at all; and as if
he were the most generous, most devoted and courageous of
patriots, he speaks in touching terms of the bravery and self-
abnegation of his soldiers, reiterates the baseless falsehood that
he and they have fought and would still fight for the liberty and
security of their fatherland ; and throws the whole blame of the
war, and the guilt of the slaughter of his people, on his enemies.

At this very time his hands were red with the blood of his
own brother, with that of the bishop, who had been his play-

fellow when a child, and his most devoted friend through life, and of the most gallant and fearless of his officers. Well was it said that language (and especially a written one) is intended to conceal our thoughts !

As soon as the fighting began at Ità Yvatè, Lopez abandoned his quarters, and had a tent erected in a wood a mile or more in the rear, and he kept on horseback ready for escape during the whole of each morning when he expected the Allies would again attempt to carry the place by a general assault. On the 25th, forty-six guns being in position, a tremendous but badly directed fire was poured into the place : shot, shell, and rockets swept the lines the whole of that day ; and on the next the Brazilians attacked, and—it is almost incredible—twenty thousand of them were hurled back in confusion by less than two thousand Paraguayans ! I have spoken again and again of the courage of that devoted race, but every word I have written seems tame and lifeless beside the bare record of such a day as that. I feel angry with myself for admiring them as I do, knowing for how pitiful a poltroon, for how baseless a lie they fought ; but I am proud of my intimacy with them, of the little help I so gladly gave them.

The fire was resumed, and continued all the next day, but the Paraguayans still fought the three or four guns they had left, firing them from the ground as they lay after they had been dismounted, and obstinately refusing to surrender. But on the 27th the Argentines, supported by their Brazilian allies, made an end of the few of the garrison left—less than a thousand— but every one cost the life of two of his foes. About three hundred who had escaped to the woods were surrounded and taken prisoners ; the rest died to a man.

Lopez fled early in the day ; he left alone that his absence should not be noticed, not even telling Madame Lynch, who had remained with him, when or where he was going, and leaving her to her fate. All his personal baggage was taken ; his treasure, that is the money he had stolen from murdered foreigners and his countrymen, had been previously sent to Pirububuy, under the care of Mc Mahon ; his papers, and lists of the prisoners who had been executed ; also a hundred pairs of boots, mostly of patent leather, which, in obedience to the native weakness I mentioned on page 39, he was especially proud of,—all fell into the hands of his enemies. He had one satisfaction, few amongst them would have a foot small enough to wear them.*

He fled, without drawing bridle, to Cerro Leon, picking up on the way a few scattered cavalry who were making for the same point ; and he fled unpursued ! As I was not there at the time, I quote the following from Col. Thompson, who was ; for the fact is difficult to understand.

He says : " Caxias states that Lopez was accompanied by scarcely ninety men, and of these only twenty-five arrived with him at Cerro Leon. This, if not quite correct, was certainly very nearly so ; and knowing it, why did not Caxias the Commander-in-chief of the allied army, being at war, ' *not with the Paraguayan nation, but with its Government*,' and having 8,000 magnificently-mounted cavalry with nothing to do, pursue Lopez, whom he might have taken without the loss of a single man ? Was it from imbecility, or from a wish to make more money out of the army contracts ? Was it to have an excuse for still maintaining a Brazilian army in Paraguay ? or was there an understanding between Caxias and Lopez ? Or was it done with the view of allowing Lopez to collect the remainder of the Paraguayans in order to exterminate them in ' civilized warfare ' ? Be this as it may, the Marquis de Caxias is responsible for every life lost in Paraguay since December, 1868, and for all the sufferings of the unfortunate men, women, and children, then left in the power of Lopez."†

On the 29th, the garrison of Angustura, which still held out, was summoned to surrender, but refused ; the next day, how-

---

* The South American Indians have remarkably small feet, the Spaniards also are favoured in this respect. Amongst the Paraguayan women I saw some of the prettiest imaginable, and as they were unspoilt by high-heeled shoes and compression, their arch and elasticity gave a singularly graceful step and carriage.

† The Paraguayan War. Lieut.-Col. Thompson. Longmans and Co.

ever, Lieut.-Col. Thompson, who commanded it, raised a flag of truce, and sent a letter to the allied generals complaining of a monitor which had misused one on the day before. This complaint was very curtly answered, and he was informed that Lopez had been completely routed and had fled to the hills, and he was again summoned to surrender. Thompson asked permission to send five officers under a safe conduct to see if this were the case ; which was granted, and they found, quite unexpectedly, that the statement was correct. On the return of the officers a capitulation was agreed to, the soldiers to march out with the honours of war, and the officers to be liberated on parole. These terms were accepted, and at 11 a.m. on the 30th of December, 1869, the last important stronghold of Lopez was given up to the enemy. The garrison numbered 1,200 effectives, but principally old men and boys, with 800 wounded ; also a great many women and children.

Lopez rode direct, as I have said, for Cerro Leon ; the deep streams he had to ford or swim somewhat checked his flight, and gave time for Madame Lynch, with Generals Resquin and Caballero, to overtake him. The latter, after meeting him, went back, and, collecting a few men, protected his retreat from the scattered bodies of Brazilian cavalry, scouring the low hills to the east ; but was forced to retreat in turn before a larger force. General Resquin had a narrow escape in trying to keep pace with Lopez, he was badly thrown, and remained stunned and insensible for some time, but at length recovered far enough to keep his seat in the saddle. Another field officer, less fortunate, I must mention,—for the accidental sight of his name recalls his fine soldierly figure so vividly that I can almost hear the cheerful "Buenos dias" with which he so often greeted me,—Colonel Toledo. He was a great favourite with Carlos Lopez, and for many years had held the important post of commandant of the President's escort. When I knew him he was a tall, handsome old man with very white hair, and with a voice and address which would have done honour to the most courtly of diplomatists. Whilst the battle of Ità Yvatè was raging, Lopez was sheltered behind two thick walls, but his guards were dropping fast; their old colonel, however, sat unmoved in the midst of them with a face as serene as if they were but drawn up for inspection; presently Lopez called to him " Go and fight," he bowed low, took a lance from a soldier near him and rode towards the enemy, but a few moments afterwards fell dead from the saddle, almost at the feet of his unpitying master.

About half way to Cerro Leon, Lopez met Colonel Caminos, who was coming from that place with 2,500 men and a few pieces of artillery, but not feeling safe even then, he continued his headlong flight almost alone, ordering them to follow as quickly as possible. The hospitals near the *cerro* were full of wounded, and from amongst them about 3,000 were found able—in some sort—to bear arms; with these and the stronger men, under the command of Caminos, the place was garrisoned and some temporary works thrown up; but on the last day of December Lopez fell back to Azcurra,* at the foot of the cordillera.

I have spoken of the picturesque wildness of the pass, and of the view over the broad and beautiful valley, from its summit, from the sparkling lake of Ypacaraì fed by the river Pirayù, which flows midway through the valley, to the swelling hills of Paraguarì and the rocky steep of Santo Tomàs. I had looked on that scene with unmingled pleasure, but the now starving Paraguayans gazed on it with far different feelings; from the palm-covered height of the pass they could see the plains of Paraguarì glowing at early morning before the midday mirage obscured the view, and more brightly still in the rays of the setting sun, with the rich yellow of ripening Indian corn; for the low alluvial valley had been planted with thousands of bushels of seed ill-spared from their scanty store, and now it was ready for the sickle. They saw it ripen in the sun, and they saw it decay in the sweeping torrents of the equinoctial rains; they died—poor creatures—by hundreds from starvation, with a thousand acres of golden wheat almost within their grasp.

Vide page 76.

A few cartloads were brought in for the use of the soldiers, and for feeding the horses of the principal officers, but the crowds of women and children who were cooped up in the hills got none; they were not allowed to harvest it, lest they should go over to the Brazilians who were encamped beyond.

The Allies, meanwhile, had moved up to Asuncion and occupied it; and the rest which the troops greatly needed having been afforded them, they made preparations for finishing the war. Their movements were greatly facilitated by the railway from the capital to Paraguarì, but the destruction of a timber bridge over a small stream by the Paraguayans, a few miles out, was a serious hindrance to them. I have been terribly taken to task for writing that the Brazilians are but poor soldiers; however, I think I am safe in saying that they are very poor engineers; for the repair of that single bridge occupied them two months, when I am certain that an English carpenter would have devised a plan for doing it in as many weeks. But they completed it at last, and reached the river Pirayù by the middle of May, upon which the Paraguayans retired about a league from their old position, to the foot of the cordillera.

A few troops were left in Cerro Leon, and on the arrival of the Brazilians a rather severe engagement, considering the few men engaged on the other side, took place. The Paraguayans retreated with heavy loss, and the same day Lopez fell back to the further side of the cordillera, destroying, before he left, every house, fence, and fruit tree, leaving, as he had ever done, a desert behind him.

About the middle of April, whilst the Paraguayans still held the railway at Paraguarì, he tried a new and rather ingenious mode of warfare. He had a heavy gun mounted on a truck at the end of a train of waggons, which were filled with men, with the engine at the other extremity; and one morning the train rattled down to the bridge, and engaged the enemy at short range. The fire, however, was returned so hotly that the Paraguayans retreated somewhat hastily, but more from the fear that the train might fall into the enemy's hands, than from any loss they had sustained.

Whilst the Brazilians were still at Pirajù a division was detached and pushed forward to Paraguari, and penetrating the cordillera at the pass Sapucaì, meeting with but little resistance, occupied the village of Ybytymì, which is about seventy-five miles from Asuncion. They marched in so unexpectedly that Lopez had not had time to order it to be evacuated and destroyed, and several native families were rescued. The Brazilians treated them kindly, giving them rations of beef and *fariña* (cassava meal), but the poor creatures had been so imbued by Lopez with the idea that they would be outraged and murdered, that many of them afterwards fled to the woods.

Caballero was sent to drive the invaders back, but he arrived too late, and they had emerged from the cordilleras, where he could have attacked them with impunity, and reached the valley of Pirajù before he came up with them. But many of the women were recaptured by him, and were cruelly tortured, and afterwards executed by Lopez for their attempt at escape. Amongst the fugitives was a señorita—whose name I cannot recall—a cousin of Gen. Caballeros'; she was seated in a bullock-cart which contained all that remained of her worldly possessions, and which, moving slowly, was falling fast to the rear, so much so that the shouts of the pursuing Paraguayans could be plainly heard ; several of her companions were lingering and looking back, undecided if they should go on or give themselves up, but she impatiently jumped out of the cart, and, opening a bundle she carried, threw them a roll of notes representing some three hundred dollars, saying, "If you intend to stay with Lopez take these, for you will need them ; I am going where I can get something to eat;" and ran off to the head of the column.

The Arsenal, established in Cāācupè in 1868, and to which a considerable part of the machinery from that in Asuncion had been removed, was kept working day and night, and in six months turned out sixty guns of light calibre, suitable for mountain warfare, many of them rifled ; the work was done by natives, under the forced supervision of English artisans. Expeditions, also, were sent to the battle-fields of Villeta, and a considerable quantity of rifles, which the Allies had not taken the trouble to collect, were recovered, lances were manufactured for those who were unprovided with muskets, and in this way Lopez was once more surrounded with an armed force. When Caxias so criminally allowed him to escape, he laughed at the idea that the Paraguayans could ever again become formidable ; forgetting the sage Spanish proverb, *No hay enemigo chico*,* and it is really marvellous how soon a new army was formed and equipped.

The next operation of the Brazilians was sending two iron-clads of light draught up a stream called Manduvirà, which drains the valleys to the north of the lesser cordillera, and falls into the Paraguay a little above Emboscada. The three small steamers left to the Paraguayans were hidden in the woody recesses of this stream, and the object of the enemy was to capture them, and at the same time to get in the rear of Lopez's position. He, however, prevented both by sinking the smaller of the three in the narrow channel, and thus effectually blocking it.

In the meantime Caxias had been recalled, and the chief command of the allied army given to the Comte d'Eu, the son-in-law of the Emperor ; and in May, 1869, his troops were concentrated in Pirayù ; a small force only being left to guard the capital, where a provisional government had been formed, pending the conclusion of the war.

A Paraguayan legion had been enrolled from prisoners and deserters, and they displayed the national flag, a tricolour of horizontal stripes with a lion guarding a cap of liberty in the centre, in their midst. Lopez was greatly enraged when this was reported to him, and he wrote to the Comte d'Eu, that if it were not immediately taken down he would order all the Brazilian and Argentine prisoners he held to be shot. The

---

* Freely : "No enemy should be despised." One seems to form proverbs almost unconsciously in the terse sentences of the Spanish tongue.

Brazilian commander replied that the Paraguayan legion was composed of volunteers, and that they, and not he, had the right to decide what flag they would use. And as for the prisoners, he doubted if any were then left alive, but if they were he was sure that they would soon die from misery without the necessity for shooting them. This was true enough, for the seventy or eighty captives Lopez then held were dying fast from disease and starvation, and they were put to death by the thrust of a lance whenever a pretext could be found for doing so; however he did not carry out his threat, but it would have been a mercy to have done so, for very few of them were in existence a month afterwards.

The sufferings of the people shared by all, now fell most heavily upon the women and children; the short supplies of beef were distributed solely amongst the soldiers, the rest had to live upon such food as the forest afforded them. The oranges, there growing everywhere by the wayside, were eaten before they were half ripe, the guava trees were stripped of their green fruit; every herb, every berry, which could yield nutriment was eagerly sought for, but the multitude was too great, the edible plants too few, and they prolonged their lives but to die the more painfully.

At sunset every evening, a long procession left the outskirts of the camp, walking slowly towards the church of Caraguatai, and stopped at the brink of a shallow pit scooped in the yielding sand. A line of half-naked women bearing each on her head a corpse tied to a plank or bamboo, so light, so attenuated by the process of slow starvation under the glowing sun, that feeble as the bearers were, they carried them alone. Their fathers, their husbands, lay in the pestilential swamps of San Fernando, and now they were thus carrying their sons to their burial. The trench they had dug with their own hands, and with weary, tearless eyes they looked upon them, ere those same hands which had fondled them as children spread over them the ruddy sand, their only shroud. Often a bearer stumbled under the light weight she carried, and another corpse was added to the tale. One could not walk a furlong in the woods without coming upon a dozen who had died whilst searching for food. "In less than six months," writes Mr. Valpy, who gives me these particulars, and who saw it all, "more than a hundred thousand women and children died in the cordillera from sheer starvation."

The widows and female relatives of the so-called conspirators had been sent to Yhū, a village about thirty leagues from Azcurra. They belonged, with few exceptions, to the best families in Paraguay, many bearing names famous in Spanish history. They were stripped of all save their *tupois* and a shawl, and made the journey on foot, often having to cross wide marshes and wade through them in four feet of water. Mrs. Stark, a British subject, and her four children, so shamefully abandoned to their fate through the craven policy of our Government, started on that journey, but reached her destination childless. The terror and anxiety depicted in the faces of these poor creatures were painful beyond expression.

In June and July expeditions were made by the Allies to San Josè and to the iron mines of Ybicuì, for the purpose of destroying the workshops and cannon foundry, giving time, however, to Lopez to remove all the guns he needed. The latter was still encamped at Azcurra, but Piribebuì had been entrenched and batteries thrown up commanding the approaches to it, and the main army there awaited the onset of the foe.

In August the Brazilians marched a column through Valenzuela, destroying the sulphur works they found there, and thence to Barrero Grande, which is some five leagues east of Azcurra. At the same time part of the Argentine troops, under General Emilio Mitrè, forced the pass of Atyrà, and occupied the village of that name lying five leagues north-east of Azcurra, and three from Barrero Grande. Thus Lopez was hemmed in on all sides: in front was the Brazilian main *corps d'armée* at Pirayù; part of the Argentines at Tacuaral and Guasuvirà; the Brazilian division and the Paraguayan legion at Barrero Grande; and the rest of the Argentines at Atyrà, with the iron-clads still lying in the Manduvirà. Nothing would have been easier or more certain than his capture or destruction. But now the Allies committed one of those enormous strategical blunders for which this war is so famous. Instead of approaching Azcurra and converging rapidly on their common centre, completely encircling Lopez and cutting off his communications with Piribebui, Mitrè marched his troops to Altos, two leagues north of Atyrà, and the Brazilians moved to Piribubui; in fact, instead of converging they opened out their lines like a broken fan, leaving a space of twenty miles in the rear of Lopez free for his escape !

On the 12th of August Comte D'Eu summoned Caballero to surrender; he, however, although he saw that resistance was useless, feared Lopez more than the Brazilians and refused to do so, and the place was carried by assault. The Paraguayans had 1,500 men, the enemy 10,000; the latter lost heavily, and the veteran General Mena Barreto was killed; of their foes scarcely one was left alive, and many women and children perished in the *mêlée*. Col. Caballero was taken alive, but was bayonetted whilst pitifully praying on his knees that his life might be spared.

On the afternoon of the same day Lopez announced that a great victory had been gained, and had a Te Deum celebrated in the camp in celebration of it; but the next morning silent preparations were made for a retreat. At ten o'clock at night he passed through Cãacupè on his way to San Joaquim, having sent some of his best troops ahead a few hours before; and a train of fifteen guns followed, dragged by the women. He reached the latter place unmolested, and has since carried on a guerilla warfare in the fastnesses of the hills, where he is to this day (March 30th, 1870) still unsubdued.

A great many native women, as well as the residue of the English *employés*, including Mr. Valpy, Mr. Burrell, and Mr. Twite, civil engineers, and Mr. Skinner, surgeon, were left in Cãacupè in a state of the greatest anxiety and uncertainty. A few troops still occupied the town, and every hour they expected to receive orders to march, with the prospect of torture or death before them for lingering behind with the intention of desertion—

as Lopez would have termed it.　An officer actually was sent by him to command them to come on; but Bacchus, to whom so many of the English had sacrificed so devoutly, laying even their lives upon his shrine—empurpled as much with blood as with wine—came to their help.　In other words, the officer fell in with a bottle of rum, and when he arrived at the encampment he was so intoxicated that he could give no intelligible orders; he was lifted from the saddle and lay in a drunken sleep on the ground, from which he awoke a prisoner in the hands of the Brazilians.

Mr. Skinner left by daylight to rejoin Lopez, Mr. Nesbit was also with him, and no news have since been received of either of them.

On the 15th of August the Brazilians came up and rescued the remainder; they were treated rather brusquely at first; which indeed is not to be wondered at, for their captors could but be aware how important the forced help of the English engineers had been to Lopez.　However they were set at liberty, and nearly all have returned to England, and either personally or by letter have given me most interesting accounts of their adventures.　To Mr. Valpy, especially, I am greatly indebted for the notes from which this chapter has been principally compiled.

I have now brought this painful story to a close.　I have tried to state the facts as I know them, the scenes as I witnessed them, and have not intentionally added one touch of exaggeration, one word which could make them more horrible than they were in their terrible reality.　My notices, rather than accounts, of some of the battles are necessarily imperfect, and may be incorrect in many particulars; for I was not present at one of them, and my sources of information were not always trustworthy: nor have I mentioned many of the incidents of the war deserving of notice;* but in representing the courage,

* Those who desire full information on these points I would refer to Lieut.-Colonel Thompson's " Paraguayan War."

the fearlessness of death, of the Paraguayans as so extraordinary, my statements are fully supported by every one, of whatever shade of opinion, who has written or spoken of this singular people.

They exist no longer—there is a gap in the family of nations; but the story of their sufferings and of their heroism should not perish with them. For myself, I think of them with regret and sorrow; the cruelties I endured at the hands of some have not changed in the least the hearty sympathy I felt for them as a people; but, at the same time, I can but feel that their destruction sooner or later would be inevitable: " the tree which will bring forth no fruit shall be hewn down, and cast into the fire." They were not capable of true civilization; they could not govern themselves; they would have remained children to the end of time. Their magnificent country remained almost a wilderness, and they would have none to do that which they would not do themselves. The foreigners, whom they distrusted and despised, will till the ground which they abandoned to tares and brambles, and enjoy the fair heritage which they were unworthy to possess.

Believing the miserable sophisms of the Church of Rome, sunk to even a lower depth, not making idolatry a part of their religion, but their religion itself, they lived practically without God, with no thought beyond the present hour.

Indolent and licentious, the population scarcely increased; and the condition of the bulk of the population was such that sound health was impossible.

Unthinking and unreasoning, they were content to remain in ignorance and barbarism, a hundred years behind their neighbours; they bowed in timid deference, in blind devotion, to any tyrant set over them, to any despot unscrupulous enough to plunder them, and would not lift a finger to rid themselves of burdens the most intolerable.

Yet I can neither entirely blame nor pity them. Their gaiety, their politeness, their unaffected kindness and charity to each other, when no shadow of the Government was upon them, their obedience to superiors, shown so strangely in the cruelties they suffered and inflicted, their love of home and country, their courage and endurance, made them too estimable for the one or the other.

The Teuton and the Anglo-Saxon will soon fill the void this war of extermination has made, and permanent prosperity will banish all trace of its devastations. It is well that it should be so ; still I feel like one who sees some old wood, once a mere waste of encumbered ground, and which could only be entered by stealth, being at length converted into the home of a busy industry, and covered with houses and streets. He admits that the change is a vast improvement ; but yet remembers, with sad regret, the picturesque beauties of the useless mossy trees, and the bright wild flowers which grew beneath them.

APPENDIX.

TRANSLATION OF THE TRIPLE ALIANZA.

"Treaty of Alliance against Paraguay. Signed the 1st of May, 1865, between the Plenipotentiaries of Uruguay, of Brazil, and of the Argentine Republic.

"The Government of the Oriental Republic of Uruguay, the Government of H.M. the Emperor of Brazil, the Government of the Argentine Republic:

"These last two being actually at war with the Government of Paraguay, the same having been declared by that Government, and the first in a state hostile to, and threatened in its internal security by, the said Government, injuring the Republic, solemn treaties, international usages of civilized nations notwithstanding; and unjustifiable acts having been committed, after having disturbed the relations of its neighbours by the most abusive and aggressive proceedings:

"Persuaded that peace, the security and wellbeing of their respective nations is impossible whilst the actual Government of Paraguay exists, and that it is an imperious necessity, demanded by the highest interests, that the Government should be changed, preserving the sovereignty, independence, and territorial integrity of the Republic of Paraguay:

"Have resolved, with that object, to enter into a treaty of alliance, offensive and defensive, and for that purpose have named their Plenipotentiaries, to wit:

"H.E. the Provisional Governor of the Oriental Republic; H.E. Dr. Don Carlos Castro, Minister for Foreign Affairs;

H.M. the Emperor of Brazil; H.E. Dr. Don T. Octaviano de Almeida Rosa, Councillor accredited to the A. G. L.* and Officer of the Imperial Order de Rosa; H.E. the President of the Argentine Republic; H.E. Dr. Don Rufino de Elizalde, his Minister-Secretary for Foreign Affairs: Who, having exchanged their respective credentials, and finding them in good and proper form, agree as follows :—

"Art. I. The Oriental Republic of Uruguay, H.M. the Emperor of Brazil, and the Argentine Republic, unite in an alliance offensive and defensive for carrying on the war provoked by the Government of Paraguay.

" Art. II. The Allies will act together with all the forces they can dispose of, by land or on the rivers, as they may find convenient.

" Art. III. The operations of the war having commenced in the territory of the Argentine Republic, or in that part of the Paraguayan territory adjoining the same, the chief command and the direction of the allied forces shall remain in the hands of the President of the Argentine Republic, General-in-Chief of its army, Brigadier General Don Bartolomè Mitre.

"·The naval forces of the Allies will be under the immediate command of the Vice-Admiral Visconde de Tamandarè, Commander-in-Chief of the squadron of H.M. the Emperor of Brazil.

" The land forces of the Oriental Republic of Uruguay, one division of the Argentine and another of the Brazilian forces, which shall be designated by the respective commanders, shall form an army under the immediate orders of the Provisional Governor of the Oriental Republic, Brigadier-General Don Venancio Flores.

" The land forces of H.M. the Emperor of Brazil shall form an army under the immediate command of his Commander-in-Chief, Brigadier Manuel Luis Osorio.

" Although the high contracting parties have agreed not to change the seat of war, nevertheless, with the object of pre-

* National Legislative Assembly.

serving the sovereign rights of the three nations, they have agreed from this date in the principle of reciprocation in the chief command, when operations may have to be carried on in Oriental or Brazilian territory.

" Art. IV. The internal military direction and economy of the allied forces shall be directed entirely by their respective commanders.

" The expenses, victualling, munitions of war, arms, clothing, equipage, and means of transport of the allied forces will be at the cost of their respective States.

" Art. V. The high contracting parties will give mutual assistance, or materials which they may have and the others require, as shall be specially stipulated.

" Art. VI. The Allies solemnly bind themselves not to lay down their arms, except by mutual consent, until they shall have destroyed the existing Government of Paraguay, and not to treat separately with the enemy, nor sign any treaty of peace, truce, armistice, or convention of any kind to put an end to, or suspend the war, unless they shall all agree to do so.

" Art. VII. The war not being waged against the people of Paraguay, but against its Government, the Allies can receive a Paraguayan legion formed of any of the citizens of that nation who may wish to unite with them for the purpose of destroying the said Government, and will supply them with all materials they need, in the form and under the conditions to be hereafter established.

" Art. VIII. The Allies engage, moreover, to respect the independence, sovereignty, and territorial integrity of the Republic of Paraguay. Consequently the Paraguayans may elect their own Government, and choose such institutions as may be convenient to themselves, and they will not be absorbed ; nor will the Allies claim a Protectorate, as a consequence of this war.

" Art. IX. The independence, sovereignty, and territorial integrity of the Republic of Paraguay shall be guaranteed collectively, in conformity with the preceding article, by the high contracting parties for a period of five years.

"Art. X. It is agreed by the high contracting parties that the exemptions, privileges, or concessions which they may obtain from the Government of Paraguay shall be common and unconditional, or compensatingly equal, if conditional.

" Art. XI. When the Government of Paraguay has ceased to exist, the Allies shall proceed to make the necessary arrangements with the constituted authorities, to secure the free navigation of the rivers Paranà and Paraguay, in such a manner that the rules or laws of that Republic shall not obstruct, embarrass, nor impede the transit, nor the direct navigation of trading or war vessels of the Allied States, on the way to their respective territories or dominions which do not belong to Paraguay : and that they shall have due guarantees for the carrying out of these arrangements, on the principle that such rules of riverine police, although made for the two rivers, and also the river Uruguay, shall be established by the common consent of the Allies and the other bordering States, for the ends stipulated, they (*the latter*) accepting the invitation made to them.

" Art. XII. The Allies reserve to themselves *(the right)* to concert the best means of preserving peace with Paraguay after the fall of the existing Government.

"Art. XIII. The Allies will name at the proper time Plenipotentiaries to make the rules, conventions, or treaties with the Government which may be established in Paraguay.

"Art. XIV. The Allies will require from that Government payment of the expenses of the war, which they have been obliged to accept ; also, in reparation, indemnity for the injuries and detriment caused to property, public and private, and to the persons of their citizens, without express declaration of war, and for the injuries and damage committed subsequently in violation of the principles which regulate the laws of war. Likewise the Oriental Republic of Uruguay will claim a proportionate indemnity for the injuries and damage caused by the Government of Paraguay, through the war into which it has been forced to enter in defence of its security, threatened by that Government.

" Art. XV. A special commission shall determine the mode and form of liquidation and payment of the above-named.

" Art. XVI. With the object of avoiding disputes or wars in which the question of limits may involve them, it is established that the Allies shall require from the Government of Paraguay that when treating of limits it shall do so on the following bases :—

" 1stly. The Argentine Republic shall be divided from the Republic of Paraguay by the rivers Paranà and Paraguay, until they reach the limits of the Empire of Brazil, such being on the right of the river Paraguay, at Bahia Negra.

" 2ndly. The Empire of Brazil shall be divided from the Republic of Paraguay, on the side of the Paranà, by the first river below the cataract of the Seven Falls, which is, according to the recent map of Manchez, the Iguraì, and from the mouth of the Iguraì, following its course, to its source.

" 3rdly. On the side of the left bank of the Paraguay by the river Apa, from its mouth to its source.

" 4thly. In the interior, from the ridge of the mountains of Maracayù. The slopes on the east shall belong to Brazil, and those on the west to Paraguay, drawing straight lines as near as possible from the said mountains to the streams of the Apa and the Iguraì.

" Art. XVII. The Allies guarantee reciprocally to each other the faithful performance of the arrangements and treaties which they may make with Paraguay, in virtue of which it is agreed that the present treaty of alliance shall always continue in full force and rigour, to the end that these stipulations shall be respected and executed by the Republic of Paraguay.

" 1stly. With the object of obtaining this result, they agree that : In case it is made impossible for one of the high contracting parties to obtain from the Government of Paraguay that which it requires, or that that Government shall seek to annul the conditions adjusted by the Allies, the others shall use their best endeavours to cause them to be respected.

" 2ndly. If those endeavours should be useless, the Allies

shall unite all their forces, in order that these stipulations shall be effectually carried out.

"Art. XVIII. This treaty shall remain secret until the principal objects of the alliance shall have been obtained.

"Art. XIX. Such stipulations of this treaty as shall require legislative authorization shall begin to have effect as soon as they shall have been approved by the respective Governments, and the others from the exchange of ratifications, which shall be done within the term of forty days, counting from the date of the said treaty, or sooner, if possible, and in the city of Buenos Ayres.

"In testimony of which the undersigned Plenipotentiaries of H.E. the Provisional Governor of the Oriental Republic of Uruguay, of H.M. the Emperor of Brazil, and H.E. the President of the Argentine Republic, in virtue of our full powers, sign this treaty, attaching our seals, in the city of Buenos Ayres, the 1st of May, in the year of our Lord 1865.

(Signed)   "CARLOS DE CASTRO.

"T. OCTAVIANO DA ALMEIDA ROSA.

"RUFINO DE ELIZALDE."

PROTOCOL.

"Their Excellencies the Plenipotentiaries of the Argentine Republic, of the Oriental Republic of Uruguay, and of H.M. the Emperor of Brazil, assembled in the Foreign Office, agree:

"1stly. That in fulfilment of the treaty of alliance of this date, the fortifications of Humaità shall be demolished, and that they will not permit that another or others be constructed to impede the faithful execution of this treaty.

"2ndly. That one of the means of guaranteeing peace with the Government to be established in Paraguay being not leaving it arms or material of war, all that they find shall be divided in equal parts amongst the Allies.

"3rdly. That all trophies and booty taken from the enemy shall be divided amongst the Allies by the captors.

" 4thly. That the Generals commanding the allied army shall concert together the best means for carrying these stipulations into effect."

Signed as before.

This treaty, having been made public prematurely at the demand of Her Majesty's Government, produced a storm of indignation throughout the greater part of South America.

It was published in the " Semanario " of the 11th of August, 1866, and did more to strengthen the hands of Lopez than anything his best friends could have devised.

The intention of Brazil to seize Paraguay eventually is transparent enough, although the treaty seems to provide against such a measure. Compare Art. 8th with the 14th, and then with the 1st and 2nd of the Protocol. The Republic is to be free and independent ; but as the Allies are to be repaid all they spent during the war, and to receive compensation for all public and private injuries, we may be quite sure that some material guarantee will be demanded ; for, as Lopez and Madame Lynch have grasped nearly every dollar of hard money, and even the rings, chains, and combs of the poor market girls, to say nothing of the valuable property belonging to foreigners abandoned by Mr. Washburn, and have succeeded in sending away or secreting a great part of it, there is nothing but the soil of Paraguay left as such security. Brazil having already, by readjusting her limits, seized the district of the yerbales—the natural woods of yerba matè, the most valuable by far of the exports of Paraguay— leaves her allies but the sandy plains of the central and the *esteros* of the southern divisions, with the Misiones as a bone of contention.

How can a beaten and weakened people, without arms, without fortifications, hope to hold their own against their turbulent and unscrupulous neighbours to the south, or even against the Indians still inhabiting the wilds on the shores of the Parana beyond the pathless forests of Caáguazu ?   Will they not perforce ask Brazil to take the little she has left of their habitable territory, and annex it as the smallest province of the empire ?

NUMBER OF PRISONERS EXECUTED.

THE following is a summary of the official list of those executed " for treason and rebellion," found amongst the papers of Lopez, after his defeat at Lomas Valentinas :

Foreigners executed 107		
,, died in prison . . . 113		
	220	
Paraguayans executed . . . 176		
,, died in prison . . . 88		
	264	
Executed August 22, 1868, nationality not being expressed 85		
Died (*i.e.* bayonetted) between San Fernando and Pikysyry 27		
	112	
Total deaths up to December, 1868 . . . 596		

After that date a great number were executed, nearly all, in fact, of those remaining of the original 700 or 800 arrested.

THE " LAMBARÈ."

THIS was a newspaper published by the Government in Guarani, and interesting as a specimen of that singular language.   It was a half demy sheet folded in two, and really got up very well. On the title-page was a rude woodcut, representing el Cacique (Chief) de Lambarè shooting with arrows a triple-headed flying dragon with a balloon at the point of its tail, typical, of course, of the Triple Alliance.   To his left is Mount Lambarè, with a puma seated at its foot, the river seemingly flowing to the top of it, and a steamer running full tilt at its side : perspective was not a strong point with the native artists. In the distance is a railway train, and some wonderful palm trees. The title is "Lambarè. Cuatia ñcè ybety rusu güi osè baè." (Lambarè. A speaking-paper, which comes from his hill).

The greater part of the articles which appeared in it were so ferocious in tone, and full of such gross indecencies, that I cannot attempt to give a version of them here ; but I append, as a specimen of the language, a literal translation of a song which appeared in it, Sep. 5th, 1867, omitting a few words.

Mburahéi osé bae ybyty rasue gui ("A song which came from the hill").

El Cacique Lambarè I huy ombohacua, Opáhaguá omondoro Las cambai rebicua.	The chief Lambarè Sharpens his arrows, To tear well The backs of the negroes.
Tounte los camba curu Na ne Rétá pota hára. Rebicua rehe onandu ne Upe hendy hae overa ba.	Let the itching negroes come Who covet our country. Their backs they will feel Pierced through and through.
Lambarè heta ete oioiái Umi camba byroton Por que ndo hecha moáiri Oipota ete ba l'Asuncion.	Lambarè mocks much These black idiots, Who, though much they wish it, Will never see Asuncion.
Oparupi rei ma oiapi Ndo icuaábei hembiapo rá Icaá pa pota ete maco Umi ana rembichyra.	They run from side to side, They know not what to do, Now is nearly finished their food, And the devil is going to roast them.
Oime oho cu iaicuaà bae Mboca rubicha guazu Toiopy que tebi Ynacio El camba rebicua pucu.	He ran away whom we know, The great captain of the guns. . . . . Ignacio* You big . . . negro.
I mbegüe caraia mbaásy Cachimbo hei ba ichupe Carumbe hae iatyta Ichugui ipyae mibe.	That sick monkey, Who is called Cachimbo,† The tortoise and the snail Go faster than he.
Oñeguáhe Curuzugüi Opama ramo opotì Hae tohoque mombyry Umi aña rymba cati,	They fled from Curuzu, When all . . . . . . Let them go far away These stinking beasts of the devil.

* Admiral Ignacio. † The Marquis de Caxias.

Mamo pa oìme Caxias	Where is Caxias
I curumbe eta ndibe?	With all his tortoises?
Mbae güi udo ieraiái	Why does he not come
I caraia eta rehebe?	With his troop of monkeys?
Ma pico Bartolo ypi	What has Bartolo* done,
Hae aeo burro monda etè	And that thieving ass
Oiée ba ichupe Flore	Whom they call Flores,
Umi aña membyre?	Those sons of the devil?
Caraia Peru tujape	To the old monkey Peter †
Mocòibe oméé oguétá	Both have sold themselves;
Hae ogüeru oincapa ete	And have brought to be killed
Umi hétá ygna cuera etá.	Very many of their countrymen.
Ibyro co umi aña cuera	What fools are these devils!
Umicha gua na ñahendui	Never has been seen their equals.
Ni aipo Neron tuia yma	Nero, of old, such as he was,
Abe pe no momboioiái!	Is not to be compared with them!
Umicha gua mborebi pe	With these (creatures) like tapirs,
Toho ute leon ñaro.	Whom the fierce lion pursues.
Ta hésái ñande Rubicha	Health to our Commander,
Hae icatu bao ña ñoràirò!	And we will go on fighting!

It is worthy of notice that *caraì*, is a man, and *caraia*, a monkey in Guaraní; the latter being a contraction, I expect, of *carai camba*, a black man, or perhaps of *carai aba*, a hairy man, the latter being the most probable. It must be remembered that the South-American Indians are brownish, or dark-olive skinned, and have no hair on their limbs.

NOTES ON THE DISEASES OF PARAGUAY.

In a work intended for general reading I can say but little on the diseases of Paraguay, and yet it will be expected that I should not pass by this subject altogether. I can mention a few of the more serious maladies, without, however, being able to do more than allude to the one which was most general, but least fatal.

Affections of the lungs were common, consumption especially

* Mitre, the President of the Argentine Republic.
† The Emperor of Brazil.

so—rather in opposition, by the way, to the theory "that it is a disease resulting from extreme civilization and too high breeding," which I heard taught in one of the first of our medical schools a few weeks ago; pneumonia and influenza were frequent in the winter, and required, almost constantly, stimulant treatment.

Yellow fever, typhus, enteric fever, were unknown, and cholera also until the middle of the war, when it was introduced by the Allies; who imported, likewise, small-pox and, perhaps, measles. The latter disease played fearful havoc amongst all classes, for the very reason that they had been carefully protected against its introduction, so instead of confining itself to children, as with us, and who are less liable to suffer from the complications which may attend it, it attacked all ages alike, and cost the lives of at least 60,000 persons.

Affections of the digestive organs, liver complaints, and so on, were not common amongst the natives, who were generally abstemious; but the English *employés* of the Government, who, as a rule, ate twice as much food as they needed, and, of course, drank a good deal more than was good for them, suffered greatly from irritation and congestion of those organs. Diarrhœa, dysentery, and colic—the latter from eating uncrushed roasted maize, and especially from using water-melons as a chief article of diet—were common enough; but if proper regimen could be adopted they readily yielded to treatment.

Ague was prevalent in the marshy districts, and sometimes appeared in the capital, if the wind blew long from the west (sweeping therefore over the fens of the Gran Chaco), but the usual treatment soon cured it.

I saw a good many cases of goître; several amongst females of good family, eating wholesome food, living in lofty rooms, not drinking snow-water (they often wished they could), living on open, sunny plains, where lime was extremely scarce, and knowing deep, rocky valleys only by tradition. So none of the usual theories will explain its occurrence amongst them; but, on the other hand, it was more common amongst the poorer classes, who lived in low, crowded, ill-ventilated huts, and led lives of brutish indolence in the forests. Dr. Stewart contributes the following singular fact to its pathology; he says, " When the Paraguayan army invaded Corrientes " (during the war with Rosas in 1856), " a considerable number of the men were attacked, almost suddenly, by goître, which disappeared, however, almost as suddenly when they returned home."*

It was never accompanied by cretinism; indeed I cannot remember to have seen, or heard of, a single idiot amongst the Paraguayans, although insanity of a violent form—which, however, always seemed to recognize the existence of police regulations—was not infrequent. This statement does not clash with my theory on page 19; the idiotism shown by the Guaiquì Indians would be of a totally different kind to that which is sometimes associated with goître. A cretin has never had an intellect to lose, that is, a brain structure to evolve it; the Guaiquis have lost the little intellectual power their parents transmitted to them. The one, I take it, has a deficiency in a structural sense, the other in a potential one. But I think the association of cretinism with goître in the relation of cause and effect is entirely gratuitous; they are sometimes found together because the same cause may simultaneously produce widely different effects by acting at the same time on distinct structures or functions, which is obvious enough, but it is surely illogical to assume that these effects, therefore, depend upon each other.

That mysterious and repulsive disease, elephantiasis (pachydermia) was occasionally met with, and all those suffering from it were exiled to a remote village in the interior, under the mistaken idea that it is contagious. The skin of those suffering from it becomes thickened, and, especially that of the face and arms, is raised in rough, dark ridges, giving the appearance the old writers termed the " leonine face." All treatment I tried, or saw tried by others, failed to relieve it.

Tetanus was not infrequent, and often seemed to be due

* Du Graty, La République de la Paraguay. Bruxelles, 1865.

to exposure of the body when heated by exercise to the south wind, which there is what the north-east is to us.

However, after this formidable list, I must add that Paraguay is one of the healthiest countries in the world, if one will but adopt reasonable sanatory precautions : that is to say, live temperately, wear flannel next the skin, bathe frequently, avoid the sun during the hotter part of the day, and keep out of the marshy districts. Except the epidemics I have mentioned, there was scarcely an ailment which could not be referred either to indolence, gluttony, or immorality. "As we are all mortal," says John Hunter, "some diseases must necessarily prove fatal;" but I am certainly of opinion that one has a better chance of a healthy life, and of dying of that malady, not so common with us as it might be, called old age, in Paraguay than in England. The idea that it is not suited to our constitutions, and that we cannot work there as we do here, is an old fallacy ; Englishmen do not work there so hard as at home simply because there is no need to do it, because wealth may be gained by an amount of exertion which here would barely win the necessaries of life ; but, at the same time, did they so work the reward would certainly repay the industry.

MR. EDEN'S ACCOUNT.

"I, William Eden, went out to Paraguay in 1861, under contract for three years to take charge of the saw-mills, and took my wife with me. When my time had expired I wished to leave the country, but was not allowed to do so; however, I was pretty well treated until the Brazilians came up and bombarded Asuncion, in February, 1868. The town was then cleared out, but we and nearly all the English took refuge in the United States Legation, as we had permission to do from Colonel Fernandez. There we were tolerably comfortable until the following May, when the police commenced annoying us, and sentries were posted all round the house. Lopez wished us to return to work, and ordered us to do so, but, as we thought he would not dare to touch us in the house of the American minister, we refused to do so, although we were glad enough to do it afterwards. On the 11th of July Mr. Washburn was written to about turning us into the streets, and, as he had no means of protecting us, he at once did so. There were there three Englishmen besides myself, John Watts, George Miles, and William Newton (the rest had thought it safer to leave the capital as ordered), with their wives and children, also two widows and several orphans.

"In the street we were at once taken into custody by a lot of policemen with drawn swords, and marched down to the railway station, where they kept us prisoners, and huddled together in a corner of the waiting-room for eight days. Then we were taken to a place called San Lorenzo, about ten miles off, and put all together in a mud hut about twelve feet square, but they let me and my wife sleep outside, under cover of a piece of old carpet we had wrapped round one of our boxes. About midnight three men with drawn swords came and dragged John Watts out of the hut, bound his arms behind him with strips of hide, and marched him away, leaving his wife and four poor children in a dreadful state of mind. We never saw him again, and heard some time afterwards that he had been shot. A fortnight later, Mrs. Watts asked Miles and Newton to break open her box for her, because her husband had taken the keys with him, and she wanted some money and clothes out of it. This was seen by one of our guards, and a few hours afterwards they and I were taken away, and put in prison, as they called it, but we were kept in the open air, and put in the stocks at night. In four days' time the chief of police and a priest came and called me on one side, and, after a few questions, told me I could return home as I had not helped to break open the box. Thus I learnt for the first time why we had been treated so badly. My companions remained as prisoners in the open air for eleven weeks longer. My wife took charge of Mr. Newton's children, and we daily sent food for him and Miles, or they would soon have died from starvation. After this they left us alone for some time, but we were ordered not to speak to any of the natives, and not to go near their houses; and we were constantly watched. During this time the foreigners who were living near us became fewer every day, and we often saw prisoners being taken away, sitting sideways on mules, with heavy irons on their legs.

"On the 5th of December, 1868, we were suddenly ordered to go to Luquè, to the police-office there. We went, and I was asked as to which part of the country I wished to go. I told them that I knew nothing about the country, for I was a stranger there, and they gave me a passport to go to Piribubuÿ, on the other side of the mountains. The officer told me we could go by train as far as the line was finished, but they made us pay heavily for it, and it took us two days to get to the nearest part of it; however, it helped us on thirty miles or so, and we were put down at a place called Tacuaràl. We saw a great many wounded Paraguayans brought to it; they were in a most horrible condition, but no one appeared to pay any attention to their wounds or to them. There we remained for ten days in the open air, without even a tree to shelter us, nothing but the long grass and bushes. We offered to pay anything they pleased for a cart to take our things on, but all the *carretas* and bullocks had been taken away for the use of the army; at last an order came to go on immediately, as the enemy was close upon us. There were several thousand fugitives, besides ourselves, of all nations, and when the order came, each took up as much as could be carried, and we hurried away like a flock of sheep. I paid some native women fifty dollars for carrying my things across a swamp, and after four days' toil we reached the great lake of Ipacaraì, which is at the foot of the mountains. We crossed it at a shallow part, in a barge which was pushed along by eight stout, nakẹd, young women, who splashed through the water nearly up to their necks; they made lots of money that day, for they charged five dollars apiece for taking us over.

In that journey I saw misery enough to break the heart of a savage; the road was strewn with dead and dying people, and there was no one to help them.

"By good fortune I met with a small bullock-cart, and hired it for thirty dollars to take our boxes over the mountains to a place called Atirà. My wife and I went on foot, but when we got there the owner of it would go no further; so I went to the chief to ask him to let us have another, but he ordered us to go on at once; that, however, was impossible, and we kept out of sight for four days, and spent our Christmas in a wretched shed, in a torrent of rain which lasted nearly forty-eight hours, and we had scarcely anything to eat.

"There we were all scattered, and I was not allowed to go with the rest of my countrymen; at last I hired another cart for fifty dollars, and I bought a horse to help us over the bad places in the road, which was only a rough, rocky path through the forests and marshes.

"After two days' toil we arrived at our destination, having been twenty-five days altogether on our journey. At Piribubuy we found Mr. Valpy and Mr. Burrell, civil engineers, who were very kind to us, and sent us food as soon as they heard of our starving condition.

"The village was full of people, of all nationalities, and in a dreadful state of destitution and disease. I got permission to live in a half-ruined house about two miles from it, with some natives, and stopped there until the end of May. We suffered great privations and hardships, two of my companions died literally from want; they had been rich men before the war commenced, but they had been robbed by Lopez of everything they possessed. My horse was taken from me when I had been there three weeks, and I had to go on foot nearly every day to the village through the sun or rain, sometimes to report myself to the police, at other times to try and buy food, but I often went back to my wife hungry and empty-handed with the money in my pocket; she was laid up with rheumatic fever, and her feet were badly wounded in walking over the mountains, and then I was struck down with fever and ague.

"At last, to save our lives, my wife determined to go to Madame Lynch, and ask her to intercede with Lopez to take me back to my employment; she received her very kindly, and gave her some little comforts which gold could not have bought, for which I shall always feel deeply grateful to her, for I believe they saved our lives.

"After some delay I returned to work at the new arsenal in Cāācupè, but had a very hard time of it; we had very long hours, very little to eat, and only half our pay. But I, and the English generally, was well off compared with the wretched natives, and especially the poor prisoners of war, who were made to work there day and night, and the horrible treatment they received was shocking beyond expression.

"The people, too, were nearly all naked and starving, and died by hundreds, so that at last the few living were not strong enough to bury the dead, and they lay about in the fields and by the roadside just as they fell, and I have often driven off the vultures from their horrid meal when going to and from my work. Sometimes a few of them would try to get away to the Brazilians on the other side, but they were almost always caught, and then were flogged nearly to death, and afterwards tied to stakes or speared as a warning to the others; both men and women were served in this way. Once, as I was going to work, a Paraguayan I knew called me to see them execute a young man I was well acquainted with. There he stood, poor fellow, with heavy irons on his legs, by the side of an open grave; they put a cloth over his eyes, and then pulled off his poncho, and I saw that his back was almost cut to pieces, and a moment afterwards, to my horror, they plunged their lances through his body, then they knocked off his fetters and threw him into the grave. I asked the man who called me what his offence was, and he said only trying to go where he could get something to eat.

"But I am sick of these horrors; I could not tell in a week of one half of the wretchedness and cruelty I witnessed in Paraguay.

But they came to an end for me on the 15th of August, 1869, when we were rescued at the last moment by the Brazilians. I never thought I should have come out alive, but God, in His great mercy, preserved my wife and me through it all."

The account given by Mr. Newton is substantially the same as the above, and, therefore, there is no need to trouble my readers by reproducing it.

EXPLANATION OF GUARANI NAMES OF PLACES, ETC.

Aguapè, Victoria Regia lily.

Aguapeì, a lake or river covered with that plant.

Apà, slow, a river so called.

Càā, a tree or plant, grass.

Càāguazù, the great wood.

Càāpucù, long grass.

Carandaì, a palm.

Carandaitì, a palm forest.

Curùpaì, an acacia, with a very astringent bark.

Curùpaiti, the acacia forest.

Caraguatà, a bromelia, wild pine-apple.

Caraguataì, the river of ditto.

Cambaì, river Negro.

Curuzù, a cross.

Guàsu, a deer.

Guasuvirà, deer-areca, a palm so called.

Guazù, big, great.

Guirà, a bird.

Hobì, green, blue.

Hu, black.

I or *Y (eù)*, water, a river.

Mi, michi, mìmi, miti, little.

Morotì, white.

Mbuyapeì, Bread River.

Nembucù, a babbler, a great talker.

Pucù, long.

Ponà, poa, beautiful.

Piri, rushes, sedges.

Piribebuì, the rushy marsh.

Peguàho, a deep morass.

Para, the sea.

Paranà, like the sea.

Parà, spotted.

Tacuàra, bamboo.

Tacuarì, Bamboo River.

Tebicuari, the name of a river.*

* The meaning of this word is rather amusingly explained by Senor Angelis, thus: "*Tebi* es una parte innoble del cuerpo humano. *qua*, es agujero, ó *i* agua ò rio, y por consiguiente. *agua que sale de un manantial qui se parece a lo que expresan las demas palabras*" !

Tobati, white face.
Tayi, lapacho, a tree.
Yaguaron, the hill of the tiger.
Yberá, shining water.
Ypoa, beautiful water.
Ypitá, Red River.
Ytá, or *itá*, a stone.

Ytàpè, a flat stone.
Ytacuà, a moving stone.
Ytapuà, an elevated rock.
Ybicui, sand.
Yuquì, salt.
Ybitimì, a pile of earth.

In Spanish y is exchangeable with i, and proper names requiring a capital are usually spelt with it; but Ybicui may be written Ibicui if preferred.

I should be taking up too much space if I were to enter into any examination of this singular and most complex language, but it has one peculiarity I ought to mention; some few words, generally expressive of affection or surprise, are reserved for the use of the women; a man would be laughed at if he were to make use of them. It is highly probable that this idiom is the result of the fusion of two languages, one of which belonged to a conquered and forgotten race.

Cuña, a woman, means loose-tongue. *Cuñatai*, a girl, tender, loose-tongue. *Cuñacarai*, an old woman, is composed of the same word, and *carai*, a man.

STEWART *v.* GELOT.

THERE is an incident connected somewhat intimately with the life of Lopez, and. illustrating as it does his unscrupulous and avaricious character, well worth recording here, although the facts are probably still fresh in the public mind. On the 21st of December, 1869, the case of Stewart *v.* Gelot was tried at Edinburgh, before the Lord Justice-Clerk and a special jury, the plaintiff seeking to remove the attachment of a sum of £5,000 standing to his credit in a private bank.

The facts deposed to during the trial are these : in Dec., 1866, Lopez was seriously ill, and he affected to believe that he had had improper medicines administered to him by his medical attendants; he accordingly summoned Dr. Stewart, who was then Director-General of the Medical Department, to his quarters, and told him, amid a torrent of invective, that he (Stewart) was trying to poison him, and that he should have him tried by court-martial for the capital offence. The doctor, who had the reputation of being as rich as he is charitable and kind-hearted, and who had married a native lady of some wealth and considerable personal attractions, left the presence of Lopez in a state of mind which I can fully realize, but which to anyone unacquainted with the state of affairs in Paraguay would seem very unnecessary alarm, seeing that he was perfectly innocent of the crime in question. Shortly afterwards, Madame Lynch sent for him, and said, " Oh, doctor, I am afraid that the President is going to do something for which I shall never forgive him." Which was by no means reassuring, and then, after a few words of sympathy, very significantly asked him for a bill for £4,000 on an English house. He hesitated a little, but, seeing the evident connection between the threat and the bill, consented to give it; but she spoke no more of it until the following May, when she reminded him of his promise. At that time the pretended charges against him were revived, and his wife, also, was charged with "want of patriotism," which was the usual prelude to arrest, perhaps death.

The bill bore on the face of it, as usual, that it was for value received, but Dr. Stewart never received one farthing on account of it; Madame Lynch, it is true, promised to send him the money, but, knowing perfectly well that if he took it the charge against him would be renewed, he never asked for it. Besides, his estates had by that time been stripped of nearly every head of cattle he possessed, not only without one dollar compensation from the Government, but without even saying, " By your leave," or getting any acknowledgment for them; and accepting any money would, probably, only have led to the coin he possessed in Paraguay taking the same road as his herds had done.

In October, 1868, whilst I was still at Villeta, H.M. gunboat

" Beacon " came up to Angustura, and, as Lopez was anxious to prove to the outside world that he was one of the justest of men, he gave permission to some of his English prisoners to remit money home, and also to write letters to their friends, which he was kind enough to read and revise before they were sent, describing how happy and contented they were (Mr. Taylor, by the way, had that gratification amongst others), and how sorry they should be to leave the service of Marshal Lopez. At the same time, he told Dr. Stewart that he might send away a few thousand dollars, and asked him to transmit £11,000 of his own to England, but in Stewart's name. This was done, and Dr. Stewart wrote a letter, which I read with great pain and regret recently, in which he also described everything in Paraguay in *couleur de rose*, and directed his brother (at Galashiels) to honour the bill enclosed, but so ambiguously that he would be sure not to do so.

The battle of Ità-Yvatè soon followed, in which Dr. Stewart was taken prisoner as he was trying to keep a few men together and to help the wounded. He was taken before Caxias, who at once sent him to Asuncion to look after the Paraguayan wounded. "Now," says our Englishman, who has never been in Paraguay, "he at once writes home, tells his brother that his previous letter was composed for the purpose of hoodwinking Lopez, and stops payment of the bill." He dared do nothing of the kind! his wife and three children were in the hands of the tyrant, and their lives would pay for any indiscretion of his; the war might last for years longer, and Lopez's good friend, General Mc Mahon, who had not yet been able to convey the money he had been entrusted with to Paris, would take care to let him know if the bill had been paid; and why should he peril their lives for such ends? Lopez,.however, anticipated the fault by its punishment; he had Stewart denounced in the " Semanario," as a deserter and a traitor; his wife was arrested and treated with the same barbarity, in all save the application of torture, as the rest of the prisoners; she lay six weeks in the summer sun, had to sell her clothes to buy food, and yet was almost starved to death. Then, as some stir was made about her by Commander Parsons, she was released, and was rescued by the Allies after the flight from Cāācupè. I am glad to add, for she is one of the most esteemed of my native friends, that she is now safe and well in Asuncion, but one of her children is dead.

Dr. Stewart came on to England, never expecting to see his wife again, but leaving one of his brothers in Asuncion to receive her if she should escape, and found that the bill had been paid by the agent of Lopez to a certain Mons. Gelot, of Paris, and that payment of it had been refused by his brother. Thereupon Gelot attaches the money lying to the credit of Dr. Stewart, and hence the action.

Now the cattle taken from the *estancias* of Dr. Stewart were worth some £20,000. Lopez seized the whole of his plate, money, and the jewellery of his wife, when the latter was arrested, and I have no doubt that the bulk of it is at this moment in Paris. Therefore, Dr. Stewart claims the £11,000 he sent from Paraguay for Lopez in part payment of the amount due to him ; and I most sincerely hope, and I am sure that everyone who believes what I have written, and which was told me by Lieut.-Col. Thompson, C.E., and by Mr. Valpy, who were with Dr. Stewart at Humaitá at the time, will echo my wish, that he may keep it.

At the trial I gave an account of the state of the country, and the reign of terror prevailing there, and my evidence was fully confirmed by Mons. Laurent-Cochelet, late *chargé d'affaires* in Paraguay, now French Consul in Glasgow, by Mr. Burrell, and Mr. Valpy, who spoke also to the main question. It is not worth while to reproduce the evidence, so I quote only the summing up of the Lord Justice-Clerk, which gives it *en précis*.

The Lord Justice-Clerk said,* "He would very shortly bring before them what appeared to him the points most deserving of consideration as to the matter of law expressed in the issues. What he had to say was this, that in regard to the first part of the first

* From the *Edinburgh Evening Courant.*

issue, an obligation obtained through force and fear was by the law a nullity, seeing all obligations required consent of the parties thereto. A subscription to a bill of exchange was a mode of giving that consent, but a subscription obtained by force and fear was not, and could not be, an indication of consent, nor constitute any obligation against the subscriber. That, he maintained, was well settled in their law. But in order to have that legal remedy, the force and fear must be considerable in degree. It had been defined as that amount of apprehension which would shake the nerves of a constant man, but they could easily imagine without any very precise definition what the law really required for that purpose. It must be considerable, and with reasonable apprehension of grave results. In the second place, the danger must be present and imminent, for mere apprehension of possible contingencies would not be sufficient; and in the third place, it must be a highly conducive cause of the obligation. In regard to the second half of the issue—whether Dr. Stewart granted the bill without having received any value therefor, it was truly a question of fact, and for the sole consideration of the jury. In regard to the second issue, the counsel on either side had agreed that the jury should return a special verdict, the effect of which he would read before they retired. The second question in the issue, as to whether there was any value given for the bill, had considerable bearing on the first, namely, whether the bill had been obtained by force and fear. As to the construction put upon the present made by Lopez to Dr. Stewart of yerba, he said that, in the first place, the jury must be satisfied whether Lopez and Madame Lynch were really to be viewed as identical in the transaction, but even if it were so, there was no evidence whatever that this yerba was at all connected with the transaction in question. A great deal of light was thrown on the granting of the bill itself by a letter of Dr. Stewart which was read by Mr. Watson ; and he was inclined to agree with him, that whatever might be the effect of that letter, it was not sufficient to say that it was written with a view to elude Lopez's inspection in the event of that letter being intercepted. It rather appeared to him that that consideration could not be put upon it. It was a letter sent by a private hand, entering very fully and freely into what the writer had been doing; but while, on the one hand, he thought they might give reasonable credit to the allegations made by Dr. Stewart in this letter as being true; and, on the other hand, while it entirely negatived the idea that Dr. Stewart himself had received value for the bill, it showed the footing on which Madame Lynch had asked for it and obtained it. Apparently that, as disclosed in the letter, was that she would give good security and good interest; that she had offered money itself, but that Dr. Stewart had told her it was of no use. If that were the state of matters, there was an end to the question of value. It was one thing to grant a bill in consideration of money received, and it was quite another to help a friend to send a remittance out of the country in the prospect and expectation of security. These were two totally different things, and if the last were true, it was quite clear that there was no value at all. But in that letter Dr. Stewart said Mrs. Lynch was the most unprincipled woman he ever knew, and that he almost blushed to tell that he gave her the bill solely for the purpose of gaining, if not her friendship, at least that she might not be hostile. Whatever effect, therefore, the promise of security might have had, if that letter was to be taken as containing a true statement of the transaction, it must be taken in all its parts. But in addition to that, they had had one or two points of evidence on this matter. They had it, in the first place, proved that although the bill had been granted on the 8th July, 1867, in a quite ambiguous manner, Dr. Stewart wrote to his brother, at Buenos Ayres, to tell his brother Robert, at Galashiels, not to accept the bill. Of course, he must have been aware, if that had been the case, any damage to which he had been exposed in Paraguay would have been tenfold increased. That being the state of the case, if it were held no value was given, the question was, why was it granted? The pursuer said it was granted by him under force and fear. The suggestion on the other side was that it was not granted through force and fear, but that Dr. Stewart, in the circumstances in which he stood, was willing to do a favour to Madame Lynch, and granted the bill for that purpose. The facts appeared to be plain enough, in the first place, that the bill was wanted to pay a debt of Madame Lynch's, and that she had no means of getting money out of the country, except by a person in Dr. Stewart's position, who had funds abroad. That was the reason of its being granted. Then the next question was, had Dr. Stewart any interest to grant that bill? He had, in that view, nothing whatever to gain by it, and the question the jury were to put to themselves was, apart from the private testimony, did they believe Dr. Stewart would voluntarily have granted this bill if there had not been some inducing cause outside? They had to consider whether that inducing cause was force and fear, not a mere vague apprehension, but a reasonable, strong, and imminent fear of immediate consequences. There were some matters on which there need really be no discussion. There was no doubt the country of Paraguay was ruled by despotism. Lopez, whatever his character, was absolute; in regard to Madame Lynch's relations with him there could be no dispute or doubt, and notwithstanding the evidence of General Mc Mahon, he thought he himself in reality had as little doubt. She was not his wife, but mistress. She had been so for years, and she had a great deal of influence over him, and it was for the jury to say whether they would trust the evidence in which she was described as a tyrant and dangerous. That being the state of matters, and there being little doubt also of the cruelty and violence of Lopez himself on many occasions, he did not go into the evidence of the two American ministers, except to make this remark, that Mr. Washburn had by far the largest opportunity of observing the state of the country, and there seemed to have been a certain amount of political jealousy and disagreement between the representatives of the United States. Whether that was enough to account for the different views they took of these particular persons was a matter the jury might consider, but he did not think they would dwell much on the abstract position of the kingdom of Paraguay. It was a more important matter for them to consider whether force was the inducing cause of Dr. Stewart's action. He was not inclined, on account of the state of the country of Paraguay, to lay down all the transactions between Lopez and Dr. Stewart to fear. What the pursuer had undertaken to prove was specific force as applicable to this specific transaction, and the question was whether he had done so. They were aware how the bill was originally applied for. It was said that Madame Lynch, at a subsequent period offered security ; and it was also equally clear that she at first asked Dr. Stewart to grant this bill without mentioning any security whatever. Dr. Stewart stated that at that time he was in danger of his life, and when the matter was subsequently renewed, he was even in greater danger. Previous to that, however, he talked the matter over with his friend Mr. Valpy, the engineer, and asked his advice. That is a most important piece of corroborative evidence, which, I think, there is no reason to disbelieve. It shows that this act was not done by the free will of Dr. Stewart, but for the purpose of preventing hostility from Madame Lynch, and the provocation he had reason to fear might on the least provocation be turned against him through Lopez, entailing the most serious consequences to him. That portion of Dr. Stewart's evidence was uncontradicted which went to show that, apart from Lopez, his life was to a large extent in the power of Madame Lynch. If they believed in the particular circumstances, as stated, under which the bill was granted, there could be no doubt as to what the inducing cause was. They would recollect that, had the pursuer fallen under Lopez's displeasure, it was not a matter alone of honour and position, but, from the example of many others, it was a matter of life and death in its most literal sense. There was one part of the case which was deserving of their most careful consideration. Supposing it were true that in May, 1867, this bill was obtained by Madame Lynch through the elements contained in the issue, it was stated on the part of the defender that a year and a half afterwards a transaction of a somewhat peculiar kind had taken place. In October, 1868, Lopez sent for Dr. Stewart, and consulted him as to the best means of sending specie out of the country, and the result of the conversation was that he entrusted no less a sum of money than £12,000 to Dr. Stewart, to be conveyed out of the country to Scotland, trusting to Dr. Stewart's discretion and honesty entirely, and taking no acknowledgment from him of any kind. It was impossible to say that that transaction did not throw a certain light on the transactions between Lopez and Dr. Stewart. It was possible that in that year they had come to be on more friendly terms than they were during the year before. There could be no doubt but that the specie had been given, and that the money had been sent through Dr. Stewart's brother at Buenos Ayres to the Royal Bank of Scotland, where it still lay. The specie realized £16,000. Of this £3,000 belonged to Dr. Stewart and Dr. Skinner, and the remainder admittedly belonged to Lopez. It is said that the pursuer wrote a letter to his brother, directing him to apply £4,000 of the money, which was admittedly the property of Lopez, in payment of that bill; and on receiving that letter the brother wrote to Monsieur Gelot to tell him that he had received such instructions, and meant to fulfil them. If the jury were satisfied that the instruction was sent by Lopez, he was not in a position to tell them that they were not entitled to give effect to that. There could be no doubt at all that whatever might have been the tyranny and arbitrary power of Lopez, if he entrusted this money to Dr. Stewart to be used for his (Lopez's) use, and Dr. Stewart undertook to do so, then Dr. Stewart was bound to fulfil his obligation. It is not so much a matter of law as a matter of common sense. If that be the fact, then Lopez was entitled to require Dr. Stewart to apply it as he (Lopez) might direct. As to the second issue, the counsel had agreed that the jury should return a special verdict. He was glad that that course had been adopted, as no little difficulty had been thereby removed. In the event of the jury agreeing to return a special verdict, he had drawn up the following, which

they could consider : " The jury find that the bill mentioned
in the second issue was received by the defender in payment of
a debt previously due to him by Madame Lynch, and that no
fresh credit was given or advance of money made by the defender
on the faith of that bill; and the jury leave it to the Court to
enter a verdict for the pursuer or defender according as they
may be of opinion whether on these facts, taken in connection
with their verdict on the first issue, the defender was or was
not the onerous and *bona fide* holder of the bill, and entitled to
recover the amount from the pursuer." Of course it was only
in the event of their coming to a verdict in favour of the pursuer on the first issue that this special verdict would be required.
For if they were of opinion that this bill was not obtained
through force or fear, but granted in the ordinary course, then
beyond all question the defender would stand in the position of
onerous and *bona fide* holder of the bill.

After the lapse of an hour the jury returned into court.

The Lord Justice-Clerk said : " Gentlemen, you have expressed a wish to know whether, when Dr. Stewart directed
payment of the bill in 1868, he was in precisely the same circumstances as when he originally granted it. That is a question in the evidence of which you are judges. It is said he
wrote the letter as he granted the bill, under force and fear, but
it will not fail, I think, to strike you that the circumstances
were by no means the same. In the one case, the bill was a
matter in which, on the evidence, the pursuer had no concern
or interest, and you may make that an element in considering
the question whether it was granted through fear. In the
second case, if you are of opinion that Lopez concurred in that
use of his money, things were very different, for then he was
the custodier of money which belonged to Lopez. Before
arriving at any conclusion on this point they should satisfy
themselves as to whether Lopez was cognizant of and concurred
in that application of his money. Because, otherwise, if it was
merely Madame Lynch, and not Lopez, then there would not be
the amount of difference in the circumstances that there would
be on the other side."

The jury retired shortly after three o'clock ; and after three hours' absence returned a verdict for the pursuer on the first issue, and in terms of the special verdict read by the Lord Justice-Clerk in his charge on the second issue.

The defendant has applied for leave for a new trial, on the score that the verdict was against the evidence ; the judges in Banco have agreed to grant it on condition that new facts not shown at the trial are brought forward, for on the question of intimidation and non-receipt of value there can be no doubt: and so the matter stands.

I have only at the last moment before going to press received the particulars of the treatment suffered by Major von Versen in Paraguay, or I should have inserted it in its proper place ; for a better example of the capricious cruelty of Lopez could scarcely be met with, nor, at the same time, could a more facile proof of its reality be afforded to those who still look upon the Dictator, either as a general or a generous man, than a reference by letter to Major Versen himself.

In 1866 the fame of the gallant defence of the Paraguayans had reached Prussia ; and Major von Versen, then on the personal staff of the commander-in-chief, was so struck with the indomitable courage displayed by them, and, what seemed to be, the admirable generalship of Lopez, that he applied to the King of Prussia for permission to go out to the seat of war, in order to study the tactics which produced results so extraordinary. The permission was given, and his Majesty furnished him with credentials to the Government of Paraguay, recommending him to its protection, and explaining the objects of his visit.

In July of the following year he reached the camp of the Allies, but was not allowed to pass beyond their lines. Watching, however, for a favourable opportunity, he succeeded in eluding the vigilance of their outposts, and gained the camp of the Paraguayans at Paso Pucù in safety. He was there, as he expected, at once taken prisoner, deprived of his horse, and, by the officer in charge of the picket, Captain Miguel Rojas, conducted to the quarters of General Resquin, who commanded. After being carefully searched, he was taken within the hut, where he found the general himself, the bishop, General Barrios, and Colonel Caminos, the latter the official secretary of Lopez. He was asked who he was, and why he had come into their camp.   In reply, he gave them his name, and referred them to his credentials for further information, as he wished to explain matters more fully to Lopez himself, to whose presence he desired them to conduct him.   They laughed in his face, told him that he was a spy and his letter a forgery, and left him under guard whilst the result of his examination was reported to the Dictator.   Now, Major von Versen has one venial weakness : he believes in homœopathy.   He had a case of the harmless little globules in his pocket, and enclosed in it a note in German of their doses and uses.   These were exhibited to Lopez, who professed to discover in them a plot to destroy his own life and poison his officers, and to believe that the hundreds-and-thousands—as children of tender years used to call them—really possessed the terrible qualities the names on the neat little tubes indicated.   His medical officers were at once summoned, and asked if arsenic, aconite, etc., were not *venenos atroces*.   " Of course they are," said one of them, whilst a shudder, initiated by the bishop, ran through the circle of listeners.   " But," continued another, pointing contemptuously to the globules, " if your Excellency thinks *those* are poisons, I will swallow the whole of them at once, to prove their perfect inertness."

Lopez reddened, and dismissing the too-zealous allopathist, sent the manuscript directions to a German, then in the camp, to translate it, and afterwards to two others successively in the capital, in order to test the truth of the first version.   The result was, of course, simply absurd, but, still refusing to believe in the *bona fide* intentions of von Versen, he kept him a prisoner, and refused to admit him to his presence.   His treatment, however, was not so severe as that suffered by many others; he was allowed to keep his money and to walk around his hut under guard ;   but six weeks afterwards he fell dangerously ill with dysentery, from bad food and bitter disappointment, and was sent to the hospital. He was there when Mr. Gould visited Paso Pucù, and that gentleman, on his return to Buenos Ayres, informed von Gülich, the Prussian minister there, of the treatment he was enduring; who thereupon wrote to Lopez, assuring him that von Versen was all that he professed to be, and begging that he might be at once set at liberty. This letter was sent through the lines, but not the slightest attention was paid to it. In March, 1868, he was sent to the *calabozo* of Humaità, and afterwards, with the rest of the prisoners, made the terrible journey to San Fernando by the Chaco route; fortunately, however, he still had a few English sovereigns left, and by their means induced some of the stronger of his companions in misfortune to carry him when his own strength gave out, and he thus escaped the thrust with a bayonet which terminated the life of so many amongst them. Shortly after the arrival of the staff on the banks of the Tebicuari, Dr. Stewart was seated in his hut with Captain C. H. Thompson, when Major Versen was brought to him to ask for some medicine, and a more affecting sight can scarcely be imagined. He was emaciated to the last degree, his clothes were in rags, and his features shrunken with misery and starvation. Dr. Stewart made a sign to his servant to treat the guards to get them out of earshot, and then gave the poor fellow a cup of coffee and a loaf of *chepa;* he eagerly swallowed the former, and raising his eyes to Heaven whilst the tears ran down his cheeks, prayed the Almighty to bless the man who had again preserved his life.* Dr. Stewart was afterwards able to supply him occasionally, but at great risk to himself, with food, and he lived through all the misery at Villeta until he was rescued by the Brazilians at Caàcupè.

Now this story would lose half its force from any commentary of mine, and I will only recommend anyone who

---

* He lately sent a handsome silver coffee-service to Dr. Stewart, " In remembrance," he wrote, " of the cup of coffee you gave me, and to which, and your kindness, I owe my life."

may desire fuller information concerning it tó write to Major von Versen, Posen, Prussia, where he is now doing duty.

Note to page 26.

One of these so-called spies was a Paraguayan named Juan Gonzales; he had left the country some time before the war without applying for a passport, and had settled in Corrientes. He was taken by the conscription into the Argentine army; and was captured by a party of his countrymen, when on sentry duty one night, on the left bank of the Paraná. Lopez wanted a pretext for putting him to death as a deserter, and he was flogged until he "confessed" that he intended to assassinate the President, and that he had swam across the Paraná, there about five miles wide, with a loaded musket held sometimes in one hand, and then in his teeth, for that purpose! He was stripped naked and thrown into the tiger's cage in the presence of a crowd of Paraguayans.

Note to page 28.

My translation of Tuyùyù is incorrect, I find, but it was the explanation a native gave me. The word really means white-mud.

Note to page 95.

This was the story as it appeared in the Argentine newspapers, and which is repeated by Thompson. But I am assured that it is not true. Leandro Gomez, the officer in question, was anxious to return to his own people, and asked the Brazilian commander to allow him to do so; he was warned that it was dangerous to attempt such a step; but he persisted, and presented himself at the Oriental head-quarters; *there* he was arrested and shot, with another officer, by a commander who had had some private quarrel with him.

Note to page 187, *line* 17.

I believed this story until lately, but am now convinced that my informant had mistaken.

FINIS.

A List of Books

PUBLISHING BY

SAMPSON LOW, SON, AND MARSTON,

Crown Buildings, 188, *Fleet Street.*

[*November*, 1869.

NEW ILLUSTRATED WORKS.

AVOURITE ENGLISH POEMS. An entirely New and Improved Edition. Complete in One Volume 8vo. of 700 pages, choicely printed in the very best style of woodcut printing, cloth extra, gilt edges, price One Guinea.

This Edition has been for a long period in preparation under a careful Editor, and comprises a Selection of 218 of the most popular Poems in the Language, from the Merle and the Nightingale of William Dunbar, to Christ's Entry into Jerusalem of Dean Milman—a period of 350 years —to which has been added (the only production given of a living Poet) the Laureate's " May Queen," with Hon. Mrs. Boyle's illustrations.

The principle of the Work has been to avoid extracts, and to give each Poem unabridged ; and the rule of the Selection, subject to length has been the simple one of *public favouritism*, and it is hoped that the extension to more than double the number of Poems in the present Edition over any previous one, the completeness of the arrangement, with Dates throughout, and good List of Contents and Index, combine to give the Work a permanent literary value.

The Illustrations comprise no less than 320 of the very best Engravings on wood ever produced, from Designs by the most eminent Artists, the whole of which, with but one or two exceptions, have been designed and engraved for the Publishers for different editions of this Work and its Contributories.

CHRIST IN SONG. Hymns of Immanuel, selected from all Ages, with Notes. By Philip Schaff, D.D. Crown 8vo. toned paper, beautifully printed at the Chiswick Press. With Initial Letters and Ornaments, and handsomely bound. 8s. 6d.

WONDERS OF ITALIAN ART. By Louis Viardot. Illustrated with Ten Autotype Reproductions of Celebrated Engravings, and Thirty Woodcuts. Handsomely bound, square demy 8vo. cloth extra, gilt edges, 12s. 6d.

A DREAM BOOK. By E. V. B. Twelve Drawings in Pen and Pencil, or Sepia, by E. V. B. illustrator of " Story Without an End," &c. reproduced in perfect Fac-simile by the Autotype process, with Letterpress descriptions. Medium 4to. handsomely bound, gilt edges, 31s. 6d.

An Elegy in a Country Churchyard. By Thomas Gray. With Sixteen Water-Colour Drawings, by Eminent Artists, printed in Colours in Fac-simile of the Originals. Uniform with the Illustrated "Story Without an End." Royal 8vo. cloth, 12s. 6d.; or in morocco, 25s.

> "*Another edition of the immortal 'Elegy,' charmingly printed and gracefully bound, but with a new feature. The illustrations are woodcuts in colours, and they are admirable specimens of the art.*"—Art Journal. "*Remarkable for thoughtful conception and all that artistic finish of which this newly-born art is capable.*"—Morning Post. "*Beauty and care visible throughout.*"—Standard.

The Story Without an End. From the German of Carové. By Sarah Austin. Illustrated with Sixteen Original Water-Colour Drawings by E. V. B., printed in Fac-simile and numerous Illustrations on wood. Small 4to. cloth extra, 12s.; or in morocco, 21s.

> *** Also a Large Paper Edition, with the Plates mounted (only 250 copies printed), morocco, ivory inlaid, 31s. 6d.

> "*Nowhere will he find the Book of Nature more freshly and beautifully opened for him than in 'The Story without an End,' of its kind one of the best that was ever written.*"—Quarterly Review.

Also, illustrated by the same Artist.

Child's Play. Printed in fac-simile from Water-Colour Drawings, 7s. 6d.
Tennyson's May Queen. Illustrated on Wood. Large Paper Edit. 7s. 6d.

Forget-me-Nots. By Mrs. Ross. With Illustrations by Richard Doyle.   [*In the Press.*

The Wood-Nymph: a Fairy Tale. By Hans Christian Andersen. Translated by Miss Plesner. With Illustrations by Simpson. Square cloth extra. 2s. 6d.

Peaks and Valleys of the Alps. From Water-Colour Drawings by Elijah Walton. Chromo-Lithographed by J. H. Lowes, with Descriptive Text by the Rev. T. G. Bonney, M.A., F.G.S. Folio, half morocco, with 21 large Plates. Original subscription 8 guineas. A very limited edition only now issued at 4l. 14s. 6d.

The Seven Churches of Asia. The result of Two Years' Exploration of their Locality and Remains. By Mr. A. Svoboda. With 20 full-page Photographs taken on the spot. Edited with a preface by the Rev. H. B. Tristram, F.L.S. 4to. cloth extra, price 2 guineas.

> "*Some time since we reviewed the photographs taken by Mr. Svoboda on the sites of the famous Christian cities of Asia Minor, and found in them much that was interesting to the Biblical student and historian. We have in the well-printed volume before us twenty of these interesting illustrations, which fairly display the present state of the ruins so deeply connected with the early history of Christianity. Of these Smyrna supplies four, Ephesus five, Laodicea two, Hieropolis one, Sardis two, Philadelphia one, Magnesia Sypilus one, Thyatira one, and Pergamos three. To these the author has attached a carefully-written and very interesting series of accounts of the ruins and their history, taken from a popular and Scriptural point of view. Mr. Tristram has done his share of the work well, and edited a capital manual which is suited not only to general readers, but as a book of reference on a subject about which little is known, and that little not available without researches which would rival those of our author.*"—Athenæum.

Illustrations of the Natural Order of Plants; with Groups and
Descriptions. By Elizabeth Twining. Splendidly illustrated in colours
from nature. Reduced from the folio edition. 2 vols. Royal 8vo. cloth
extra, price 5 guineas.

Choice Editions of Choice Books. New Editions. Illustrated by
C. W. Cope, R. A., T. Creswick, R. A., Edward Duncan, Birket Foster,
J. C. Horsley, A. R. A., George Hicks, R. Redgrave, R.A., C. Stonehouse,
F. Tayler, George Thomas, H. J. Townshend, E. H. Wehnert, Har-
rison Weir, &c. Crown 8vo. cloth, 5s. each; mor. 10s. 6d.

Bloomfield's Farmer's Boy.	Keat's Eve of St. Agnes.
Campbell's Pleasures of Hope.	Milton's l'Allegro.
Cundall's Elizabethan Poetry.	Rogers' Pleasures of Memory.
Coleridge's Ancient Mariner.	Shakespeare's Songs and Sonnets
Goldsmith's Deserted Village.	Tennyson's May Queen.
Goldsmith's Vicar of Wakefield.	Weir's Poetry of Nature.
Gray's Elegy in a Churchyard.	Wordsworth's Pastoral Poems.

Bishop Heber's Hymns. An Illustrated Edition, with upwards
of one hundred Designs. Engraved in the first style of Art. New Edition. Small 4to. price 7s. 6d.; morocco, 15s.

The Divine and Moral Songs of Dr. Watts: a New and very
choice Edition. Illustrated with One Hundred Woodcuts in the first
style of Art, from Original Designs by Eminent Artists. Small 4to.
cloth extra, 7s. 6d.; morocco, 15s.

Christian Lyrics. Chiefly selected from Modern Authors. 138
Poems, illustrated with upwards of 150 Engravings, under the superintendence of J. D. Cooper. Small 4to. cloth extra, 10s. 6d.; morocco, 21s.

Light after Darkness: Religious Poems, by Harriet Beecher
Stowe. With Illustrations. Small post 8vo. cloth, 3s. 6d.

The Abbey and Palace of Westminster, with Forty National
Photographs. By John Harrington. Royal 4to.; morocco, 5 guineas.

A Search for Winter Sunbeams in the Riviera, Corsica, Algiers,
and Spain. By the Hon. Samuel S. Cox. With numerous graphic
Woodcuts, Chromolithographs, and Steel Engravings. 8vo. cloth extra,
16s.

Normandy Picturesque; a New Artistic Book of Travel. By
Henry Blackburn, Author of "Artists and Arabs," &c. Small demy 8vo.
cloth extra, with numerous Illustrations, 16s.

The Pyrenees; 100 Illustrations by Gustave Doré, and a Description of Summer Life at French Watering Places By Henry Blackburn. Royal 8vo. cloth, 18s.; morocco, 25s.

Artists and Arabs; or Sketching in Sunshine. Numerous
Illustrations. Demy 8vo. cloth. 10*s*. 6*d*.

Also by the same Author.

TRAVELLING IN SPAIN, illustrated, 16*s*. or Cheaper Edition, 6*s*.

Milton's Paradise Lost. With the original Steel Engravings of
John Martin. Printed on large paper, royal 4to. handsomely bound,
3*l*. 13*s*. 6*d*.; morocco extra, 5*l*. 15*s*. 6*d*.

The Gentle Life. A Special and entirely New Edition; comprising *portions of both series* in One Volume. *Dedicated, by express permission and desire*, to Her Most Gracious Majesty the Queen. Choicely
Printed in New Type, with Initial Letters and Ornaments. Small 8vo.
[*In preparation*.

Schiller's Lay of the Bell. Sir E. Bulwer Lytton's translation;
beautifully illustrated by forty-two wood Engravings, drawn by Thomas
Scott, and engraved by J. D. Cooper, after the Etchings by Retzsch.
Oblong 4to. cloth extra, 14*s*.; morocco, 25*s*.

Edgar A. Poe's Poems. Illustrated by Eminent Artists. Small
4to. cloth extra, price 10*s*. 6*d*.

Marvels of Glass-Making : its Description and History from the
Earliest Times to the Present. By A. Sauzay. With 47 Illustrations
on Wood, and 8 Autotype Copies of the Best Examples of Roman, Vene-
tian, and German Glass in the South Kensington Museum. Square
demy 8vo. handsomely bound, cloth extra, gilt edges, price 12*s*. 6*d*.

A New and Revised Edition of Mrs. Palliser's Book of Lace,
comprising a History of the Fabric from the Earliest Period, with upwards of 100 Illustrations and Coloured Designs, including some Interesting Examples from the Leeds Exhibition. By Mrs. Bury Palliser.
1 vol. 8vo. cloth extra, One Guinea.

The Royal Cookery Book. By Jules Gouffé, Chef de Cuisine of
the Paris Jockey Club. Translated and Adapted for English use. By
Alphonse Gouffé, Head Pastrycook to Her Majesty the Queen. Illustrated with large Plates beautifully printed in Colours, and One Hundred and Sixty-One Woodcuts. Super-royal 8vo. cloth extra, 2*l*. 2*s*.
Household Edition in one handsome large type book for domestic use.
Price 10*s*. 6*d*., strongly half-bound.

Victor Hugo's Toilers of the Sea. New Edition, with 60 graphic
Illustrations by Chifflart, beautifully printed on toned paper Square
demy 8vo. cloth extra, 10*s*. 6*d*.

The Bottom of the Sea. By M. Sonrel. Translated by Elihu
Rich. Small Post 8vo. cloth extra, with numerous woodcut Illustrations.
5*s*.

The Bayard Series.

COMPRISING

PLEASURE BOOKS OF LITERATURE PRODUCED IN THE CHOICEST STYLE, AS COMPANIONABLE VOLUMES AT HOME AND ABROAD.

Price 2s. 6d. each Volume, complete in itself, printed at the Chiswick Press, bound by Burn, flexible cloth extra, gilt leaves, with silk Headbands and Registers.

THE STORY OF THE CHEVALIER BAYARD. By M. De Berville.

DE JOINVILLE'S ST. LOUIS, KING OF FRANCE.

THE ESSAYS OF ABRAHAM COWLEY, including all his Prose Works.

ABDALLAH; OR, THE FOUR LEAVES. By Edouard Laboullaye.

TABLE-TALK AND OPINIONS OF NAPOLEON BUONAPARTE.

VATHEK : AN ORIENTAL ROMANCE. By William Beckford.

THE KING AND THE COMMONS: a Selection of Cavalier and Puritan Song. Edited by Prof. Morley.

WORDS OF WELLINGTON : Maxims and Opinions of the Great Duke.

DR. JOHNSON'S RASSELAS, PRINCE OF ABYSSINIA. With Notes.

HAZLITT'S ROUND TABLE With Biographical Introduction.

THE RELIGIO MEDICI, HYDRIOTAPHIA, AND THE LETTER TO A FRIEND. By Sir Thomas Browne, Knt.

BALLAD POETRY OF THE AFFECTIONS. By Robert Buchanan.

COLERIDGE'S CHRISTABEL, and other Imaginative Poems. With Preface by Algernon C. Swinburne.

LORD CHESTERFIELD'S LETTERS, SENTENCES AND MAXIMS. With Introduction by the Editor, and Essay on Chesterfield by M. De St. Beuve, of the French Academy.

OTHER VOLUMES IN ACTIVE PROGRESS.

A suitable Case containing 12 volumes, price 31s. 6d.; or the Case separate, price 3s. 6d.

EXTRACTS FROM LITERARY NOTICES.

" The present series—taking its name from the opening volume, which contained a translation of the Knight without Fear and without Reproach—will really, we think, fill a void in the shelves of all except the most complete English libraries. These little square-shaped volumes contain, in a very manageable and pretty form, a great many things not very easy of access elsewhere, and some things for the first time brought together."—Pall Mall Gazette. *" We have here two more volumes of the series appropriately called the ' Bayard,' as they certainly are ' sans reproche.' Of convenient size, with clear typography and tasteful binding, we know no other little volumes which make such good gift-books for persons of mature age."*—Examiner. *" St. Louis and his companions, as described by Joinville, not only in their glistening armour, but in their every-day attire, are brought nearer to us, become intelligible to us, and teach us lessons of humanity which we can learn from men only, and not from saints and heroes. Here lies the real value of real history. It widens our minds and our hearts, and gives us that true knowledge of the world and of human nature in all its phases which but few can gain in the short span of their own life, and in the narrow sphere of their friends and enemies. We can hardly imagine a better book for boys to read or for men to ponder over."*—Times. *" Every one of the works included in this series is well worth possessing, and the whole will make an admirable foundation for the library of a studious youth of polished and refined tastes."*—Illustrated Times.

The Gentle Life Series.

Printed in Elzevir, on Toned Paper, handsomely bound, forming
suitable Volumes for Presents.

Price 6s. each; or in calf extra, price 10s. 6d.

I.

THE GENTLE LIFE. Essays in aid of the Formation of
Character of Gentlemen and Gentlewomen. Ninth Edition.

> *" His notion of a gentleman is of the noblest and truest order. The
> volume is a capital specimen of what may be done by honest reason, high
> feeling, and cultivated intellect. A little compendium of cheerful philo-
> sophy."* —Daily News. *" Deserves to be printed in letters of gold, and
> circulated in every house."* —Chambers' Journal.

II.

ABOUT IN THE WORLD. Essays by the Author of " The
Gentle Life."

> *" It is not easy to open it at any page without finding some happy idea."*
> —Morning Post.

III.

LIKE UNTO CHRIST. A new translation of the " De Imita-
tione Christi," usually ascribed to Thomas à Kempis. With a Vignette
from an Original Drawing by Sir Thomas Lawrence. Second Edition.

> *" Evinces independent scholarship, a profound feeling for the original,
> and a minute attention to delicate shades of expression, which may well
> make it acceptable even to those who can enjoy the work without a trans-
> lator's aid.* —Nonconformist. *" Could not be presented in a more exquisite
> form, for a more sightly volume was never seen."* —Illustrated London
> News

IV.

FAMILIAR WORDS. An Index Verborum, or Quotation
Handbook. Affording an immediate Reference to Phrases and Sentences
that have become embedded in the English language. Second and enlarged Edition.

> *" Should be on every library table, by the side of ' Roget's Thesaurus.' "*
> —Daily News.

V.

ESSAYS BY MONTAIGNE. Edited, Compared, Revised, and
Annotated by the Author of " The Gentle Life." With Vignette Portrait.
Second Edition.

> *" We should be glad if any words of ours could help to bespeak a large
> circulation for this handsome attractive book ; and who can refuse his
> homage to the good-humoured industry of the editor."* —Illustrated Times.

VI.

THE COUNTESS OF PEMBROKE'S ARCADIA. Written
by Sir Philip Sidney. Edited, with Notes, by the Author of " The Gentle
Life." Dedicated, by permission, to the Earl of Derby. 7s. 6d.

> *" All the best things in the Arcadia are retained intact in Mr. Friswell's
> edition, and even brought into greater prominence than in the original, by
> the curtailment of some of its inferior portions, and the omission of most of
> its eclogues and other metrical digressions."* —Examiner.

VII.

THE GENTLE LIFE. Second Series. Third Edition.

" *There is the same mingled power and simplicity which makes the author so emphatically a first-rate essayist, giving a fascination in each essay which will make this volume at least as popular as its elder brother.*"
—Star.

VIII.

VARIA : Readings from Rare Books. Reprinted, by permission, from the *Saturday Review*, *Spectator*, &c.

" *The books discussed in this volume are no less valuable than they are rare, but life is not long enough to allow a reader to wade through such thick folios, and therefore the compiler is entitled to the gratitude of the public for having sifted their contents, and thereby rendered their treasures available to the general reader.*"—Observer.

IX.

A CONCORDANCE OR VERBAL INDEX to the whole of Milton's Poetical Works. Comprising upwards of 20,000 References. By Charles D. Cleveland, LL.D. With Vignette Portrait of Milton.

. Affords an immediate reference to any passage in any edition of Milton's Poems.

" *By the admirers of Milton the book will be highly appreciated, but its chief value will, if we mistake not, be found in the fact that it is a compact word-book of the English language* "—Record.

X.

THE SILENT HOUR : Essays, Original and Selected. By the Author of " The Gentle Life." Second Edition.

" *Out of twenty Essays five are from the Editor's pen, and he has selected the rest from the writings of Barrow, Baxter, Sherlock, Massillon, Latimer, Sandys, Jeremy Taylor, Ruskin, and Izaak Walton. . . . . The volume is avowedly meant 'for Sunday reading,' and those who have not access to the originals of great authors may do worse on Sunday or any other afternoon, than fall back upon the ' Silent Hour' and the golden words of Jeremy Taylor and Massillon. All who possess the ' Gentle Life' should own this volume.*"—Standard.

XI.

ESSAYS ON ENGLISH WRITERS, for the Self-improvement of Students in English Literature.

" *The author has a distinct purpose and a proper and noble ambition to win the young to the pure and noble study of our glorious English literature. The book is too good intrinsically not to command a wide and increasing circulation, and its style is so pleasant and lively that it will find many readers among the educated classes, as well as among self-helpers. To all (both men and women) who have neglected to read and study their native literature we would certainly suggest the volume before us as a fitting introduction.*"—Examiner.

XII.

OTHER PEOPLE'S WINDOWS. By J. Hain Friswell. Second Edition.

" *The chapters are so lively in themselves, so mingled with shrewd views of human nature, so full of illustrative anecdotes, that the reader cannot fail to be amused. Written with remarkable power and effect. ' Other People's Windows' is distinguished by original and keen observation of life, as well as by lively and versatile power of narration.*"—Morning Post.

LITERATURE, WORKS OF REFERENCE, ETC.

THE Origin and History of the English Language, and of the early literature it embodies. By the Hon. George P. Marsh, U. S. Minister at Turin, Author of " Lectures on the English Language." 8vo. cloth extra, 16s.

Lectures on the English Language; forming the Introductory Series to the foregoing Work. By the same Author. 8vo. Cloth, 16s. This is the only author's edition.

Man and Nature; or, Physical Geography as Modified by Human Action. By George P. Marsh, Author of " Lectures on the English Language," &c. 8vo. cloth, 14s.

The English Catalogue of Books: giving the date of publication of every book published from 1835 to 1863, in addition to the title, size, price, and publisher, in one alphabet. An entirely new work, combining the Copyrights of the " London Catalogue" and the " British Catalogue." One thick volume of 900 pages, half morocco, 45s.

⁎ The Annual Catalogue of Books published during 1868 with Index of Subjects. 8vo. 5s.

Index to the Subjects of Books published in the United Kingdom during the last Twenty Years—1837-1857. Containing as many as 74,000 references, under subjects, so as to ensure immediate reference to the books on the subject required, each giving title, price, publisher, and date. Two valuable Appendices are also given—A, containing full lists of all Libraries, Collections, Series, and Miscellanies—and B, a List of Literary Societies, Printing Societies, and their Issues. One vol. royal 8vo. Morocco, 1l. 6s.

⁎ Volume II. from 1857 in Preparation.

Outlines of Moral Philosophy. By Dugald Stewart, Professor of Moral Philosophy in the University of Edinburgh, with Memoir, &c. By James McCosh, LL.D. New Edition, 12mo. 3s. 6d.

Art in England. Essays by Dutton Cook. Small post 8vo. cloth, 6s.

A Dictionary of Photography, on the Basis of Sutton's Dictionary. Rewritten by Professor Dawson, of King's College, Editor of the " Journal of Photography;" and Thomas Sutton, B.A., Editor of " Photograph Notes." 8vo. with numerous Illustrations. 8s. 6d.

Dr. Worcester's New and Greatly Enlarged Dictionary of the English Language. Adapted for Library or College Reference, comprising 40,000 Words more than Johnson's Dictionary. 4to. cloth, 1,834 pp. price 31s. 6d. well bound.

" The volumes before us show a vast amount of diligence; but with Webster it is diligence in combination with fancifulness,—with Worcester in combination with good sense and judgment. Worcester's is the soberer and safer book, and may be pronounced the best existing English Lexicon."—*Athenæum.*

The Publishers' Circular, and General Record of British and Foreign Literature; giving a transcript of the title-page of every work published in Great Britain, and every work of interest published abroad, with lists of all the publishing houses.

Published regularly on the 1st and 15th of every Month, and forwarded post free to all parts of the world on payment of 8s. per annum.

A Catalogue of a Selection of Works in the French, German, Italian, Spanish, and other Langnages that Messrs. Low and Co. keep in Stock, to which is added a List of Grammars and Dictionaries for the use of English Students in Anglo-Saxon, Arabic, Chinese, Danish, Dutch, French, German, Greek, Hebrew, Icelandic, Italian, Latin, Portuguese, Russian, Sanskrit, Spanish, Swedish, Syriac, &c. which they will have pleasure in forwarding, post free, on receipt of Address with stamp.

Low's Monthly Bulletin of American and Foreign Publications, forwarded regularly. Subscription 2*s.* 6*d.* per annum.

A Handbook to the Charities of London. By Sampson Low, Jun. Comprising an Account of upwards of 800 Institutions chiefly in London and its Vicinity. A Guide to the Benevolent and to the Unfortunate. Cloth limp, 1*s.* 6*d.*

Sir J. D. Coleridge on Convents, the Speeches of H.M. Solicitor-General, containing all that may be considered of importance in the lengthened Examination of Witnesses in the case of Saurin *v.* Starr. 8vo. 5*s.*

Prince Albert's Golden Precepts. *Second Edition,* with Photograph. A Memorial of the Prince Consort: comprising Maxims and Extracts from Addresses of His late Royal Highness. Many now for the first time collected and carefully arranged. With an Index. Royal 16mo. beautifully printed on toned paper, cloth, gilt edges, 2*s.* 6*d.*

Our Little Ones in Heaven: Thoughts in Prose and Verse, selected from the Writings of favourite Authors; with Frontispiece after Sir Joshua Reynolds. Fcap. 8vo. cloth extra. Second Edition. 3*s.* 6*d.*

The Authorized English Version of the New Testament; with the various Readings from the most celebrated Manuscripts, including the Sinaitic, the Vatican, and the Alexandrian MSS., in English. With Notes by the Editor, Dr. Tischendorf. The whole revised and carefully collected for the Thousandth Volume of Baron Tauchnitz's Collection. Cloth flexible. gilt edges, 2*s.* 6*d* ; cheaper style, 2*s.* ; or sewed, 1*s.* 6*d.*

The Origin and History of the New Testament. By Professor C. E. Stowe. 8vo. Illustrated Edition, with numerous Facsimiles from Original MSS., Early Editions, &c. Price 10*s.* 6*d.* ; or without the plates, 8*s.* 6*d.*

> " *The work exhibits in every stage the stamp of untiring industry, personal research, and sound method."*—London Review. " *The author brings out forcibly the overwhelming manuscript evidence for the books of the New Testament as compared with the like evidence for the best attested of the profane writers."*—Churchman. " *We have no hesitation in recording our judgment that this is one of the most useful books which our times have produced."*—Watchman.

Latin Proverbs and Quotations, with Translations and Parallel Passages, and a copious English Index. By Alfred Henderson. Fcap. 4to., 530 pp., price 16*s.*

> " *The book is, we should imagine, the best of the kind that has yet been issued from the press."*—Examiner. " *We trust that many will be induced by the taste of good things that we have given them to go to the book itself, which is well worth possessing."*—Spectator. " *A very handsome volume in its typographical externals, and a very useful companion to those who, when a quotation is aptly made, like to trace it to its source, to dwell on the minutiæ of its application, and to find it illustrated with choice parallel passages from English and Latin authors."*—Times. " *A book well worth adding to one's library."*—Saturday Review.

BIOGRAPHY, TRAVEL, AND ADVENTURE.

 THE Last of the Tasmanians: a History of the Black War in Van Dieman's Land. By James Bonwick, F.R.G.S., Fellow of the Ethnological Society, &c. &c. With numerous Illustrations, 16s.

Notes in England and Italy. By Mrs. Nathaniel Hawthorne (Widow of the Novelist). Crown 8vo. cloth. *[Just ready.*

The Bye-Ways of Europe. Visits by Unfrequented Routes to Remarkable Places. By Bayard Taylor, Author of "Views Afoot." 2 vols. post 8vo. 16s.

*" His approach to the Republic of Andorre by the southern route from Barcelona, adopted in the teeth of all his friends' advice; his exciting ride up the valley of the Cardoner and the perilous gorge of the Rio Segre; and his final experiences among the people of that singular fossil republic, which is now threatened with invasion by the homeless tribes of punters and croupiers:—all these things are told by our author in a way that will make his readers long to be upon his footsteps."—*Pall Mall Gazette.

The Life of John James Audubon, the Naturalist, including his Romantic Adventures in the back woods of America, Correspondence with celebrated Europeans, &c. Edited, from materials supplied by his widow, by Robert Buchanan. 8vo. With portraits, price 15s.

*" A readable book, with many interesting and some thrilling pages in it."—*Athenæum. *" From first to last, the biography teems with interesting adventures, with amusing or perilous incidents, with curious gossip, with picturesque description."—*Daily News. *" But, as we have said, Audubon could write as well as draw; and while his portfolio was a cause of wonder to even such men as Cuvier, Wilson, and Sir Thomas Lawrence, his diary contained a number of spirited sketches of the places he had visited, which cannot fail to interest and even to delight the reader."—*Examiner.

Leopold the First, King of the Belgians; from unpublished documents, by Theodore Juste. Translated by Robert Black, M.A 2 vols. 8vo. With portraits. 28s.

*" A readable biography of the wise and good King Leopold is certain to be read in England."—*Daily News. *" A more important contribution to historical literature has not for a long while been furnished."—*Bell's Messenger. *" Of great value to the future historian, and will interest politicians even now."—*Spectator. *" The subject is of interest, and the story is narrated without excess of enthusiasm or depreciation. The translation by Mr. Black is executed with correctness, yet not without a graceful ease. This end is not often attained in translations so nearly verbal as this; the book itself deserves to become popular in England."—*Athenæum.

Fredrika Bremer's Life, Letters, and Posthumous Works. Edited by her sister, Charlotte Bremer; translated from the Swedish by Fred. Milow. Post 8vo. cloth. 10s. 6d.

Remarkable Life and Discoveries of Sebastian Cabot, of Bristol, the Founder of Great Britain's Maritime Power, Discoverer of America and its First Colonizer. By J. F. Nicholls, City Librarian, Bristol. Square crown 8vo. printed at the Chiswick Press, with Marginal Notes, &c. Price 7s. 6d.

Our New Way Round the World. Two Years of Travel by Charles Carleton Coffin. 8vo., with 100 Illustrations and Maps, 12s.

Two Years Before the Mast and Twenty-four Years After. An entirely New Edition of Mr. Dana's Narrative extended. With Notes and Revisions. Copyright Edition. Fcap 8vo. 6s.

" It would be impertinence to praise so well known a book as Mr. Dana's, but we may say that his added chapter to this edition is of very rare interest "—Spectator. ;" Remember, it was an undergraduate of Harvard University who served as a common seaman two years before the mast, and who wrote about the best sea book in the English language."—Mr. Charles Dickens, at the Dinner to the Oxford and Harvard Crews, Aug. 31.

Plutarch's Lives. An entirely new Library Edition, carefully revised and corrected, with some Original Translations by the Editor. Edited by A. H. Clough, Esq. sometime Fellow of Oriel College, Oxford, and late Professor of English Language and Literature at University College. 5 vols. 8vo. cloth. 2l. 10s.

Social Life of the Chinese: a Daguerreotype of Daily Life in China. Condensed from the Work of the Rev. J. Doolittle, by the Rev. Paxton Hood. With above 100 Illustrations. Post 8vo. price 8s. 6d.

The Open Polar Sea: a Narrative of a Voyage of Discovery towards the North Pole. By Dr. Isaac I. Hayes. An entirely new and cheaper edition. With Illustrations. Small post 8vo. 6s.

The Physical Geography of the Sea and its Meteorology; or, the Economy of the Sea and its Adaptations, its Salts, its Waters, its Climates, its Inhabitants, and whatever there may be of general interest in its Commercial Uses or Industrial Pursuits. By Commander M. F. Maury, LL.D. New Edition. With Charts. Post 8vo. cloth extra, price 6s.

Captain Hall's Life with the Esquimaux. New and cheaper Edition, with Coloured Engravings and upwards of 100 Woodcuts. With a Map. Price 7s. 6d. cloth extra. Forming the cheapest and most popular Edition of a work on Arctic Life and Exploration ever published.

A History of the Island of Cape Breton, with Some Account of the History and Settlement of Canada, Nova Scotia, and Newfoundland. By Richard Brown, F.G.S., F.R.G.S. 8vo. cloth, 15s.

Lost Amid the Fogs: Sketches of Life in Newfoundland, England's Ancient Colony. By Lieut.-Col. R. B. M'Crea, Royal Artillery. 8vo. 10s. 6d.

Christian Heroes in the Army and Navy. By Charles Rogers, LL.D. Author of " Lyra Britannica." Crown 8vo. 3s. 6d.

The Black Country and its Green Border Land; or, Expeditions and Explorations round Birmingham, Wolverhampton, &c. By Elihu Burritt. Second and cheaper edition, post 8vo. 6s.

A Walk from London to John O'Groats, and from London to the Land's End and Back. With Notes by the Way. By Elihu Burritt. Two vols. price 6s. each, with Illustrations.

Notes on Yachts. By Edwin Brett. With Frontispiece drawn by John Brett, and engraved by J. D. Cooper. Fcap. cloth, 6s.

The Voyage Alone; a Sail in the " Yawl, Rob Roy." By John M'Gregor. With Illustrations. Price 5s.

Also, uniform, by the same Author, with Maps and numerous Illustrations, price 5s. each.

A Thousand Miles in the Rob Roy Canoe, on Rivers and Lakes of Europe. Fifth edition.

The Rob Roy on the Baltic. A Canoe Voyage in Norway, Sweden, &c.

NEW BOOKS FOR YOUNG PEOPLE.

WILD Life under the Equator. By Paul Du Chaillu, Author of "Discoveries in Equatorial Africa." With 40 Original Illustrations, price 6s.

> " *M. du Chaillu's name will be a sufficient guarantee for the interes' of Wild Life under the Equator, which he has narrated for young people in a very readable volume."*—Times. " *M. Du Chaillu proves a good writer for the young, and he has skilfully utilized his experience for their benefit."* —Economist.

Also by the same Author, uniform.

Stories of the Gorilla Country, 36 Illustrations. Price 6s.

> " *It would be hard to find a more interesting book for boys than this."*— Times. " *Young people will obtain from it a very considerable amount of information touching the manners and customs, ways and means of Africans, and of course great amusement in the accounts of the Gorilla. The book is really a meritorious work, and is elegantly got up."*—Athenæum.

Lost in the Jungle. By P. Du Chaillu. Numerous Illustrations.
6s.   *[In the Press.*

Cast Away in the Cold. An Old Man's Story of a Young Man's Adventures. By the Author of "The Open Polar Sea." With Illustrations. Small 8vo. cloth extra, price 6s.

> " *The result is delightful. A story of adventure of the most telling local colour and detail, the most exciting danger, and ending with the most natural and effective escape. There is an air of veracity and reality about the tale which Capt. Hayes could scarcely help giving to an Arctic adventure of any kind. There is great vivacity and picturesqueness in the style, the illustrations are admirable, and there is a novelty in the 'dénouement' which greatly enhances the pleasure with which we lay the book down. This story of the two Arctic Crusoes will long remain one of the most powerful of children's stories, as it assuredly deserves to be one of the most popular."*—Spectator.

The Autobiography of a Small Boy. By the Author of " School Days at Saxonhurst." Fcap. 8vo. cloth, 5s.

Also now ready.

Alwyn Morton, his School and his Schoolfellows. 5s.
Stanton Grange; or, Life at a Tutor's. By the Rev. C. J. Atkinson. 5s.

The Story of a Bad Boy—not a *very* Bad Boy. By Thomas Bailey Aldrich. With 30 Illustrations. Small post 8vo. cloth, price 5s.
     [Just ready.

Lost; or, What Came of a Slip from Honour Bright. By Rev. J. C. Atkinson. Small post 8vo. with Illustrations, cloth extra, price 5s.
     [Just ready.

The William Henry Letters. By Mrs. Diaz. With numerous Illustrations.

The Silver Skates; a Story of Holland Life. By Mrs. M. A. Dodge. Edited by W. H. G. Kingston. Illustrated, cloth extra, 3s. 6d.

Life amongst the North and South American Indians. By George Catlin. And Last Rambles amongst the Indians beyond the Rocky Mountains and the Andes. With numerous Illustrations by the Author. 2 vols. small post 8vo. 5s. each, cloth extra.

> " *An admirable book, full of useful information, wrapt up in stories peculiarly adapted to rouse the imagination and stimulate the curiosity of boys and girls. To compare a book with ' Robinson Crusoe,' and to say that it sustains such comparison, is to give it high praise indeed."*— Athenæum.

The Voyage of the Constance; a tale of the Polar Seas. By
Mary Gillies. With 8 Illustrations by Charles Keene. Fcap. 3s. 6d.

Our Salt and Fresh Water Tutors; a Story of that Good Old
Time—Our School Days at the Cape. Edited by W. H. G. Kingston.
With Illustrations, price 3s. 6d.

  "*One of the best books of the kind that the season has given us. This
little book is to be commended warmly.*"—Illustrated Times.

The Boy's Own Book of Boats. A Description of every Craft
that sails upon the waters; and how to Make, Rig, and Sail Model
Boats, by W. H. G. Kingston, with numerous Illustrations by E. Weedon.
Second edition, enlarged. Fcap. 8vo. 3s. 6d.

  "*This well-written, well-wrought book.*"—Athenæum.

Also by the same Author,

Ernest Bracebridge: or, Boy's Own Book of Sports. 3s. 6d.
The Fire Ships. A Story of the Days of Lord Cochrane. 5s.
The Cruise of the Frolic. 5s.
Jack Buntline: the Life of a Sailor Boy. 2s.

What are the Stars? a Treatise on Astronomy for the Young.
By M. E. Storey Lyle. Fcap. 8vo. with numerous Illustrations. Cloth,
extra, gilt edges, 3s. 6d.

Phenomena and Laws of Heat: a Volume of Marvels of Science.
By Achille Cazin. Translated and Edited by Elihu Rich. With
numerous Illustrations. Fcap. 8vo. price 5s.

Also, uniform, same price.

Marvels of Optics. By F. Marion. Edited and Translated by C. W.
Quin. With 70 Illustrations. 5s.

Marvels of Thunder and Lightning. By De Fonvielle. Edited by Dr.
Phipson. Full of Illustrations. 5s.

Stories of the Great Prairie. From the Novels of J. F. Cooper.
Illustrated. Price 5s.

Also, uniform, same price.

Stories of the Woods, from the Adventures of Leather-Stocking.
Stories of the Sea, from Cooper's Naval Novels.
The Voyage of the Constance. By Mary Gillies. 3s. 6d.
The Swiss Family Robinson, and Sequel. In 1 vol. 3s. 6d.
The Story Without an End. Translated by Sarah Austin. 2s. 6d.

Adventures on the Great Hunting-Grounds of the World. From
the Frence of Victor Meunier. With additional matter, including the
Duke of Edinburgh's Elephant Hunt, &c. With 22 Engravings,
price 5s.

  "*The book for all boys in whom the love of travel and adventure is
strong. They will find here plenty to amuse them and much to instruct
them besides.*"—Times.

Also, lately published,

One Thousand Miles in the Rob Roy Canoe. By John Macgregor, M.A. 5s.
The Rob Roy on the Baltic. By the same Author. 5s.
Sailing Alone; or, 1,500 Miles Voyage in the Yawl Rob Roy. By the
same Author. 5s.
Golden Hair; a Tale of the Pilgrim Fathers. By Sir Lascelles Wraxall. 5s.
Black Panther: a Boy's Adventures amongst the Red Skins. By the
same Author. 5s.

Jacob and Joseph, and the Lesson of their Lives for the Young.
By Elihu Burritt, Author of "Old Burchell's Pockets, &c." Numerous
Illustrations, price 3s. 6d.

Also beautifully Illustrated :—

Little Bird Red and Little Bird Blue. Coloured, 5s.
Snow-Flakes, and what they told the Children. Coloured, 5s.
Child's Book of the Sagacity of Animals. 5s.; or coloured, 7s. 6d.
Child's Picture Fable Book. 5s.; or coloured, 7s. 6d.
Child's Treasury of Story Books. 5s.; or coloured, 7s. 6d.
The Nursery Playmate. 200 Pictures. 5s.; or coloured, 9s.

Anecdotes of the Queen and Royal Family of England Collected,
arranged, and edited, for the more especial use of Colonial Readers, by
J. George Hodgins, LL.B , F.R.G.S., Deputy-Superintendent of Education for the Province of Ontario. With Illustrations. Price 5s.

Geography for my Children. By Mrs. Harriet Beecher Stowe.
Author of "Uncle Tom's Cabin," &c. Arranged and Edited by an Eng-
lish Lady, under the Direction of the Authoress. With upwards of Fifty
Illustrations. Cloth extra, 4s. 6d.

Child's Play. Illustrated with Sixteen Coloured Drawings by
E. V. B., printed in fac-simile by W. Dickes' process, and ornamented
with Initial Letters. New edition, with India paper tints, royal 8vo.
cloth extra, bevelled cloth, 7s. 6d. The Original Edition of this work
was published at One Guinea.

Little Gerty; or, the First Prayer, abridged and adapted for
a Sunday School Gift Book, from "The Lamplighter." By a Lady
Price 6d.

Great Fun and More Fun for our Little Friends. By Harriet
Myrtle. With Edward Wehnert's Pictures. 2 vols. each 5s.

BELLES LETTRES, FICTION, &c.

OLD Town Folks. By the Author of "Uncle Tom's
Cabin." New and Cheaper Edition. With Frontispiece by
Sidney P. Hall. Small post 8vo. cloth. 6s.

*" This story must make its way, as it is easy to predict it will, by its in-
trinsic merits."*—Times. *"A novel of great power and beauty, and something more than a mere novel—we mean that it is worth thoughtful
people's reading. . . It is a finished literary work, and will well repay the
reading."*—Literary Churchman.

Hitherto: a Novel. By the Author of "The Gayworthys," &c.
3 vols. post 8vo.

Longleat: a Novel. By Elleray Lake. 3 vols. post 8vo.

David Lloyd's Last Will. By Hesba Stretton. 2 vols. post 8vo.

Lorna Doone. A Romance of Exmoor. By R. D. Blackmore.
3 vols.

" Continually reminds us of the best of Scott's novels.—Spectator.

The Log of my Leisure Hours: a Story of Real Life. By an
Old Sailor. 3 vols. post 8vo. 24s.

David Gray ; and other Essays, chiefly on Poetry. By Robert
Buchanan. In one vol. fcap. 8vo. price 6s.

The Book of the Sonnet; being Selections, with an Essay on Sonnets and Sonneteers. By the late Leigh Hunt. Edited, from the original MS. with Additions, by S. Adams Lee. 2 vols. price 18s.

Lyra Sacra Americana: Gems of American Poetry, selected with Notes and Biographical Sketches by C. D. Cleveland, D.D., Author of the " Milton Concordance." 18mo., cloth, gilt edges. Price 4s. 6d.

Poems of the Inner Life. Selected chiefly from modern Authors, by permission. Small post 8vo. 6s.; gilt edges, 6s. 6d.

English and Scotch Ballads, &c. An extensive Collection. With Notices of the kindred Ballads of other Nations. Edited by F. J. Child. 8 vols. fcap. cloth, 3s. 6d. each

Lyrical Pieces, Secular and Sacred, from the Home Circle of a Country Parsonage. Edited by the Rev. Abner W. Brown, M.A., Vicar of Gretton, Northamptonshire, and Hon. Canon of Peterborough. With numerous Illustrative Vignettes, and with Archæological and other Notes. Crown 8vo. bevelled boards, price 8s. 6d.

The Autocrat of the Breakfast Table. By Oliver Wendell Holmes, LL.D. Popular Edition, 1s. Illustrated Edition, choicely printed, cloth extra, 8s.

The Professor at the Breakfast Table. By Oliver Wendell Holmes, Author of "The Autocrat of the Breakfast-Table." Cheap Edition, fcap. 3s. 6d.

Bee-keeping. By "The Times" Bee-master. Small post 8vo. numerous illustrations, cloth, 5s.

The Blackbird of Baden, and Other Stories. By Robert Black, M.A. Price 6s.

> "*A pleasant book, deserving honest praise.*"—Athenæum. "*Furnishes a few hours of genuinely pleasant recreation.*"—Star. "*It is unquestionable that whether Mr. Black writes a dismal tale or a bright one, he possesses the art of story-telling.*"—Daily News.

Queer Little People. By the Author of " Uncle Tom's Ca" Fcap. 1s. *Also by the same Author.*
The Little Foxes that Spoil the Grapes, 1s.
House and Home Papers, 1s.
The Pearl of Orr's Island, Illustrated by Gilbert, 5s.
The Minister's Wooing. Illustrated by Phiz, 5s.

The Story of Four Little Women: Meg, Joe, Beth, and Amy. By Louisa M. Alcott. With Illustrations. 16mo, cloth 3s. 6d.

> "*A bright, cheerful, healthy story—with a tinge of thoughtful gravity about it which reminds one of John Bunyan. Meg going to Vanity Fair is a chapter written with great cleverness and a pleasant humour.*"—Guardian.

Also, Entertaining Stories for Young Ladies, 3s. 6d. each, cloth, gilt edges.
Helen Felton's Question: a Book for Girls. By Agnes Wylde.
Faith Gartney's Girlhood. By Mrs. D. T. Whitney. Seventh thousand.
The Gayworthys. By the same Author. Third Edition.
A Summer in Leslie Goldthwaite's Life. By the same Author.
The Masque at Ludlow. By the Author of " Mary Powell."
Miss Biddy Frobisher: a Salt Water Story. By the same Author.
Selvaggio; a Story of Italy. By the same Author. New Edition.
The Journal of a Waiting Gentlewoman. By a new Author. New Edition.
The Shady Side and the Sunny Side. Two Tales of New England.

Edelweiss; a Story of Swiss Life. By Berthold Auerbach. Fcap. 8vo. 5s.

New and Cheaper Edition of "A Mere Story." By the Author of "Lady Grace," "Twice Lost," &c. Third Edition, fcap. 8vo. with Frontispiece by Sidney Hall. 6s.

> "*A story that we strongly recommend our readers to procure. . . . Altogether it is a very pleasant little book, sparkling and original, which no one will read without a good deal of enjoyment.*"—Guardian.

Marian; or, the Light of Some One's Home. By Maud Jeanne Franc. Small post 8vo., 5s.

Also, by the same Author.

Emily's Choice: an Australian Tale. 5s.
Vermont Vale: or, Home Pictures in Australia. 5s.
Minnie's Mission, a Temperance Story. 4s.

Tauchnitz's English Editions of German Authors. Each volume cloth flexible, 2s.; or sewed, 1s. 6d. The following are now ready :—

1. On the Heights. By B. Auerbach. 3 vols.
2. In the Year '13. By Fritz Reuter. 1 vol.
3. Faust. By Goethe. 1 vol.
4. Undine, and other Tales. By Fouqué. 1 vol.
5. L'Arrabiata. By Paul Heyse. 1 vol.
6. The Princess, and other Tales. By Heinrich Zschokke. 1 vol.
7. Lessing's Nathan the Wise.
8. Hacklander's Behind the Counter, translated by Mary Howitt.
9. Three Tales. By W. Hauff.
10. Joachim v. Kamern: Diary of a Poor Young Lady. By M. Nathusius.
11. Poems by Ferdinand Freiligrath, a selection of Translations. Edited by his daughter.
12. Gabriel: a Story of Magdeburgh. From the German of Paul Heyse. By Arthur Milman.

Low's Copyright Cheap Editions of American Authors. A thoroughly good and cheap series of editions, which, whilst combining very advantage that can be secured by the best workmanship at the lowest possible rate, will possess an additional claim on the reading public by providing for the remuneration of the American author and the legal protection of the English publisher. Ready :—

1. Haunted Hearts. By the Author of "The Lamplighter."
2. The Guardian Angel. By "The Autocrat of the Breakfast Table."
3. The Minister's Wooing. By the Author of "Uncle Tom's Cabin."
4. Views Afoot. By Bayard Taylor.
5. Kathrina, Her Life and Mine. By J. G. Holland.
6. Hans Brinker; or, Life in Holland. By Mrs. Dodge.
7. Men, Women, and Ghosts. By Miss Phelps.

To be followed by a New Volume on the first of every alternate month. Each complete in itself, printed from new type, with Initial Letters and Ornaments, price 1s. 6d. enamelled flexible cover, or 2s. cloth.

LONDON : SAMPSON LOW, SON, AND MARSTON,
CROWN BUILDINGS, 188, FLEET STREET.

English, American, and Colonial Booksellers and Publishers.

Chiswick Press:—Whittingham and Wilkins, Tooks Court, Chancery Lane.